ARABIA FELIX

ARABIA FELIX

An exploration of the
archaeological history
of Yemen

Alessandro de Maigret

STACEY INTERNATIONAL

To Sabina

ARABIA FELIX
Alessandro de Maigret

First published by Rusconi Libri s.r.l. 1996

This edition published by
Stacey International
128 Kensington Church Street
London W8 4BH
Tel: 0207 221 7166 Fax: 0207 792 9288
e-mail: enquiries@stacey-international.co.uk

ISBN: 1 900988 070

Translated by Rebecca Thompson

Edited by Alison Feldman and Caroline Singer
Designed by Kitty Carruthers

British Library Cataloguing-in-Publication Data
A catalogue record for this publication is available from the British Library

Printed and Bound by Tien Wah Press, Singapore

The publishers would like to express special thanks to Carl Phillips for his work in checking this translation.

PUBLISHER'S NOTE

This book is a direct translation of *Arabia Felix - un Viaggio nell'Archeologia dello Yemen* written and published in Italian in 1996. Alessandro de Maigret's text remains the same in this English language version as it appeared in the 1996 publication, since the information contained within the book is as valid today as it was six years ago. However, it is important to note that since *Arabia Felix* was written, there has been a considerable amount of activity taking place in the field of South Arabian archaeology. International teams are continuing the work of previous archaeological pioneers profiled in this book, deepening our knowledge and understanding of the pre-Islamic culture in Yemen.

The Russian-French team have completed his surveys of the ancient Ḥaḍrami port of Qana and the hilltop fortress of Husn al-Ghorab on the Indian Ocean coast, (see for example, 'Sea Trade of the Ḥaḍramawt Kingdom from the 1st to the 6th centuries AD' by Alexander Sedov in *Profumid'Arabia Atti del Convegno*, edited by Alessandra Avanzini, Rome 1997, pp. 365-77), and the Russian-Yemeni team has finished its excavations of the Hadrami city of Raybun.

One of the most exciting developments to have been initiated in the last five years is the re-excavation of the Awwam temple in Mārib. A team has been assembled by the American Foundation for the Study of Man (AFSM) in collaboration with Calgary University, led by Merilyn Phillips Hodgson and Dr William Glanzman. They are using the very latest ground-penetrating radar technology to examine the remains of the great pilgrimage temple dedicated to the Sabaean god Almaqah, famously excavated by AFSM's Wendell Phillips and his team in 1951-2 (see page 91 *et seq*). Details of the first three years' work have been published in *PSAS* volumes 28, 29 and 30 (1998-2000).

In November 2000 a ceremony took place to mark the completion of the German Institute of Archaeology's excavations and restoration work at the other major Sabaean temple in Mārib, the Bar'an Temple. The German team are currently in the process of excavating the necropolis of the Awwam temple (see for example, 'The 1997 Excavations of the German Institute of Archaeology at the Cemetery of Awwam in Marib' by Holger Hitgen in *PSAS* volume 28 1998).

While many details of South Arabian history are now well-established facts, the study of pre-Islamic Yemen is still, comparatively speaking, in its infancy. Our field of vision is widening all the time, and the picture – still patchy in many places – is becoming ever clearer. Continued excavations of these important South Arabian sites will shed vital new light on what we already know about the rulers, deities and citizens of the kingdoms of Saba, Awsān, Qatabān, Ḥaḍramawt, Ma'īn and Himyar.

ARABIC LETTERS AND THEIR PRONUNCIATION

ā, ī, ū	A lengthening of the vowels *a, i, u*. In speech these long vowels tend to determine the position of the tonic accent in the word.
th	A hard English '*th*' sound, as in 'thing'.
j	As in 'jury'.
h	A lightly aspirated '*h*' as in the German 'haben'.
ḥ	A heavily aspirated '*h*', similar to the hard '*c*' in 'Tuscany'.
kh	Similar to the Spanish '*j*', a fricative velar '*h*'.
dh	A soft English '*th*', as in 'then'.
z	A soft '*z*', as in 'rosy'.
s	As in 'assassin'.
sh	As in 'shine'.
ṣ, ṭ, ḍ, ẓ	More emphatic, rounded pronunciation of the consonants *s, t, d* and *z*.
ʿ	A deep, resonant gutteral consonant, exclusive to Arabic.
gh	A hard fricative '*g*', pronounced like a voiced '*kh*'.
q	An emphatic hard '*c*', pronounced at the back of the throat.

The remaining letters (b, t, d, r, f, k, m, n, w, y) correspond to the same letters in the English language.

N.B. *wiyān* is the plural of *wādī, sibākh* is the plural of *sabkhah.*

TABLE OF CONTENTS

Part Three: The Kingdoms of Arabia Felix

Part Four: Religion and Material Culture

SELECTED LIST OF ILLUSTRATIONS

Maps and Plans

Tables and Charts

INTRODUCTION

Considering a Discovery

"Do you really think nobody's been here before us?"

"Nobody has, Francesco. At least, no explorer has discussed it."

"But how could an entire city have passed unnoticed, especially one as big as this, with its huge walls, and all the surrounding dams, farms and temples? Antonio was right when he said that Yemen is archaeology's last frontier!"

"It certainly seems so. Well, goodnight and thanks for everything."

This was the brief conversation I had with Francesco Di Mario, an expert in prehistoric stone tools, as we sank, exhausted, into our sleeping bags. It was the 25th of July, 1985, and that day we had discovered the great complex of Sabaean antiquity that spreads the length of Wādī Yalā, about thirty kilometres south of Mārib, the ancient capital of the kingdom of Saba[1].

Next to us on the pale sand lay the geologist Enzo Francaviglia, and 'Uthmān al-Khalīfah, an official from the Department of Antiquities in Ṣan'ā whose job was to accompany us on our exploratory journey. A little further away, in the light of a small oil lamp, our guide Ḥussayn al-Zamlī was chatting animatedly with the sheikh of the village of Yalā and other men from the small Al-Ṭāhir tribe. The light flickered on the guns and on the brightly coloured clothes of the women who sat apart, listening and giggling. The occasional muffled bleat reached us from the little stone and thatch hut behind us.

Lying there with my eyes closed, I was gloriously aware of the lovely fortified city that lay at the base of the little rocky outcrop where we were camped. "Archaeology's last frontier." The phrase sounded a bit sinister to me. Antonio Solazzi, the Italian archaeological mission's photographer, would probably have said "archaeology's last paradise". But maybe he had avoided the word "paradise" on purpose, to emphasise that besides this unique and wonderful opportunity to be involved in something new, rich and untouched, there were also difficult and demanding moments ahead, and hard, lonely conditions under which our research mission would have to operate. During the vigil in that lost village in Yemen's hinterland, I was suddenly overcome with anxiety. The mass of library material, the emotional impact on the local community, and the numerous technical, logistical, methodological and political problems that I would have to face flooded all at once into my head. I felt overwhelmed by the fame and the mystery surrounding Arabia Felix, and by the mildly ironic, expectant presence of those early explorers who had preceded me, by the neatly arranged histories of other Middle Eastern countries, and by the brief and enigmatic presentation of existing information on the ancient kingdoms of South Arabia. All this appeared in an unnerving flash, unsettling my rationality and intuition.

The next morning, the desert sun rose over the gleaming granite mountains and lit up the golden valley with its ancient and mysterious city. My anxieties dissolved. The valley rang with the strange, melodious songs of unknown birds. The sheikh's wife emerged from the circle of thatch that served as a kitchen, bearing an aluminium tea urn and some flat loaves. A little girl clutched a plastic bottle full of milk. We ate breakfast sitting on the ground by the only true hut on the plain, and various armed men joined us from the tents dotted across the valley. They assured us that it was the first time Europeans had come here, and asked me which country we were from. We pointed to the north-west and told them that it took eight to nine hours to get here from Italy by plane. I thought of the French explorer Thomas Arnaud who had reached Mārib about one hundred and forty years earlier; the intervening years had not altered the receptive attitude towards foreigners.

"Italians *kwayis*! We shall take you to Shi'b al-'Aql!" said the sheikh.

"Where? What is at Shi'b al-'Aql?"

"*Āthār muhimm jiddan*! [very important antiquities]."

Our Land Rover descended the slope accompanied by three pick-ups packed with armed bedouin. We skirted the ancient fortified city, and stopped at the foot of a gorge that wound to the east through mountains that separated the valley of Wādī Yalā from the great dunes of the Ramlat Sab'atayn desert. Leaving the vehicles, we entered a deep, narrow, rocky ravine. It was an enchanting sight: the crevasse, coloured a thousand shades of pink, opened like a wound in the shiny black flank of the mountain. Centuries of wind and water had carved out surreal forms from the high walls – it reminded me of Henry Moore. This symphony of pink was brilliantly punctuated by bright blue pools of water scattered about the bottom of smooth steps that led up the slope of the *wādī* bed. A beautiful stone building stood in an opening to the left. Its form struck me, and for an instant I was fooled by the regular, well-cut blocks of stone into thinking it was a modern building. But something made me turn back. The only settlements around here were huts and tents; this was definitely not modern! This building was a small but sumptuous Sabaean villa, intact right up to roof level, and complete with doors, windows and stairs. The dating was confirmed by the discovery of Sabaean earthenware among the ruins.

We climbed on for about a kilometre. The gorge opened out into a wide rocky plain framed by long, low borders of dark granite. In the middle, a pool lay in a large natural basin, and we stopped for a break nearby. The heat was already intense, but the pause allowed us to admire the stunning view afforded by the valley at our backs. We were roused by the cries of the bedouin, who had meanwhile climbed onto a ledge above the basin.

"*Nuqūsh, nuqūsh* [inscriptions]," they shouted.

We clambered up, and found to our amazement that the vertical rock surfaces were covered with marks. The inscriptions, worked into the glassy black of the granite, had brought out the underlying pink of the rock, but the intervening centuries had obscured the colour contrast and they were now difficult to decipher. I am not an epigrapher, but I realised immediately that we were dealing with very ancient Sabaean inscriptions. Their palaeography was comparable in age to ancient pottery found among the ruins of the city near Yalā.

Once again I was roused by calls from our escorts, who had climbed further up. I followed up a long and vertiginous stone stairway and emerged on a sort of artificial platform, in the centre of which stood three great segments of parallel walls. Nearby were the remnants of a white limestone ritual basin. A sanctuary!

We immediately decided that this had been a sacred place, although for the moment we lacked corroboration. The atmosphere of the place was enough. The view from here took in the entire pink length of the gorge right down to the Sabaean villa at the bottom. The basin of Wādī Yalā with its dams, ancient farms and fortified city spread into the distance. Behind us lay the suffocating dunes of the Ramlat Sab'atayn desert, antechamber to the immense, terrifying desert of the Rub' al-Khālī. On the magical boundary between the two places, representing life and death respectively, ancient man had turned to God, and the kings of Saba – as we were to discover later, once the inscriptions had been interpreted – had used the place to perform the mysterious rituals of the sacred hunt.

Befuddled by the heat and our discoveries, and tired by the state of constant tension needed to absorb as much as possible in a limited time, we descended towards the Sabaean villa. An old shepherd had set up camp nearby with a hut, two wives, a few children and a flock of goats. He invited us to rest in the small clearing between the rocks. Had it not been for the tyre I was leaning against, the surroundings and people could have been those of two or three thousand years ago. One of the women was starting a fire in the thatch hut, the other sat spinning wool, the children played with the goats, and the shepherd, calm and smiling, chewed some *qāt* leaves. All around was peace and quiet. The woman from the kitchen took a block of rock salt and dissolved little pieces into a clay pot. At the smell of the salt, the goats clambered onto us, fearlessly trying to get their muzzles into our mugs. The women and children laughed. The shepherd was talking to our guide and 'Uthmān al-Khalīfah, and he pointed out to them a high dark peak above us. On closer inspection one could almost make out a human form, and the summit resembled the head of an old man. 'Uthmān explained to me that the shepherd considered this mountain sacred. I thought that this feature must certainly have existed in Sabaean times and that it confirmed the sacred nature of the place in the distant past.

Despite the rather frightening salty drink, I felt a sense of gentle peacefulness. It was a magical moment, and the very opposite of the previous night. Everything now seemed obvious and easy. Precedents and assumptions, actions and proceedings, consequences and results all became clear and practicable. At that moment I felt initiated and ready to take part in unravelling the secrets of Saba.

An Eccentric Culture

The archaeological mission that I found myself in charge of had been founded in 1980[2].

However, 1985 was the first year that research had focused on the antiquities of the Sabaean – or pre-Islamic South Arabian – period, the first of the two great phases that cover the historic period of Yemen. The previous seasons' research had centred on the earlier prehistoric and protohistoric periods of Yemen.

The reason we had spent the first few years of research on the oldest periods was that, from the moment I decided to dedicate myself to South Arabian archaeology, I sensed a strange contradiction in the cultural development of the ancient civilisations of that particular region[3].

We know that a society is usually referred to as a "state" once the specialisations and differences within it are of a type and number that make it necessary to form levels of hierarchy within that society. The appearance of writing in ancient civilisations, determined by the need for keeping abreast of this newly complicated socio-economic structure, usually shows that they have reached this level of "state"[4].

The Egyptian and Mesopotamian cultures of the great river valleys of the Nile, Tigris and Euphrates reached and surpassed this level of social development from the beginning of the third millennium BC . A little later, as trade and commerce grew on account of the surplus produced by these riverside communities[5], we find a similar structural metamorphosis in other communities situated between these "wet" zones. During the third and second millennia BC we find city-states appearing in Syria, Palestine and Anatolia.

Throughout the first millennium BC these city-states – despite their changing political structure – characterised the history of the ancient Near East. At this time we find evidence of the emergence of a new form of writing in the far south-west corner of the Arabian Peninsula. This confirms the existence of complex societies that reached the level of state essential for their participation in the historic scene of ancient Asia. This development is in a sense unexpected, anomalous and surprising.

It is surprising for two reasons: firstly, the geographical

position of these new states: they developed separately from the older centres which were spread along the same stretch of land, appropriately named the Fertile Crescent. And secondly, the spontaneity of their appearance: they grew up suddenly and apparently without the preparatory phase that we find to some degree in all other states[6]. My own professional experience began in 1976 in Syria, where for many years I took part in the Italian Archaeological Mission of the University of Rome's excavations at Ebla. The excavation of this impressive royal palace and its highly elaborate economic archives showed that the Syrian city had achieved an unexpected level of state organisation by about the middle of the third millennium BC[7].

The discovery was especially surprising because it happened in Syria, an area hitherto credited with adopted, rather than independently developed, civilisation. But the cultural phenomenon itself was no surprise, if seen within the general historical and archaeological framework already familiar to scholars of that particular field. The discovery of Ebla was important, not because it revealed a new cultural manifestation, but rather because it enormously enriched our existing picture of the ancient Near East. Although exceptional, the culture brought to light at Ebla seemed to fit into a logical framework, whereas the culture of South Arabia did not.

The polemics generated by the discovery of the royal archives at Ebla brought to an end, among other things, my involvement with the Italian Archaeological Mission in Syria, and gave me time for a more in-depth study of the literature relating to the research carried out so far in the relevant part of the southern Arabian Peninsula.

I found myself faced with a store of knowledge much wider than I could have expected. But as I read, I gradually became aware of the flimsiness of the information and of a distinct imbalance in the subjects treated. The scholars' attention seemed to be directed mainly at the textual evidence and as a result their arguments ran chiefly along philological and linguistic lines. Apart from the odd excavation report, the archaeological content was limited to a few magazine articles relating mostly to marginal or tiny details of a vast and remarkable historical and artistic patrimony. Due to this disjointedness, and to the fact that the written evidence – the most popular area of study – was mostly composed of dedications, there was a peculiar lack of cohesion in the history of South Arabia, particularly in areas such as society, economy, art, philosophy and everyday life. That the subject had already aroused widespread interest, and continued to do so, was obvious from the many accounts of visits and journeys, the numerous photographic studies, and even a few books of the paranormal variety. The Queen of Sheba had emerged as the central figure, and in her name were written the only cohesive histories, which unfortunately, in an attempt to fill in the gaps, stumbled into uncertainty, relying more on legend than fact.

My increasing sense of dissatisfaction with these publications derived from the fact that the studies carried out on the texts, although serious, led to a terrible *impasse* regarding the chronology of the few reconstructable historical events. The impression I got from these works was that they were incomplete (partly because I was able to make comparisons with other areas of the Middle East). I thought this was largely due to the scarcity of archaeological publications. But I also understood that it was not entirely a result of the scholars' inclination towards written evidence, but was also dependent on other factors, above all the particular political position and surroundings that had always characterised Yemen. I therefore felt it was important to study previous excavations and explorations in order to be familiar with the facts and to be able to assimilate them easily into any future discoveries.

It seemed obvious that, lacking archaeological data, it would be impossible to reconstruct the birth, development, maturity, decline and death of Yemen's great ancient civilisations. I compared it to Palestine, where, apart from the Bible, there were very few written documents, but where intense archaeological activity had succeeded in perfectly reconstructing the chronology, history and culture of the country. This comparison turned out to be very useful as increased archaeological research would later bring rewarding results.

A Land of Many Parts

My archaeological experience in Syria had given me the opportunity to study the distribution of ancient settlements

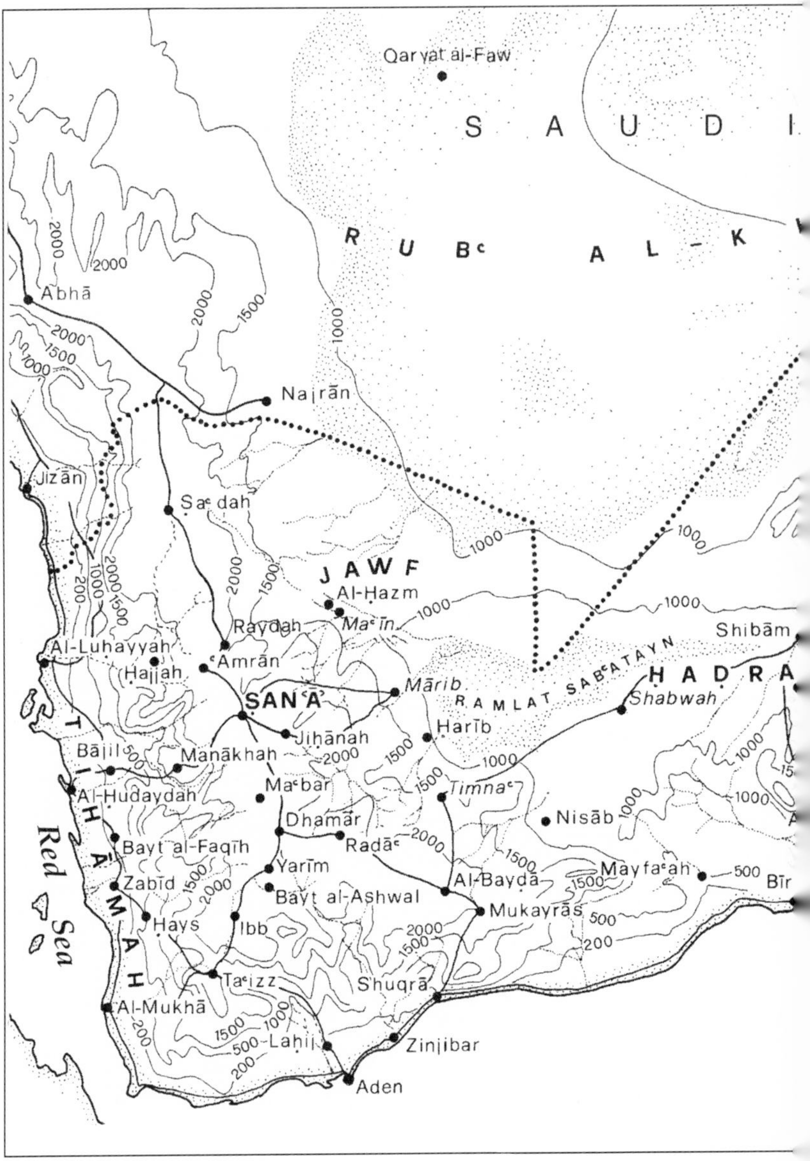

Figure 1
Map of the Republic of Yemen

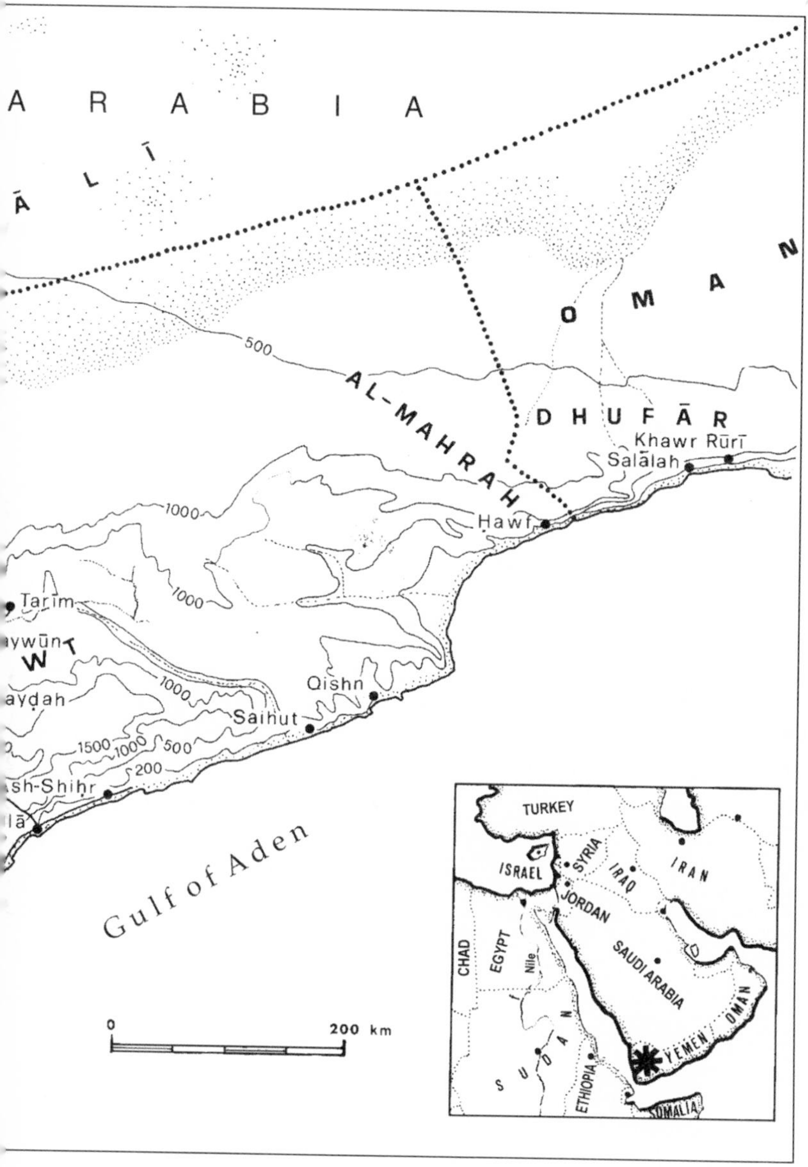
A R A B I A
Ā L Ī
O M A N
500
AL-MAHRAH
D H U F Ā R
Khawr Rūrī
Salālah
1000
Hawf
1000
Tarim
aywūn
W T
1000
Qishn
aydah
Saihut
1500
1000
500
200
sh-Shihr
lā
Gulf of Aden
0
200 km
TURKEY
SYRIA
ISRAEL
IRAQ
IRAN
JORDAN
SAUDI ARABIA
CHAD
EGYPT
Nile
OMAN
YEMEN
SUDAN
ETHIOPIA
SOMALIA

in the territory south of Aleppo. I had seen that the complex structural and geographical homogeneity of the Syrian environment had not prevented human occupants, over the centuries and millennia, from establishing types of settlements that differed according to their time and place. Surely a proper analysis of these differences could provide me with a lot of useful information on the ways in which man gradually adapted and used his environment, and therefore, the various technological, economic and organisational systems adopted in ancient times by the various communities[8]. Analysis of the fluctuation of settlements did, in fact, lead to interesting results, which proved the validity of the original hypothesis.

Since the geography of Yemen is so much more diverse than that of Syria, the contrast between the two seems striking. One would therefore imagine that the enormous geographical variation that characterises Yemen has played an important role in the history of the settlement of the area.

These variations are due to a particular set of geological circumstances involving the whole of the Arabian Peninsula, but specifically the south-west section[9]. The peninsula forms part of the East African shield, an extensive region of Precambrian rock that was largely levelled during the course of the Palaeozoic era and then re-covered in layers of sediments in the Jurassic and Cretaceous periods. At the end of the Cretaceous and the start of the Tertiary era, the western part of the peninsula and the corresponding East African table were pushed upwards and began to break into separate chunks. Rivers of lava began to flow along the geological fissures, giving rise to extensive layers of tufa and lava that covered both the pre-Cambrian base rock and the later deposits of Mesozoic sediment.

These volcanic layers, which reached impressive heights in Yemen (up to 1500 metres), fractured during the course of the Tertiary era along the deep faults caused by gradual movement away from the African peninsula. This is how the Red Sea and the Gulf of Aden were born. The fractures lying parallel to these new pools crossed each other almost at right angles, breaking the mountains into huge square blocks that began to move vertically and independently. In some places this vertical movement has created a disparity in the height of ancient geological layers, which can rise above 2000 metres. As a result, the pre-Cambrian base rock and the Mesozoic sediments rise to different heights in each mountain range and the elevation changes suddenly, with dramatic and precipitous drops from the high plateaux to the sedimentary plains stretching along the marine basins.

These slow but catastrophic developments resulted in the dramatic contrasts that today characterise the geography of the Yemeni landscape (Fig.1). Firstly, then, there is a *coastal strip*, originally formed by the progressive deposits of fine material carried down by mountain water. This extends west and south of the Yemeni mountains (Tihāmah), and rises only a few metres above sea level. The coastal strip is host to the country's principal port towns (Al-Hudaydah, Al-Mukhā, Aden and Al-Mukallā) and to numerous smaller but historically important centres (Zabīd, Bayt al-Faqīh, Hays, Bājil, Laḥij, Zinjibār, Shuqrā, Mayfa'ah, Bīr 'Ali, and Al-Shiḥr).

Then follows an intermediate strip of land *between the mountains and the plain*, which, although restricted by the sheer drop from the high mountains to the coastal plain, accounts for the majority of Yemeni agriculture, as it benefits from the most rainfall. Here are the "green cities" of northern Yemen, like Ta'izz, Jiblah, Ibb, Manākhah, Al-Maḥwīt, Ḥajjah, cities that travellers regularly had to negotiate after arriving by sea on their way to meet the monarch of Ṣan'ā.

Then there is the *highland region*, which has an average height of over 2000 metres and so does not suffer from the suffocating heat of the coast. It also has less rain, and is therefore less fertile. This is the most densely populated part of Yemen today. Many great cities were founded there, like Ṣan'ā, Ṣa'dah, Raydah, 'Amrān, Dhamār, Yarīm, Radā', and Al-Bayḍā.

The *middle highland strip* (where the river valleys run down the mountainside) is less steep than the highland region, but also much more extensive. This territory, where one can make out ancient geological strata as one descends, is riven by numerous deep *wādīs* that become fewer and fewer as they flow down towards the desert, while their valleys get gradually wider. This area is much less densely populated. The settlements lie within the erosive valleys and canyons, where the water essential for survival can be found.

While in northern Yemen there seems to be a distinction between modern and ancient population densities, in southern Yemen these seem to be comparable. (It was here, where this area meets the desert, that the major pre-Islamic centres were founded.) Thus, for example, in the great valleys of the Ḥaḍramawt and its main tributaries, we still find some of the most heavily populated cities in Yemen, like Tarīm, Saywūn and Shibām.

And finally, there is the *desert.* Enclosed by the mountains of Yemen, the Ramlat Sab'atayn forms a sandy pocket that medieval Arab geographers named the "Sayhad Desert". In prehistoric times, the climate was more humid, and this was a great lake fed by the *wādī*s that ran from the mountains down through Wādī Ḥaḍramawt towards the sea. A little further north, rising just above the 1000 metre level that is average for the Ramlat Sab'atayn, lies the vast stretch of sand of the Rub' al-Khālī, the great desert that covers a third of the surface area of Saudi Arabia.

The area spanning the desert and the internal foothills saw the foundation, development and prosperity of the only state cultures of Arabia: the Minaeans of the Jawf; the Sabaeans of Wādī Dhanah; the Qatabanis of Wādī Beihan; and the Hadramis of Wādī Ḥaḍramawt (Figs 1 and 3). Sheltered from the dangers of the sea by the impenetrable mountain shield, and protected against overland incursions by the immense desert, these communities found the will and the means to cross the threshold of state progress. Their success was partly due to their secluded and naturally protected position in this ecological pocket. But while their isolation was a benefit to them, for us it represents a serious, and sometimes insurmountable obstacle to understanding their culture.

Footnotes:

1. de Maigret, A., "The Sabaean Antiquities in the Wādī Yalā Area", *EW* 35 (1985), p. 345-351.
2. de Maigret, A., "Prospezione geo-archeologica nello Yemen del Nord. Notizia di una prima ricognizione, *OA* 19 (1980), p. 307-313.
3. de Maigret, A., "Die Sabäer vor der Königin von Saba", in W. Daum (ed.), Die Königin von Saba: Kunst, Legende und

Archäologiezwischen Morgenland und Abenland (Stuggart-Zurich: Belser, 1988), p. 36-39.

4. Johnson, G.A., Local Exchange and Early State Development in Southwestern Iran (Anthropological Papers 51, Museum of Archaeology, University of Michigan, 1973), p. 2.
5. Wittfogel, K.A., "The Hydraulic Civilizations," in W.L. Thomas (ed.), *Man's Role in Changing the Face of the Earth* (Chicago: University of Chicago Press, 1956), p. 152-164.
6. de Maigret, A., "Ricerche archeologiche nella Repubblica Araba Yemenita. Notizia di una seconda ricognizione", *OA* 21 (1982), p. 237-253.
7. For further reading, see Pettinato, G., *Ebla: Nuovi orizzonti della storia* (Milano: Rusconi, 1986).
8. de Maigret, A., "Il fattore idrologico nell'economia de Ebla" *OA* 20 (1981), p. 1-36.
9. See Steffen, H., *Population Geography of the Yemen Arab Republic* (Wiesbaden: L. Reichart, 1979); Dequin, H., *Arabische Republik Jemen. Wirtschaftgeographie eines Entwicklungslandes* (Riyadh, 1976); and Schoch, R., *Regional Gliederung der Arabischen Republik Jemen mit Hilfe van Landsat-Bildern* (Zurich, 1977).

PART ONE

Piecing Together the Picture

I

ARABIA FELIX BEFORE OBLIVION

The Classical World and Arabia Felix

For around a millennium Europeans regarded Arabia as an unknown entity. With the end of Roman civilisation, which was swept aside by the barbarian hordes of the fourth and fifth centuries, the gravitational centre of Europe shifted to the continent, away from the Mediterranean and the East. This new position was further strengthened by the progressive and unstoppable rise of Islam. These Arabs had developed a prestigious and thriving civilisation, and as they founded cities in their newly-acquired territories, they gradually began to forget their arid homeland.

Though the first modern explorers of Yemen were, in fact, Arabs – Ibn al-Mujawir (thirteenth century) and Ibn Baṭṭūṭah (1328) – Muslim authors were not studied in Europe until much later, which preserved the mystique surrounding Arabia. Not until the late fifteenth century, with the Renaissance's burning desire for knowledge, did this veil of obscurity start to lift.

Arabia excited increasing interest, not only because it was an immense and largely unknown continent, but also because it formed the backdrop for two great cultures: the modern Islamic world that has always had a strong influence on the development of Europe, and the other, ancient world, famous for being one of the richest civilisations of antiquity.

The rediscovery of this ancient civilisation revived the myth of Arabia Felix, a concept born of the wealth and rarity of the merchandise brought from there to the West. The Greeks and Romans referred to it as if it belonged to another world, like the great Erythrean Sea (from the Greek word *erythra*, meaning "red") that the ancients believed stretched to the edge of the world[1].

A Carian Greek called Scylax explored the coastline from the mouth of the Indus to Arsinoe (near Suez) in about 510 BC. His journey probably formed the basis for Herodotus' famous accounts of Arabia (*c.* 484-425 BC). Halicarnassus' great historian, though, seems to have been

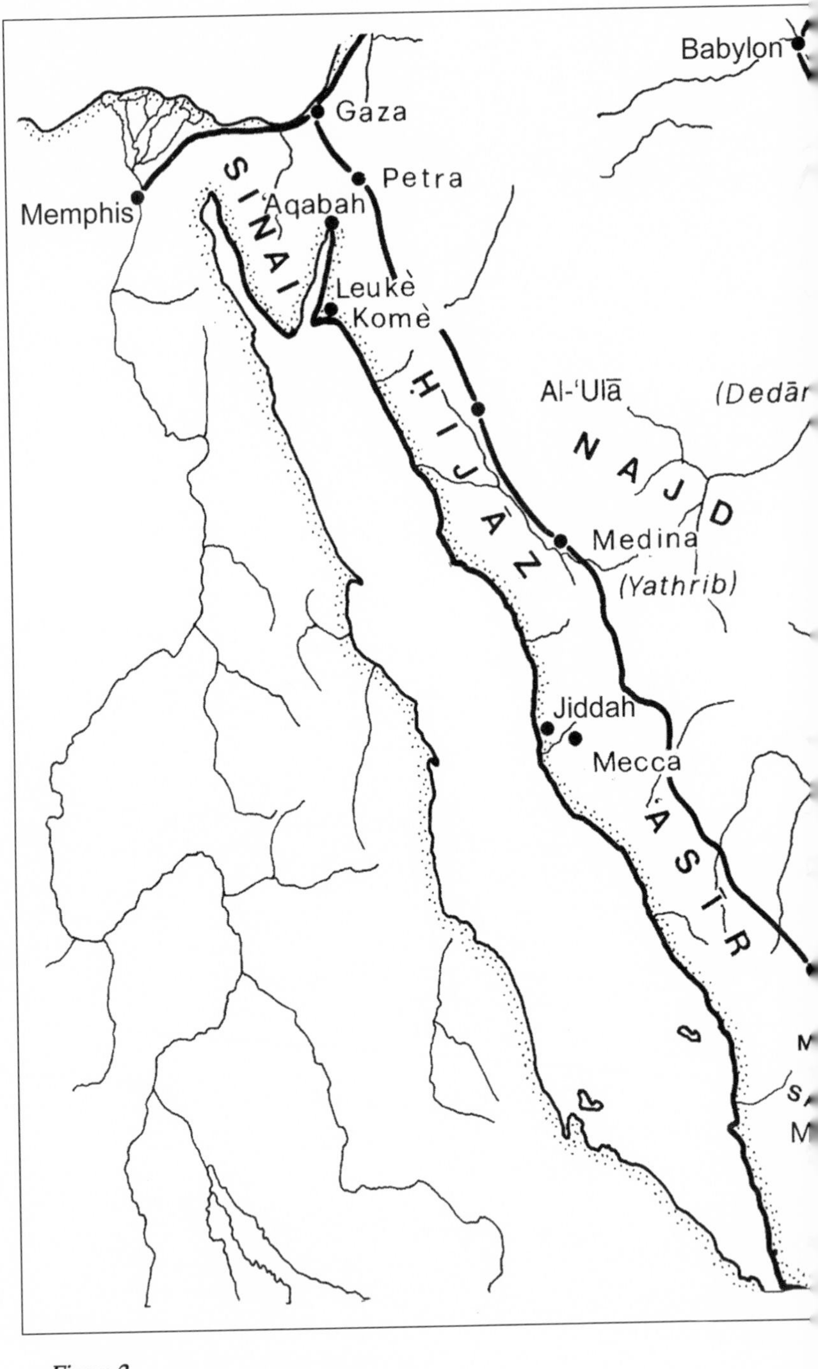

Figure 2
Incense routes on the Arabian Peninsula

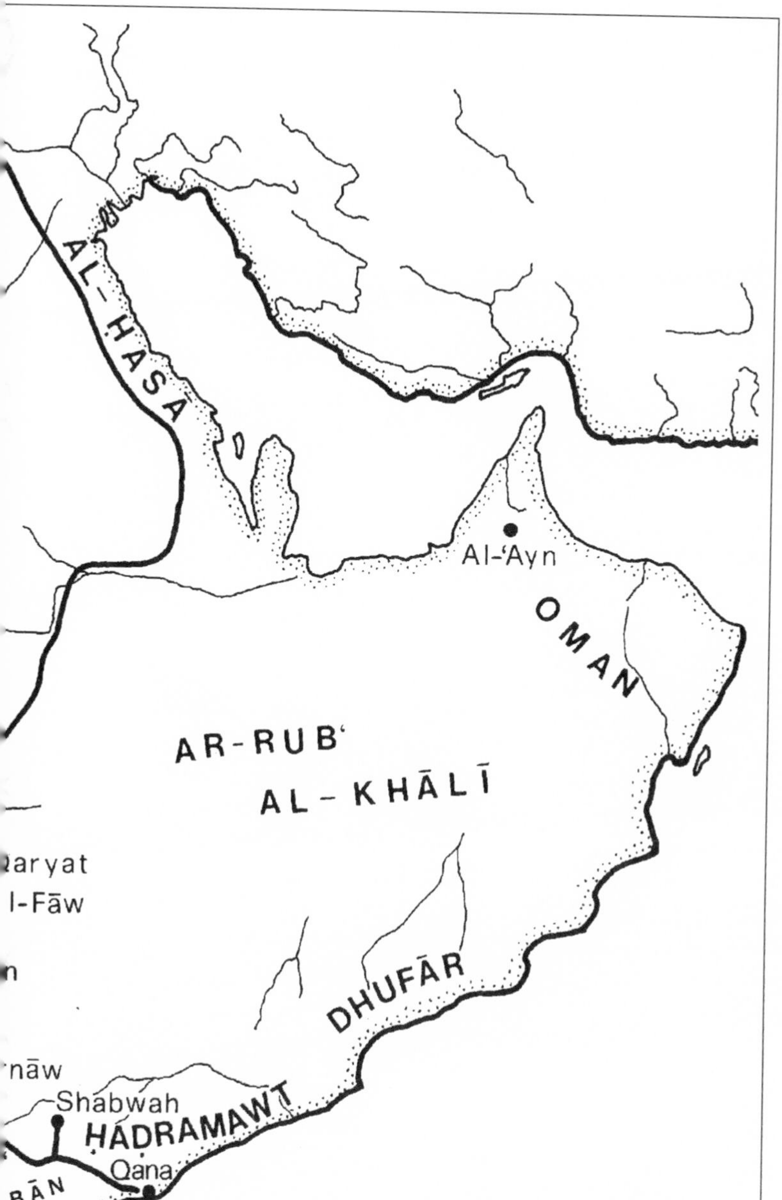
AL-HASA
Al-'Ayn
OMAN
AR-RUB'
AL-KHĀLĪ
ar yat
l-Fāw
nāw
Shabwah
ḤAḌRAMAWT
DHUFĀR
Qana
BĀN
0
300
600
km

rather confused, mistaking, for example, the Arab nomads of the north and centre of the peninsula for the people of southern Arabia[2]. He was a diligent reporter of the second-hand news that he learnt during his Persian journeys, as we can tell from the amazing detail with which he describes the land of spices, incense, myrrh, cassia, cinnamon and laudanum.

In 325-4 BC Alexander the Great's admiral, Nearchus, carried out a reconnaissance of the coastline as far as southern Arabia; further information on the region was provided by the Greek naturalist Theophrastus (*c.* 287 BC). This pupil of, and successor to, Aristotle devoted part of his *De Historia Plantarum* [Enquiry into Plants] to the famous perfumes of Arabia and the inhabitants of the regions where they were produced (the Sabaeans).

During the Hellenistic era, the director of the vast library at Alexandria, Eratostenes of Cyrene (died *c.* 195 BC), incorporated numerous details on Arabia into his great geographical survey. He was perhaps the first to use the term "Arabia Felix" and to position it correctly in the south of the Arabian Peninsula. He describes it as a fertile land, rich in fauna and populated by four distinct peoples, located in four separate provinces. He called those peoples the Minaeans, Sabaeans, Kattabaneans and the Khatramotites, and their capitals were Karna, Mariaba, Tamna and Sabota.

Further important geographical details were provided shortly afterwards by Agatharchides of Cnidus (*c.* mid-4th century BC). He positions Arabia Felix in the south of the peninsula, and names the Sabaeans as the most important tribe. This great Alexandrian geographer was extensively cribbed from by later writers – principally, in the subsequent century, by Diodorus Siculus (*c.* 80-20 BC) who reproduced the main points in his *Bibliotheca Historica* [Historical Library].

The significant consumption of aromatic produce during the Roman Empire, due specifically to the increase in cult rituals and to the ruling classes' immoderate dedication to luxury, led Augustus to take pains to ensure that the Empire retained absolute control over this precious and lucrative produce.

At the very start of his reign, Augustus instructed Aelius Gallus, the Prefect of Egypt, to gather together an army and set out to conquer Arabia Felix. Along with around 10,000 men, mostly Egyptian Romans, Nabateans and Judaeans, Aelius Gallus crossed the Red Sea and landed in northern Arabia at the port of Leukè Komè (the "White City")[3].

Gallus left Leukè Komè in the spring of 24 BC and headed south. After endless trials he reached the city of Najrān (now the ruins of Al-Ukhdūd), which he occupied and destroyed. A week later and further south, in the Yemeni Jawf, the Romans had their first true encounter with the Arab warriors of Arabia Felix. It was an easy victory; the Arabs lost over 10,000 men, while the Romans suffered only two casualties.

Following this victory, Aelius Gallus took Nasca (now Al-Bayḍā) and Athrula (Yathil, modern-day Barāqish). Leaving behind garrisons, and armed with wheat and dates, he journeyed on to Marsiaba (probably Mārib), which he besieged for six days, but then had to abandon for lack of water. Meanwhile, his vanguard had reached Caripeta (possibly Haribat, now Ḥinū al-Zurayr), only two days' march away from the land of incense. The return journey was swift: while it had taken them six months to reach Marsiaba, they would need a mere sixty days to return to base[4].

The two most important historians to write about southern Arabia during the imperial era were Strabo and Pliny the Elder. Their work was greatly enhanced by the information that Aelius Gallus brought back. Strabo of Amasia (*c.* 60 BC-AD 20) incorporated many of these new details, almost certainly taken from primary sources, into his *Geographica*. For example, he proposed that southern Arabia should be divided not into four ethnically distinct kingdoms as was traditional, but into five states, according to the division of labour: warriors, farmers, artisans, myrrh producers and incense producers.

Aelius Gallus was also one of the many sources for Pliny the Elder's (AD 23-79) *Historia Naturalis* [Natural History]. Pliny was a great encyclopaedist and has left us a wealth of information, some of which is confused, but important because it has survived to this day.

This period also saw an increase in the Roman Empire's commercial activity in the Erythrean Sea. Trade routes became easier and more direct, and as a result the traffic increased in both directions. An anonymous text of uncertain date (probably, as we shall see further on, from around AD 45-50) clearly shows that these journeys must have become commonplace. An invaluable guide for merchants, *The Periplus of the Erythrean Sea* starts from the Egyptian ports on the Red Sea, and describes the stages on the long coastal voyage to India[5]. It does not limit itself to the sea journey and landing points, but offers detailed information on the merchandise imported and exported from the various ports, as well as relevant comments on the political situation of these places that would be useful to merchants plying their trade.

Claudius Ptolemy wrote his famous *Geographia* [The Geography] towards the middle of the second century AD. The book included coverage of Arabia, and must have been based on works like the *Navigation.* Ptolemy was a great Alexandrian mathematician and astronomer, and the first to incorporate all the known world into a system of parallels and meridians. Using the distance charts provided by the various itineraries, the instructions in pilots' books, and travellers' accounts, he managed to produce an entirely new sketch map of the known world which was amazingly comprehensive for its time[6].

Ptolemy's work is, as far as we know, the last reference to Arabia Felix in the ancient world. With the passing of the centuries, the book was forgotten like many of its predecessors, and was not rediscovered until the Renaissance.

The Bible and the Queen of Sheba

The oldest reference to the Sabaeans is in the Bible. The Queen of Sheba's visit to King Solomon of Israel is described in I Kings (10:1-13), and reproduced almost word for word in II Chronicles (9:1-12). The account was probably compiled around the fourth century BC, but it certainly refers back to older texts, some of which may have been contemporary with the events they describe, in other words with King Solomon's reign in Jerusalem (*c.* 960-920 BC).

The episode is undoubtedly of immense historic value. Under Solomon, the united state of Israel created by David entered a phase of mature consolidation, and the Biblical episode of the Queen of Sheba, or Saba, seems to reflect an attempt to control the commercial policy of southern Arabia, which produced gold, incense and myrrh. So, if we are to believe that the account is historically accurate, we must accept that the kingdom of Saba existed in the tenth century BC and that it held a monopoly over the incense route.

The Sabaeans are mentioned elsewhere in the Bible. In the Book of Genesis, Sheba and Dedan are numbered among the descendants of both Ham (10:7) and Abraham and therefore Shem (25:3). It seems likely that the names Sheba and Dedan were used to refer to the inhabitants of the west coast of the Arabian Peninsula, and that in particular Dedan refers to the northern tribes, and Sheba to those further south. Also, the Book of Genesis links Sheba to Ḥaṣarmawet, or the Ḥaḍramawt (10:26), which confirms that it was a southern kingdom.

The intense commercial activity of the Sabaeans is well documented in the Bible. Their caravans were convoys of merchandise which skirted the desert, transporting gold (I Kings 10:2; Psalms 72:10,15; Isaiah 62:6), incense (Isaiah 60:6; Jeremiah 6:20), perfume and spices, jewels and precious stones (I Kings 10:2; Ezekiel 27:22).

Towards the end of the last century, research into the origins of the South Arabian states started to become more scientific. This research tried to interpret these various Biblical passages so as to prove that in the early centuries of the first millennium BC the Sabaeans were confined to the north-west of the Arabian Peninsula, and that they only ventured south later, around 500 BC, into the hinterland of what is today Yemen, to found the kingdom of Saba itself[7]. Actually, this is not at all what the Bible says. We shall come back to the idea that the Sabaeans were confined to the north in ancient times. This concept lies at the heart of one of the two theoretical chronologies of the origins of the southern Arabian kingdoms.

The Qur'an, Arab Tradition and Bilqīs

As in the West, the image of the Queen of Sheba had a great impact in the East, where she became an important figure in literature and the subject of elaborate myths. We should bear in mind, however, that in Arabia, with the rise of Islam and the formalisation of Arabic as a written language towards the middle of the seventh century AD, ancient texts were soon forgotten. In fact, the only information to survive from the "period of ignorance" (*jahiliyyah*) was handed down by word of mouth, which inevitably led to a certain distortion in the reconstruction of events.

The story of the Queen of Sheba and her meeting with Solomon was still fresh in people's minds, as we can see from the first complete version of the episode, given in the Qur'an (Sura of the Ant, 27:16-45). The holy book recounts an episode that happened sixteen centuries beforehand, and it comes as no surprise to find that this version is significantly different from the Biblical version written at least twelve centuries earlier.

In fact, the Qur'anic version is an abbreviation of a story which originated in the Talmūd (discussions of Jewish law and legend), composed from the first century AD onwards. Jewish sages of the period, commenting on the Bible, concluded that Solomon governed over all earthly creatures, and was particularly helpful to birds and demons, to whom he gave superior speed.

Later Jewish tradition adopted this new version of the famous Biblical episode and incorporated it into the Targūm, that is, into the late Aramaic tradition drawn from the Bible probably around the sixth century AD. The concept of Solomon as master of demons had also entered into Christian tradition, as is proven by various apocryphal texts (excluded from the canon of the Sacred Scriptures) dating from the fourth and fifth centuries AD[8]. The account in the Qur'an owes much to these fabulous inventions.

The story of the Queen of Sheba became famous with its inclusion in the sacred book of Islam, and in the centuries that followed, the theme was taken up by the first Arab writers and historians. Their deference and devotion to the Qur'an led them to attribute historic meaning to the episode, and to give the Queen a name, Bilqīs. The name has stuck, especially in the Arab world, and refers not only to the Queen in the Qur'an, but also to the Biblical one.

The great historian Ibn Isḥāq was probably the first to mention Bilqīs, at the time of the Abbasid Caliph Al-Manṣūr (AD 754-775). Almost nothing remains of his work, but over a century later another great historian, Al-Tabarī (AD 838-923) made many references to him in his *Tarikh al-rusul wa al-muluk* [History of the Prophets and Kings]. From this we deduce that Ibn Isḥāq related a meeting between Bilqīs and Solomon, basically staying close to the Qur'anic version, but adding a few toponymic details that give the meeting a likely date of around the second to third century AD, much later than that in the Bible.

Bilqīs must, however, have been a real person, and must have lived at about this time. In the chronology of Ibn Wādīh al-Ya'qūbī (AD 832) we see that a Bilqīs reigned shortly before King Yāsir Yuhan'im, a well-known name among Himyarite sovereigns who was in power in Yemen in the third century AD[9].

But if Bilqīs was effectively a sovereign of Himyar, what do we make of Solomon? Scholars such as Jacqueline Pirenne and H. St. J. B. Philby have quoted the verses of a later historian, Nashwān ibn Sa'īd Al-Ḥimyāri (d. 1177), who declared himself a descendant of this same Bilqīs, in which he says that she "came from Mārib to visit Solomon at Palmyra"[10].

Who was this king of Palmyra then, whom Arab tradition had named Solomon, possibly out of respect for the ancient scriptures? He must be none other than King Ḥassān ibn Udhaynah, better known as Septimius Odaenathus, who reigned over the Syrian city from AD 258 to 268[11].

Following a victory over the Persians, he assumed the title of "King of Kings" and was honoured by Emperor Gallienus with the title of "co-ruler of the Orient" for his reconquest of the Empire of Mesopotamia. Like Solomon of Israel, he was seen as the powerful, wise king who would restore order to the Orient. This, therefore, is the "Solomon" that Bilqīs went to visit.

We cannot conclude this study of the ancient Arab writers without mentioning at least two other historians, both of them serious and scrupulous, who wrote about Arabia before the time of Muḥammad. The first is Ibn al-Kalbī (d. 819), whose *Kitab al-asnam* [Book of Idols] is perhaps the most important surviving text on the religious practices of pagan Arabia[12]. The second is Al-Hasan ibn Ahmad Al-Hamdānī (d. 945), one of the most prolific and versatile of ancient Arab scholars. His *Sifat Jazirat al-Arab* [Geography of the Arabian Peninsula] is the oldest and most complete Arabic study of the geography and tribal relations of Arabia, including Yemen, while the eighth book of his *Al-Iklīl* [The Crown] is a priceless source of information on the historical topography of southern Arabia of the Himyarite period[13]. The latter most directly concerns us: in it Al-Hamdānī describes the ruins, castles and ancient sites which he visited in person. We are concerned less with the history of these ruins than with his precise and accurate description of them.

Footnotes:

1. Kiernan, R.H., *L'exploration de l'Arabie, depuis les temps anciens jusqu'à nos jours* (Paris: 1938), 17.
2. Rodinson, M., "L'Arabie du Sud chez les auteurs classiques", in J. Chelhod (ed.), *L'Arabie du Sud, histoire et civilisation: 1. Le peuple yéménite et ses racines* (Paris: G.P. Maisonnneuve et Larosse, 1984), p. 55-89.
3. Strabo in Conti Rossini, C., *Chrestomathia arabica meridionalis epigraphica* (Rome: Istituto per l'Oriente, 1931), p. 13.
4. Pirenne, J., "Les montagnes dans la religion sudarabiques", in R. Stiegner (ed.), *Al-Hudhud: Festchrift Maria Höfner zum 80* (Graz: Karl-Franzens-Universitat , 1981), 263-282.
5. Schoff, W.H. (ed.), *The Periplus of the Erythean Sea, Travel and Trade in the Indian Ocean by a Merchant of the First Century* (New York: Longmans,Green & Co., 1912).
6. Rodinson, "L'Arabie du Sud chez les auteurs classiques", in Chelhod, p. 68.
7. Philby, H. St. J., *The Queen of Sheba* (London: Quartet Books, 1981), p. 37-*38; and Eph'al, I., The Ancient Arabs: Nomads on the Borders of the Fertile Crescent 9th-5th Centuries B.C.* (Leiden: E.J. Brill, 1982), p. 88.
8. Pirenne, J., "Bilqīs et Salomon", *DA* 33 (March-April), p. 9.
9. Philby, *Queen of Sheba,* p. 67.
10. Pirenne, "Bilqīs et Salomon", p. 6-10.
11. Philby, *Queen of Sheba*, p. 83.
12. Ibn Al-Kalbī, Hishām, *The Book of Idols*, trans. N.A. Faris (Princeton: Princeton Oriental Texts, 14, 1952).
13. Hamdānī, Al-Hasan ibn Aḥmad, *The Antiquities of South Arabia (being a translation from the Arabic, with linguistic, geographic, and historical notes of the Eighth Book of al-Hamdānī's Al-Iklīl]*, trans. N.A. Faris (Princeton: Princeton Oriental Texts, 3, 1938).

II

THE REDISCOVERY OF YEMEN

The First Westerner: Lodovico de Varthema

The intellectual revival of the fifteenth century that swept Europe, and Italy in particular, saw the world of classical antiquity as a perfect model of existence, leading to an idealised view of the ancients. Humanism favoured the establishment of schools and academies for classical studies, where works that had been considered permanently lost were rediscovered. The new knowledge was met with great enthusiasm and wonder. But at these schools for the study of classical authors there was now a new concern for the truth. Every piece of information had to be verified, and scholars were determined to do this themselves. Out of this grew a real enthusiasm and need for the great journeys that would later take them along new routes and bring them into contact with new people, habits and customs. Southern Arabia was included in this desire for direct authentication, partly because the peninsula lay on the route to the most interesting and inaccessible destinations of all, the sacred sites of the Muslim east, bordering the area that Europe had always found most hostile.

The first European explorer to reach Mecca and Yemen was an Italian, Lodovico de Varthema, who set sail from Italy and rounded the Cape of Good Hope a few years after Vasco da Gama had opened up the route to India. Probably born in Bologna between 1461 and 1477, he visited Egypt, Syria, Persia, India and Ethiopia. His *Itinerario* [Itinerary], published in 1511, was a great success and was used for at least two centuries by geographers and map-makers.

He was the first European to visit Muḥammad's tomb at Medina and the Ka'aba, the sacred building at Mecca containing the holy black stone. He then set sail from Jiddah and reached the port of Aden. De Varthema noted the importance of the port, which sheltered vessels from India, Ethiopia and Persia. Unfortunately, as a result of one of his companions calling him "Christian dog", the explorer was bound in chains and borne to the palace of the vice-sultan[1]. Once there, he gained the favour of one of the vice-sultan's wives and was subsequently set free to explore at will the most important cities of Yemen. Leaving Aden, his first stop was the oasis of Lahej, thence Yarīm, Ṣan'ā, with its impressive mud walls, Ta'izz, Zabīd and Ḍhamār.

His account of this journey is careful and precise. The few personal asides, which help us to understand the mentality and customs of the country, are always written with his main aim in mind: to travel and to relate all that he saw and heard.

Opportunities for Travel: The Portuguese, the Dutch and the English

In the sixteenth century the Portuguese had absolute naval supremacy over the coastal waters of Arabia. However, we know little or nothing of Yemen in this period. The written records that remain mostly concern the coastline of the Red Sea, for example Alfonso de Albuquerque's *Commentarios*, the *Roteiro* of Joao de Castro, an official-cum-mathematician, or the *Voyages* of an anonymous Venetian sailor on board a Turkish ship during a military expedition to Yemen[2].

One document in particular stands out. This is the first eyewitness account of the ruins of Mārib, the ancient capital of Saba. Two Jesuit missionaries, Montserrate and Paez, sent in 1589 to strengthen a mission in Ethiopia, were shipwrecked off the Kuria Muria islands, taken prisoner by the Arabs and conveyed to Dhofār, the land which today forms the border between Oman and Yemen.

After a summary trial, conducted by allies of the Turks, they were dispatched to the Sultan of Haynān. So it was that the two poor Jesuits embarked on a terrible journey that took them first to Tarīm in Wādī Ḥaḍramawt, and then on to Haynān. They were brought into the presence of the local sultan, who rather unwillingly handed them over to his Turkish governors. So, after four months in the Ḥaḍramawt, the two missionaries set off on foot for Ṣan'ā. Ṗero Paez, who was later to recount his adventures, was struck by the aridity and poverty of the region. Listing the local produce, he mentions an "infusion made with the skin of a fruit called Bunnā"[3]. This is the first known reference to coffee.

They marched for five days and five nights through the barren desert (the Ramlat Sab'atayn), and on the sixth day reached a place called Melchis, where they saw "impressive ruins of large buildings and many rocks with ancient letters, that the natives of the place could neither read nor decipher"[4].

This was Mārib, the capital of Saba, and the ruins were those of the great temple Awwam that Yemenis nowadays call "Maḥrām Bilqīs", or "the sanctuary of Bilqīs".

The two priests eventually reached Ṣan'ā, and found that the city had fallen into some disrepair since de Varthema's time, probably as a result of the Turkish occupation. They were kept in Ṣan'ā for five years, initially as prisoners and then as labourers. Finally they were sent to Al-Mukhā, where they were set free at last.

Ṣan'ā was the seat of the Turkish pasha, and a favourite destination for Western travellers from the beginning of the seventeenth century onwards: ships' commanders and Dutch and English commercial fleets came from Aden and Al-Mukhā to gain the pasha's permission to establish emporiums along the coast or to gain less demanding customs duties. They were given warm and often sumptuous receptions by the local governors and the ruler of Ṣan'ā[5].

Men like John Jourdain, Henry Middleton and Pieter van den Broecke described their experiences at al-Mukhā while they awaited the pasha's reply, the adventures on their travels through Zabīd, Ta'izz, Ibb and Dhamār, and their impressions of the lovely town of Ṣan'ā[6].

The discovery of coffee in southern Arabia in the eighteenth century aroused further interest in the area. Special expeditions were organised to gather supplies of this precious Yemeni crop, and it is interesting to see how some of the leaders – among them the captain of the *Grelaudiere* who, in La Roque's famous *Voyage de l'Arabie Heureuse* published between 1708 and 1713, arrived in Ṣan'ā from the port of Al-Mukhā – described how Yemen was under the rule of Arab sovereigns, who had defeated the Ottoman Turks. Pomp and splendour had been replaced by the greatest simplicity. The royal palace was now sober and unadorned and the king's clothing was reduced to a simple length of silk. Visitors noticed for the first time that the imām had an air of religious royalty.

But while their accounts of everyday life and customs are interesting in the same way as the earlier accounts written by members of the Compagnie delle Indie, they do not give us any new information on the country's geography. The trade routes remained the same, and there was no reason to change them.

Acknowledging the Problem: Carsten Niebuhr

January 1761 was an important year because it marked the beginning of a truly scientific exploration in southern Arabia. This expedition was led by a group of scholars who turned out to be splendid examples of the adventurous spirit of the Enlightenment.

The instigator was King Frederick V of Denmark. Acting on the idea of the Semitic scholar J.D. Michaelis of the University of Gothingen, he compiled a whole series of questions on subjects ranging from geology to philology, from astrology to history, from religion to natural history. A scientific mission was sent to southern Arabia to answer these questions. The various roles were assigned to Peter Forskal, doctor, botanist and a pupil of Linnaeus; Christian Cramer, surgeon and zoologist; Frederick von Haven, philologist and orientalist; George Baurenfeind, geographer and topographer; and, finally, Carsten Niebuhr, engineer, geographer and topographer. The group was completed by a young Swede, Berggren, in the role of cook and domestic help[7].

The outward journey passed calmly and without incident. None of the members of the group was the type to go looking for adventure or danger unless it was required

Plate 1
Carsten Niebuhr

Key to Fig.3. (pp48-49)

1 - Al-Ukhdūd = *Najrān*
2 - Ḥizmat Abī Thawr
3 - Al-Bayḍā = *Nashq*
4 - As-Sawdā = *Nashan*
5 - Kamnah = *Kaminahū*
6 - Kharibat Hamdān = *Haram*
7 - Ma'īn = *Qarnāw*
8 - Inabbah
9 - Barāqish = *Yathil*
10 - Darb aṣ-Ṣabī
11 - Shaqab al-Manassah
12 - Jidfir Bin Munaykhir
13 - Kharibat Sa'ūd = *Kutal*
14 - Al-Asāḥil = *'Ararat*
15 - Al-'Alam
16 - Jabal Ruwayk
17 - Kāniṭ
18 - Na'iṭ
19 - Shibām Kawkabān
20 - Ḥāz
21 - Ḥuqqah
22 - Shibām al-Ghirās
23 - Ghaymān
24 - Ar-Raqlah
25 - Wādī Yanā'im
26 - Al-Masannah
27 - Al-Makhdarah
28 - Al-Kharibah = *Ṣirwāḥ*
29 - Mārib
30 - Yalā/Ad-Durayb = *Ḥafarī*
31 - Al-Masājid
32 - Hajar ar-Rayhānī
33 - Hajar at-Tamrah
34 - Ḥinū az-Zurayr = *Haribat*
35 - Hajar Kuḥlān = *Timna'*
36 - Madīnat al-Ahjur
37 - Baynūn
38 - Kharibat al-Ahjār
39 - Qāniyah
40 - Al-Mi'sāl = *Wa'lān*
41 - Ẓafār
42 - Ash-Shumah
43 - Mawza'
44 - Muhamdid al-Hamilī
45 - Sawā
46 - Ṣubr
47 - Ghanam al-Kuffār
48 - Al-Binā
49 - Al-Barīrah
50 - Al-'Uqlah
51 - Shabwah = *Shabwat*
52 - Al-'Abr
53 - Al-Ḥurayḍah = *Madhab*
54 - Raybūn
55 - Hajrah
56 - Ḥuṣn al-'Urr
57 - Makaynūn
58 - Bā Qutfah
59 - Ḥuṣn al-Qays
60 - Al-Binā = *Qalat*
61 - Ḥuṣn al-Ghurāb = *Qana*
62 - Ḥayd Bin 'Aqīl
63 - Hajar Bin Ḥumayd
64 - Mayfa'ah = *Mayfa'at*
65 - Riyām

Place names in alphabetical order

Al-Asāḥil = *'Ararat* (14)
Al-'Abr (52)
Al-'Alam (15)
Al-Barīrah (49)
Al-Bayḍā = *Nashq* (3)
Al-Binā (48)
Al-Binā = *Qalat* (60)
Al-Ḥurayḍah = *Madhab* (53)
Al-Kharibah = *Ṣirwāḥ* (28)
Al-Makhdarah (27)
Al-Masājid (31)
Al-Masannah (26)
Al-Mi'sāl = *Wa'lān* (40)
Al-Ukhdūd = *Najrān* (1)
Al-'Uqlah (50)
Ar-Raqlah (24)
As-Sawdā = *Nashan* (4)
Ash-Shumah (42)
Barāqish = *Yathil* (9)
Baynūn (37)
Bā Qutfah (58)
Darb aṣ-Ṣabī (10)
Ghanam al-Kuffār (47)
Ghaymān (23)
Hajar ar-Rayhānī (32)
Hajar at-Tamrah (33)
Hajar Bin Ḥumayd (63)
Hajar Kuḥlān = *Timna'* (35)
Hajrah (55)
Ḥayd Bin 'Aqīl (62)
Ḥāz (20)
Ḥinū az-Zurayr = *Haribat* (34)
Ḥizmat Abī Thawr (2)
Ḥuqqah (21)
Ḥuṣn al-Ghurāb = *Qana* (61)
Ḥuṣn al-Qays (59)
Ḥuṣn al-'Urr (56)
Inabbah (8)
Jabal Ruwayk (16)
Jidfir Bin Munaykhir (12)
Kamnah = *Kaminahū* (5)
Kharibat al-Ahjār (38)
Kharibat Hamdān = *Haram* (6)
Kharibat Sa'ūd = *Kutal* (13)
Kāniṭ (17)
Madīnat al-Ahjur (36)
Makaynūn (57)
Ma'īn = *Qarnāw* (7)
Mawza' (43)
Mayfa'ah = *Mayfa'at* (64)
Muhamdid al-Hamilī (44)
Mārib (29)
Na'iṭ (18)
Qāniyah (39)
Raybūn (54)
Riyām (65)
Sawā (45)
Shabwah = *Shabwat* (51)
Shaqab al-Manassah (11)
Shibām al-Ghirās (22)
Shibām Kawkabān (19)
Ṣubr (46)
Wādī Yanā'im (25)
Yalā/Ad-Durayb = *Ḥafarī* (30)
Ẓafār (41)

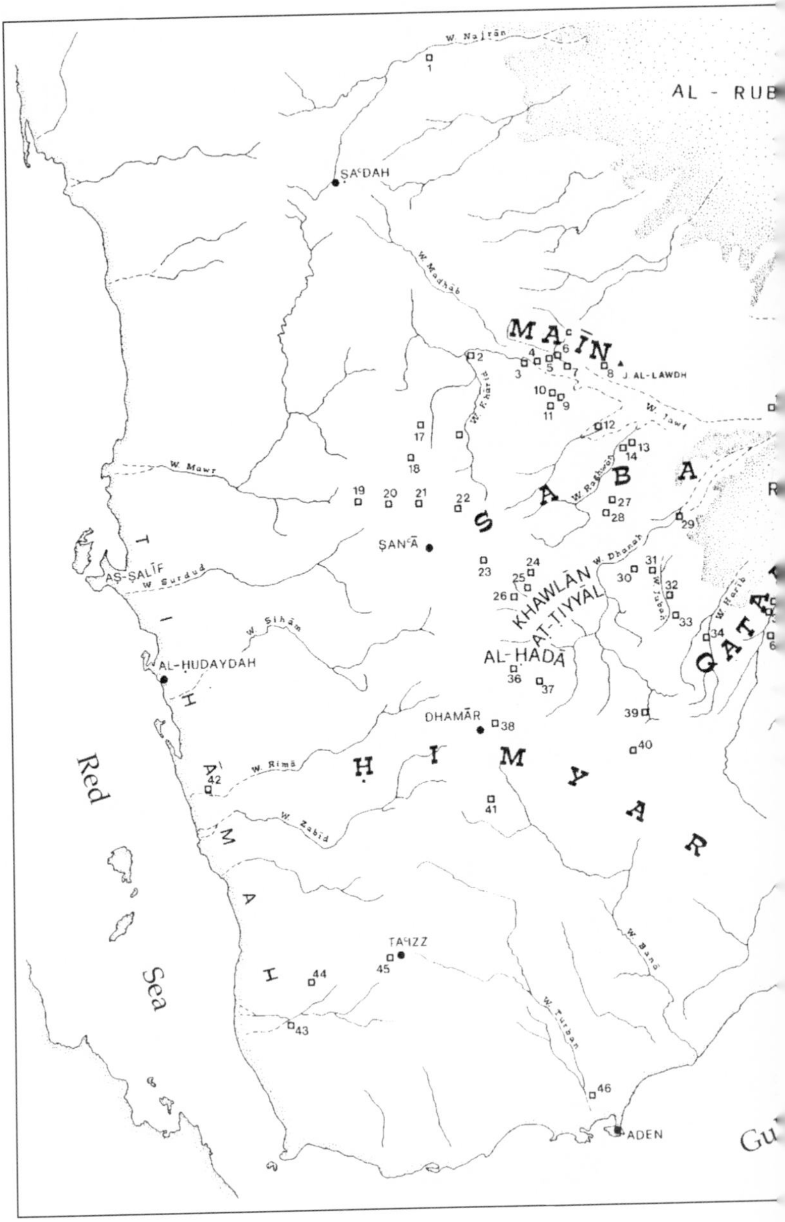

Figure 3.
The South Arabian kingdoms and archaeological sites

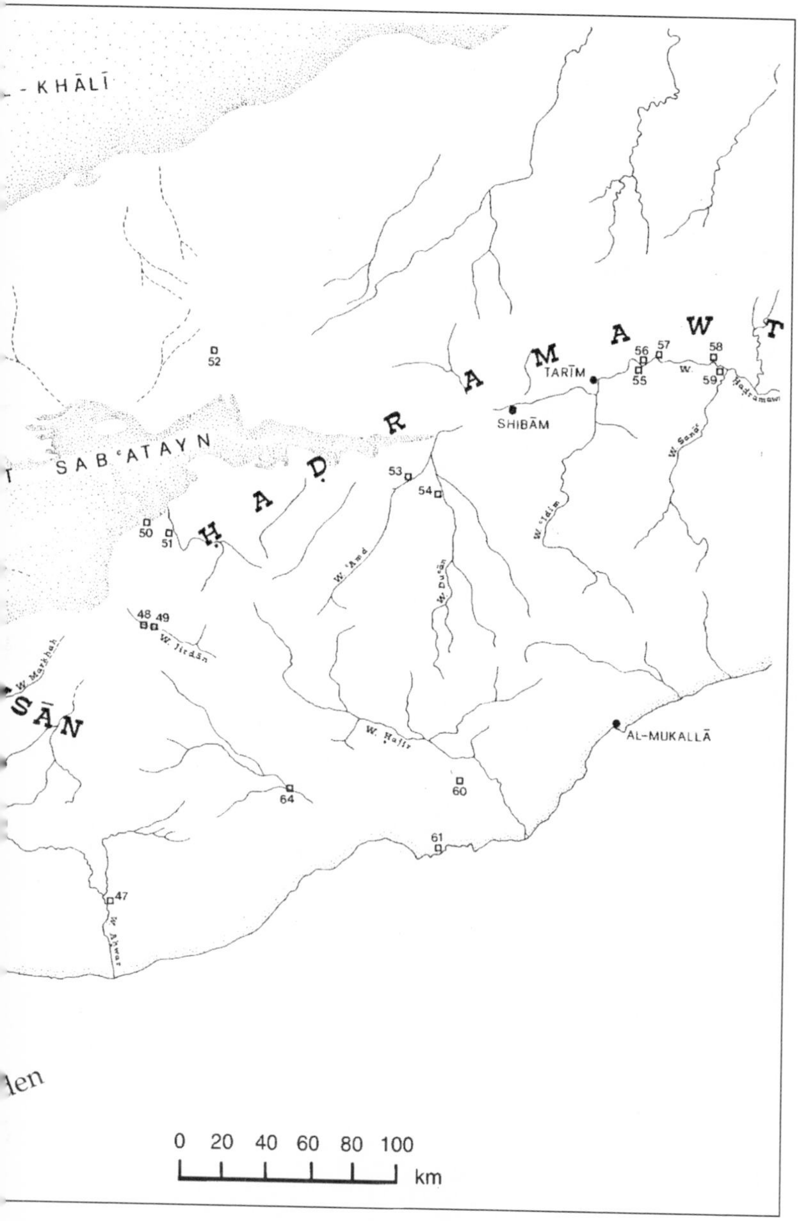

KHĀLĪ
SABʿATAYN
ḤAḌRAMAWT
TARĪM
SHIBĀM
AL-MUKALLĀ
W. ʿAmd
W. Duʿān
W. ʿIdim
W. Sanāʾ
W. Ḥajr
W. Jirdān
W. Markhah
W. Ḥaḍramawt
W. Aḥwar
47
48 49
50
51
52
53
54
55
56
57
58
59
60
61
64
0 20 40 60 80 100 km

by the nature of their science. After a stop at Jiddah they reached Luhayyah and then al-Mukhā. But the expedition that began so happily was destined to end in tragedy: of the six members of the mission, only Niebuhr survived. All the others succumbed to illness and died.

Their visit to Yemen was altogether brief, and dealt only with those sites and cities already repeatedly visited by European commercial envoys. However, Niebuhr's *Travels through Arabia and other Countries in the East* (Edinburgh, 1792) contains such gaps in the development of his arguments and questions that he seems to be talking about completely different places.

During their stay at al-Mukhā and at Bayt al-Faqīh, the Danes separated in order to explore the Tihāmah and the mountains as far as Zabīd and Ta'izz. From al-Mukhā they headed for Ṣan'ā, where they were received by the imam, who gave them permission to stay in the city and explore at their leisure. They stayed for ten days, pushing themselves to gather as much information as possible on the town and its surroundings.

Their return to al-Mukhā gave Niebuhr the opportunity to describe the place and its intense commercial activity, which was mostly controlled by the English. From here, the mission set off for India, although Niebuhr was the only member to arrive alive. After more than a year in Bombay, he finally made it back to Europe, stopping in Oman, Syria and Iraq on the way.

Despite the journey's short duration, the fact that they visited places already known, and their bad luck, the Danish expedition furnished Europe with an extraordinary wealth of new knowledge. Niebuhr's book was published in German in 1772, in French two years later, and in English in 1792. It was a huge success, mostly because it offered the West a new, complete and honest portrait of the Arabs.

Following in Niebuhr's footsteps, Ulrich Jasper Seetzen visited Transjordan and north-west Arabia and reached Al-Ḥudaydah in March 1810. Educated at the University of Ġothingen (as was J.D. Michaelis, the inspiration for Niebuhr's expedition), Seetzen had arranged to travel as the correspondent for a scientific review directed by H. von Zach, Grand Marshal of the court of Saxony-Gotha. Unfortunately, the only records we have of his visit are his letters to his patron. He was prevented from writing a complete account of his finds by his sudden death a year later in Ta'izz.

On his travels, Seetzen visited Zafār (*Fig. 3*), the famous capital of the kingdom of Himyar. Here he found inscriptions in blocks of stone, reused to build new houses, that proved to him that he was standing on the site of the ancient city. He was amazed that the city had left no ruins. (We now know that the stones of Zafār were completely re-used to build neighbouring villages, especially Bayt al-Ashwal.) He copied the unknown letters down as best he could, and as he was leaving, one of the locals gave him an inscribed stone. Once back in al-Mukhā, he had time to make a more exact copy of the characters engraved on his newly-acquired stone, and send the results to his patrons in Germany.

So, for the first time, a written document of the pre-Islamic period found its way to Europe, and Seetzen may therefore be considered the pioneer of South Arabian epigraphy.

Symbols and Words: the Officers of the Palinurus

This was the point at which people started to take an interest in the archaeology of southern Arabia. The excitement engendered by contemporary finds in Egypt, Syria and Ethiopia affected everybody, even explorers who had come to Arabia for quite different reasons. In 1831, an English ship belonging to the East India Company, the *Palinurus*, was sent to survey the coast of southern Arabia. Three of her officers were keen to follow up the ideas in Seetzen's written records. These officers were J.R. Wellsted, J.G. Hulton and C.J. Cruttenden. On 6 May 1834, with their ship anchored in the bay at Bir Aliand and protected by the volcanic cliffs of Husn al-Ghurāb, they found a long and clearly engraved inscription on a high spur of rock[8]. They copied it down accurately and noted that there were numerous ruins both on the summit of the rock and around its base. The three Englishmen could not have known then that they had found the ancient port of Qana, the famous emporium where ships would arrive from Dhofār full of incense, and from where spices would leave on the great camel caravans.

The following year the officers of the *Palinurus* discovered the first great city of southern Arabia, Mayfa'at, known by the Arabic name of Naqīb al-Hajar (*Fig. 3*). The ancient site was surrounded by an impressive set of walls, built of carefully squared and smoothed limestone blocks. On one of these blocks, near the old north gate, they found a long and perfectly engraved inscription. Inside the walls stood the ruins of many buildings, including one thought to be a temple, whose corners faced the cardinal points.

Two years later Wellsted published his description of the city and transcripts of the inscriptions[9]. Other texts, copied by his colleague Cruttenden during a trip to Ṣan'ā (although they are probably from Mārib), were published slightly later[10]. The stock of material discovered was growing, and the first attempts were being made in Europe to decipher the Himyaritic alphabet.

In 1841 W. Gesenius was able to submit a first tentative translation of the South Arabian alphabet to the Royal Asiatic Society in London. His work was based on the analogy between the South Arabian alphabet and that of ancient Ethiopia, and succeeded to the extent that twenty out of the twenty-nine characters had been correctly interpreted. That same year, E. Rödiger published a small volume establishing the correct reading of a further three characters[11].

The material brought back by the officers of the *Palinurus* was still too little to take the work any further. The definitive decoding appeared only after journeys by Thomas Arnaud and Joseph Halévy, which brought the number of known texts to more than eight hundred.

Footnotes:

1. de Varthema, L., *Itinerario*, edition of Paolo Giudici (Milan: 1929), p. 133.
2. Pirenne, J., *A là découverte de l'Arabie. Cinq siècles de science et d'aventure* (Paris: Le Livre contemporain, 1958), p. 44.
3. Ibid. p. 47.
4. Kammerer, A., "Le plus ancien voyage d'un occidental en Hadramaout (1590), le P. Pero Perez de la Compagnie de Jésus", *BSRGE* 18 (1933), p. 164.
5. Beckingham, C.F. and R.B. Serjeant, "Dutch Travellers in Arabia in

the Seventeenth Century", *JRAS* (1951), p. 64-81 and p. 170-181.
6. Foster, W., *The Journal of John Jourdain 1608-1617 Describing His Experiences in Arabia, India, and the Malay Archipelago* (London: 1905).
7. Freeth, Z. and Winstone, H.V.F. , *Explorers of Arabia from the Renaissance to the End of the Victorian Era* (New York: Holmes and Meier, 1978), p. 61.
8. Wellsted, J.R., "Account of Some Inscriptions in the Abyssinian Character Found at Ḥassān Ghorab Near Aden on the Arabian Coast", *JASB* 3 (1834), p. 554-556.
9. Wellsted, "Narrative of a Journey from the Tower of Ba'-l-haff on the Southern Coast of Arabia, to the Ruins of Nakab al Hajar in April 1835", *JRGS* 7 (1837), p. 20-34.
10. Cruttenden, C.T., "Narrative of a Journey from Mokha to Ṣan'ā by the Tarik she-Sham or Northern Route, in July and August 1836", *JRGS* 8 (1838), p. 267-289.
11. Rodiger, E., *Versuch über die himjaritschen Schriftmonumente* (Halle: 1841).

III

EPIGRAPHY YIELDS ITS CLUES

Sabaean Antiquities: Thomas Arnaud

During the 1830s and 1840s, the French consul at Jiddah was Fulgence Fresnel, an Arabist with a particular interest in pre-Islamic antiquities and the historical geography of Arabia. Fresnel wrote up the scientific content of Thomas Arnaud's journey to Mārib in July 1843, which signalled the real beginning of southern Arabian archaeology and epigraphy.

Arnaud was in Yemen in 1835. He spoke fluent Arabic, and gained the trust of the imām of Ṣan'ā as a pharmacist. Having found himself a guide, and dressed in local garb, he paid to join a small caravan of camels descending from the high plains to the desert.

After four days' travelling in Wādī Sirr, which Arnaud describes vividly in his notes published two years later, the caravan finally arrived on the Mārib plain[1]. His first stop was at his guide's tribal camp, where he was received with warmth and hospitality. He was subjected to an onslaught of bedouin curiosity and masses of questions, which were sometimes difficult or dangerous to answer. Meanwhile, the *sharīf* of Mārib had been informed of his arrival, and gave him permission to enter the city. First though, he decided to hire members of the various tribes to protect him on his way. The following morning Arnaud set off on foot, along part of Wādī Dhanah and through the narrow passage between the two sections of Jabal Balaq. He eventually reached the famous ruined dam, and managed to examine both the south and north sluices.

In Mārib, Arnaud was free to visit the ruins of ancient Saba (as he called the capital city), and "the Pillars" and the "Haram Bilqīs", the two temples outside the city walls, respectively the Bar'an temple and the oval Awwam temple.

However his main interest was in inscriptions, and his accounts have little space for archaeological descriptions. For him, the city ruins did not offer much beyond "little mounds of earth"[2]. The Bar'an temple is mentioned only in connection with two inscriptions found nearby, and the

Plate 2
Joseph Halévy

Awwam temple only because, having got there, he was forced to leave before making copies of three inscriptions.

It is curious that the French explorer did not feel the need to dedicate even one word to the rows of monolithic pillars embedded in the sand, which are still today the symbol of archaeology in Yemen. But Arnaud had only two aims: to copy down as many inscriptions as possible for Fresnel, and more importantly, to remain alive and well long enough to hand them over.

On his way back from Mārib, Arnaud stopped briefly at Al-Kharibah, or Ṣirwāḥ, which was for some time the capital of the kingdom of Saba. His predilection for inscriptions was here rewarded with an important discovery in a private house. This was one of the rarest and most complete of all: a long and historic inscription relating to Karib'īl Watar, King of Saba (RES 3495), which, once it had been copied in full by Eduard Glaser, was to provide us with an important addition to ancient South Arabian history. In all, Arnaud brought copies of 56 inscriptions back to Europe, which Fresnel published a couple of years later[3].

In the Kingdom of the Minaeans: Joseph Halévy

The race for inscriptions had started, but Arnaud's experiences had also highlighted some of the serious problems associated with it. Immersing oneself in the territory east of Saba meant abandoning oneself to the mercy of the bedouin tribes, and cutting off all contact with the city. Ṣan'ā and its sovereign wielded no power over the area bordering the desert, nor over the main town, Mārib, which maintained relations of sorts with the central government due to its salt trade.

Joseph Halévy, another Frenchman, was in Ṣan'ā in 1869, about to undertake a journey which, besides producing remarkable results in the fields of archaeology and geography, led to great advances in the ethnographic understanding of the bedouin and Jewish communities of Yemen. Halévy was a Semitist, capable of deciphering the inscriptions that he found. He was also a Jew, and he realised that during his travels he would be able to count on the support of various Jewish groups which, due to their skills as artisans, were scattered throughout the land, down to the smallest inland oasis. So he took on the dress and bearing of a humble Yemeni Jew and, armed only with a pencil, a few pieces of paper and a great capacity for adapting to every situation with patience and wisdom, he set off towards Mārib.

He took the northern road, and as a result became the first European to explore the true paradise of South Arabian antiquities, the Jawf. Here he uncovered the fabulous texts of the Minaeans, and was the first to recognise from the inscriptions that they had a special dialect, different from the Sabaean.

His discoveries are still used today as the basis of all research in the area. We might appreciate the value of Halévy's work by noting that the first real update and re-working of his *Rapport sur une mission archéologique dans la Yemen* (1872) and his *Voyage au Nedjrân* (1873) occurred only with the Egyptian Aḥmad Fakhry's expedition of 1947.

During his stay at Al-Ḥazm, the main centre of the Jawf, in April and May 1870, Halévy explored a lot of the valley. He discovered six cities: ancient Haram, which consists of an artificial hill (now occupied by a modern village, Kharībat Hamdān) and at its foot, the remains of a spectacular temple with a huge stone portal and pilasters decorated with inscriptions and delicate figurative motifs; Qarnāw, the capital of the Minaean kingdom (which the bedouin call Ma'īn), which crowns the high, imposing hill with its ruins, and whose enclosing walls and two monumental gateways are still standing, along with an internal and external temple; Inabbah, between Ma'īn and Jabal al-Lawdh, perhaps identifiable with Ptolemy's Inapha; Kharibat al-Sawdā, ancient Nashan; Kamnah (Kaminahū), Pliny's Caminacum; and finally, the largest of all, Kharibat al-Bayḍā (Nashq), Pliny's Nasca, encircled by a fairly well-preserved ring of walls, enclosing numerous ruins including a temple[4].

After a time, having skirted the desert and seen Bilad Najrān and the ruins of ancient Nagara (Najrān), Halévy returned to the Jawf, entering the valley from the west, in other words, from the plateau. This enabled him to explore all the ruins scattered about in what he called the upper Jawf[5].

Reaching the village of Al-Ghayl, he continued his research in the lower Jawf. Here, having been told by a member of the Jewish community that there had been an ancient Jewish city nearby, he discovered the splendid city of Barāqish, previously called Yathil or Athrula, the city taken by Aelius Gallus after Nasca on his march to Mārib. He journeyed on towards Mārib, the final goal of his travels, crossing Wādī Raghwān and discovering the great Sabaean city of Kharibat Sa'ūd on his way.

At Mārib, Halévy visited the ruins of the city. But he was rather disappointed in them, perhaps because everything seemed so buried in the sand or maybe because, for him, the pinnacle of discovery had been the inscriptions he had seen in the Jawf. He took 685 inscriptions back to the Académie des Inscriptions et Belles-Lettres in Paris, of which 670 were unedited. This was a great success, and he was awarded a chair for South Arabian antiquities at the Sorbonne.

He did however make one small mistake due, unfortunately, to excessive pride and ambition. He erased from his records all mention of a Jewish guide from Ṣan'ā who had accompanied him to the Jawf, Najrān and Mārib, in other words for almost the whole duration of his trip. This guide, Ḥayyim Ḥabshush, perhaps out of resentment for this slight, wrote an account of his journey with Halévy, which only appeared in Europe in 1939, when it was discovered and published by S.D. Goitein[6]. His account tells how Halévy taught him to read and copy down the inscriptions and how he would often be sent off alone to likely sites. Ḥabshush was paid according to the number of copies he brought back. He rather honestly admits that if he found the inscriptions too long he would divide them into shorter pieces to earn more money[7].

So Halévy did not personally see many of the places he describes, which explains why his archaeological descriptions tend to be rather vague and generic. By contrast, Ḥabshush's account, although it is simply written – he was a mason by trade – is full of his impressions of the ruins and cities that he visited, heedless of danger and hardship, to earn his keep and please his master. He seems never to have lost respect for Halévy, despite having his role unfairly and ungratefully deleted.

The discovery of this manuscript rounded off Halévy's work, providing the first ever account of the true archaeological nature of the Jawf antiquities. For example, when describing Barāqish Ḥabshush shows remarkable intuition in divining the site's progressive strata: three discernible layers from the Islamic period, on top of a Minaean layer. Our excavations at Barāqish in 1990 and 1992 would provide exactly the same results.

Collecting the Inscriptions: Eduard Glaser

A few years later, the already vast store of inscriptions collected by Halévy was further enlarged by an Austrian explorer named Eduard Glaser. Glaser was born into a middle-class Bohemian family and from an early age he showed a keen interest in exploring distant lands, especially Arabia. But, perhaps for economic reasons, he was never able to completely dedicate himself to these studies[8].

He went on to study maths, physics and geodesy at Prague Polytechnic, and then became an assistant at the astronomy observatory of the University of Vienna. With enormous perseverance and self-sacrifice, Glaser completed his education on his own, in order to fulfil his ambitious desire to conduct a scientific study of Yemen.

His first expedition (1882-1884) covered the region north-west of Ṣan'ā, taking in Tawīlah, Ḥajjah, Sūdah, Raydah, Dhī Bīn and Riyām. The second (1885-1886) concerned the area west and south-west of Ṣan'ā, between the coastal strip, at the elevation of Bājil, and the highlands at the same elevation as Ṣan'ā, and included the cities of

Plate 3
Eduard Glaser

Manākhah, Mafḥaq and Sūq al-Khamīs. The third (1887-1888) explored the vast area between Ṣan'ā and Mārib; and the fourth and final expedition (1892-1894), covered the Aden-Ṣan'ā route and the cities of Lahej, Ta'izz, Ibb, Yarīm, Dhamār and Ma'bar[9].

Glaser had a good eye for topography and geography, as is apparent in his notebooks (not all published). His incessant, thorough use of sextant, chronometer, compass, aneroid and thermometer enabled him to collect accurate and precise topographical data, which is still used today in drawing up the country's maps. His notes also accurately relate climatic data, astronomy, linguistics, ethnography and archaeology. Archaeology was, in fact, what made his trip to Mārib unforgettable.

Glaser took a new route to the Sabaean capital, south of the mountainous range of Jabal al-Ṭiyāl, and passing through the Khawlān region and Ṣirwāḥ, making him the first to enter the catchment basin of Wādī Dhanah. This is one of the great watershed areas of inland Yemen, and the innumerable little *wādī*s that intersect it become fewer and fewer as it descends towards the desert, until the whole vast system of streams converges on the one great *wādī* (Wādī Saba or Wādī Dhanah) which reaches as far as Mārib, and which the Sabaeans blocked at the mouth of Jabal Balaq with the great dam, visited by Arnaud and Halévy before Glaser.

He was the only explorer to venture into this tortuous region of bleak mountains, intersected by sheer cliffs and deep canyons. Incidentally, this was one of the reasons why almost a century later the Italian mission chose to explore the Khawlān area, and it was here that we came across the first important traces of Yemeni prehistory and protohistory.

More than his study of the monuments, Glaser's great achievement was that he was the first to record his findings in a number of topographical plans. His topographical observations are impressively accurate and thorough. Unfortunately though, Glaser's account of this trip to Mārib was the only part of his notes ever published[10].

The Austrian scholar never managed to achieve his true goal of entering the Jawf, the forbidden zone that had been the making of Halévy. Still, he had the ingenious idea of teaching the bedouin to make calculations and copy down inscriptions[11]. This method led, for example, to his discovery of more than one hundred Qatabanian inscriptions, which gave Europe a first glimpse of the history of this unknown people.

Equally remarkable was the work that Glaser did during his final expedition, discovering, describing and positioning on his charts the many toponyms quoted in the work of Al-Hamdānī, an Arab historian of the tenth century AD, as well as putting together numerous collections of Arabic manuscripts, sculpture, inscriptions and coins that today grace the Library and History of Art Museum in Vienna. Unfortunately his notes were never published, apart from the previously mentioned account of his trip to Mārib, and it was only much later, beginning in 1961, that a collection of his inscriptions began to appear in a collection of the Osterreichische Akademie der Wissenschaften in Vienna, the fourteen-volume work, *Sammlung Eduard Glaser* (SEG 1961-1981).

The Académie des Inscriptions et Belles-Lettres in Paris, beginning in 1899, published *Corpus Inscriptionum Semiticarum* (CIS 1890-1932), and beginning in 1900, *Répertoire d'Épigraphie Sémitique* (RES 1900-1968), which together comprised all the known South Arabian inscriptions. The material was provided thanks to the splendid work of the three great pioneers of South Arabian epigraphy.

During this period, the South Arabian texts were backed up by further texts from northern Arabia, like those discovered by the great English explorer Charles Doughty[12] and by the French expedition led by A. Jaussen and R. Savignac[13]. Material held in museums and various other collections has provided the basis for a growing number of publications.

More Ancient Texts: Assyrian and Aksumite Sources

While work on local epigraphy continued in Arabia, in Mesopotamia, cuneiform texts found during excavations were gradually being deciphered. The Sabaeans and their monarchs made several appearances in the long inscriptions which the Assyrian kings used to list their civil and military feats.

The oldest text was produced by the Assyrian king Tiglath-Pileser III (744-727 BC), who had conquered territories as far away as southern Palestine. In the text, he recounts his invasion of the territories of Massa, Teima and Saba[14] in around 735-733 BC. However, we cannot be sure if he is referring to the kingdom of Saba in Yemen. Considering that the Massa and Teima tribes were based in northern Arabia, he may have been referring to Sabaean nomads, who were also to be found in the north.

Sargon II (721-705 BC) also produced a text, in which he mentions a certain "Ita'mar, the Sabaean", who in 716 BC brought precious gifts to the king including gold, silver and spices[15]. Even without a royal title (which at this period in Saba was *mukarrib* rather than "king", which would not have been recognised by the Assyrians, and explains why they left it out), his name is similar to the Yatha'amar, *mukarrib* of Saba, whom we know from Yemeni texts.

Our final text was produced by Sennacherib (704-681 BC) to commemorate the completion of the New Year temple of Assur. In it he records that precious stones and spices were sent by another south Arabian monarch, King Karibilu of Saba[16]. This is another common name in South Arabian inscriptions and it is tempting to compare it with the name Karib'īl, used by several *mukarribs* of Saba. He may in fact be none other than Karib'īl Watar, the great king of Saba and author of the famous inscription of Ṣirwāḥ (RES 3495).

These allusions to the Sabaeans in the Assyrian texts appeared to provide a good, solid basis for scholars attempting to reconstruct the dynasties. But there were some who were less keen to accept these historical parallels, and serious, lasting scientific disagreements emerged as a result.

Meanwhile with the publication in 1913 of the Deutsche Aksum Expedition's account of the excavations carried out in Abyssinia under the guidance of D. Krencker[17], there was increasing interest in the African facies of Sabaean culture, many examples of which appeared on the other side of the Red Sea, especially in the highlands of northern Ethiopia (Tigray).

The new chronological data and the evidence of the diffusion of their culture fuelled the debate over the origins of the South Arabian peoples. The boundaries of the debate widened to include the controversy over the relations between the Semites and the Hamites. The eminent Italian scholar of Ethiopia, Carlo Conti Rossini, took up the discussion in the 1920s and concluded that during the first millennium BC groups of southern Arabs penetrated the northern Ethiopian highlands for commercial purposes, gradually subduing the local Hamite people (the Cushites). The newcomers grew increasingly powerful, and the region became a true Sabaean colony in the fifth century BC[18].

This would explain why we find works in Ethiopia (architecture, statuary, votive altars, bronze seals and especially inscriptions), which are entirely South Arabian in style[19]. However, there are also local elements – like the pottery for example – which are evidence of the subjugation of the native population.

With the weakening of the Sabaean kingdom towards the end of the millennium, the indigenous tribes seem to have regained control and gradually organised themselves into a strong kingdom called Aksum. In the second and third centuries AD this kingdom expanded its domain as far as the Nile valley to the north and beyond the Red Sea to the east, gradually imposing its power over the whole of southern Arabia.

Footnotes:

1. Arnaud, T., "Relation d'un voyage à Mareb (Saba) dans l'Arabie méridionale, entrepris en 1843 par M. Arnaud", *JA* 5 (1845), p. 211-245 & p. 309-345.
2. Ibid. p. 324.
3. Fresnel, F., "Recherches sur les inscriptions himyariques de Ṣan'ā, Kariba, Mareb, etc.", *JA* 6 (1845), p. 169-237.
4. Halévy, J., "Voyage au Nedjrân", *BSGP* 6th Series (1873), p. 600-604.
5. Halévy, "De Sana au Nedjrân", *BSGP* 6th Series (1877), p. 466-479.
6. Ḥabshush, H., *Masot Habshush: sipuro shel Reb Hayim ben Yahya Ḥabshush al masaotav im Yosef ha-Levi be-Teman ha-mizrahit ve-al haye ha-Yehudim veha-Arvim sham* (Tel Aviv: A.Y. Shtibel, 1939).
7. Moscati Steindler, G., *Hayyim Habšuš, Immagine dello Yemen* (Ricerche dell'Istituto Orientale di Napoli, 11, 1976), p. 93.
8. Werdecker, J., "A Contribution to the Geography and Cartography of North-West Yemen (based on the results of the exploration by Eduard Glaser undertaken in the years 1882-1884)", *BSRGE* 20 (1939), p. 16-20.
9. Ibid. p. 20.
10. Glaser, E. *Eduard Glaser's Reise nach Mârib; hrsg. von Dav. Heinr. v. Muller und N. Rhodokanakis; nebst 4 Kartographischen und topographschen Beilagen und 3 Skizzen der Dammbauten bei Mārib* (Wien: A. Holder, 1913).
11. Weber, "Eduard Glasers Forschungsreisen in Südarabien", *Der Alte Orient* 10, no. 2 (1909), p. 23-25.
12. Doughty, C.M., *Travels in Arabia Deserta* (Cambridge: University Press, 1888).
13. Jaussen, A. and Savignac, R., *Mission Archéologique en Arabie*, Vol. I-III (Paris: P. Geuthner, 1909-1922).
14. Eph'al, I., *The Ancient Arabs: Nomads on the Borders of the Fertile Crescent 9th-5th Centuries B.C.* (Leiden: E.J. Brill, 1982), p. 15, 88.
15. Ibid, p. 36, 39.
16. Ibid, p. 43.
17. Krencker, D., *Deutsche Aksum-Expedition, Vol. II: Ältere Denkmäler Nordabissiniens* (Berlin: G. Reimer, 1913).
18. Conti Rossini, C., *Storia d'Etiopia (Parta prima: Dalle origini all'avvento della dinastia salomonide* (Bergamo: Istituto italiano d'arti grafiche , 1928), p. 99.
19. Pirenne, J., "Sabea d'Etiopia, arte", *Enciclopedia dell'Arte Antica Classica e Orientale*, vol VI (Rome: Istituto della Enciclopedia Italiana), p. 1044-48.

IV

EARLY EXCAVATIONS AND THE ANCIENT CAPITALS

The Ḥuqqah Excavations: a Temple Brought to Light

The excavations in Yemen were started by two geologists from Hamburg University, Carl Rathjens and Hermann von Wissmann. Arriving in Ṣan'ā in 1927, they were warmly received by Imām Yaḥyah who, despite not granting them leave to visit the Jawf, proposed the idea of conducting excavations at Ḥuqqah, a site not far from the capital.

The excavations yielded some fascinating results, despite being run by non-specialists in extremely precarious conditions. The two German naturalists uncovered the foundations of a temple, whose inscriptions date it to the first century BC or first century AD, and tell us that it was dedicated to the "sun goddess" Dhat Ba'adan[1].

The building consisted of a square courtyard with columns along three sides (Figs. 4 and 5). On the open side there stood a 5 metre-wide cell with a central door which was reached through a sort of covered platform. The portico was flanked to the north and south by two rectangular rooms. The structure was 28 metres wide and 22 metres deep and the entrance stood in the middle of the eastern side. The columns were evenly-spaced and octagonal and supported square capitals surmounted by a

Plate 4
Hermann von Wissmann

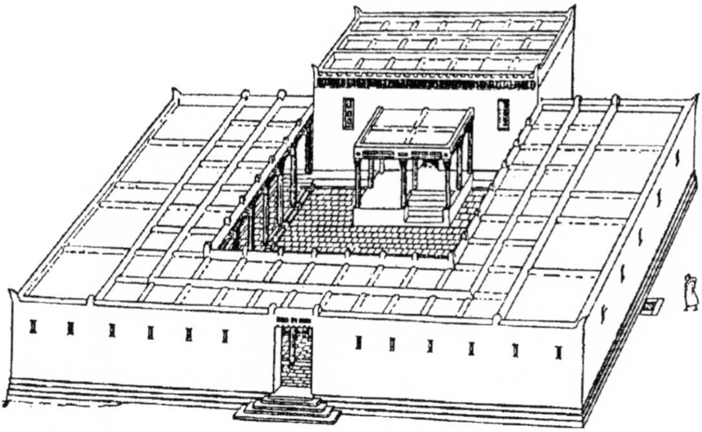

Figure 4
Reconstruction of the Temple of Ḥuqqah

band of decorative indentations. The floor of the portico was higher than the central courtyard and was paved with stone slabs.

During this first expedition, Rathjens and von Wissmann also had the opportunity to visit Hāz and Shibām al-Ghirās, two important South Arabian sites not far from Ṣan'ā. They returned to Europe in 1928 and published three reports: one on the inscriptions (they found 170 new examples[2]), one on the excavation of the temple of Huqqah[3], and the third on points of geological, meteorological and topographical interest in the regions visited[4].

It is, of course, the second volume (*Vorislamische Altertümer*) that interests us most, as it is the first true archaeological report on pre-Islamic Arabia. Published in 1932, it provided the first direct evidence of a culture that until then had only been known through its inscriptions.

The two German geologists returned to Yemen in 1931 with the Dutchman Daniel van der Meulen, and led an important first expedition to the Ḥaḍramawt. That same year, Rathjens furthered the exploration of the region, focusing on the area that Glaser had seen, north-west of Ṣan'ā. He made return trips in 1934 and 1937[5], collecting a huge amount of new material, some of it from the antiques

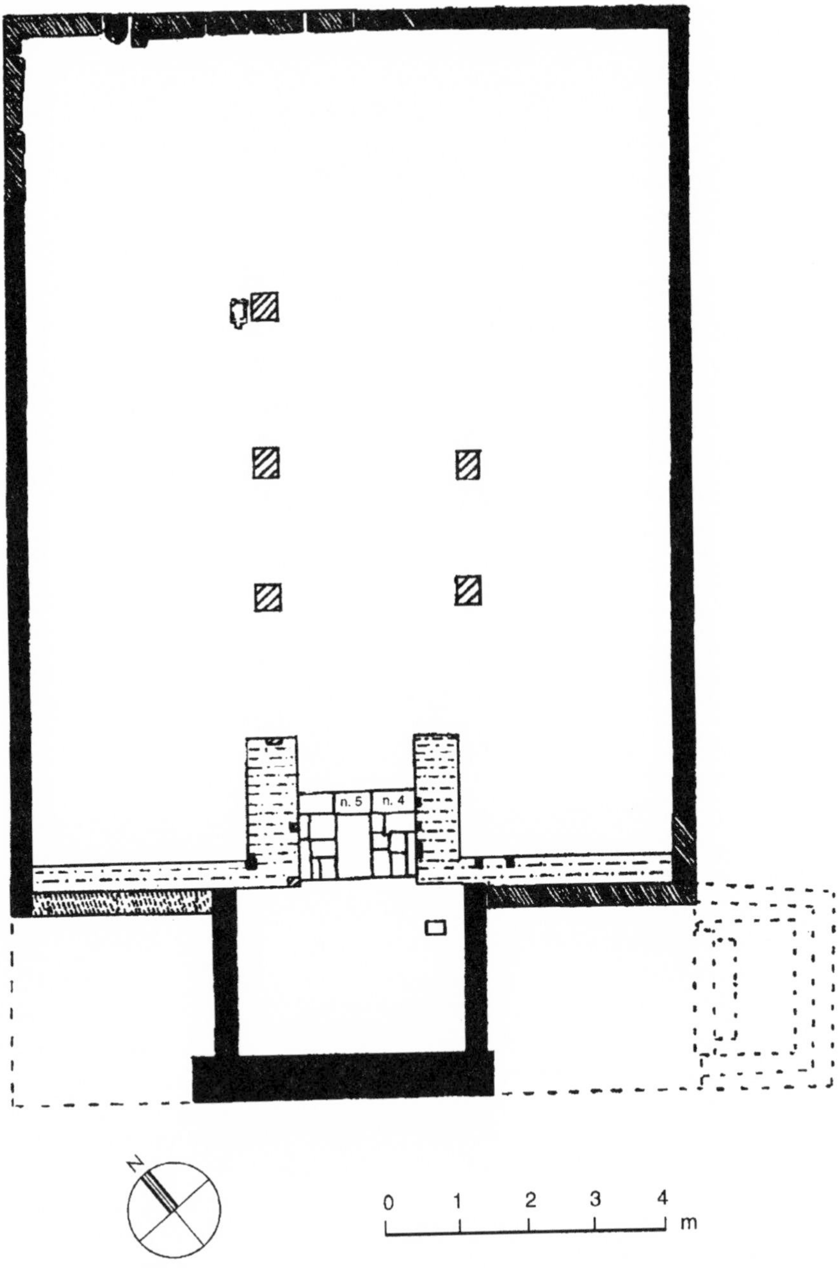

Figure 5
Plan of the Temple of Ḥuraydah/Madhab

market, which he subsequently published in a valuable volume[6]. Besides inscriptions, many other works were thus brought to light, especially in the minor arts, for example clay figurines, statuettes and funerary stelae, seals, amulets, tools and especially pottery.

Science in the Ḥaḍramawt: the Ḥurayḍah Excavations

In fact, research on a collection of pottery had been published during the previous decade by the English scholar, Gertrude Caton Thompson. Her report in 1944 followed her excavation in early 1938 of the site at Ḥurayḍah in the Ḥaḍramawt. This was the first real report of an excavation in Yemen[7].

The expedition included the famous traveller and writer Freya Stark and the geology and sedimentary expert Elinor Gardner. Caton Thompson had originally studied prehistoric sciences, which is why her results were so exceptionally accurate and reliable. She attempted to reconstruct the methods of irrigation and agriculture used by the Hadramis by concentrating particularly on the region's environmental aspects. In fact, her reconnaissance missions in the Wādī 'Amd valley found strong evidence of the presence of ancient man and provided an insight into ancient methods of exploiting resources.

This study was the first to portray the ancient Sabaeans as able and tireless hydraulic engineers. The huge remarkable Mārib dam, which was considered a miracle by Arnaud, Halévy and Glaser, could now be placed in its true functional context.

Apart from its environmental research, the English mission also brought to light an interesting temple complex, situated on an artificial mound in the *wādī* bed, whose inscriptions show that it was dedicated to the lunar god Sin[8].

The temple was rectangular in shape (12.5 x 9.5 metres), and stood on a raised stone platform approximately four metres high. Its corners were oriented towards the cardinal points (Fig. 5). The building consisted of a single room paved with stone slabs, whose ceiling was supported by six, probably wooden, pillars, five of whose stone bases remain. Over time, the chamber was enlarged by moving the entrance on the short south-west side out by about 2.5

metres, while two flights of steps were built to reach the entry platform.

Stone reliquaries and altars were then built in front of the temple. Here the mission discovered various anthropomorphic stelae, a betyl, some stone incense-burners, a few ceramic shards and many inscriptions.

The texts were studied and published in a report by Gonzague Ryckmans, the Belgian Arabist who had taken on the difficult task of gathering and studying all the inscriptions that were filtering through to Europe from Yemen. The vast majority of the Ḥuraydah texts were in the Hadrami dialect, which introduced an element of novelty and interest.

Besides the name of the god to whom the temple was dedicated (now, as we shall see, identifiable with the sun god Sayyin), the inscriptions also bore the ancient name of the site, Madhab, which, judging from the extent of its ruins, must have been a place of considerable importance and was perhaps a commercial centre.

Unfortunately, their time was limited and the English mission had to choose quickly between several options: to extend the excavation of the temple, to dig a new trench at the Madhab site, or to search out other antiquities in the valley.

In order to prove the chronology of her moon temple, Gertrude Caton Thompson decided to excavate two tomb chambers that had been identified by Gardner at the northern edge of the *wādī*. The first of these tombs, dug out of the rock, was intact[9]. Inside were the remains of forty-two people and their belongings. The excavation report by an anthropological expert included an analysis of the bones, giving the first insight into the physical characteristics of the people of South Arabia. As many as eighty-seven vases were found intact in this mass grave and catalogued. The second grave, which seemed to have belonged to a wealthier family, was not entirely excavated and showed evidence of having been plundered in antiquity. Among the possessions of the three occupants were vases similar to those in the first tomb, as well as a pair of seals, an engraved silver amulet and a multi-coloured glass vase[10].

The finds were datable to the sixth century BC, and it was obvious that the tombs were contemporary with the oldest phase of the temple's use. This led the English archaeologist to date the temple to the fifth to fourth century BC, and to conclude that the enlargements at the rear of the temple and the external sanctuaries and altars probably remained in use throughout the third century BC[11].

Philby at Shabwat

In 1935 Freya Stark visited the Ḥaḍramawt and its three principal cities, Tarīm, Saywūn and Shibām[12], but she never got as far as Shabwat (now Shabwah), capital of the ancient kingdom of Ḥaḍramawt.

Harry St. John Philby, the great explorer of central Arabia and the only European to gain the friendship and protection of King Ibn Ṣa'ūd, founder of the Kingdom of Saudi Arabia, was aware of Stark's unrealised goal. That same year, he accepted Ibn Ṣa'ūd's request that he should go to Asīr and redraw the boundary following a victory over the imām of Yemen. Once there, Philby began to nurture an ambitious dream, to discover a South Arabian city, just as Arnaud (Mārib) and Halévy (Qarnāw) had done[13].

His journey in 1936 was a success, partly because motorised vehicles were used for the first time. From the Najrān region he crossed the desert area of Dahm, skirting the sands of the Rub' al-Khālī, and coming to the entrance of Wādī Ḥaḍramawt, where he succeeded in finding Shabwat. He was disappointed by the small scale of the site, and could not come to terms with Pliny's assertion that

Plate 5
Harry St John Philby

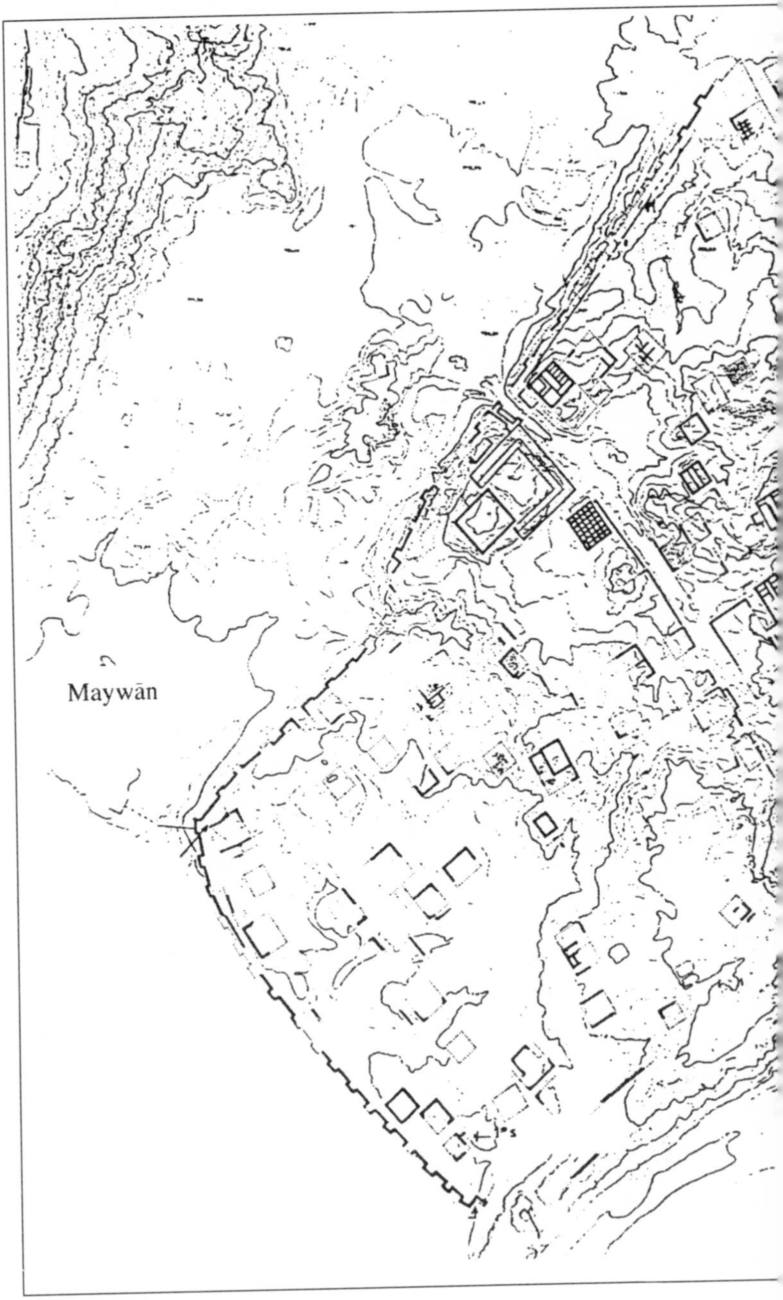

Figure 6
Plan of Shabwah/Shabwat

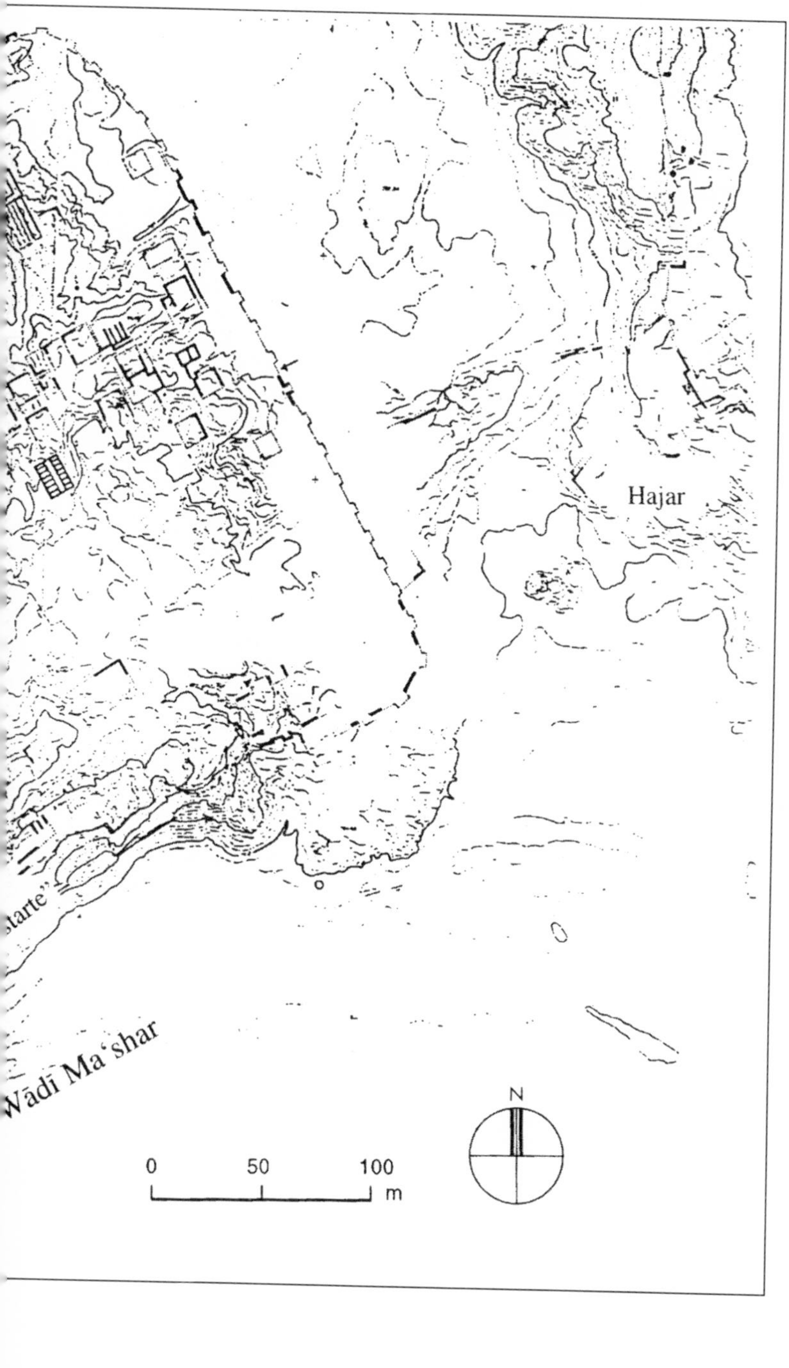
Hajar
"Astarte"
Wādī Ma'shar
N
0
50
100
m

"Sabota contained sixty-five temples"[14].

Philby's disappointment is perhaps understandable. It is a feeling often experienced by explorers discovering South Arabian antiquities, due to subconscious comparisons being drawn with the mythical fame of Saba and the other kingdoms. Besides, Philby was neither an archaeologist nor a philologist but a brilliant explorer, competent geographer and expert on Arab customs; he could not help but expect more of his discovery. Nevertheless, his description of the site is pretty conscientious and leaves us with a complete picture of Shabwat's topography and archaeology.

The ancient capital occupied the southernmost of a group of hills surrounded by two *wādī*s, Wādī Mihbadh and Wādī Ma'shar. The fact that the hills contained ancient salt mines led Philby to believe that the site had first been settled for the salt trade. But its position in the far west of the kingdom – which extended beyond Wādī Ḥaḍramawt as far as the sea to the east – is better understood as meeting a political need to stay in touch with the other capital cities of South Arabia.

The ancient city of Shabwat was bounded to the west by the village of Maywan, and to the east by that of Hajar. It stretched over a rectangular site (about 550 x 300 metres) that rose gently towards the south, ending in a long narrow plateau with a vertical drop down to the ancient fields of Wādī Ma'shar (Fig. 6).

To the north stands a magnificent large gate, constructed from well-cut blocks of smooth stone, from which a straight "street" leads southward, cutting the city into two approximately equal halves. This passes in front of what Philby called the Temple of Astarte.

The street leads to a monumental staircase, about ten metres wide, flanked by two enormous rectangular plinths, supporting niches for sculptures (possibly bronze ibex). At the top of the steps stands a row of four rectangular bases for similar statues. These stand on a level with a long terrace (16.5 x 2.25 metres) ending in a wall to the south with a gateway in the middle, aligned with the bases. It is difficult to make sense of this majestic and complex entrance without the help of excavations. Philby's theory on the function of the temple is worth verifying, however[15].

There is another noteworthy building in the east of the city near the main street. Philby thought that this too could be a temple. In 1938 an English army officer named R.A.B. Hamilton, stationed at Aden as Political Officer, conducted a short excavation here which unfortunately shed no light on the building's function[16].

Necropolises in the Desert

Leaving Shabwat, Philby turned east towards the Yemeni Jawf. Crossing the desert of Ramlat Sab'atayn he stopped at the foot of Jabal Ruwayk, a black granite hill standing among the dunes. To his great surprise he noticed that the summit of the main peak of Ruwayk was dotted with curious circular towers that reminded him of the "pill-boxes" (or blockhouses) of the First World War[17].

Rejecting the possibility that these were irrigation or military installations, Philby considered the possibility of a ceremonial function, and then, having also visited those lining the summit of the nearby limestone ridge of 'Alam al-Abyaḍ, firmly identified them as tombs. Philby remained astonished by the extent of these necropolises in the middle of the desert and was unable to find an explanation. As we shall see, the Italian mission was able to

Plate 6
View of the walls of Al-Asāḥil/'Ararat

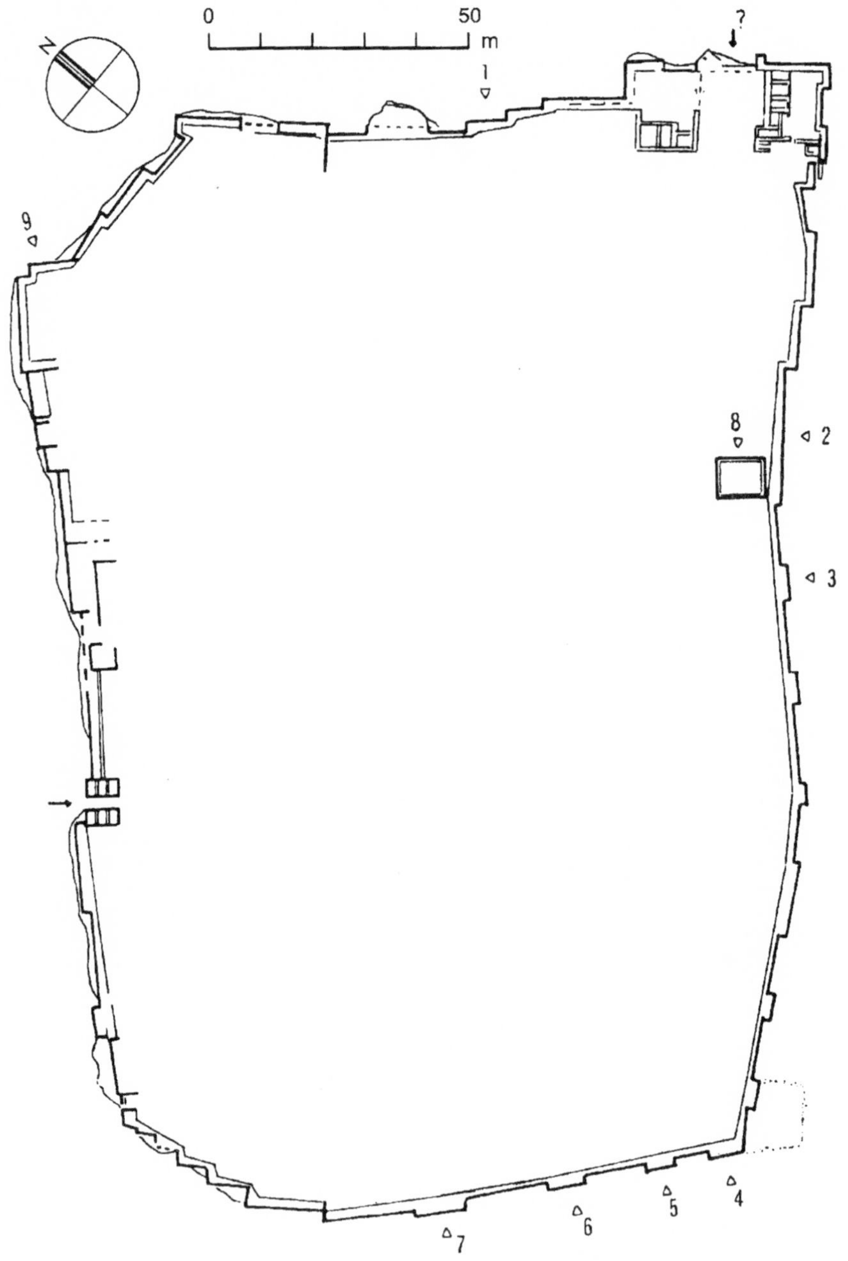

Figure 7
Plan of Al-Asāḥil/'Ararat

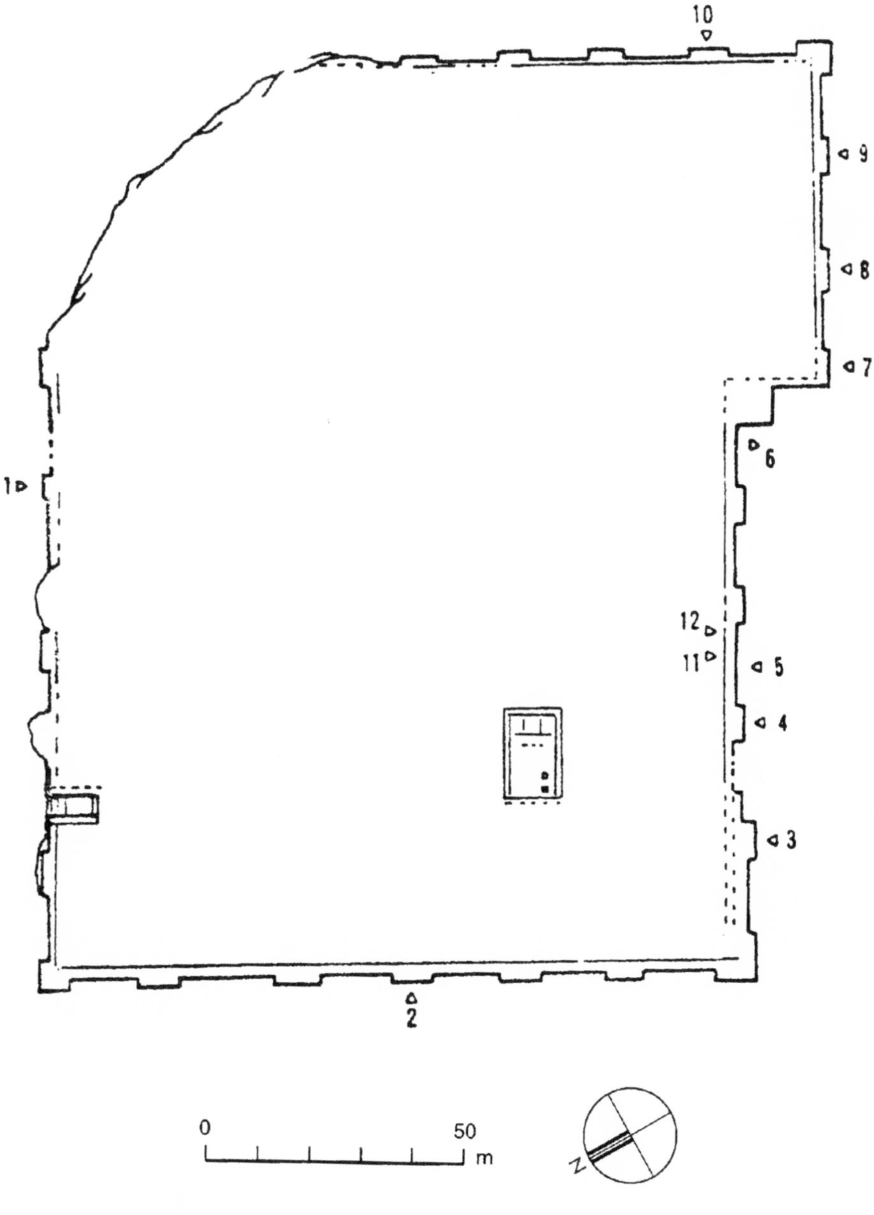

Figure 8
Plan of Kharibat Sa'ud/Kutal

excavate some of these tombs and we can now advance a few hypotheses on their origin and nature.

'Ararat and Kutal

In the Jawf, Philby spent a few days in Wādī Raghwān, where he examined the ruins of the two Sabaean cities of 'Ararat (Al-Asāḥil) and Kutal (Kharibat Sa'ūd)[18].

The site of Al-Asāḥil is covered with the ruins of a great fortified city (Fig. 7). The walls are made of roughly-hewn blocks of stone, encircling a basically rectangular area of about 170 x 230 metres. Philby found several inscriptions on these walls and came to the conclusion that the old name of the city was Ḥarib.

Kharibat Sa'ūd, situated about two and a half kilometres south-west of Al-Asāḥil, is a smaller site (about 145 x 185 metres). It has a neat rectangular shape, except for an extension to the south-east perimeter wall (Fig. 8). The uniform alternation of buttresses and recesses, finishing at the corners in square bastions, gives the impression that the city was planned as a whole and built all at one time, unlike Al-Asāḥil. There is very little debris within the walls; just in front of the entrance in the south-west wall the remains of a building are clearly visible. Judging by the fragments of architectural decoration, this was probably a temple.

Philby also found inscriptions on the walls of Kharibat Sa'ūd that led him to identify it with the ancient city of Yaliṭ. The plans of the two cities were drawn up in 1964 by Hermann von Wissmann on the basis of Philby's own descriptions[19]. On reconsidering the discovery, von Wissmann corrected Philby's historical conclusions. The names Ḥarib and Yaliṭ were simply used in the dedications on parts of the walls or individual bastions, and a careful study of the inscriptions, completed in 1980 by the Frenchman Christian Robin and the Belgian Jacques Ryckmans, now identifies Al-Asāḥil with ancient 'Ararat, and Kharibat Sa'ūd with ancient Kutal[20].

Fakhry at Qarnāw

In the 1940s, Imām Yaḥyah, who had always cautiously guarded the country against external influences, began to

Plate 7
The extramuros temple of Ma'in/Qarnāw (temple of 'Athtār)

allow the occasional visit to his country's antiquities, probably to enable him to assess their value for himself. Permission was granted to the entomologist Muḥammad Tawfīq in 1944, and to the Egyptian archaeologist Aḥmad Fakhry in 1947.

Although full of an amateur's mistakes, the brief report in Arabic that Tawfīq published in 1951[21] demonstrated a knowledge of Qarnāw far surpassing the scant, outdated information provided by Halévy and Ḥabshush. The following year his information was corrected and published by Fakhry, who made good use of a short visit to Ṣirwāḥ, Mārib and the Jawf, organised for him by the same imām[22].

Despite the many visits to Ma'īn by scholars, we still do not have a complete description of Qarnāw, and so Fakhry's account is still our sole point of reference. He describes the fortified city as built on a plateau, which rises about 10 metres above the surrounding plain. It has a rectangular plan and measures about 350 x 240 metres.

Plate 8
View of the south sluice of the Mārib dam

Plate 9
Ruins of the Awwam temple at Mārib

There are two principal entrances: the eastern gate, facing the desert, is flanked by two towers which still stand about 12 metres high and show an exceptional skill in military architecture. The western entrance is more elaborate. Passing between two bastions, one emerges into a portico covered with inscriptions, which then narrows into a passageway leading to the city (Fig. 11).

The houses and palaces are in ruins and only excavations will reveal the original plan of the city. There are rows of columns and pillars still standing though, and in the northern sector are the ruins of a large limestone temple. Part of this is still standing: a room containing six square pillars which support the roofing slabs, reached through two open courtyards. Nearby, two further temples are almost completely buried. Only the roof slabs are visible on the surface.

About 800 metres outside the eastern gate stand the ruins of a temple dedicated to ‘Athtar. It consists of a prostyle of four large monolithic pillars which, with the jambs of the double door behind them, support the beams and architraves that have been elaborately arranged between them. Inside are six large pilasters whose flat surfaces are engraved with complicated decorative motifs including recumbent oryx, entwined serpents, stylised jars and dancing figures (Fig. 78).

Fakhry's account has an admiring, almost awestruck tone when describing the impressive ruins of Qarnāw, but it lacks precision, which is a common trait among travellers in the Jawf when faced with so many fabulous ruins in such a short space of time.

A plan of Ma‘īn produced by the French archaeological mission (Fig. 12) allows us to correct Fakhry on several points. For example, the city is essentially square in shape rather than rectangular and none of the sides is more than about 220 metres long. The work published by the German archaeological mission means that we can now also modify the plans of the temples both within and outside the city walls (Fig. 13). The dimensions in Fakhry's plans were inexact, and he tended to push his hypothetical reconstructions too far, resulting in sketches that actually had little to do with the true nature of the temples[23].

Plate 10
Locus 14 of Al-Raqlah after the excavation (Bronze Age)

Plate 11
View of the city of Yalā/Al-Durayb, ancient Hafarī

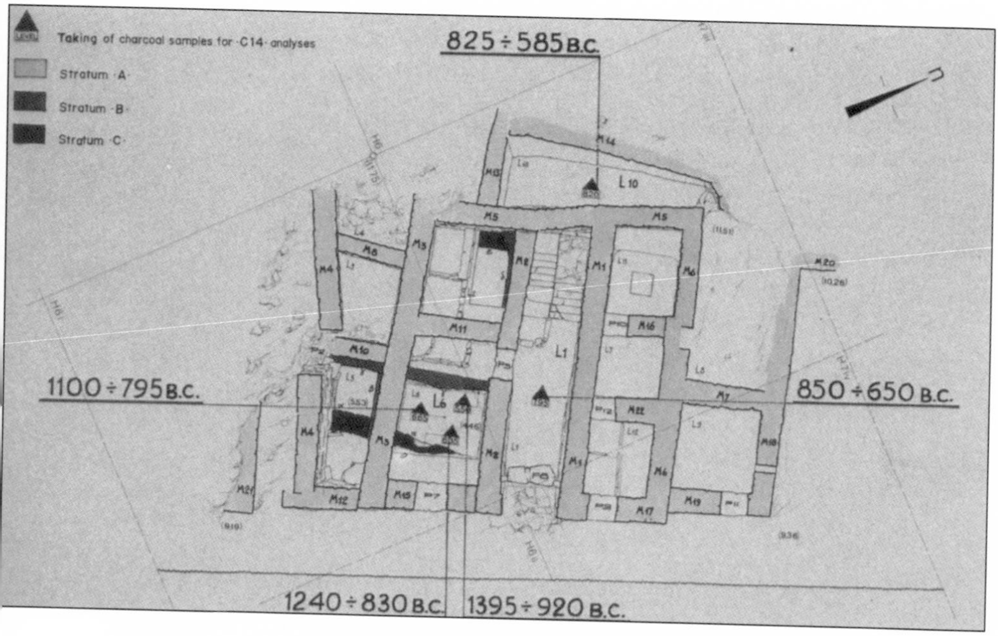

Figure 9
View of house A in Yalā/Al-Durayb, excavated by the Italian archaeological mission in 1987

Ṣirwāḥ

Besides Ma'īn, Fakhry visited several other ruined cities that Halévy had seen, including the site near the south-west edge of Al-Ḥazm, where the village of Kharibat Hamdān (previously Haram) now stands; that of Barāqish (previously Yathil); and further west, the cities of Kamnah (Kaminahū), Al-Sawdā (Nashan), and Al-Bayḍā (Nashq).

The descriptions are too vague to give the reader even the faintest idea of what these cities must have been like. To his credit, however, Fakhry found many new inscriptions (which were published at the end of G. Ryckmans' report), and made detailed drawings such as the interesting decoration engraved on a large stone doorway which may have belonged to an extramural temple at Haram. This was similar to the decoration found on the external temple of Ma'īn.

Fakhry brought back further useful, if succinct, pieces of information from Ṣirwāḥ and Mārib, which he passed

Plate 12
View of house A in Yalā/al-Durayb after the excavation

Plate 13
Terracotta religious panel found in house A at Yalā/Al-Durayb

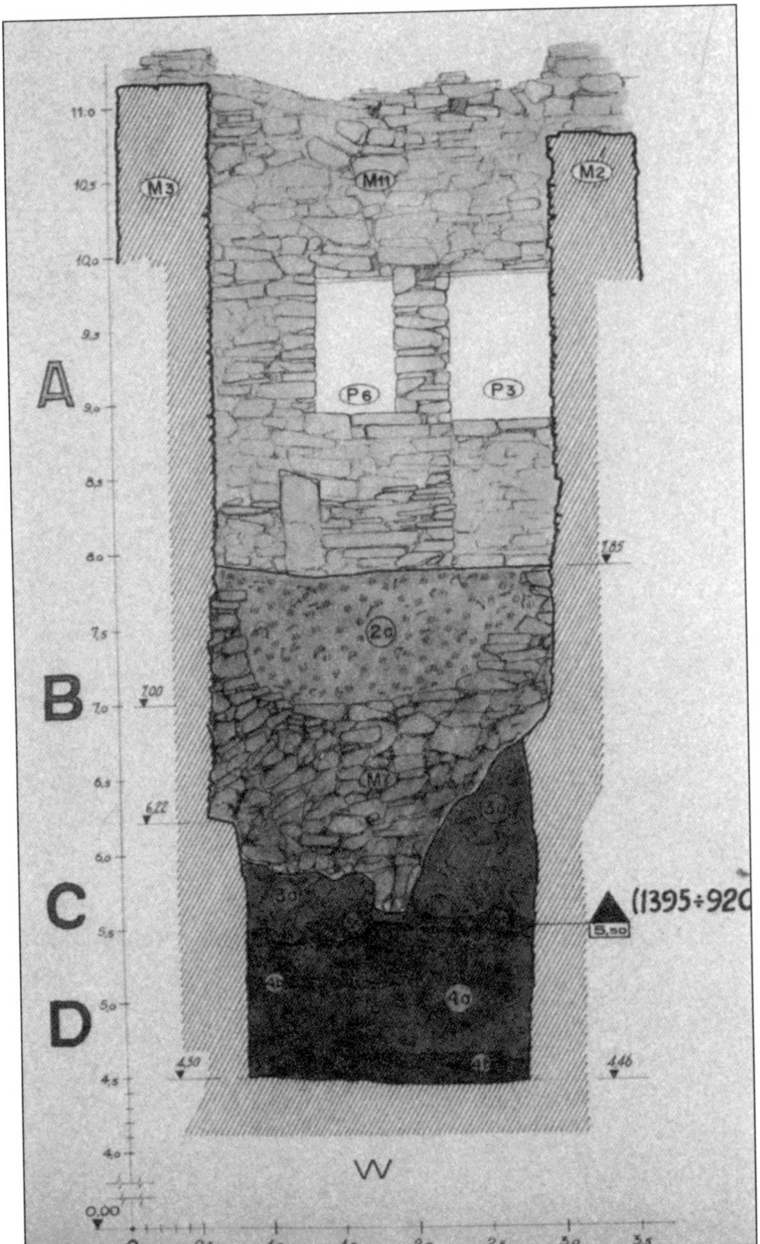

Figure 10
Stratigraphic section from the probe (in L6) under house A at Yalā/Al-Durayb

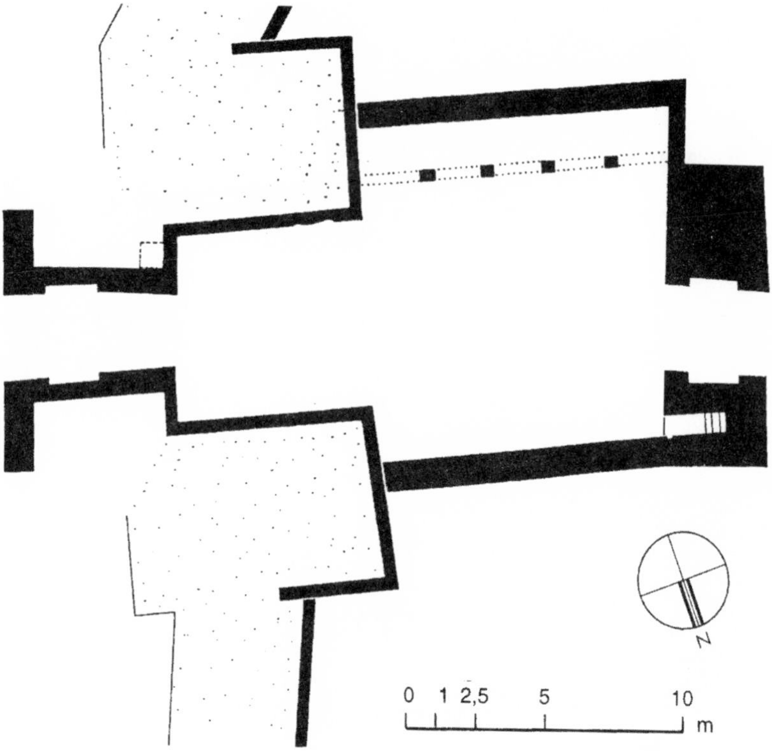

Figure 11
The west gate of Ma'īn

through before immersing himself in the Jawf. He provided the first summary sketch of the antiquities found at Al-Kharibah (Ṣirwāḥ), a plan of Mārib showing the topographical distribution of monuments, a few diagrams of the dam and a couple of comprehensive surveys of the two oval temples at Ṣirwāḥ (Temple of Almaqah) and Mārib (Temple of Awwam or Maḥrām Bilqīs).

Ṣirwāḥ, once the capital of Saba, had a square plan (about 210 metres per side) and its ruins stand on a platform about eight metres higher than the surrounding ground level (Fig 15). This platform looks man-made but Fakhry noticed outcrops of rocks here and there that show it was probably a natural structure[24].

The site is covered with the ruins of large structures, originally temples and important public buildings. The

Plate 14
The west gate of Ma'īn/Qarnāw

Plate 15
The intramuros temple of Ma'īn/Qarnāw

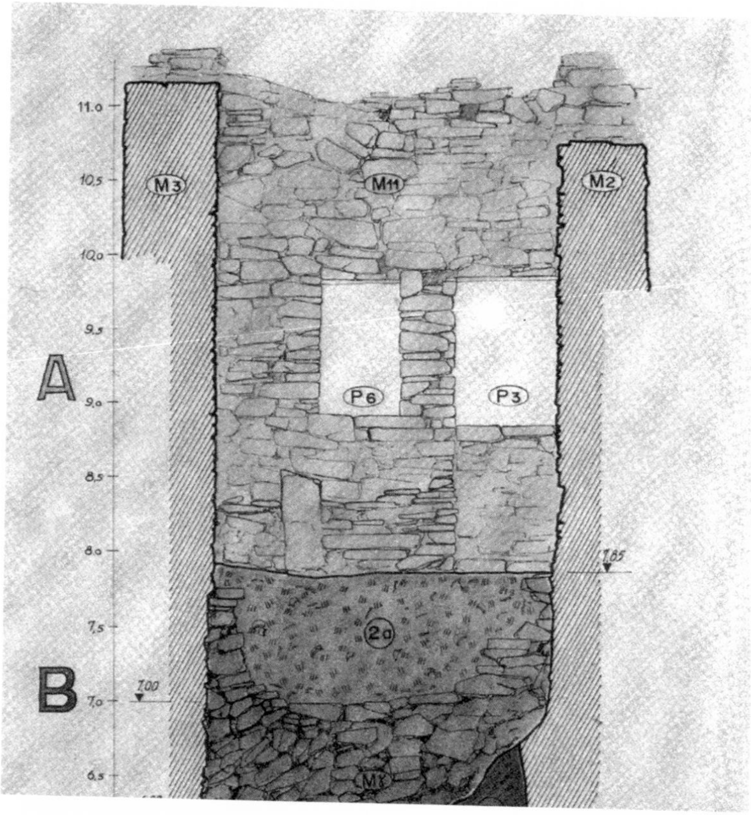

Figure 12
Plan of Mai'īn/Qarnāw

most spectacular of these is the oval temple dedicated to the god Almaqah, in the south-west corner of the city (Figs. 14 and 15). It consists of a large apse, 34 metres deep by 33 metres wide, whose western side was probably connected to a series of annexes. We do not know the layout of these annexes but their presence is indicated by several rows of monolithic columns. The apsidal wall is a sort of casemate, covered by well-connected, smooth stones. Above it runs a frieze of ibex heads. The entrance in the south wall of the apse is still just about visible, although it now leads to a modern home set up inside the temple[25]. In the courtyard of this house is the famous, lengthy inscription RES 3945, seen by Arnaud and Halévy and copied in full by Glaser.

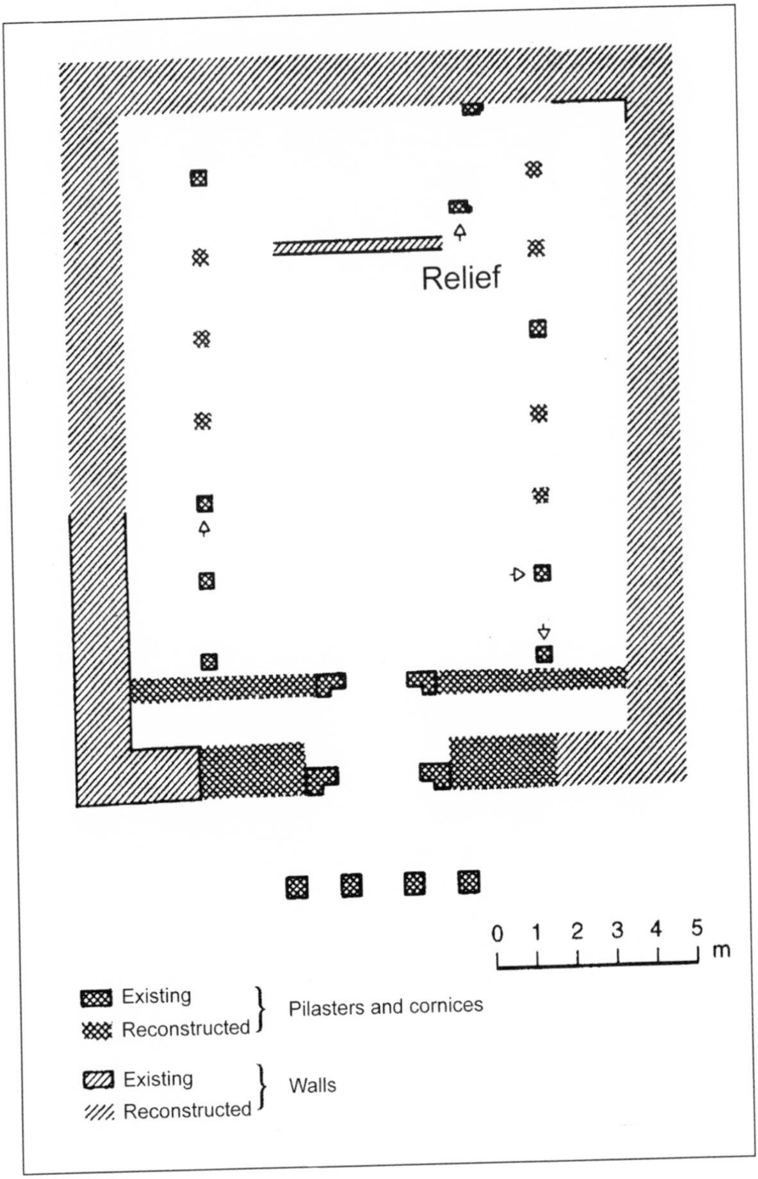

Figure 13
Plan of the extramuros temple of Ma'īn/Qarnāw

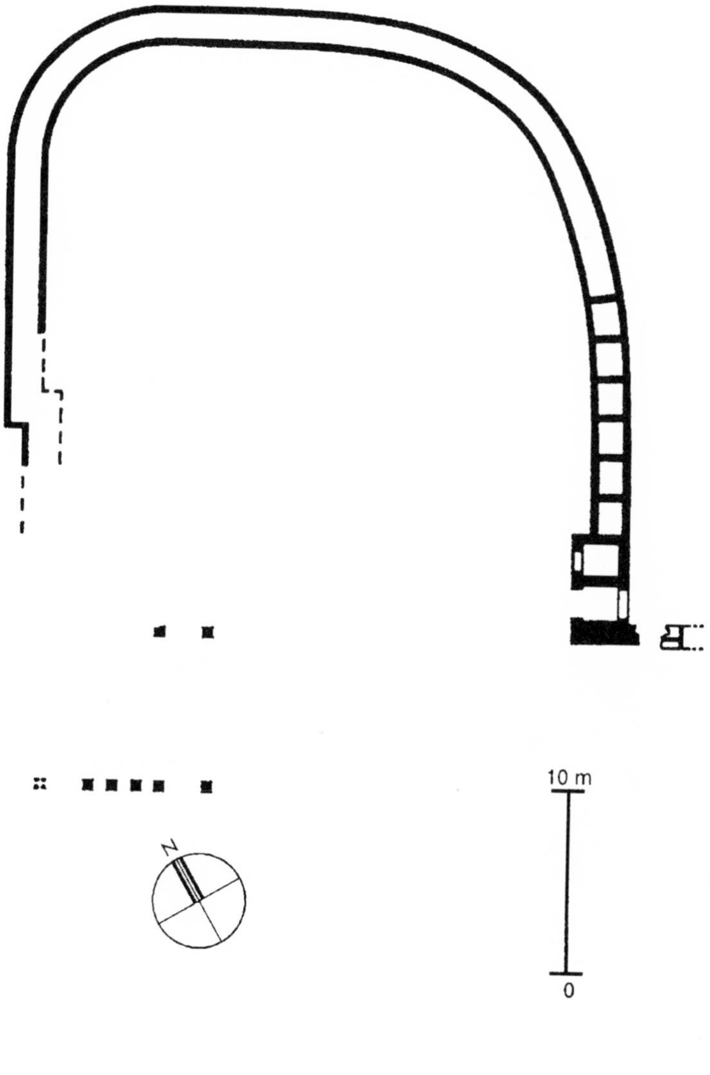

Figure 14
Plan of the temple of Almaqah at Al-Kharibah/Ṣirwāḥ

Figure 15
Sketch plan of Al-Kharibah/Ṣirwāh

Plate 16
The temple of Almaqah at Ṣirwāḥ

Plate 17
Detail of the Temple of Almaqah at Ṣirwāḥ

Plate 18
Inscription RES 3945 inside the temple of Almaqah at Ṣirwāḥ

To the east of Ṣirwāḥ, the ruins of Mārib are scattered the length of Wādī Dhanah, and may be divided topographically into three principal groups: the dam, the city and the external temples (Fig. 16).

Mārib relied on the dam for its prosperity, and indeed its very existence. Because of the dam, Mārib could stay rooted in the desert, like a port in a sea of sand, far enough east to intercept the commercial caravans returning north.

The dam was built by closing off Wādī Dhanah, one of the most water-rich in all Yemen, at the point where, having crossed the final mountainous barrier (Jabal Balaq), it spills into the desert to be swallowed up by the sands of the Ramlat Sab'atayn (Fig. 17). The project required a vast embankment about 700 metres long, faced with stone slabs and a cement-like mixture, stretching between two intricate sluices to the north and south, which were built using carefully cut and smoothed stone blocks. The earth embankment has now

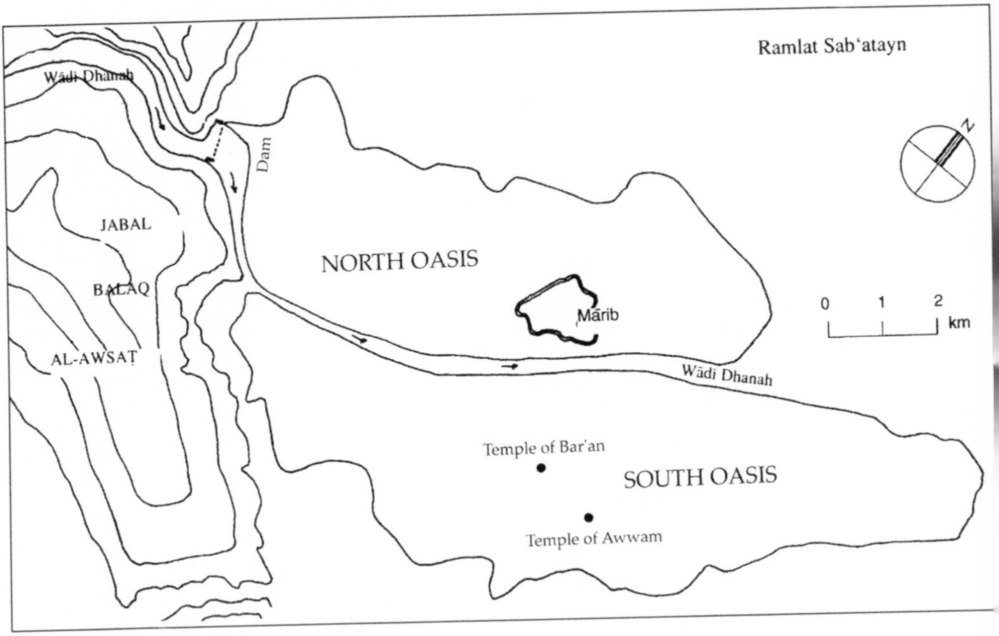

Figure 16
Map showing the distribution of antiquities around Mārib

disappeared and we are left with the two monumental sluices as testimony to the scale of the project.

The purpose of the dam was to retain the flood waters that flowed down the *wādīs*, reduce their speed and force them between the sluices. These had to be placed high enough to give the water sufficient head to flow through a system of channels, which divided into many smaller channels as they spread across the plain to irrigate the fields north and south of Mārib. The water carried with it a great quantity of silt and clay which was deposited on the fields and served as fertiliser. The Qur'an mentions the "garden on the right" and the "garden on the left" (Sura 24: 15-16) and tells how the ancient city was surrounded with luxuriant crops.

Turning from the dam towards Mārib, one can still see the retaining walls that controlled the flow of the precious water. One can observe how the channels grew progressively smaller in size and greater in number as they approached the desert. The channels fanned out like tendrils to irrigate the extensive surface area of the plain. This painstaking channelling must

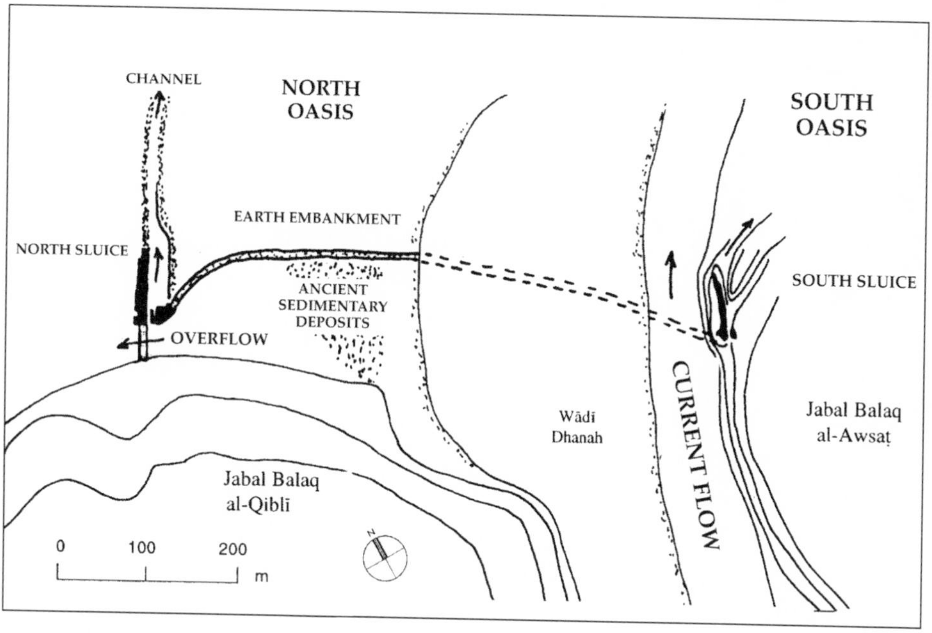

Figure 17
General plan of the Mārib dam

have called for a complex central bureaucracy to control and regulate the sluices and channels. Add to this the controls over the commercial activity of Mārib, and a good idea of the complexity of the Sabaean state emerges.

Inscriptions carved into the stones of the sluice tower tell us that the dam was constructed in three separate phases[26]. It was destroyed by floods at least four times, and was built increasingly higher to guarantee an ever greater water capacity. The scale of the work is reflected in the inscriptions, which proudly record the superhuman effort needed to build, maintain and reface the dam. Besides, the city depended on the dam for its very existence, and it is understandable that the community would dedicate a large part of the city's resources to ensuring it was kept in good order.

The dam's structure was threatened not so much by the dramatic and sudden floods of the summer monsoons as by the gradual build-up of sediments. Silt and clay, which annually fertilised the fields of the two oases, slowly accumulated to create thick banks of earth below the dam. As the sediments rose, they gradually cancelled out the vital difference in height between the fields and the storage area of the dam. Every time this happened, they had to increase the height of the dam to ensure that the system of connecting channels was reactivated and the water could revert to irrigating the land, filtering down to the most peripheral little channels.

Eventually there came a point when the engineering of the day was no longer capable of raising the dam high enough to meet the changing geomorphic conditions, particularly as this was now a culture in decline. Thus the dam was abandoned, possibly, according to the Qur'an, at the time of its final collapse (Chap. 34:14-20).

The City and Temples of Mārib

A dozen kilometres east of the dam, at the southern edge of the "garden of the north", stood Mārib, the largest fortified city of southern Arabia (Fig. 18). The city walls were discovered by Glaser, who located eight gates among the ruins. Fakhry reduced the number of gates to four, one in each of the four sides of the huge, roughly rectangular site (about 1500 x 1000 metres). The walls covered over 70

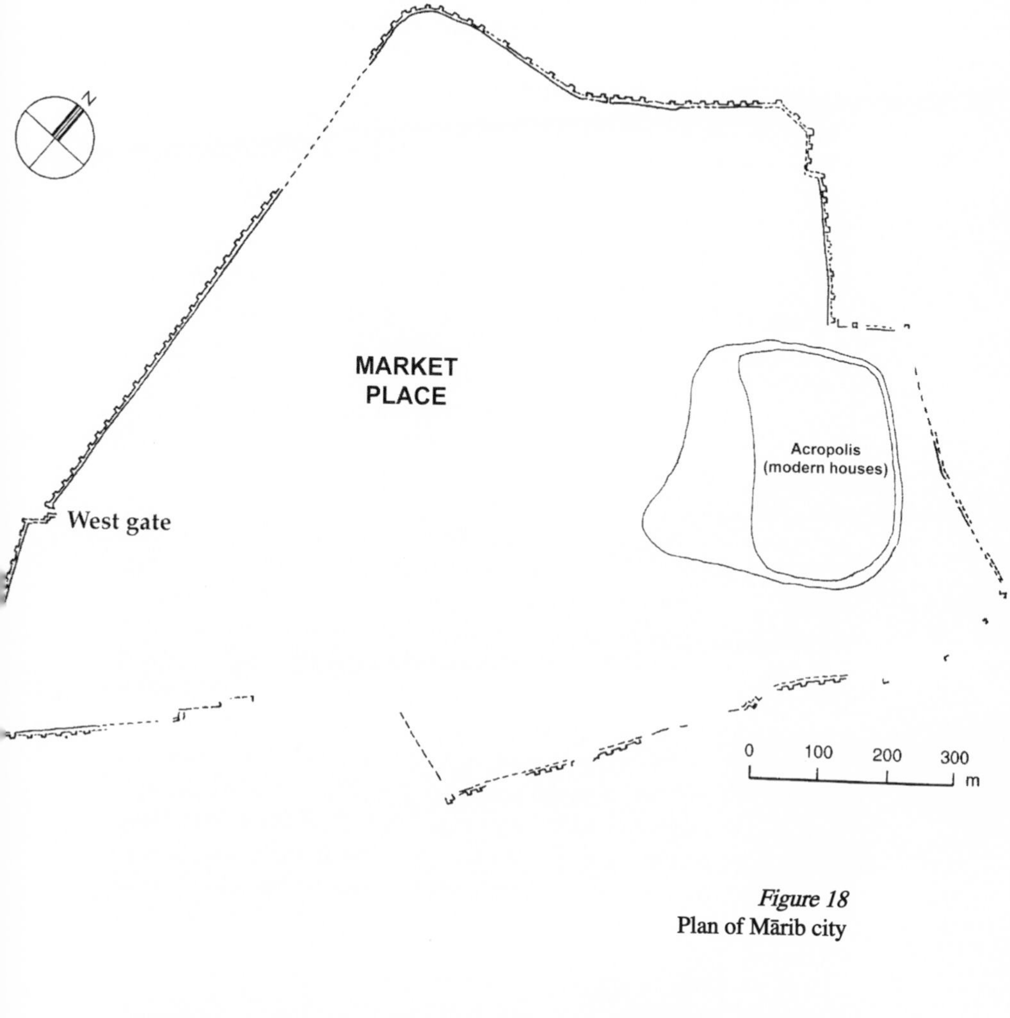

Figure 18
Plan of Mārib city

hectares, were about 1 metre thick. Their facade consisted of huge limestone slabs (1.5 metres long and 50 centimetres thick), while their foundations were made of similarly-sized conglomerate rocks. Rectangular buttresses protruded from the walls at regular intervals, giving Mārib the appearance of a great, many-towered city. The west gate was protected by two bastions, and is still visible today.

Modern aerial photographs have confirmed the layout of the city as described by Glaser and Fakhry, showing that the walls ran around the edge of a wide plateau, which rises above the surrounding fields. It is easy to make out the outlines of various large building complexes within the walls.

Not far from the modern village stands a ruined temple, now used as a mosque called Masjid Sulaymān. The temple had a propylaeum with eight pillars, now incorporated into the mosque's north wall[27].

About 3.5 kilometres south-east of the city, i.e. on the other side of Wādī Dhanah, is a temple that the locals call Maḥrām Bilqīs (Fig. 16) but is now known as the Awwam Temple. Glaser found an inscription on the outside wall that says the temple was built in honour of the god Almaqah by the mukarrib of Saba, Yada'īl Dhariḥ, son of Sumhu'ali[28]. This temple stands in a huge open space, oval in shape and enclosed by sturdy walls. The clearing measures about 100 metres on the east-west axis and 75 metres on the north-south axis. An elaborate rectangular entrance hall in the north-eastern section of the walls leads into the oval clearing[29].

This hall had not yet been found when Fakhry visited in 1947; it was discovered shortly afterwards by the American excavations led by Wendell Phillips. Fakhry saw only the propylaeum with its eight pillars of limestone, and a row of smaller pillars inside the entrance to the oval.

The Awwam Temple's unusual layout proves that, unlike other south Arabian temples, it must originally have been a sacred or religious precinct. The thick surrounding walls have been seriously damaged by the people of Mārib, who have plundered them for building materials, but they must originally have stood about 10 metres high, with a facade of 34 rows of smooth stone slabs. Glaser describes seeing a "parapet, or crown, of a double row of squared stones like cubes, with small spaces between them"[30] atop the eastern section of the wall. This was a common form of architectural decoration, found in other important Sabaeo-Minaean monuments, for example, the temple of Almaqah, and the walls of Barāqish, and particularly on the rectangular capitals typical of South Arabia (Figs. 80-83).

About one kilometre west of The Awwam Temple stand the ruins of a temple known as Al-'Amaid, five of whose pillars still stand in a high propylaeum[31]. There must

Plate 19
The west gate of Mārib

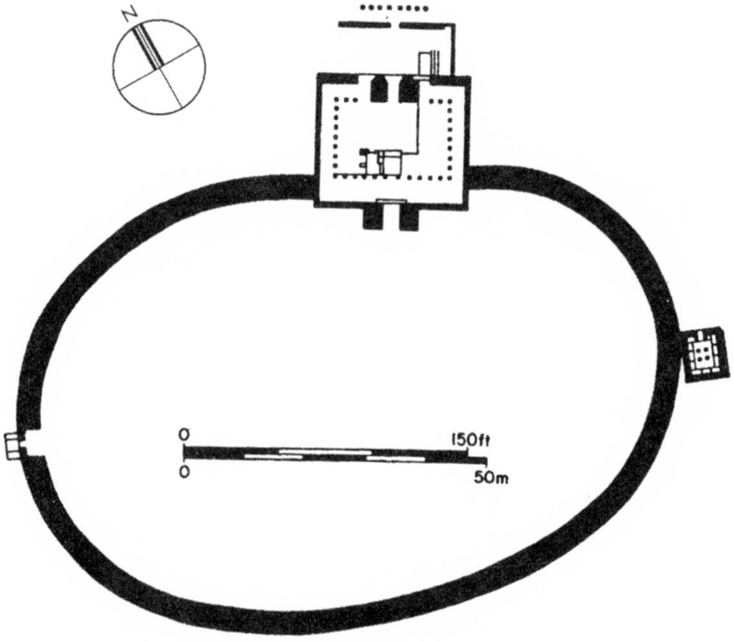

Figure 19
Plan of the oval temple of Awwam

Plate 20
The pilasters of the propylaeum of the temple of Bar'an at Mārib

originally have been more, given the presence of a sixth column base. Unlike those at Awwam, which culminate in square tenons designed to accommodate an architrave, these have indented capitals, and cannot therefore have been attached to anything above. The only traces of the temple that Fakhry found were a few inscriptions and numerous fragments of architectural decoration. The ancient name of the complex was Ba'ran and it was dedicated to Almaqah. The whole sanctuary area has recently been thoroughly excavated by a German archaeological mission.

Footnotes:

1. Rathjens, C. and von Wissmann, H., *Rathens - v. Wissmannsche Südarabien-Reise, Band 2; Vorislamische Altertümer* (Hamburg: Friedrichsen, de Gruyter & Co., 1932), p. 27.
2. Mordtmann, J.H. and Mittwoch, E., *Rathjens - v. Wissmannsche Südarabien - Reise, Band 1: Sabaische Inschriften* (Hamburg: Friederichsen, 1931-1934).
3. Rathjens and von Wissmann, *Rathjens - v. Wissmannsche Südarabien-Reise, Band 2; Vorislamische Altümer* (Hamburg: Friederichsen, 1932).
4. Rathjens and von Wissmann, *Rathjens - v. Wissmannsche Südarabien-Reise, Band 3; Landeskundliche Ergebnisse* (Hamburg: Freiderichsen, 1934).
5. Rathjens, C., *Sabaeica, Bericht über die archäologischen Ergebnisse seiner zweiten, dritten und vierten Reise nach Südarabien, I. Teil: Der Reiseberich* (Hamburg: Kommissionsverlag L. Appel, 1953).
6. Rathjens, *Sabaeica, Bericht über die archäologischen Ergebnisse seiner zweiten, dritten und vierten Reise nach Südarabien, II. Teil: Die unlokalisierten Funde* (Hamburg: Kommissionsverlag L. Appel, 1955).
7. Caton Thompson, G., *The Tombs and Moon Temple of Hureidha (Hadhramaut)* (Oxford: Reports of the Research Committee of the Society of Antiquaries of London, 13, 1944).
8. Ibid, p. 19.
9. Ibid, p. 65.
10. Ibid, p. 85.
11. Ibid, p. 153.
12. Stark, F., *The Southern Gates of Arabia: A Journey in the Hadhramaut* (London: J. Murray, 1938).
13. Philby, H.St.J., *Sheba's Daughters, Being a Record of Travel in Southern Arabia* (London: Methuen & Co., 1939), p. 5.
14. Pliny, *Historia Naturalis,* VI (32: p. 153).
15. See also Doe, B., *Southern Arabia* (London: Thames & Hudson, 1983), p. *136-141.*
16. Hamilton, R.A.B., "Six Weeks in Shabwa", *GJ* (1942), p. 107-123.
17. Philby, *Sheba's Daughters,* p. 371.
18. Ibid, p. 381.
19. von Wissman, H., *Zur Geschichte und Landeskunde von Alt-Südarabien* (Wien: H. Bohlas Nacht, 1964), p. 215.

20. Robin, C. and Ryckmans, J., "Les inscriptions de Al-Asāḥil, Ad-Durayb et Hirbat Sa'ūd", *Raydan* 3 (1980), p. 113-181.
21. Tawfīq, M., *Les monuments de Ma'īn (Yémen)* (Cairo: l'Institut Francais d'Archeologie Orientale, 1951).
22. Fakhry, A., *An Archaeological Journey to Yemen* (March-May, 1947) (Cairo: Government Press, 1951-52).
23. Schmidt, J. "Der 'Attar Tempel bei Ma'īn", *ABADY* I (1982), 143-152; and "Der Stadttempel von Ma'īn", *ABADY I*I (1982), 153-155.
24. See also Doe, B., *Monuments of South Arabia* (Naples: Falcon, 1983), p. 124.
25. See also Robin, C., "Résultats épigraphiques et archéologiques de deux bref séjour en République Arabe du Yémen", *Semitica* 26 (1976), p. 176.
26. Ryckmans, J., "Le barrage de Mārib et les jardins du Royaume de Saba", *DA* 33 (March/April, 1979), p. 28-35.
27. Robin, C., "Le Royaume de Saba", *Bible et Terre Sainte* 177 (1976), p. 15.
28. Glaser, E., *Eduard Glaser's Reise nach Mārib; hrsg. von Dav. Heinr. v. Muller und N. Rhodokanakis; nebst 4 Kartographischen und topographschen Beilagen und 3 Skizzen der Dammbauten bei Mārib* (Wien: A. Holder, 1913), p. 43-46.
29. Doe, B., *Southern Arabia*, p. 160-64.
30. Müller, D.H. and Rodokanakis, N., *Eduard Glaser's Reise nach Mârib.*

V

THE FIRST ATTEMPTS AT MODERN ARCHAEOLOGY

American Excavations in Wādī Beihan

In 1947, Wendell Phillips, a rich young American and enthusiastic researcher, left Aden and flew in an R.A.F. plane to Wādī Beihan, on the border between the English protectorates of the south and the Kingdom of Yemen (the same area that was once the cradle of the Kingdom of Qatabān). Here he visited the great site of Hajar Kuhlan, and decided to set up an archaeological mission to initiate excavations in Yemen along the lines of those underway in Palestine (Fig.20).

Back in the United States, Phillips immediately established the American Foundation for the Study of Man, appointing as vice-president William Foxwell Albright, one of the most eminent Biblical archaeologists in the world. He then set about getting funding. Phillips was shrewd enough to forge financial links between the South Arabian enterprise and a Palestinian expedition that was microfilming thousands of manuscripts in the monastery of Saint Catherine at the foot of Mount Sinai, and which found patrons easily on account of the Biblical connections.

The mission members landed at Al-Mukhālla on the

Plate 21
Wendell Phillips

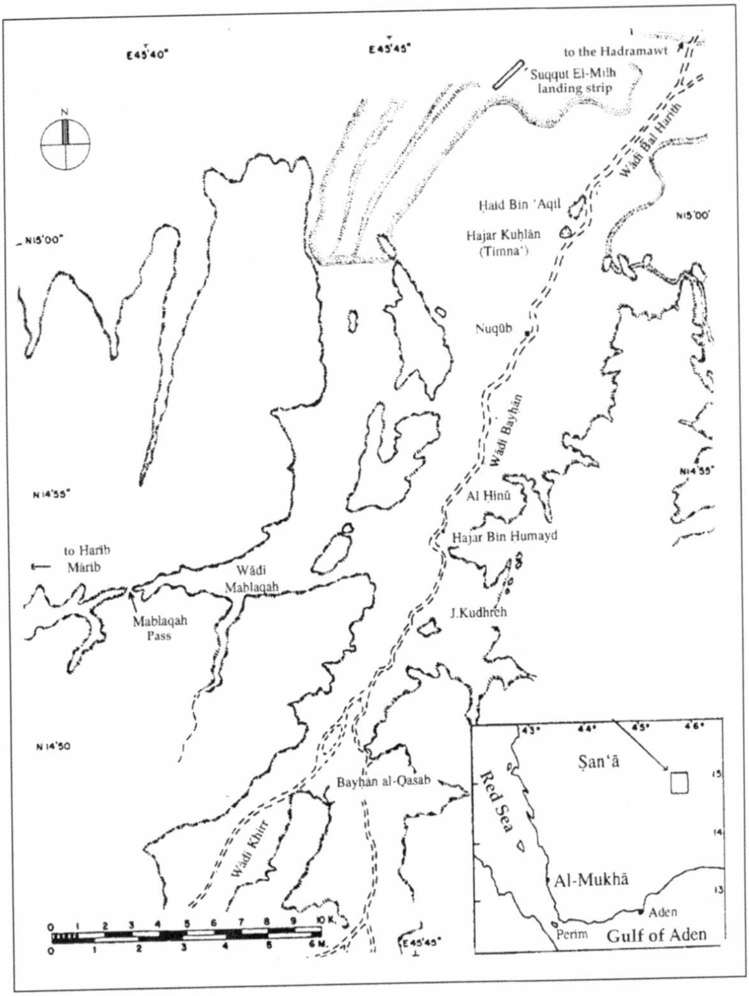

Figure 20
Map of Wādī Beihan

south coast of Yemen with all their equipment, and started north on 20 February 1950, heading for Wādī Ḥadramawt. In its first phase, the mission consisted of fourteen members: an expedition leader (Phillips), chief archaeologist (W.F. Albright), two epigraphists (A. Jamme and A. Honeyman), two archaeologists (R. Bowen and K. Brown), a geologist (F. Heybroek), a site director (W. Terry), plus a photographer, an administrator, two doctors and two mechanics. Twelve trucks specially equipped for the desert carried the expedition members and their equipment, which included generators, radios, guns, refrigerators, tape recorders, cameras, typewriters, petrol, oil, medicines, and of course a huge amount of food. The government of Aden sent the convoy a guard of fifteen bedouin.

This great deployment of resources showed the pragmatism of the American team and demonstrated their commitment to the enterprise. Their intentions could not have been better, but they found that their approach was way ahead of the times, as Yemen was still firmly stuck in the Middle Ages. This had a serious effect on the scientific results of their mission.

Timna'

The ruins of Hajar Kuhlan were first visited by the Englishman George W. Bury in 1899, during his expedition to Wādī Beihan[1], on behalf of an expedition sent to Aden by the Viennese Academy of Science, and directed by D.H. Muller[2]. On that occasion, Bury took photographs of the ruins and made casts of several Qatabanian inscriptions[3].

Another Englishman, S. Perowne, visited the site in 1936 as political envoy to Beihan[4]. But he was preceded by about a decade by an Austrian scholar of Greek origin, Nikolaus Rhodokanakis, who established, on the basis of the inscriptions, that this was the site of ancient Timna'[5].

The Americans carried out a series of excavations on two parts of the Timna' site during the expeditions of 1950 and 1951, when Albright and Jamme were joined by four new archaeologists, one of whom was Gus van Beek. Along with Mārib and Shabwat, this site is among the most extensive in southern Arabia (Fig. 21). The site is a large oval (about 450 x 700 metres) lying about 26 metres above the Beihan valley floor. It is covered with the remains of many ancient buildings, including two ruined town gates, one to the south-west (commonly called the south gate) and one to the north[6].

The American excavations focused on the south gate and on a large building embedded in the sand in the middle of the clearing. Unfortunately, to this day no report has ever been published on the excavations at Timna', and our knowledge is therefore based on Wendell Phillips' popular

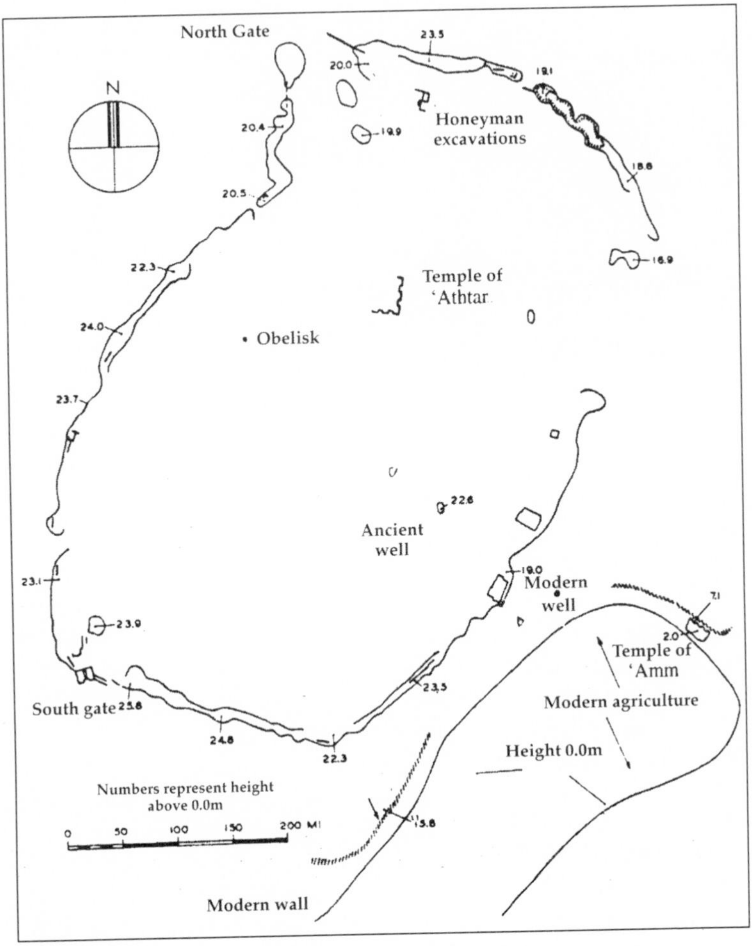

Figure 21
Plan of Hajar Kuhlan/Timna'

1955 book, *Qatabān and Sheba: Exploring the Ancient Kingdoms on the Biblical Spice Routes of Arabia*, and on an article by Gus van Beek in the American journal *The Biblical Archaeologist*[7]. There are not even any maps of the excavated areas, and we only know the position of the buildings from the rare photographs that accompany van Beek's article.

The excavations near the south gate covered an area about 65 x 60 metres, although only the top layer, which related to the last phase of the city's occupation, was excavated. Here there is evidence of a large quantity of ash

Plate 22
The south gate of Hajar Kuhlan/Timna'

and carbon, indicating that Timna' was destroyed by fire. The gateway was paved with thick stone slabs, and two benches were placed by the towers, where presumably men would sit and discuss their commercial activity. Further inside the city there is a wide courtyard where the various streets of the city converged. The excavations uncovered part of the street that joined the courtyard in front of the town gate, and part of another street, parallel and to the west. Also discovered were part of the building that separated them (building A) and part of a building situated to the west of the second street (building B). We know from the inscriptions that the houses belonged to two rich families. The first was named the house of Yaf'am after its owner, and the second the house of Yafash.

On the ground by the second house the mission found two beautiful bronze lions surmounted by two cherubs, which had perhaps fallen from an upper-floor terrace, and clearly show a strong Hellenistic influence[8]. There are identical inscriptions on the lions' bases which record the artisan's name. Comparisons with other inscriptions found in the area enabled the American archaeologists to date the two statues to the time of the Qatabanian king Shahr Yagul Yuhargib (first century BC).

It is obvious that the city was destroyed by a great fire, and we can assume "on the basis of fragments of imported Roman pottery, of a type known as *terra sigillata*" that this occurred during Augustus' reign in

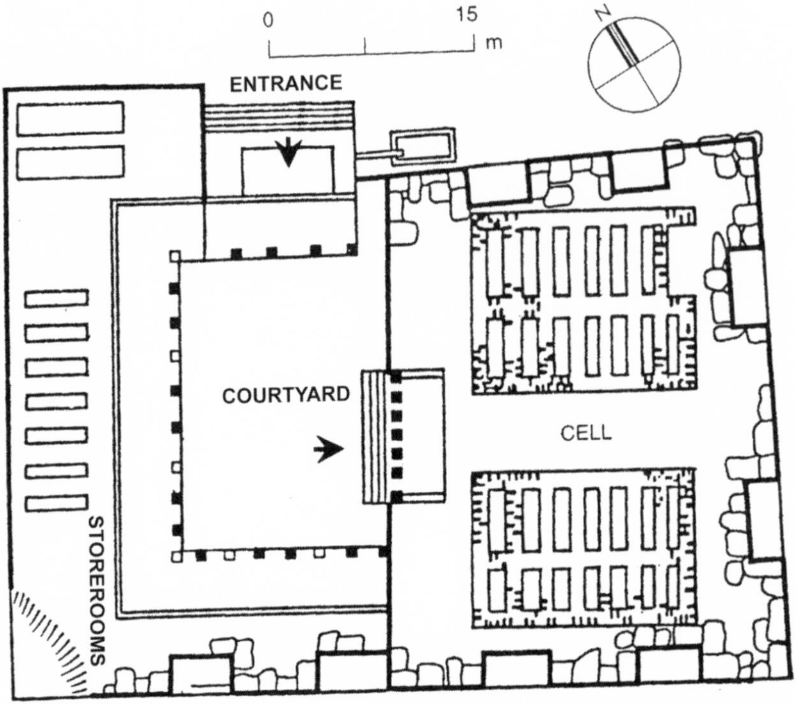

Figure 22
The so-called temple of 'Athtar at Timna'

Rome, which lasted from 31 BC to AD 14[9].

The second part of Timna' that the Americans excavated was the so-called temple of 'Athtar (Fig.22). This large rectangular building stood in the north-east of the city and was built on an east-west axis. No plan was published of this building either so the only information available is van Beek's brief description[10], and a map first published by the Englishman Brian Doe in 1971[11], and then updated by him in 1983. The complex can be divided into three parts: the temple proper to the east, a central courtyard and the warehouses to the west.

By examining the various buildings, the Americans established that the temple of 'Athtar was built in four separate phases. The oldest phase of construction dates from the seventh century BC and is represented by a solid building discovered under the eastern wall of the temple.

The second phase, dating from the sixth century BC, included work on the basement of the temple itself, using buttresses and indentations. The courtyard and its two entrances date from the third phase, around 300 BC , and the fourth and final phase saw the construction of the warehouses, from the first century BC onwards[12].

The Ḥayd Bin 'Aqīl Necropolis

During the excavations of 1950-1951, the mission also discovered the necropolis of Timna', just over one kilometre north of the city. This covered most of the slope of a rocky outcrop known as Ḥayd Bin 'Aqīl. Here they excavated many buildings which all seemed to be connected to the cult of the dead. Besides tombs, they found funerary chapels, two small temples designed for burial rites (one prostyle and the other hypostyle), public squares and streets. This was truly a city of the dead, and its discovery provided the first ever insight into the religious beliefs of the ancient Qatabanians.

The tombs are quite unusual (Fig. 23). There are a lot of them, all square in shape and close together. Each one consists of a central corridor with three to five rooms opening off it to each side. These rooms were each about 60 centimetres wide and two metres long, and high enough to be sub-divided horizontally with stone shelves, allowing several bodies to be buried in each chamber. In all, they found about eighty graves, but few of the skeletons were complete as the necropolis seems to have been systematically plundered in ancient times.

The possessions that Qatabanians buried with their dead were remarkably sumptuous, like the fabulous gold necklace with an inscribed, crescent-shaped pendant that was found in one of the tombs, having miraculously escaped the raiders' attention. The success of the excavation was assured by the discovery of many other objects, including splendid alabaster votive sculptures, original stelae featuring bulls' heads, many friezes featuring rows of ibex heads; inscriptions and pottery. These finds were later published by R.L. Cleveland in a fully illustrated catalogue[13].

As the cemetery was built on a hill, the archaeologists noticed that many of the tombs and other structures had been built on top of each other. Evidently, the necropolis

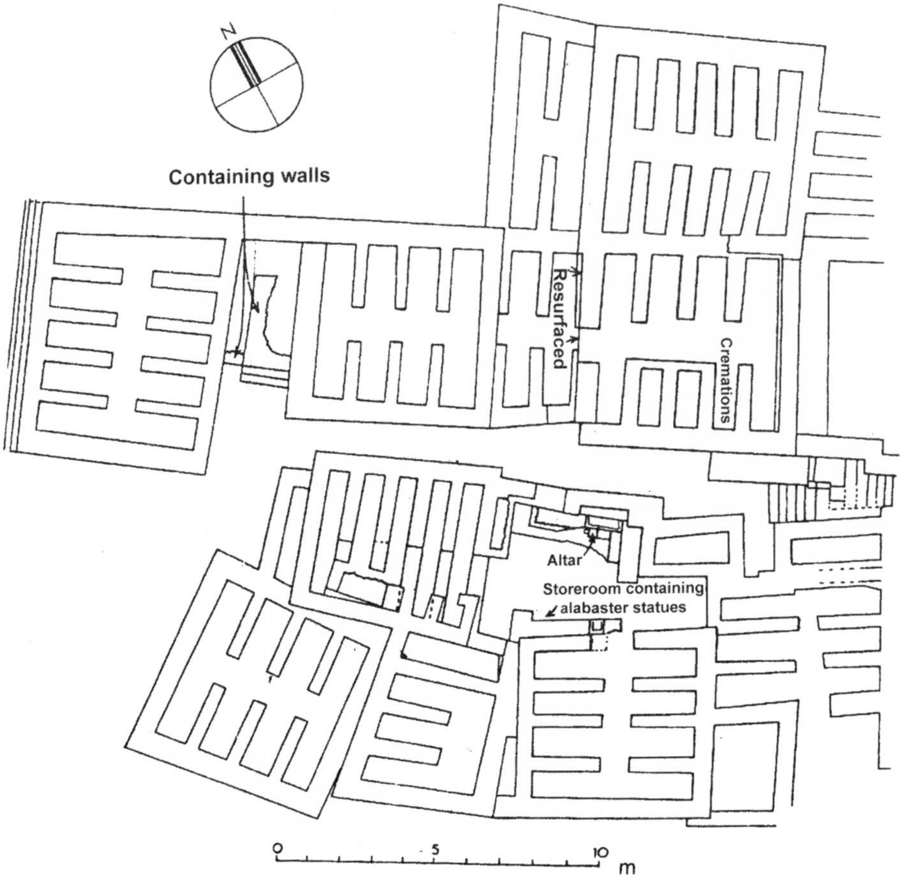

Figure 23
The Necropolis of Ḥayd Bin 'Aqīl, near Timna'; detail of the tombs in the northern sector.

was used over a long period. Comparing the pottery with stratified objects from the neighbouring site of Hajar Bin Ḥumayd, they deduced that burials had started at Ḥayd Bin 'Aqīl before the first millennium BC and had continued throughout the occupation of Timna'.

Hajar Bin Ḥumayd

One of the American Foundation's most important projects in Wādī Beihan was the excavation of Hajar Bin Ḥumayd, an artificial hill about 15 kilometres south of Timna'

Plate 23
Tombs in the necropolis of Ḥayd Bin ʻAqīl, near Timnaʻ

(Fig.24). W. F. Albright chose the site on account of its unusual shape, which was similar to a Palestinian tell. His intention was to extract a complete stratigraphy, something which had never been done before in southern Arabia.

Hajar Bin Ḥumayd was in fact a proper tell, oval in shape (about 280 x 180 metres) and standing about 15 metres above the plain. Its north-west edge had been washed away by water flooding in the *wādī*, exposing a high vertical section. It was obvious that many successive settlements were superimposed on each other. An excavation close to this section ran from the summit of the tell to the foot of the hill and brought to light a long and complete stratigraphy.

In 1969, van Beek published a complete account of the excavation, along with an accurate study of the pottery found at the site[14]. The earliest occupation of Hajar Bin Ḥumayd was during the eleventh century BC, and the most recent somewhere between the second and fifth centuries AD.

Besides their excavations, the Americans carried out important geo-archaeological reconnaissance work throughout the valley of Wādī Beihan, with the aim of establishing how ancient peoples used their environment.

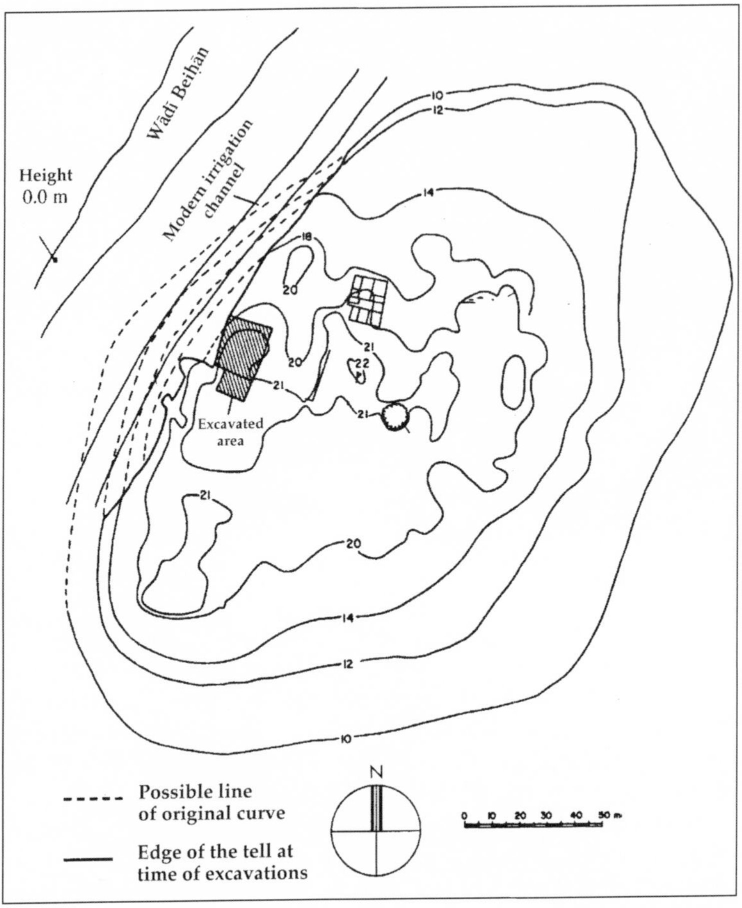

Figure 24
Plan of Hajar Bin Ḥumayd

Thus Richard Bowen carried out some brief excavations of a few of the small mounds of ruins that are scattered between Timna‘ and Hajar Bin Humayd[15]. The remains were small but significant, revealing some of the ancient systems of water management used to intercept and channel the great mass of water that flooded down the *wādīs* in the spring from the southern mountains. It seems from the number of these that in ancient times the entire valley resembled a great garden.

Bowen published his findings in 1958, definitively confirming what the geologist E. Gardner had already said

Plate 24
The Hajar Bin Ḥumayd site during the excavations

about the Ḥuraydah area, and anticipating the results of subsequent studies carried out by German geomorphologists in the oases of Mārib. He concluded that the success of the southern Arabian states was partly due to commercial luck, but primarily to their remarkable methods of irrigation. Using a highly advanced technological system, they had not only solved the problem of providing food, but had also successfully settled in this climatically hostile area, where they could intercept the caravan trade.

Modern reconnaissance work has revealed the dual character of all the major southern Arabian sites: besides its walls, temples and ruins, each city site has a corresponding "agricultural area" consisting of fields, irrigation systems and channels. The buildings cannot be studied in isolation from the agricultural systems.

The Mārib Affair

It is unclear why Wendell Phillips thought that two seasons' excavations at Timna' were enough. It is a shame that he did because Timna' and its satellite sites deserved much more time, and the scientific results would certainly have been of greater import.

We know that, well before the end of the second season at Beihan, Phillips wrote to the imām requesting leave to carry out excavations at Mārib[16]. The king's attitude to foreigners had changed. Aḥmad, who had succeeded his father Yaḥyah in 1948, had no reservations, and an agreement on Mārib was signed by the government of His Majesty the Imām of the Mutawakilite Kingdom of Yemen and the American Foundation for the Study of Man.

Phillips was overwhelmed with joy and enthusiasm. He closed the excavations at Timna' forthwith and instructed Robert Carmean, a specialist mechanic, and the photographer Chester Stevens to go to Mārib and set up the mission's headquarters. Meanwhile, he rushed back to the United States to gather funding, equipment and new archaeologists. This was in July 1951, and the head of the mission did not get back to Mārib until late January of the following year. Nonetheless, he arranged for Carmean to get to work immediately that first August, on the excavations at Maḥrām Bilqīs.

This initial rush had unfortunate results, which were compounded by a series of disastrous setbacks due to the difficult social and political situation in Yemen at the time. The mission's fortunes rapidly declined, despite its being joined by scholars like Albert Jamme and Frank P. Albright (unrelated to W.F. Albright) in 1952, and in the end its members fled into South Yemen.

This is not the place to examine how and why the research proposals failed, especially as the group was rich, well-prepared, and lucky in that they had gained authorisation for the excavations at Mārib. Suffice it to say that the episode caused – and still does to a certain extent – a great outcry. Each side levelled virulent accusations at the other. The Yemenis were accused of being an uncivilised nation that orchestrated the whole affair to gain control over the archaeological finds and the technical equipment that the Americans had been forced to abandon at Mārib. They were also accused of harassment motivated by Yemen's internal politics, in particular Ṣan'ā's desire to control Ta'izz, and therefore Prince Ḥassān's aim to control his brother, Imām Aḥmad. The Americans, on the other hand, were accused of using their flight as an excuse to carry off a large amount of precious finds, of failing to pay their workers; and worst of all, taking advantage of a country which was not yet ready to play host to this kind of operational mission.

One of the worst effects of this unfortunate incident was that North Yemen, despite its more open republicanism from 1962 onwards, became extremely reluctant to allow foreign missions to carry out any research. All archaeological research came to a complete halt in the winter of 1952, and only started up again in the late 1970s, when French and German teams managed to get tentative permission for reconnaissance work. Excavations were not started again in earnest until 1987, when the Italian archaeological mission was granted a brief season of excavations inside the Sabaean city of Yalā.

However, the excavations did have some positive results, despite everything. Of course, the incident meant that the published report of 1958[17] was reduced to a brief and succinct document backed up by little evidence and lacking detailed analysis. It merely reproduced the excavation notes from Frank Albright's diary (even though he was a late arrival on the scene), and Phillips himself admitted to its inadequacies in the preface. Nonetheless, this is one of very few reports on a South Arabian excavation, and remains of fundamental importance mainly for the information it provides on the architecture of the wonderful Awwam temple of Almaqah.

The Awwam Temple Excavations

The focus of the excavations was the complex structure that spanned the north-eastern opening into the great eastern enclosure, which served as an entrance to the temple (Fig.19). It consisted of a large rectangular building (about 26 x 22 metres) in front of which stood a smaller avant-corps (about 20 x 8 metres) and a row of eight monolithic square pillars. The impressive rectangular hall itself stood on the other side of the opening, within the oval temple walls, and comprised a hypostyle central courtyard surrounded by a peristyle corridor with a flat roof.

A triple door led into the hall from the north-east, flanked by two sturdy rectangular piers set well back into the entrance. From the hall, a narrow and deep-set doorway opened into the inner sanctum. The central courtyard was surrounded by thirty-two pillars; those along the sides on an axis with the doors were 5.3 metres, and those along the other two sides were 4.9 metres tall.

The pillars were different heights because they were

Plate 25
The entrance hall of the Awwam temple of Mārib during the American excavations of 1951-1952

joined to the perimeter walls by stone girders which supported the roofing slabs, and so the roof over the north and south sides had to be high enough to overlap the roof over the other sides, where they met at the corners. The walls of the hall must have been just over five metres high, about five metres lower than the temple's great elliptical walls. The interior facade of the entrance hall was decorated with 64 sculpted panels depicting false windows, a characteristic geometric motif often found in architectural decoration in southern Arabia.

The excavations showed that for a long time there had been a stream running through the entrance hall which petered out north of the temple. The water ran into a bronze basin, which people probably used for their ablutions before entering the sacred area to the south. The water may have come from a well in the unexcavated area within the oval walls.

The entrance hall yielded many important inscriptions, remarkable bronze statues including the famous figure of Ma'ādī Karib, alabaster statues, stone vases and pottery.

The archaeologists showed that the hypostyle access room was constructed later than the oval building of the temple proper, and various inscriptions proved that the complex was in use until at least the first century AD. The purpose of the oval enclosure remains unclear for now, since the excavations were interrupted. We can suppose that the religious focus of the entire complex was the point at which the long axis of the ellipse crosses the axis of the hypostyle entrance hall.

The excavations have not been resumed, and so theories put forward by various scholars explaining the structures' peculiarities remain unproved to this day. The most authoritative is that by A. Grohmann suggesting that the Awwam temple derived from the oval presargonic temples of Mesopotamia[18].

American Excavations in Dhofār: Khawr Rūrī

To make up for his disappointment in Yemen, Phillips decided in 1952 to seek the Sultan of Oman's permission to explore Dhofār. This region, in the south of the country and bordering on South Yemen, has always aroused curiosity because it has been famous since antiquity for producing a huge amount of incense.

Oman's Sultan Sayyid Bin Taimur, an old friend of Phillips, agreed to the proposed reconnaissance, and the mission immediately decamped to Muscat and thence to Salālah, capital of Dhofār. F.P. Albright was placed in charge as director of operations.

The region was basically uncharted territory, apart from its few appearances in the *Periplus of the Erythrean Sea*, so the American archaeologists were overjoyed to find the remains of a small but well-preserved South Arabian city (Fig. 25), on the banks of an inlet called Khawr Rūrī (35 kilometres east of Salālah). Despite his limited resources and reduced team, Albright managed to sustain a more or less continuous excavation for 13 months (1952-1953). He had some good results, including the discovery of the ancient name of the city, Samhar (also known as Samhuram), the name of the principal deity, Sin (Sayyin) and the name of his temple, Ilum[19].

The citadel of Samhar was built to dominate and protect an important port for the export of incense, and the excavations showed that it was an outpost of the kingdom of Ḥaḍramawt, established to receive and control the incense gathered in the hinterland. Grains of incense were found all over the site, which suggests that the product was stored within the city before being shipped to those south Arabian ports nearest the caravan routes to the interior[20].

Samhar was surrounded by a solid wall of rough-hewn stone over 2.5 metres thick. The only entrance was in the north wall, and the site was more or less rectangular, about 130 metres long by about 70 metres wide[21]. The walls were graduated for extra strength and protected by two square towers on the north-east and north-west corners of the city. The complexity of the sole entrance proves that the site's main purpose was defence. Protected from the outside by a free-standing transverse wall, the entrance consisted of a passage with a guard tower on the left, which led into a sort of oblong forecourt on the right. From here the gateway proper opened into the city walls. The passage, less than two metres wide at this point and protected by two bastions, led into a small rectangular atrium from which a final door led west into the city.

So, to get inside the fortress, one had to change direction a good four times, and go through at least three separate wooden doors. A series of inscriptions carved into the upper walls accompanied the journey. Once inside, one faced a sturdy rectangular building set against the north wall of the city. The walls are intact up to about five metres, and their remarkable width (over five metres on the south side) indicates that this was once a high tower. Inside, a flight of steps along the east wall of the room indicates the start of a stairway, which must have risen in a spiral as work progressed. Access from the outside was through a narrow, split entrance, with a door that was only 50 centimetres wide.

Inside the one, large room (about 12 by 11 metres) are two stone bases, possibly for altars. In the middle stood a square well in a neatly cut stone border, and near it a stone basin. Animal bones and ashes were found around the altar bases, and various cult objects around the well and basin, which help identify the building as the temple Ilum, sacred to the god Sayyin.

A Belgian Mission in 'Asīr: the City of Najrān

Late in 1951, the famous Belgian epigraphist Gonzague Ryckmans, who had been the undisputed expert in South

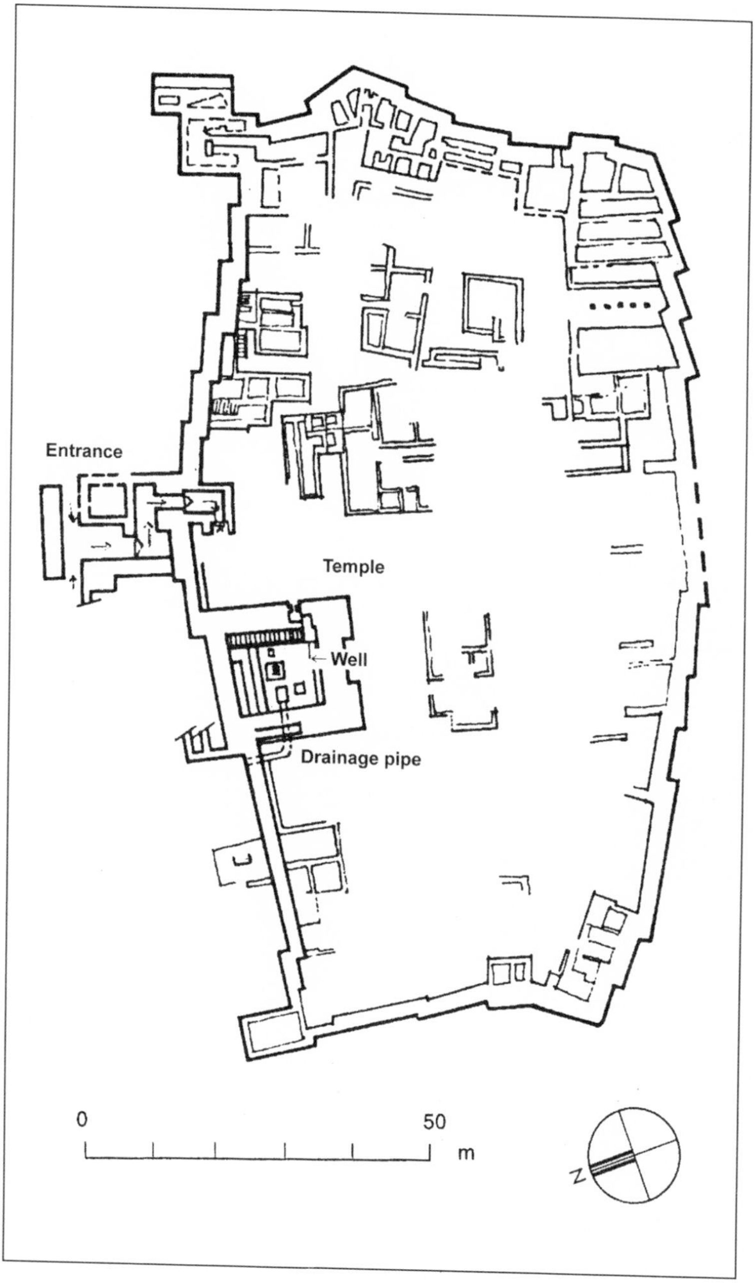

Figure 25
Plan of Khawr Rūrī/Samhar

Arabian studies for years, made plans to carry out reconnaissance work in Saudi Arabia with Philby. Philby's friendship with the ageing king Ibn Ṣa'ūd meant that they could count on getting permission for the exploration, as well as the funds to carry it out. They chose the area between Jiddah, Najrān and Riyadh, in other words the south-west of Saudi Arabia. Their aim was to establish how far north the influence of the South Arabian states had spread in the pre-Islamic period. Two other Belgians participated in the three-month trip: Phillippe Lippens and Jacques Ryckmans, a young orientalist who was also Gonzague's nephew.

Leaving Jiddah, their first port of call was the 'Asīr mountains, where they found a great many Thamudic (pre-Islamic Arabic) inscriptions on the rocks. They then visited the ancient city of Najrān on the Yemeni border, famous since the time of Aelius Gallus and home in the sixth century AD to the Christian community cruelly persecuted by Dhū-Nuwās, the Himyarite king who converted to Judaism. Large numbers of Christians were burnt alive and tossed into mass graves, earning the site the name of Al-Ukhdūd ("the trench"), by which it is still known today. The expedition then skirted the Rub' al-Khālī desert and following Jabal Tuwayq as far as Riyadh. The journey was difficult, but yielded good results in the form of important South Arabian inscriptions and a lot of graffiti which testified to the influence of the Sabaeans over the centre of the Arabian Peninsula. Equally, they produced a lot of geographical data that served to fill in the map of these areas, which had hitherto been practically blank[22].

According to drawings made by the Belgian mission, the fortified city had a square plan, about 250 metres to a side, enclosed by irregularly bastioned walls[23]. These walls are probably irregular because they followed the lines of an older system of defence, consisting simply of a line of houses. It seems that the corners of the square were protected by towers which would have had a prominent role in the defence of the city (Fig. 26).

The main city gate stood halfway along the western side. Protected by two strong bastions, the gate allowed for only a narrow and well-guarded passage. Inside the city are the ruins of many buildings, whose refined construction is reminiscent of the temples of the great southern cities. Many further ruins are scattered outside the city walls.

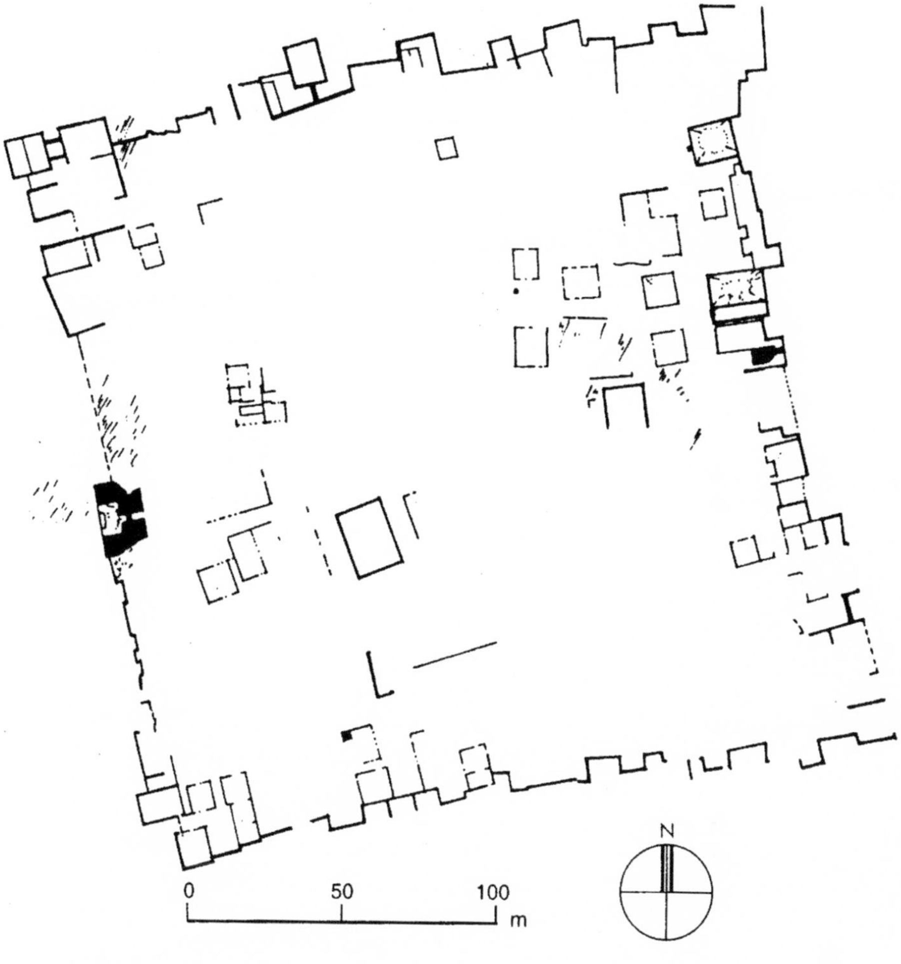

Figure 26
Plan of Al-Ukhdūd/Najrān

The ancient settlement at Najrān lasted until the sixth century AD. We know from the Byzantine historian Procopius that the Himyarite king Dhū-Nuwās was killed in battle in AD 525 by the Ethiopian general Abrāhā, who had been sent by his ruler to help the Christian community in Najrān. A large inscription made by Abrāhā was found by the Belgian mission slightly north of Najrān, on Jabal Qarah. In it, the general confirms that in AD 547 he carried out an expedition against the Arab tribes. We can therefore assume that the city of Najrān was still occupied at this time.

From Najrān, Ryckmans and his party headed for Riyadh, probably following the ancient caravan route to Gerrha, on the Persian Gulf. En route they discovered another important Sabaean city, the mass of ruins known as Qaryat al-Fāw, located near the southern slope of Jabal Tuwayq, on the edge of the Rub‘ al-Khālī desert. Recently Saudi archaeologists have undertaken regular excavations there, which have turned up a great wealth of objects. This shows that the South Arabian states were still flourishing at this late stage and on this secondary trade route[24].

Archaeology in Yemen Today

By the late 1970s, the political situation in Yemen seemed to have stabilised. The republican revolution of 1962 had triumphed, despite strong armed opposition during the subsequent years. Under the direction of the *Ismā‘īl al-Akwa‘*, the General Organisation for Antiquities and Libraries was established at Ṣan‘ā with the aim of supervising and protecting the country's fine archaeological heritage. Western missions and experts found that doors were beginning to open to them. Two foreign missions, French and German, set up permanent research centres in the capital from where they could send out regular escorted reconnaissance trips.

This also renewed the tradition of studies that had been upheld in Italy since the early 1930s by orientalists like Leone Caetani, Ignazio Guidi, Carlo Alfonso Nallino and

Plate 26
Renzo Manzoni

especially Carlo Conti Rossini[25]. It was a tradition established by great travellers like Renzo Manzoni[26] (nephew of the more famous Alessandro Manzoni,); Carlo Guarmani, who looked far beyond the original search for Arabs of pure descent[27]; and Lodovico de Varthema himself.

This tradition ended with the enthusiastic work of two merchants, Luigi and Giuseppe Caprotti, who, at the turn of the century acquired the collection of Yemeni manuscripts that are now the pride of the Biblioteca Ambrosiana in Milan[28]. They also acquired a book on the history of Yemen by one of the imām's doctors, Cesare Ansaldi[29], and they brought back the only archaeological finds now held in Italy, which reside in Rome's Museum of Oriental Art.

The new atmosphere in Yemen in the early 1970s enabled Giovanni Garbini of the University of Naples, to revive this tradition by undertaking reconnaissance work in Yemeni territory and allowed Paolo Costa, an archaeologist with long experience in Iraq, to spend several years living in Yemen. Among other things, he tried to organise the archaeological section of the National Museum of Ṣan'ā[30].

Finally, the time had come to descend once more on the ancient land of Arabia Felix. The philologists were the first to start, as they were keenest to find the answers to their great dilemmas. Christian Robin's discoveries in Al-Mi'shal and Jabal al-Lawdh which, as we shall see, were enormously useful in reconstructing the history of South Arabia during the first centuries of the decadent era, simply emphasised the enormous potential of (even superficial) archaeological evidence and the need for work to be done on site[31].

So it was not until the 1980s that true, systematic research began in Yemen, far later than in other Near Eastern countries. At least 15 new excavations were opened in the 1980s (as opposed to six in the previous decades) and regular archaeological missions began to excavate parallel to each other, providing scholars with new and ever more consistent data.

Thus we can list the French excavations of Shabwat (1976-1981)[32] and the temple of 'Athtar near Al-Sawdā (from 1988)[33]; the American excavations at Hajar al-Tamrah and Hajar al-Rayhānī in the Al-Jubah region south of Mārib (1983-1984)[34]; the Soviet excavations at Raybun and Qana (from 1983)[35]; and the German excavations of the temples of Waddum dhū-Masma'im and Bar'an, near Mārib (from 1988). Finally, there were the Italian excavations of the prehistoric sites of Khawlān, Tihāmah and Ramlat Sab'atayn; the protohistoric sites in the Al-A'rūsh area (1983-1985); the necropolises of Waraqah (1985-1986), Al-Makhdarah (1986-1987), and Yalā (1987); and the temple of Nakrah at Barāqish (1989-90, 1992).

All these excavations have contributed new data for a debate which can finally take its lead from archaeology. Of course, archaeological data is not easy to interpret. Those accustomed to working solely with epigraphy often find the information too generic and vague. On the other hand, it is true that radiocarbon dating can fluctuate greatly, that the finds cannot immediately tell us about political history, and that it takes time to create ceramic sequences. Nonetheless, after a decade of regular research and excavations, this kind of evidence ought to form part of the basic knowledge of scholars in the field.

Archaeology, in its narrowest sense, has contributed little to uncovering the history of later (Himyarite) periods. Research has focused mainly on the antiquities and stratigraphy of the oldest periods, possibly because these areas presented the most problems, and the resulting information has helped to clear up some chronological problems. The discovery of the prehistory and protohistory of the area has also turned up new data which illustrates the origins of South Arabian culture in the most objective way possible.

So, in the light of these archaeological advances, we can now trace the development of the cultural and political history of ancient southern Arabia from the earliest times, which commence with the prehistoric finds recently unearthed by the Italian archaeological mission.

Footnotes:

1. Bidwell, R., *Travellers in Arabia* (London: Hamlyn, 1976), p. 175-177.
2. Macro, E., "The Austrians in South West Arabia, 1897-1900", *PSAS* 20 (1990), p. 101-109.

3. Bury, G.W., *The Land of Uz* (London: Macmillan & Co., 1911), p. 231.
4. Perowne, S., "Im'adiya and Beihan, Aden Protectorate", *Antiquity 13 (1939), p. 133-137.*
5. Rhodokanakis, N., *Die Inschriften an der Mauer von Kohlan-Timna* (Wien: Holder-Pichler-Tempsky, 1924).
6. Bowen, R.L., "Archaeological Survey of Beihan", in Bowen and F.P. Albright (eds), *Archaeological Discoveries in South Arabia* (Baltimore: Johns Hopkins Press, 1958), p. 5-6; and Doe, B., *Monuments of South Arabia* (Naples: Falcon, 1983) p. 129-132.
7. van Beek, G., "Recovering the Ancient Civilization of Arabia", *BA* 15 (1952), p. 2-18.
8. Segall, B., "The Lion-Riders from Timna'", in Bowen and Albright (eds.), *Archaeological Discoveries in South Arabia,* p. 155-182.
9. van Beek, G., "Recovering Ancient Civilization", p. 10.
10. Ibid, p. 10-13.
11. Doe, B., *Southern Arabia* (London: Thames & Hudson, 1971), p. 219.
12. van Beek, G., "Recovering Ancient Civilization", p. 12-13.
13. Cleveland, R.L., *An Ancient South Arabian Necropolis: Objects from the Second Campaign (1951) in the Timna' Cemetery* (Baltimore: Johns Hopkins Press, 1965).
14. van Beek, G., *Hajar Bin Humeid, Investigations at a Pre-Islamic Site in South Arabia* (Baltimore: Johns Hopkins Press, 1969).
15. Bowen, R.L., "Irrigation in Ancient Qataban (Beihan)", in Bowen and Albright (eds.), *Archaeological Discoveries,* p. 43-132.
16. Phillips, W., *Qataban and Sheba: Exploring Ancient Kingdoms on the Biblical Spice Routes of Arabia* (New York: Harcourt, Brace, 1955), p. 192-93.
17. Albright, F.P., "Excavations at Mārib in Yemen", in Bowen and Albright (eds.), *Archaeological Discoveries,* p. 215-268.
18. Grohmann, A., *Arabien* (München: Beck, 1963), p. 178-79.
19. Phillip W., *Qataban and Sheba,* p. 337-340.
20. Albright, F.P., *The American Archaeological Expedition in Dhofār* (Oman), 1952-1953 (Washington: American Foundation for the Study of Man, 1982).
21. Doe, B., *Monuments of South Arabia* (Naples: Falcon, 1983), p. 147-150.
22. Lippens, P., *Expédition en Arabie Centrale* (Paris: Adrien-Maisonneuve, 1956).
23. Doe, B., *Monuments of South Arabia,* p. 150-152.

24. Ansary, A.R., *Qaryat al-Fau: A Portrait of Pre-Islamic Civilisation in Saudi Arabia* (Riyadh: University of Riyadh, 1982).
25. Garbini, G., "Recent South Arabian Studies in Italy", *Raydan* 2, (1979), p. 153-161.
26. Manzoni, R., *El Yémen: Tre anni nell'Arabia Felice* (Rome: 1884).
27. Guarmani, C., *Il Neged settentrionale* (Jerusalem: 1866).
28. De Leone, E., "I fratelli Caprotti di Magenta nel Yemen", in *Atti del Convegno di studi su la Lombardia e l'Oriente* (Milan:1963), p. 129-132.
29. Ansaldi, C., *Il Yemen nella stories e nella leggenda* (Rome: Sindicato Italiano Arti Grafiche, 1933).
30. Costa, P., *The Pre-Islamic Antiquities of the Yemen National Museum* (Rome: L'erma di Bretschneider, 1978).
31. Robin, C. "Les inscriptions d'al-Mi'sal et la chronologie de l'Arabie méridionale au III siècle de l'ère chrétienne", *CRAIBL* (1979), p. 174-203; and Robin and J.F. Breton, "Le sanctuaire préislamique du Jabal al-Lawd (Nord Yemen)", *CRAIBL* (1982), p. 590-629.
32. Breton, J.F., *Shabwa, Deux campagnes de fouilles,* 1980-81 (Aden: 1981); "Shabwa capitale antique du Ḥaḍramawt", *JA* 275, 13-29; and *Fouilles de Shabwa, II. Rapports préliminaires* (Paris: 1992). See also Pirenne, J., *Fouilles de Shabwa, I. Les témoins écrits de la région de Shabwa et l'histoire* (Paris: P. Geuthner, 1990).
33. Breton, J.F., "Le sanctuaire de 'Athtar dhu-Risaf d'As-Sawdā (République du Yémen)", *CRAIBL* (1992), p. 429-53.
34. Blakely, J., "The Stratigraphic Probe at Hajar at-Tamrah", in J. Blakely, J. Sauer, M. Toplyn (eds.), S*ite Reconnaissance in North Yemen* (1985), p. 55-145. See also Glanzman, W. and Ghaleb, A., *Site Reconnaissance in the Yemen Arab Republic*, 1984: *The Stratigraphic Probe at Hajar Ar-Rayhānī* (Washington: American Foundation for the Study of Man, 1987).
35. Sedov, A., "Raybun. A Complex of Archaeological Monuments in the Lower Reaches of Wādī Dau'an and Certain Problems of its Protection and Restoration", in *Ancient and Mediaeval Monuments of Civilization of Southern Arabia* (Moscow: 1988), p. 61-66.

PART TWO

Prehistory and Protohistory

VI

PREHISTORY IN YEMEN

Defining the Field of Research

Until 1981, our knowledge of the prehistory and protohistory of Yemen was limited to a few palaeolithic pieces found by Gertrude Caton Thompson in the Ḥaḍramawt[1], the megalithic complex found in the 1960s by G. Benardelli (the Italian ambassador to Ṣan'ā) in the Muhamdid al-Hamilī area[2], and the lithic tools that the Frenchman R. de Bayle des Hermens gathered during his brief forays into Yemen in the 1970s[3].

In 1981, the Italian archaeological mission, founded under the auspices of the Istituto per l'Oriente of Rome, began to investigate the Khawlān region, particularly the territory along the road from Ṣan'ā to Mārib, which passed through Jiḥanah, Banī Sulayḥ and Ṣirwāḥ (Fig. 27).

This expedition was a result of my first brief visit to Yemen the previous year[4]. The plan was to examine how human occupation within a particular geographical area had changed over the ages, to establish the different kinds of economy adopted over time by the various communities, and so to understand the principal characteristics of the development of South Arabian civilisation.

These communities developed advanced water-management techniques to make the land productive in an area where monsoon cycles guaranteed large volumes of water, but where extreme contrasts in the physical environment meant that the water was lost to the desert at an alarming rate. Man could live under these conditions only by developing technology that would let him make the most of the soil. Evidence of the level of technology reached were right before our eyes. However, this was clearly the end result of a long process, and we had yet to discover the missing links.

We were clearly going to need to understand this development before we could fully appreciate the type and extent of the domestic economic system. This must have been an impressive system because a well-developed internal economy was essential for any civilisation wishing to dedicate itself wholeheartedly to commerce. The state must have grown out of the peaceful symbiosis of these two separate aspects of the economy, one agricultural and domestic and the other commercial.

Ismā'īl al-Akwa', then director of the General Organisation for the Antiquities and Libraries of Ṣan'ā, looked favourably on my request that an exclusive permit be granted for the Italian mission to explore the areas of Khawlān and Al-Ḥadā. There were two reasons for my choosing this part of Yemen. Firstly, apart from Glaser's journey to Mārib along the Jiḥanah road, the area was virgin territory; and secondly, the area covered most of the catchment area of Wādī Dhanah. In other words, the place had a precise, homogeneous hydrological identity and seemed to be ecologically suited to an environment-based study of the way in which the various centres of human habitation moved around over the years (Fig.27).

The Palaeolithic Period

In September 1981, I embarked on my first trip with two students from Rome University, Francesco Di Mario and Michael Jung, which resulted in our first tangible evidence of Yemen's remote past. We also saw how the distribution of human settlements had changed over time within the different ecozones of the Dhanah watershed, from the innumerable small streams in the mountains east of the Ṣan'ā-Dhamār road, down to the single great valley where water flows into the desert at Mārib. We found the first traces of the Bronze Age and the prehistoric period in Yemen during this trip.

Climbing down into the canyon of the fabulous Wādī Ḥabābiḍ, we discovered that at a certain point the rock walls were covered with flint nodules, which we thought was an excellent material for weapons and utensils of the prehistoric period. We climbed up again to a plateau called Ḥumayd al-'Ayn and to our delight found ourselves in an immense workshop where for thousands of years Stone Age man had chipped away at flint to produce tools. Thousands of flint flakes and cores were strewn at our feet. There were very few finished tools, though, since they would have been taken away by the hunters who had stopped here to produce them.

Plate 27
Stone tools of the middle palaeolithic period, from Ḥumayd al-'Ayn in the Khawlān al-Tiyal

However, we did find unfinished and badly-made ones which had been abandoned on the spot.

Since I am not an expert in prehistory myself, I put together a comprehensive collection of samples of this work and took it to Rome. There, at the Museo Pigorini, my friends Marcello Piperno and Grazia Bulgarelli, who had done extensive work on the palaeolithic period in Ethiopia, examined the material and recognised the objects as the earliest examples of the middle palaeolithic in Yemen (about 50,000 years ago)[5].

The Yemenis were very enthusiastic about the discovery of their country's prehistory and protohistory, and the whole of 1982 was taken up with arranging a five-year plan of cooperation between the Yemeni and Italian Governments. This accord's aims were to continue the research, and particularly to train local archaeologists so that they would be able to oversee the country's rich heritage of antiquities, including the prehistoric. The Istituto Italiano per il Medio ed Estremo Oriente (IsMEO),

Plate 28
Stone tools of the lower palaeolithic period found on the plain of Qā‘ Jahrān, near Ma‘bar

directed by Professor Gherardo Gnoli, took over as the governing body of the project on behalf of our ministry, and I was made director of the Italian Archaeological Mission in the Arab Republic of Yemen (MAIRAY).

So it was that in the following season (1983) Bulgarelli was able to study the Ḥumayd al-'Ayn workshop in depth. During the same season, while on a reconnaissance trip to the Qā‘ Jahrān plain on the Ma‘bar plateau, she discovered the first site in North Yemen dating back to the lower palaeolithic period (about 200,000 years ago).

The Neolithic Period on the Plateau

Meanwhile I pressed on, exploring the area covered by our permit and travelling further south into the Al-Ḥadā area (Fig. 27). Here I found some ten sites: at the foot of Jabal Sha'ir, on the slopes of Jabal A‘mās (near the village of Beihan) and in the valleys parallel to Wādī al-'Ish. These were very different from the later sites that were slowly but

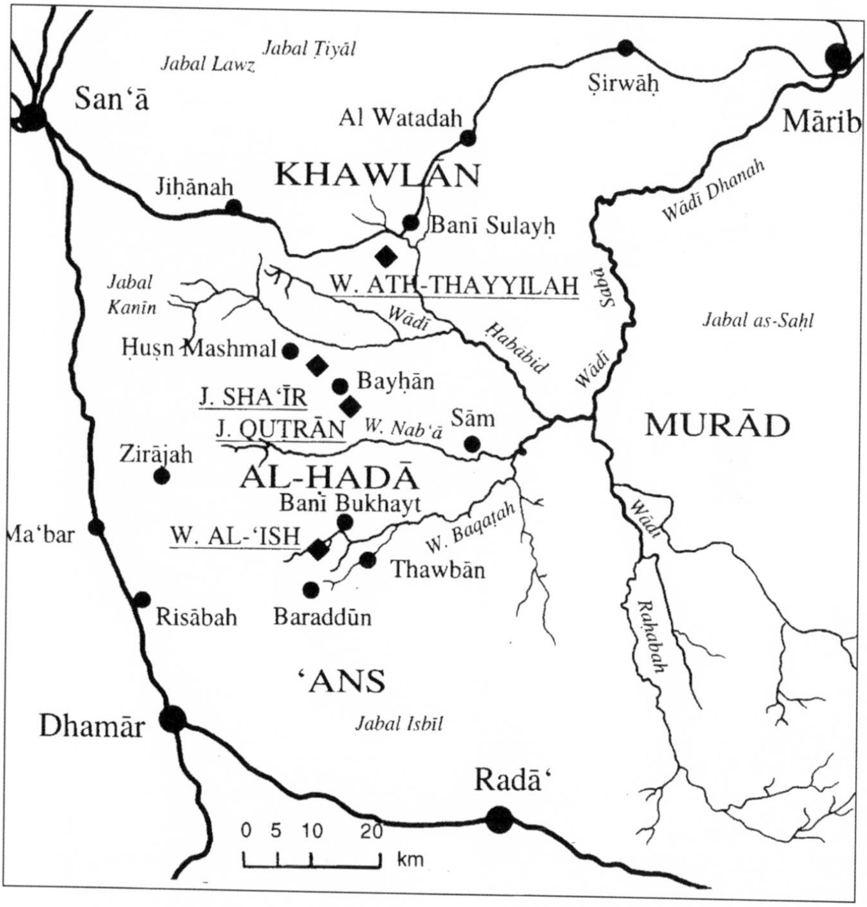

Figure 27
Map of the Wādī Dhanah basin with the neolithic sites found in 1983

surely covering our map of Bronze Age settlements.

Whereas the houses in later sites were linked together in a village structure, these new sites contained small oval huts (whose foundation stones were still in place) standing a little way apart from each other on artificial terraces cut into the hillside. The long axes of the huts always followed the contour line. We found no pottery shards around the huts, only evidence of stone-working including a profusion of bifacial points, which were clearly different from the type usually found in Bronze Age villages.

To get a better understanding of these tools, myself and

Annalisa Zarattini, an expert in neolithic artefacts, decided to undertake a brief trial excavation. This was based on a house in the Jabal Qutran site which was distinctive on account of its greater dimensions and because it had an original carving on one of the foundation stones showing five superimposed sets of horns. Material gathered during the excavation (obsidian bifacials, basalt and flint tools, scrapers, hammer-stones and many animal bones) confirmed our original hypothesis: we had discovered evidence of the neolithic period in Yemen.

But we still found this culture so enigmatic! Isolated as it was in the vast Arabian subcontinent, we had nothing to compare it to and therefore were unable to attempt a chronology. Furthermore, a study of prehistoric culture was impossible without some knowledge of the related paleo-environmental data, and at that time we knew absolutely

Plate 29
Flint and obsidian bifacials of the neolithic period on the plateau, from sites in the Khawlān and Al-Ḥadā

nothing about that aspect of Yemen. We were even ignorant of the geography of our area of research. As I remember, our only orientation aid was a series of aerial photographs from which we drew up topographical maps full of names of villages, mountains and water courses, which are still unique in the cartography of the region.

This in-depth study of such an unknown chapter of Yemeni history persuaded me to include Francesco Fedele in the staff of the mission the following year. He was a specialist in the neolithic culture of Europe and had also worked in Africa.

Having examined the material found in 1983, he immediately decided to analyse one of the sites we had found with a systematic study. Thus began the excavation of site no. 3 in Wādī al-Thayyilah (WTHiii), continuing throughout 1985 and closing in 1986[6]. The WTHiii site (Fig. 28) covered a third of a hectare, containing around ten principal structures and an array of stone blocks, set on a gentle slope halfway down Wādī al-Thayyilah. The excavations were done in three stages, with a total of 30 days on the site, a first for prehistoric archaeology in Yemen. The results are described by Fedele below:

> The three elliptical huts excavated turned out in fact to be houses, at least so we thought at first. The foundation wall was formed of stone blocks, with an opening on one side ... The hut must have been roofed with some sort of vegetation and possibly animal hides, and was supported by an almost central pole standing on a stone slab. Beside one of the large ellipses were found traces of adjacent rooms, which had been constructed from wooden stakes and other light materials. It seems evident, then, that stone houses were only one element of a village, the most notable perhaps, but not necessarily the most common, nor indeed the most important.
>
> These findings in 1985 spurred us on to the next excavation. It emerged that most structures in a village like this one would indeed have been made of ephemeral, lightweight materials, erected in the gaps between the stone houses. Some of these light structures seemed to be mere shelters made of vegetation, with a bare, sunken floor, a stone grinder in the corner, a hearth and domestic debris strewn

around. Alongside these residential structures were others, both lightweight and stone, with linear ground plans, or even openplan, which had repeatedly fallen down and been rebuilt. All this shows a long and involved use and re-use of the available space, and probably a rich community life, which we hadn't expected. This is perhaps the most important discovery as regards the neolithic period on the plateau.

Inside some of the stone huts were hearths and abandoned tools. Cinders from the fireplaces furnished carbon dating material, along with the names of the plants that had been burnt. We found various tools, including cleavers, large flakes of stone and an arrowhead, as well as a stone bracelet similar to those

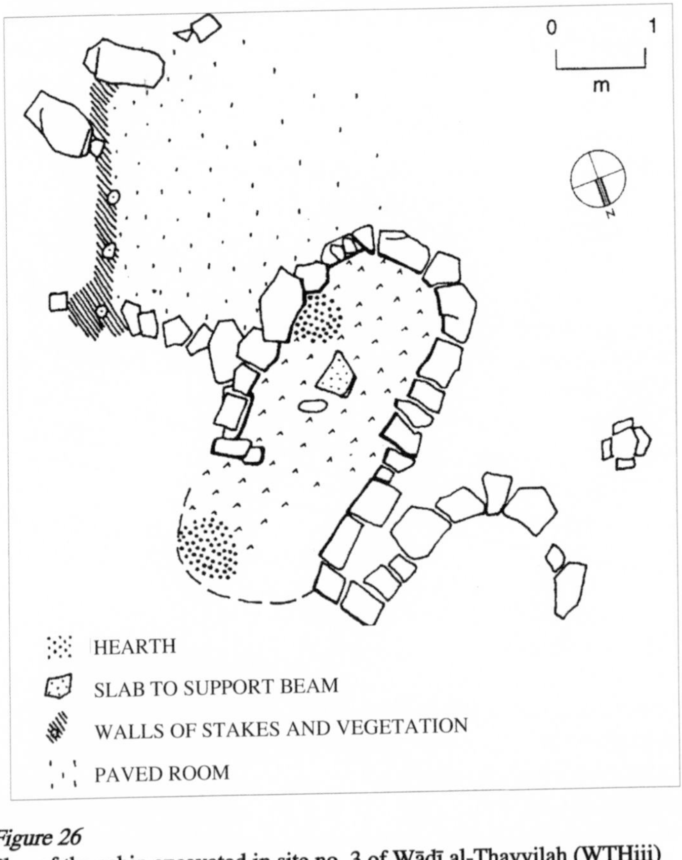

Figure 26
Plan of the cabin excavated in site no. 3 of Wādī al-Thayyilah (WTHiii)

of the late fifth millennium in Palestine or the Nile valley. There were also bone fragments belonging to cattle, sheep and domestic goats, all in such a bad state of repair that they had to be reconstituted on site...

Elsewhere on the site we found fragments of worked stone, left over from making composite tools, which have enabled us to establish the entire toolkit of a neolithic village for the first time. These included scrapers, burins, drills/bores, serrated tools for working wood, and pieces of blades used for harvesting ... These excavations led to the interesting discovery of solid, heavy tools made of local granite (cleavers, hammers, scrapers) which would not have been recognisable as tools had they not been found in context. The whole range of tools was made of many different kinds of stone, including the mediocre local flint, obsidian from quite far away, metamorphic quartzite and even solid granite.

Overall, WTHiii seems to have been a pastoral-peasant community quite well adapted to life on the plateau. The villages contain several types of buildings, both ephemeral and lasting. Besides durable, well- made objects we found makeshift tools for immediate use in food preparation and a host of other activities, which certainly included woodwork and the treatment of animal skins. Other implements suggest harvesting, although it is impossible to say of what. The bones found show that they kept a lot of cattle and a smaller number of sheep and goats, while hunting seems to have been totally absent. This economic framework has immediate environmental implications: cattle grazing tells us that the neolithic landscape was substantially different from today's sub-arid scenery[7].

All the major archaeological finds on the site were embedded in grey clayey soil, as opposed to the sandy yellow that covers the ground today, which indicates that the landscape was different during the heyday of WTHiii. As Fedele observed, this grey layer belongs to a period of geomorphological stability, which would have seen a considerable covering of vegetation. This wetter period could perhaps be linked to the mid-Holocene pluvial, a recognised period in the soil stratigraphy of the Afro-Asiatic tropical zone. If the correlation is correct, this grey Yemeni layer and therefore the principal neolithic phase of WTHiii dates from between the sixth and fourth millennium BC.

In an eroded trench in the upper part of the site, at a deeper and therefore earlier level than the grey layer, Fedele unearthed a truly unique piece: a female figurine made of unfired clay. Albeit tiny and incomplete, it may give us an idea of the period in which WTHiii was first settled. The only comparable pieces actually come from pre-pottery B neolithic (PPNB) in Palestine, which dates from the seventh millennium BC.

The first chapters of prehistory on the plateau of Yemen were gradually becoming clearer. But could our sequence hold true for other regions in a country of such physical contrasts? Surely in areas totally different from the plateau, like the Tihāmah or the desert, different types of culture would have developed, with different histories?

Figure 29
Reconstruction of a neolithic village of Al-A'rūsh (drawing by P. Smith)

The Neolithic Period on the Coast

Maurizio Tosi, an expert in the prehistory and protohistory of Asia with extensive research experience in the Near East, accepted my proposal to explore the Tihāmah region. From 1985 onwards he undertook a series of reconnaissance missions throughout the lower and middle coastal strips bordering the Red Sea, from Al-Mukhā in the south to the Al-Ṣalīf peninsula in the north[8] (Fig. 3).

Archaeological research was not an easy matter in that intensely hot and humid region, mainly because the lack of any pre-existing information made it hard to guess the position of potential prehistoric sites within the current landscape. The Tihāmah has undergone enormous changes over time, especially near the coast. The mass of alluvial sediment from the neighbouring mountains has gradually encroached on the sea; a slow tectonic lifting of the mountains has given rise to lakes and *sibākh* (pools of brackish water); monsoon winds, especially widespread and violent on the south coast, have caused an enormous amount of erosion; and human occupation, in cultivating the oases along the various *widyān* (*wādīs*) running from east to west across the Tihāmah region, has caused extensive destruction to the few traces of ancient settlements which do exist.

Prehistoric sites are often no more than slightly lighter patches on the ground. Looking for them at random in a vast tract of land like the Tihāmah would have been like searching for the proverbial needle in the haystack. So, the mission had first to evaluate and understand the ecological factors responsible for the changes in the landscape. Only then, having identified potential sites, could the archaeological reconnaissance begin in earnest.

There were two particular areas where neither wind nor man had managed to obliterate all traces of the sites: along the northern bank of Wādī Rimā and in the area stretching east of the Al-Ṣalīf peninsula to the north of Wādī Surdūd. The shell middens (heaps of waste from the shellfish that the village-dwellers of the Tihāmah fed on in neolithic times) found in Wādī Rimā were over ten km from the sea, which shows how far soil deposition has extended the coastline. The discovery of shells of the *Terebralia palustris L* species gives us an insight into the ecological system that surrounded prehistoric man. Throughout the Indo-Pacific region, this mollusc lives in symbiosis with mangroves which grow in lagoon zones with strong tides, and its presence here is proof that our Yemeni sites once stood in a mangrove environment[9].

By analysing the distribution and quantity of the man-made (pottery, worked stones, remains of ovens and post-holes) and natural objects (shells, bones, ostrich eggs, coprolites) that one can still find on the surface of the sites we have been able to reconstruct some of the activities that took place in prehistoric settlements. For example, at site no. 1 of Wādī Surdad (*SRDi*), there are well-defined areas for the various crafts, including a specific area for making beads out of ostrich eggshell and chalcedony, and another area for the manufacture of circular scrapers, possibly used to work leather and hides.

At first we thought that the community must have had a fishing economy, on account of the profusion of shells, although in a few places we had found some mammal bones. A lucky break while excavating the Al-Shumah (*ASH*) site, north of Wādī Rimā, produced surprising results. Under the surface crust, composed of shells compacted and broken up by the wind, Tosi came upon something he could never have expected: a substantial quantity of animal bones. Sandor Bökönyi, the palaeozoologist from Budapest who identified the bones, found in his report that samples showed that wild donkeys were hunted, but also that there was a certain number of domesticated donkeys. He also concluded that besides the marine resources, hunting these wild donkeys provided over 90 percent of the meat eaten by the site's population, and that the only domestic animals were cattle and, probably, dogs. Apart from the wild donkeys, he reported, wildlife was limited to aurochs (*Bos primigenius*), gazelles and, perhaps, wild goats.

It seems, then, that the Al-Shumah site – which dates from a very ancient period (6684-6475 BC) according to radio-carbon analyses of the shells – was a kind of seasonal base for hunters, whose main quarry was the wild donkey that, it seems, frequented Yemen's coastal strip at that time. The animals were hunted, but – as far as Bökönyi could tell from studying the bones – were not always killed. They were sometimes captured and farmed. Here we have early evidence of the domestication of donkeys.

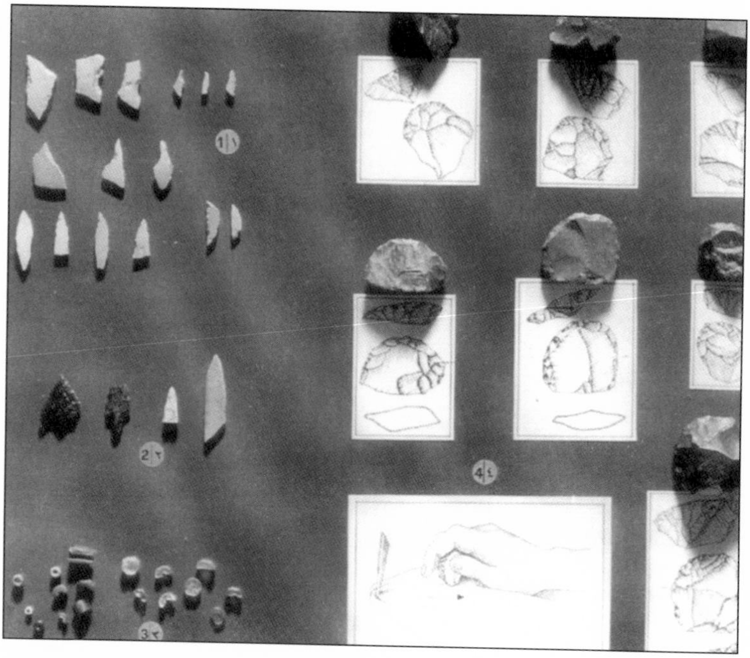

Plate 30
Stone tools, ostrich eggshell tools and beads from the prehistoric sites of Tihāmah

Unfortunately, the particular environmental conditions of the Tihāmah region precluded the possibility of taking soil stratigraphies comparable to those taken on the plateau. We cannot therefore see the two cultural facies side by side. But the considerable environmental differences must have led to substantially different lifestyles and means of subsistence. The absence of hunting on the plateau indicates a static lifestyle with an economy dominated by herding and perhaps agriculture. The people of Tihāmah, on the other hand, mainly supported themselves by fishing and hunting. This would have led to settlements which were probably not of a permanent nature, though this would have changed with the start of farming. Besides Al-Shumah, which dates to the lower Holocene period, Tosi also found sites from the middle Holocene period, but their condition has so far prevented us from establishing whether they were seasonal bases or permanent settlements.

The Neolithic Period in the Desert

To complete our picture of Yemeni prehistory we still needed information on the third ecozone, the internal deserts.

The Rub' al-Khālī had already yielded some lithic tools[10], some of them from the south-west (Ramlat Sab'atayn), but the sporadic nature of these finds (mostly by people working for the oil companies) meant that we had no information on the circumstances or contexts of the discoveries. One day in the Organisation for the Antiquities of Ṣan'ā I was delighted to see some exquisite flint arrowheads lying on the desk of the head of the Excavation Section. They had been brought in by some bedouin from Mārib, who claimed to have found them in the Ramlat Sab'atayn, south of Safir, where there is now an oil refinery. This was in the autumn of 1986, and I decided to set out on a brief visit to the area with Francesco Di Mario, who was by now an expert on the lithic industry of Yemen.

One has only to look at a map to see what the Ramlat

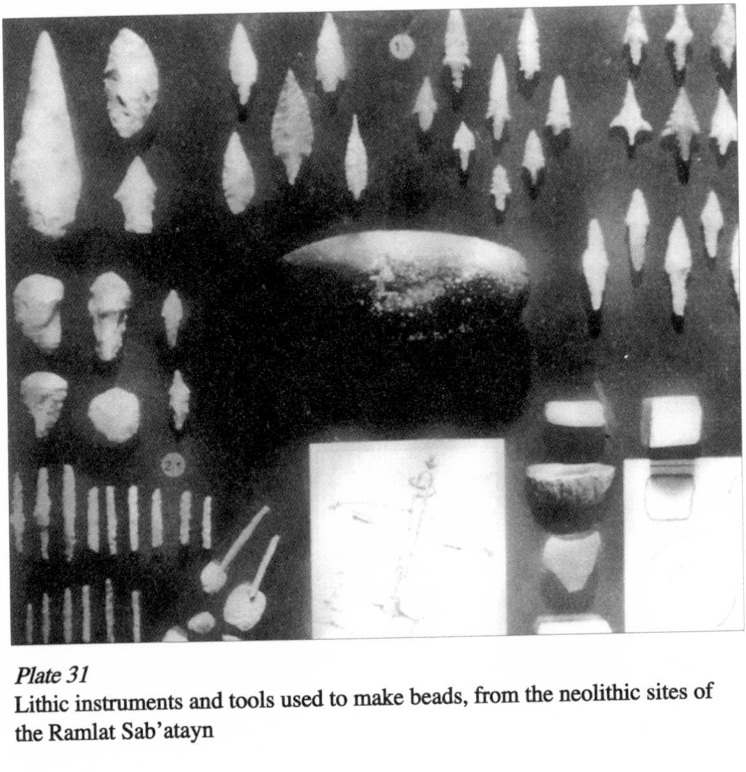

Plate 31
Lithic instruments and tools used to make beads, from the neolithic sites of the Ramlat Sab'atayn

Sab'atayn must once have been, in a wetter age. Hemmed in by the mountains of Yemen to the east, south and west, and separated from the Rub' al-Khālī proper to the north by a low watershed that stretched from Jabal al-Lawdh to the hills of Al-'Abr, it must have consisted of a huge flood basin, receiving all the rainwater of Yemen's mountainous interior. In the distant past, when there was greater rainfall, the water would have accumulated and formed a large lake before dispersing through the single outlet, Wādī Ḥaḍramawt. The increasingly dry climate caused the lake to dry out, becoming first a sort of savannah, and ultimately, as the winds and increasingly dramatic daily temperature ranges crumbled the earth and rocks, a desert of towering sand dunes. However, the wind gently moves these dunes, making them "roll" across the solid, argillaceous base that was at first a lake bed and then the savannah floor. The slow but inexorable march of the dunes is well-documented at the Awwam temple at Mārib, now unfortunately in ruins and entirely covered by sand again after the American excavations of 1952.

Dunes, therefore, create gaps or valleys as they move, exposing the ancient grey floor. We know from studying the soil of these valleys that the wind acts mainly on the sand, leaving any large or heavy objects in place. Lying there in full view were fossilised bones and flints among other things; the first precious pieces of information on the environment and lifestyle of the middle Holocene period in Yemen.

Climbing one sand dune after another we made our way south from Safir, filling plastic bags with our finds, until we found ourselves crossing Wādī Ḥarib, which Phillips' trucks had crossed so many times, shuttling between Mārib and Beihan. I couldn't help thinking for a second that only a few kilometres to the south, in the inaccessible (for us) Popular Democratic Republic of Yemen, lay the heart of Qatabān, the glorious capital of Timna' and Hajar Bin Ḥumayd.

Di Mario roused me from my daydreams by pointing out a wide greyish patch on the golden slope of the *wādī*'s north bank. The gradual wind erosion had given us *HARii*, a site almost entirely composed of splendid neolithic artefacts.

I was astounded by the number of complete, perfect arrowheads. In one spot there was a mass of borers that, although all made of the same beige-hazelnut coloured flint, were of an absolutely amazing length.

Sabina Antonini and I launched ourselves into an enthusiastic harvest, but Di Mario immediately told us to leave the objects where they were. He drew a long rectangle on the ground and began combing the surface and filling bags. The results of this systematic search are now published in the first report on the so-called neolithic of the Ramlat Sab'atayn[11]. They tell us that the local communities, possibly contemporary with the neolithic people on the plateau and the coast (although the dates are not yet certain), hunted gazelles and wild donkeys and collected ostrich eggs. Their environment was much greener than it is now, and they moved around, setting up seasonal bases, where they would stay whilst hunting and carrying out other jobs, like butchering the animals they killed and making their weapons and tools, or fashioning beads of amazonite, a craft which is well-documented in all its stages at *HARii.*

Here, like at Al-A'rūsh and in Tihāmah, we had opened up a whole new field of study. Over the course of a few years the Italian mission had discovered Yemen's great prehistoric heritage, quite equal to that of other, better-known Middle Eastern countries.

Footnotes:

1. Caton Thompson, G., "Some Palaeoliths from South Arabia", *PPS* 19 (1953), p.189-218.
2. Benardelli, G. and Parrinello, A.E., "Note su alcune localitàarcheologiche del Yemen, I", *AION* 30 (1970), 117-120; and "Note su alcune località archeologiche del Yemen, II", *AION* 31 (1971), p. 111-118.
3. de Bayle des Hermens, R., "Prémière mission de recherche préhistoriques en République Arabe du Yémen", *L'Anthropologie* 80, p. 5-39. See also de Bayle des Hermens and Grebenart, D. "Deuxième mission de recherches préhistoriques en République Arabe du Yémen", *L'Anthropologie* 84 (1980), p. 563-582.
4. de Maigret, A. "Prospezione geo-archeologica nello Yemen del Nord. Notizia di una prima ricognizione", *OA* 19 (1980), p. 307-313.

5. de Maigret, A. "Two Prehistoric Cultures and a New Sabaean Site in the Eastern Highlands of North Yemen", *Raydan* 4, (1981), p. 191-204.
6. Bulgarelli, G., "Evidence of Paleolithic Industries in NorthernYemen", in W. Daum (ed.), *Yemen: 3000 Years of Art and Civilization in Arabia Felix* (Frankfurt: Umschau-Verlag, 1987), p. 32-33.
7. Fedele, F., "North Yemen: The Neolithic", in Daum (ed.), *Yemen:3000 Years of Art and Civilization in Arabia Felix*, p. 34-37.
8. de Maigret, A. Di Mario, F. and Fedele, F., "Lo Yemen prima del regno di Saba", *Le Scienze* 234 (1988), p. 20-22.
9. Tosi, M., "Tihāmah Coastal Archaeology Survey", *EW* 35 (1985), p. 363-369; and "Survey and Excavations on the Coastal Plain (Tihāmah)", EW 36 (1986), p. 400-414.
10. Tosi, M. "Tihāmah Coastal Survey", p. 364.
11. Zeuner, F., "Neolithic Sites from the Rub' al-Khālī, Southern Arabia", *Man* 54 (1954), p. 1-4.
12. Di Mario, F., "The Western ar-Rub' al-Khālī (Neolithic): New Data from the Ramlat Sab'atayn (Yemen Arab Republic)", *AION* 49 (1989), p. 109-148.

VII

THE BRONZE AGE

First Bronze Age Site

The year 1981 was an important one for archaeology in Yemen, as it brought the discovery both of the country's prehistory and of the Bronze Age. The most important date for the Italian mission was 12 December of that year, the day that we came upon a site which seemed to correspond exactly to what we had envisaged. As we saw in the previous chapter, our aim in excavating the Khawlān site was to identify the cultural antecedents of the South Arabian kingdoms. The ruin that we found on 12 December, which we called WYi (or site 1 of Wādī Yanā'im, which runs across this north-western corner of the Al-A'rūsh region) appeared to be the first pre-Sabaean site discovered up until then in southern Arabia.

There were two principal reasons why I made this chronological assumption: 1) The presence of surface pottery different from the Sabaean type meant that WYi could not belong to the classical South Arabian period; 2) The presence of a lithic industry different from that found at the few prehistoric sites known up to that time in North Yemen (we had not yet identified the neolithic sites on the plateau), showed that the site did not belong to the neolithic period.

This impression was strengthened by the excavations of subsequent years, when the dates provided by radiocarbon analysis and the kind of objects that we found appeared to justify and confirm our belief in a Yemeni culture dating from the third to second millennium BC, a previously unknown period in the archaeology of southern Arabia. My enthusiasm at this discovery is obvious in the title of the first report I published on the subject: *A Bronze Age for Southern Arabia*[1].

Research on the site was resumed in 1983 and continued until 1985. As a result we can claim that our system, a combination of on-the-spot research, reconnaissance and excavations using all the scientific methods available to archaeology (geomorphology, soil science, mineralogy, palaeozoology, palaeobotany) has produced very useful

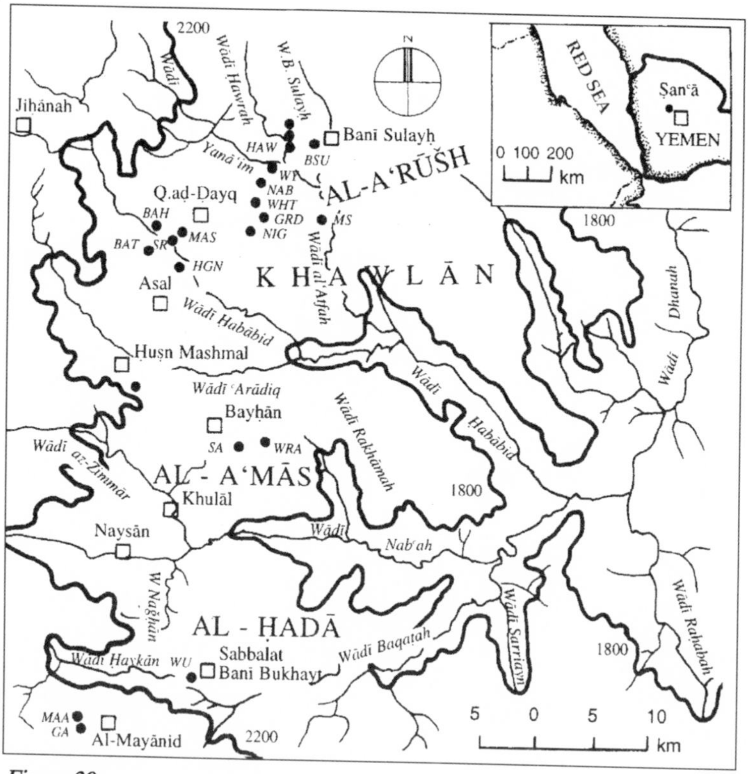

Figure 30

Bronze Age sites in the Wādī Dhanah basin

results and has enabled us to recreate the essential elements of this forgotten society.

Interdisciplinary Reconnaissance

Reconnaissance missions were concentrated on the Al-A'rūsh region (Fig. 30), where we had found WYi, and from there spread west (Suhmān) and south (Jabal al-A'mās, Al-Ḥadā). These missions gave us a clearer picture of the distribution of settlements in relation to the natural environment and we gained a basic idea of the architecture and relative chronology from a comparison of the sites' plans and from samples of pottery found on the surface.

We excavated three sites in Al-A'rūsh (WYi, *RAQi* and *NABvii*), and one site in the Suhmān (MASi) and were therefore able to see the architecture and objects –

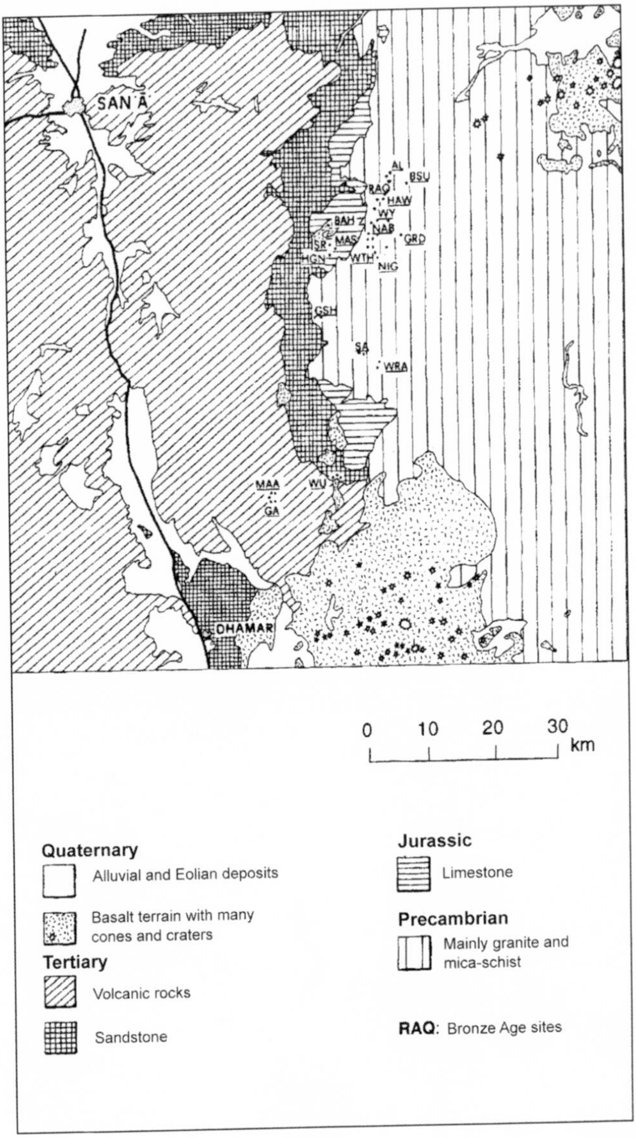

Figure 31
Bronze Age sites in their geological context

particularly pottery – within their archaeological contexts, to understand the position of the Bronze Age strata compared to those of older periods (*NABvii*) and, finally, to gather the organic matter we needed to study the fauna and produce radiocarbon analyses[3].

Almost all the forty sites belonging to this period were found immediately east of the geological zone of tertiary sandstone called the "Tawīilah group", which stretches from Jabal Ṭiyāl in the north down to the great quaternary lava plain of Jabal Isbil in the south (Fig. 31). Standing on Precambrian granite, Yemen's base rock, the settlements were established in a line, staying fairly close to the sedimentary rocks of the Tawīilah. Local geological features include the two broad, isolated tables of Jurassic limestone (the 'Amrān series) comprising the Suhmān/'Urqūb to the north and the Dula' al-Amas/Banī Bukhayt to the south. Settlements were generally established close to the widyān that followed the tectonic fracture lines in the base rock.

The geology of the area is very important. We can learn more about the economy of the communities in question from studying the composition and disposition of rock formations than from anything else. For this I have to thank Bruno Marcolongo, a geomorphologist from Padua, who accompanied us on our explorations and broadened the rather blinkered vision of the archaeologists, helping us to see the ancient evidence that we were turning up in paleo-ecological terms. Now the palaeo-environmental picture began to take shape, and with it our first conclusions on the principal palaeo-economic aspects of the pre-Sabaean population of Khawlān.

Another geologist and soil scientist, Alberto Palmieri, helped to study the sediments and found that the valleys of the region contained an unusual alternation of sedimentary layers, which had been highly valuable in the past because they drew water away from the shallow underground aquifers that originated in the limestone massifs west of the sites and channelled it towards the crops. The early settlers had seen the value of these aspects of their environment and had learned to farm successfully. This was confirmed by the results of the archaeological study[4].

We found 24 sites along the fault between Jabal 'urqūb and the Al-A'rūsh region. This is in striking contrast to the two solitary villages that stand there today and shows us how, in the past, alluvial sediments played an important role in maintaining population density. Samples of these sediments were found on the sides of the valleys and in the dried-up river beds. A study of their cross-sections showed us what the countryside must once have looked like. A yellowish layer with a sandy consistency, between 40 and 60 cm thick, lay on top of a dense, dark-grey layer, composed mostly of clay. This second layer, formed in a period with wetter climatic conditions, then formed an impermeable barrier, which would not absorb the water flowing down from the limestone area to the west. The water gradually soaked into the sandy yellow layer that formed above the clay during a drier period. This topsoil, kept damp by the impermeable layer beneath, constituted the basis for Bronze Age agriculture.

A Stratigraphy

In August 1984 we excavated a trench in site no.7 of Wādī al-Najid al-Abayd (*NABvii*) which proved that our theories were correct. (Fig. 32). We found that the stratigraphic sequence of the valleys could also be found in an archaeological site. This was very important because it enabled us to compare the sedimentary layers with the archaeological finds. In particular, it showed that the Bronze Age structures were contemporary with the yellow layer, which was the layer with the greatest agricultural potential. We were then lucky enough to find, in the grey layer underneath, unmistakable signs of human occupation, in the form of lithic tools, which were reminiscent of the neolithic sites found in 1983 further south. So, at *NABvii* we had a precious stratigraphy which proved that there was a double link: yellow layer/Bronze Age and grey layer/neolithic. This second assumption was definitively proven in October of that year by Fedele's excavation at WTHiii. The little site of NABvii was also important partly because it yielded a bronze burin, or engraving tool, which convinced us to use the term "Bronze Age" for these protohistoric antiquities of Yemen.

Settlement Patterns

Throughout the territory, the settlements appear to have been arranged with three principal criteria in mind: 1) the

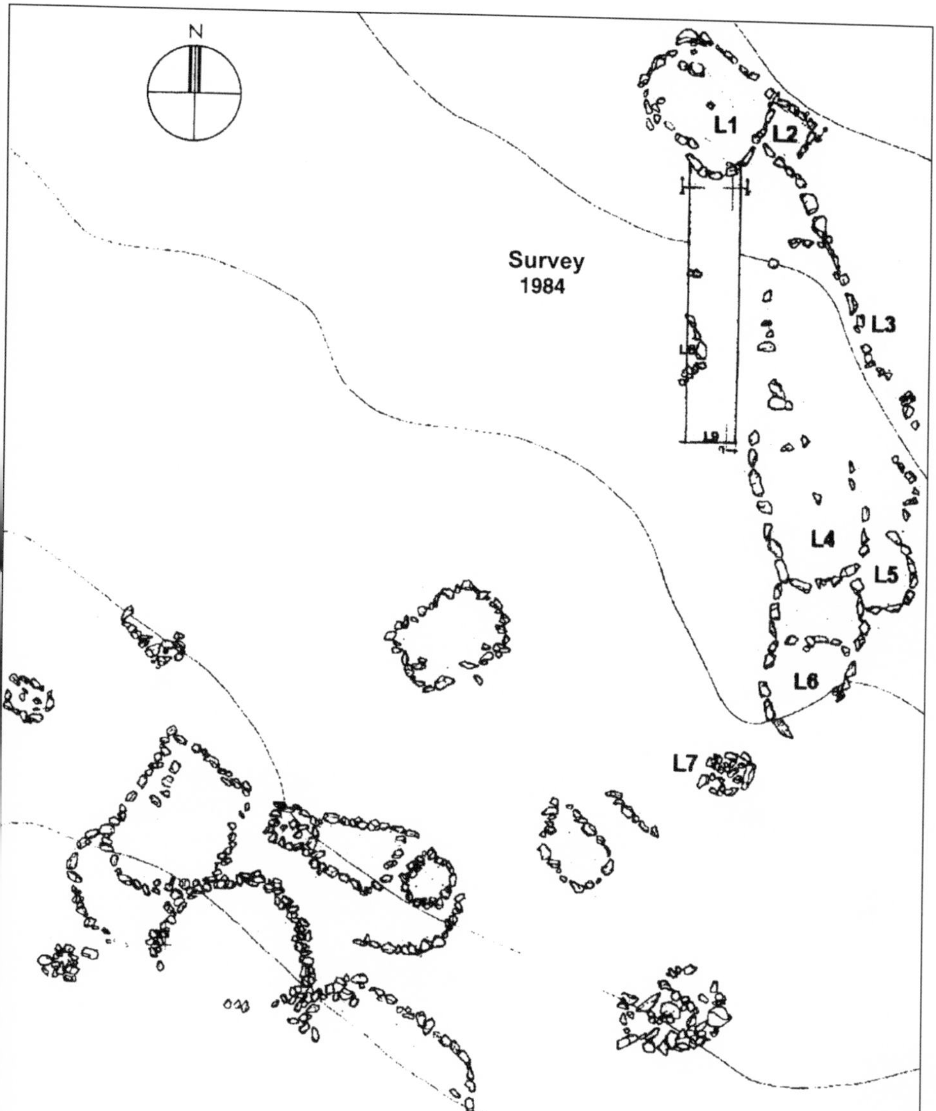

Figure 32
Plan of site 7 in Wādī al-Najid al-Abyaḍ

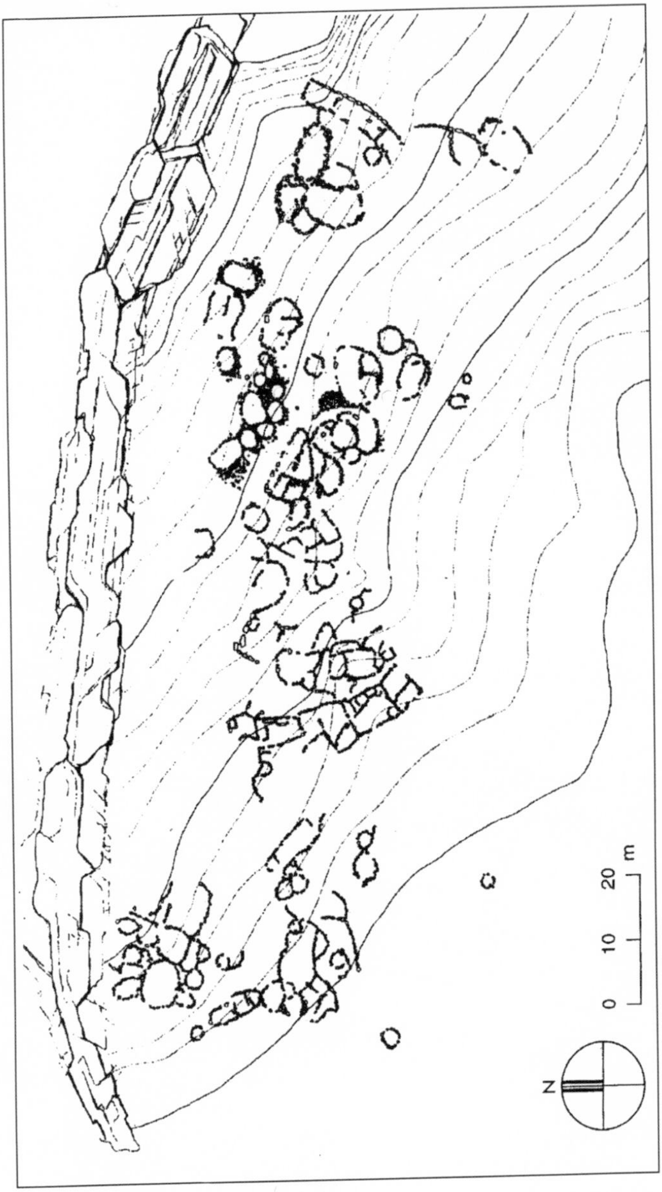

Figure 33
Plan of site 1 of Al-Raqlah (RAQi)

Plate 32
Foundations of a Bronze Age house from site 5 of Wādī al-Najid al-Abyaḍ (NABv) in Al-A'rūsh (Khawlān al-Tiyal)

need for a certain amount of farmable land; 2) the ready availability of building materials; 3) the ability to defend the position. The first criterion is clearly suggested by the sites' regular distribution along the valleys. It is worth noting that the villages can be divided into two categories: small sites, with an area of less than 1000 square metres, and large sites, with an area greater than 10,000 square metres. These larger sites are situated at wide but regular intervals along the valleys and seem to have dominated huge territories, within which the smaller sites were distributed.

Farming considerations must only have determined the distribution pattern to a certain extent. A degree of flexibility was needed in order to meet the next criteria: the availability of building materials. Of course, these were not in short supply, given the rocky nature of the region. However, in most cases the sites tended to be

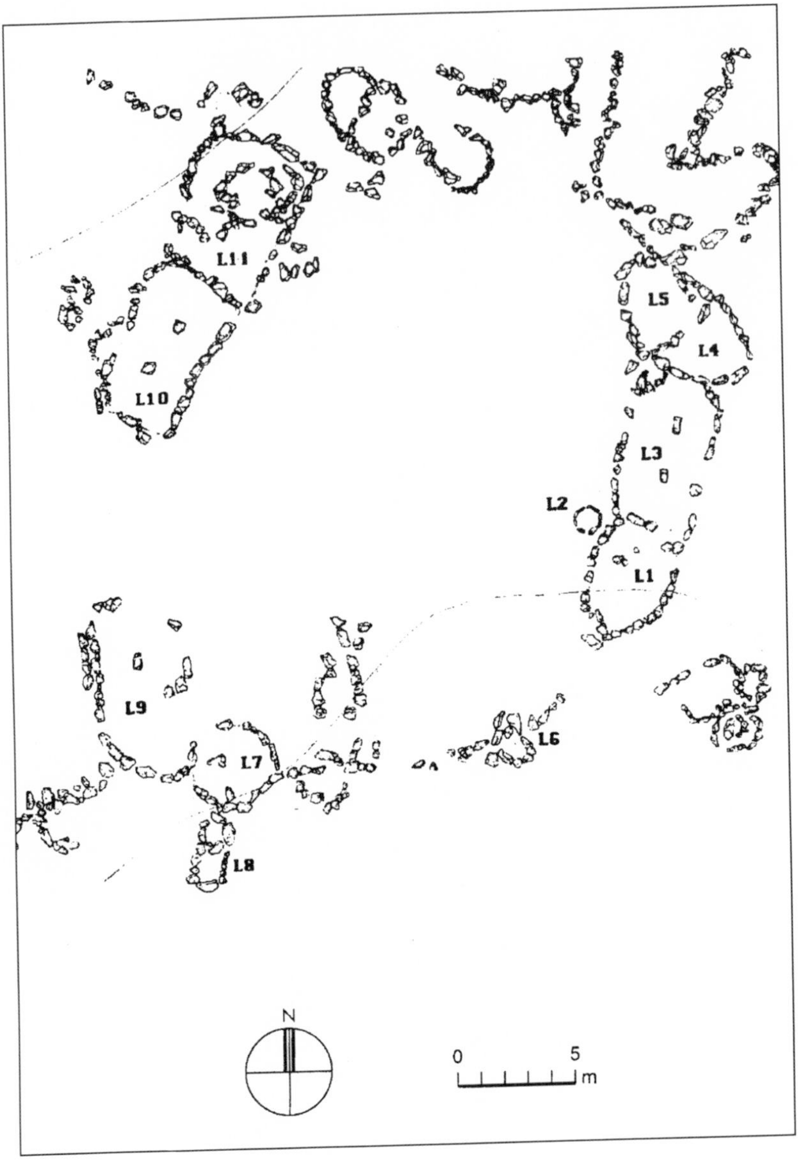

Figure 34
Plan of Unit A in Wādī Yanā'im (WYi)

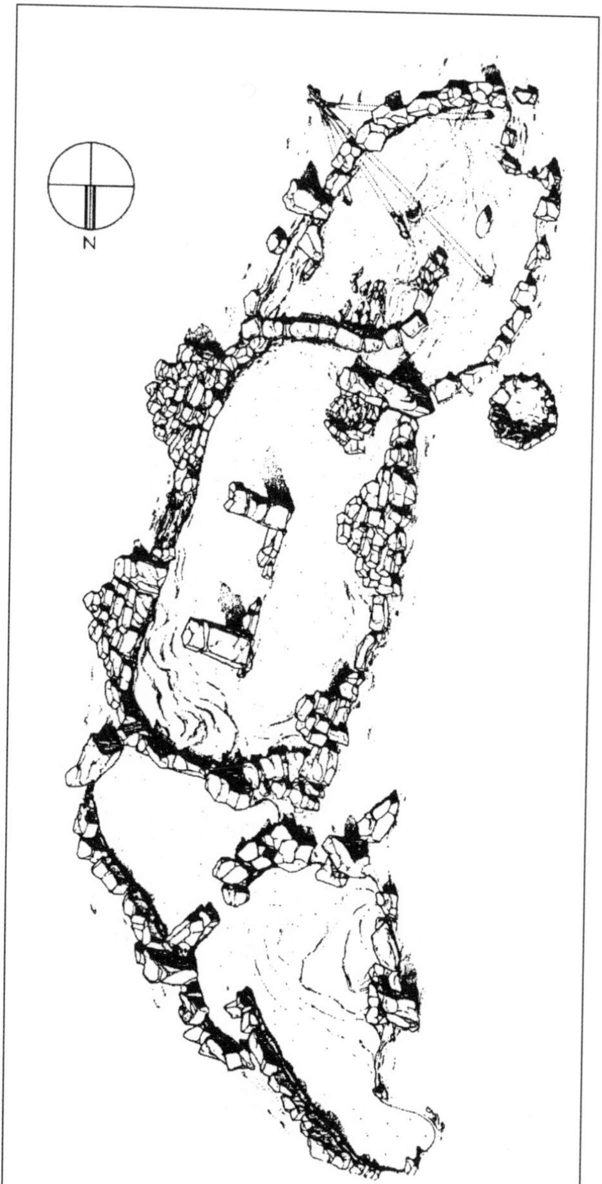

Figure 35
Axonometric view of a house of unit A in Wādī Yanā'im (al-'Arush, Khawlān al-Tiyal)

situated on slopes surmounted by ancient lava flows which had solidified into narrow faults in the granite base rock (Fig. 33). This guaranteed the inhabitants a good source of building materials close at hand, which they used to build the elliptical or sub-rectangular foundations of the houses (Plate 32). At the same time, they could fulfil the third criterion, defence, since the bank of lava offered the villages protection from the rear.

The sites can be divided into two categories not only by their size, but also their layout. The small sites consist of a circular clearing surrounded by a ring of basically interconnecting rooms (Fig. 32). The large sites are made up of clusters of this type of arrangement. Here, the individual units are sometimes simply juxtaposed, but in some cases the plans suggest an embryonic form of town planning.

Plate 33
Some rooms in Unit A of site 1 in Wādī Yanā'im

Architecture

Architectural details were revealed by excavating individual units of the large sites of *MASi* and *RAQi*. The excavation of unit A of WYi (Fig. 34) shows that houses usually consisted of two connecting oval rooms, both opening onto a central courtyard, one of which comprised the living quarters (L3, L10) while the other was used for producing and storing food (L1, L11). The foundations of the houses were made of large blocks of stone, unworked, but squared off as far as possible; the walls were made of smaller stones held together with mud; the roof, probably of thatch, was held up by two central wooden posts, with stone bases still visible now in the middle of the rooms (Fig. 35). The beaten earth floors were about 30 centimetres below ground level, making the houses seem rather low when seen from outside (Plate 33).

Inside, the most common features are low dividing walls, benches around the edges, doors with thresholds, jambs and hinges, and receptacles for grain and the like. Among the objects most commonly found in the storerooms are pottery, all sizes and shapes of grindstones, lithic tools and bones. The position of three holes, designed to receive poles, dug out of the rock underneath a room in WYi (L1), testify to the presence there of a high wooden trestle, probably used for butchering. Outside, there is almost always a small pit, dug out of the earth or rock, lined with slabs of rock arranged like the staves of a barrel, and used for cooking meat (cooking pits).

Some sites contain buildings more imposing than, and isolated from, the surrounding houses. These might have had a different function from the simple dwellings. An example is locus 14, excavated at *RAQi* (Plate 10). Although the few objects found inside were not much help in identifying its function, particular architectural characteristics (such as benches along the walls, freestanding monoliths, etc.) suggest that the building had a public use.

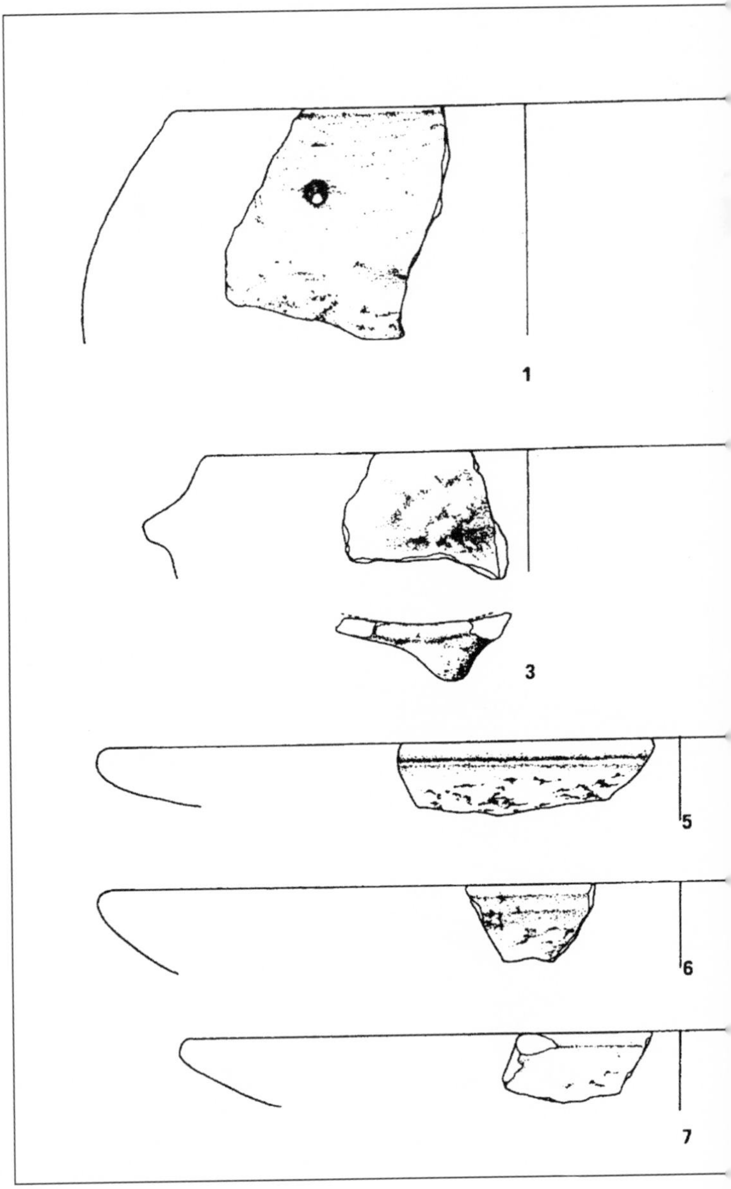

Figure 36
Bronze Age Yemeni ceramics

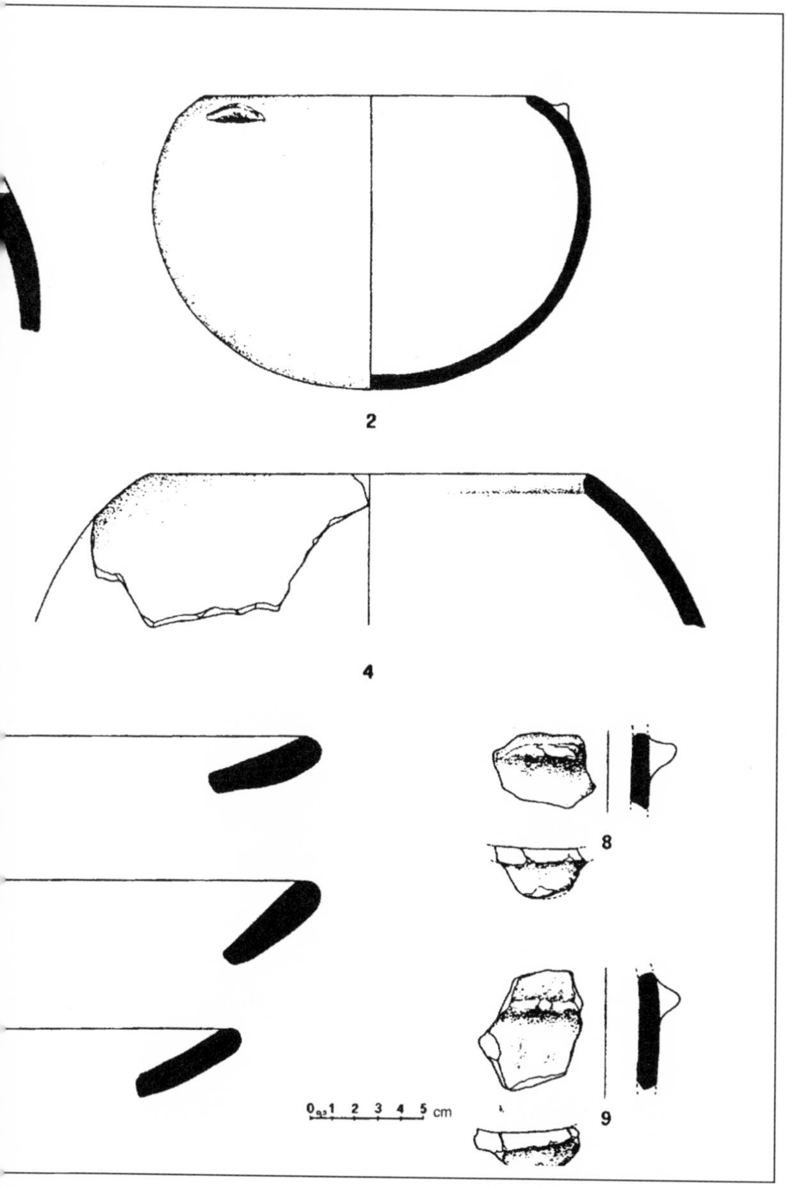
2
4
8
9
0 0.5 1 2 3 4 5 cm

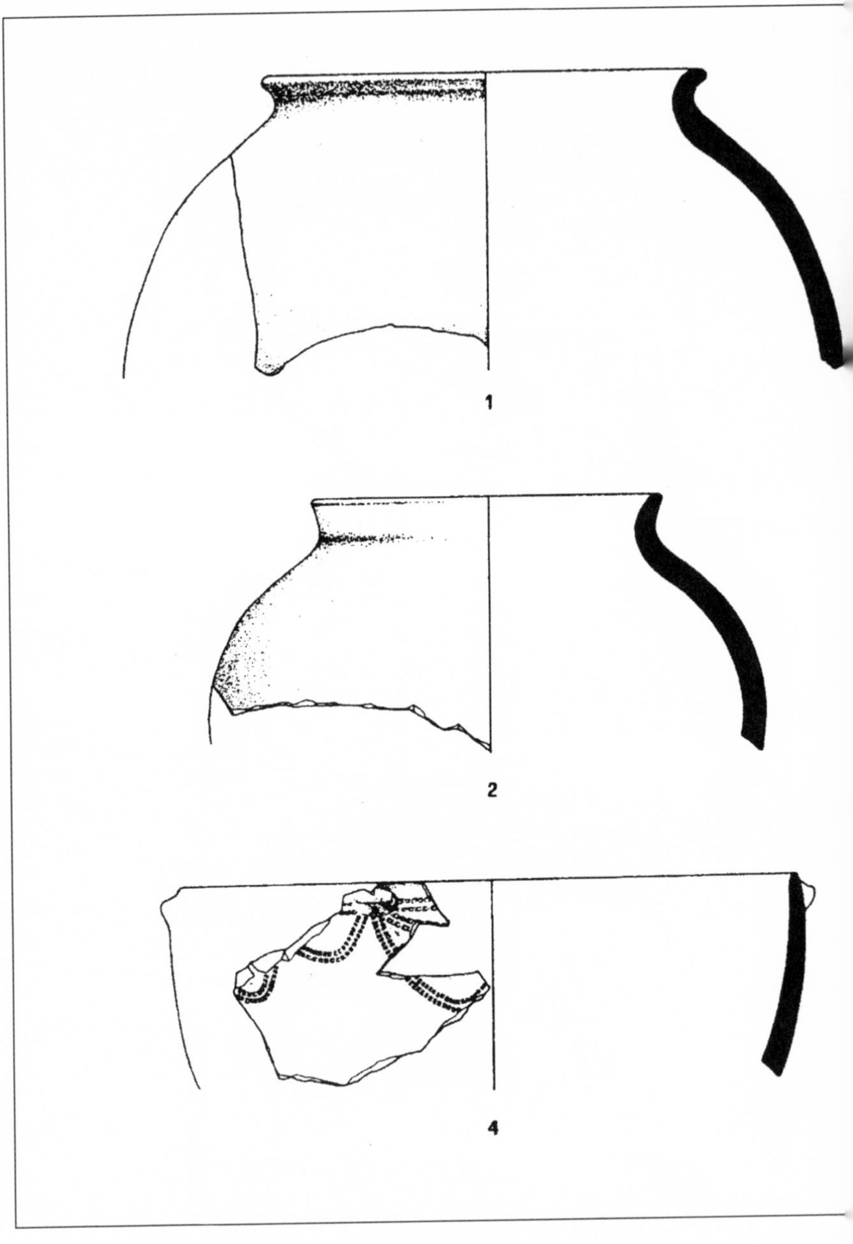

Figure 37
Bronze Age Yemeni ceramics

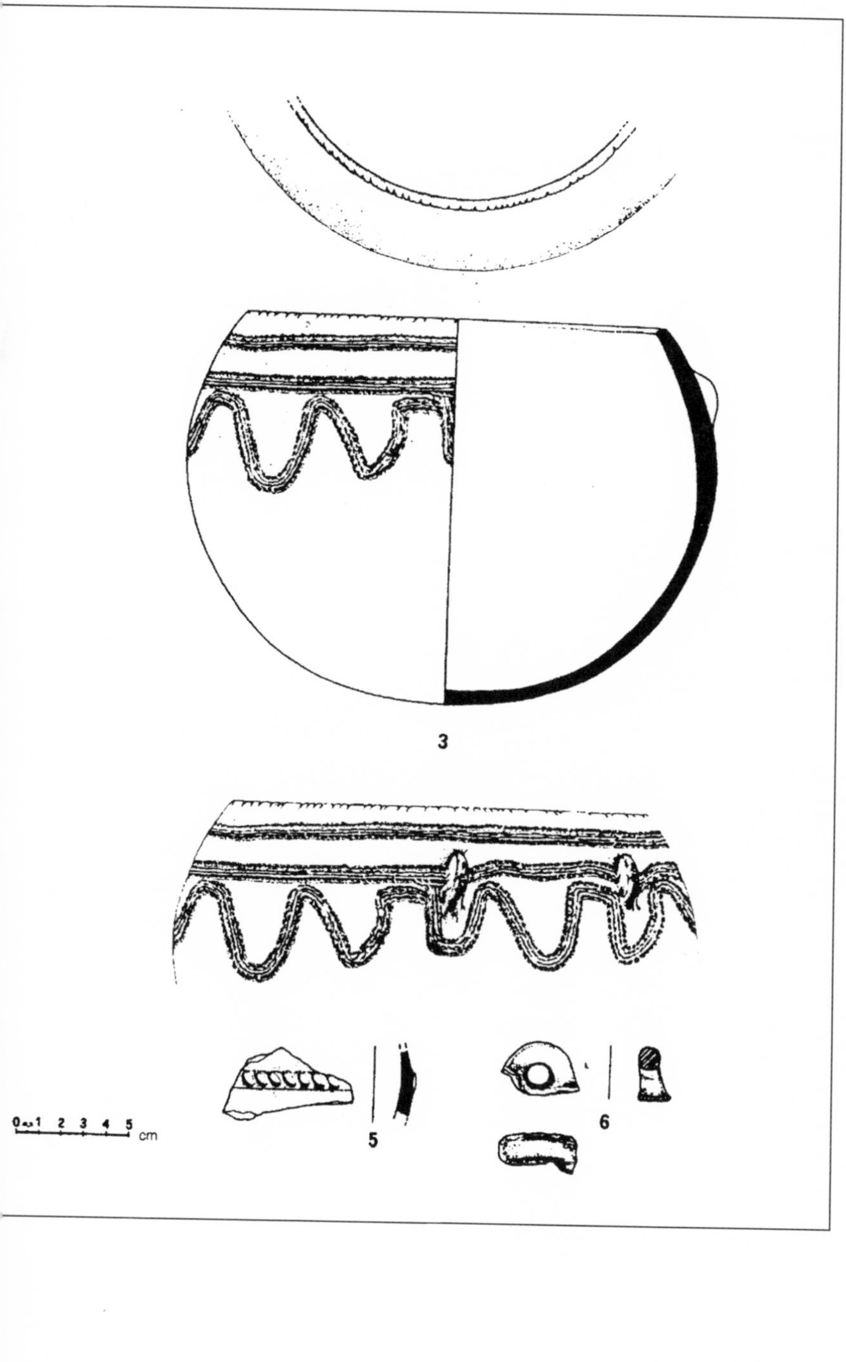
3
5
6
0 1 2 3 4 5 cm

Material Culture

The pottery found on the surface – which was a completely unknown type and convinced us, in 1983, that we were dealing with a new Arabian culture – and especially that found in excavations, which was better preserved, differed in many respects from that of the South Arabian period (Figs. 36 and 37). Its heaviness, the red-brick colour, the presence of inclusions of coarse granitic sand often protruding from the roughly-finished surfaces, all give this ware a very recognisable character, making it easy to identify, even when dealing with just a few shards.

The pottery was never produced on a wheel and can be divided into two principal groups: 1) The so-called "kitchen" pottery was made of clay and is coarse-grained, devoid of surface treatment, and with a great many mineral inclusions. Characteristic shapes are an olla (a hole mouth vessel) with no rim, a simply rounded bottom and, often, horizontal handles; and large plates with slightly thickened rims. 2) Pottery with a finer texture is better fired, and has polished surfaces, often altering the natural reddish colour of the clay to darker shades of orange, brown, or dark hazelnut. Typical of this work are the many little spherical jars with turned-out rims, and some deep cups without bases but with handles placed horizontally just under the rim, which often show signs of surface polishing and occasionally an unusual type of decoration, pressed into the clay with a rolling instrument.

Stone tools, common both on the surface and in excavations, can be distinguished from those of the earlier and more sophisticated neolithic phase in that they are basically discarded flint, quartz and obsidian flakes, retouched and adapted to function as scrapers, borers and saws. Some of these flakes probably belonged to composite tools.

The Economic Framework

We finished gathering the information outlined above in 1985, at which point we began the work of analysis and study. Apart from the archaeologists dealing with the architecture, pottery and miscellaneous artefacts, I was joined by other scientists (B. Marcolongo and A. Palmieri on geomorphology and sedimentology; F. Fedele and S. Bökönyi on palaeozoology; L. Costantini on paleobotany, and V. Francaviglia on sources of obsidian). The architects and artists of the mission dedicated themselves to making

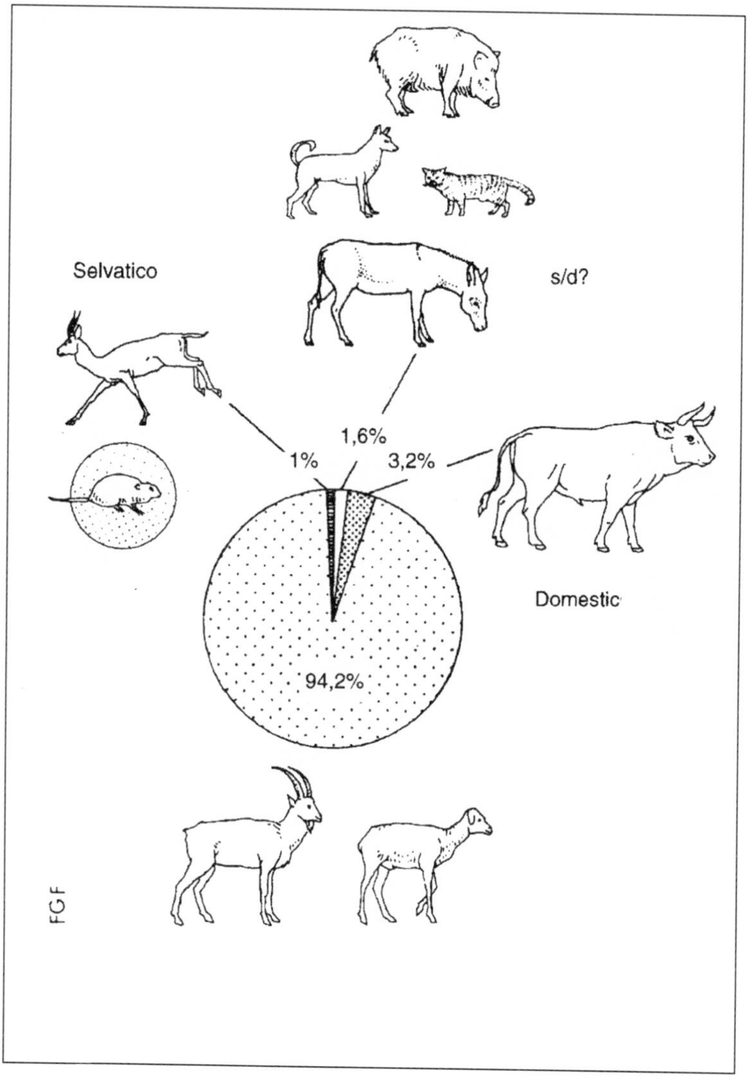

Figure 36
Occurrence of animal species found in Bronze Age sites in Wādī Dhanah

drawings of all the pottery, flints and other artefacts, and particularly to producing fair copies of our many plans and topographical maps. Thus, in 1990, the first definitive report was published – with an Arabic translation – on Yemeni culture in the Bronze Age, *The Bronze Age Culture of Hawlan at-Ṭiyāl and Al-Ḥadā*.

My conclusions at the end of that volume were that the general socioeconomic framework of these Bronze Age Yemeni cultures is typical of static communities dedicated to farming and animal husbandry. The presence of farming is demonstrated first and foremost by the distribution of the settlements, which were spaced evenly across the whole area of cultivable land. Also, studies carried out in Wādī al-Najid al-Abyaḍ show that excellent hydro-geological conditions for plant cultivation existed in the area which contains our sites. The worked stone tools and grindstones reflect changes in lifestyle occasioned by agricultural development. Grindstones in particular are evidence of two phases of cereal production: first, crushing the grains (mortars) and then grinding them (grindstones)[4]. Many tools of this sort were found at WYi (Plate 36), a large quantity in storeroom L11, along with some unusual fitments, which led us to identify the room as a mill. Some of the pottery contained seeds and imprints of plants, proving that farming was well-developed and intensive[5].

During the excavations, we discovered special rooms (L1 of WYi) and structures – like the cooking pits containing animal bones found at WYi, RAQi and MASi – which reflect stages in the production of meat-based food, in itself evidence of intensive animal husbandry. Further proof of this was provided by some remains of animal bones[6]. These belonged mostly to sheep and goats (Fig. 38). They were slaughtered at a predetermined age, which suggests that they were kept primarily for meat. Cattle and pigs were also probably kept for their meat. Stone tools – both flaked and polished – suitable for working animal hides are evidence of a secondary use for the animals, and the presence of donkeys may indicate that animals were used for transport.

The presence of beasts of burden is important, as it confirms that merchandise was transported, which can be deduced anyway from purely archaeological evidence.

Think, for example, of the distribution of the settlements, with the larger sites sitting astride the only communication routes between the desert and the plateau. Settlements like WYi, RAQi and WTHv were well-placed to intercept trading convoys, which in turn meant that these sites grew and prospered faster than others. To judge from material found during excavations (bronze, shells, semi-precious stones, obsidian etc.), trade routes were well established in this period. Analysis of the obsidian objects has proved that trade routes existed and seem to have extended further than we thought, in that the majority of the specimens studied seem to have originated from sources beyond the current borders of Yemen[7]. The import of foreign goods suggests that the agropastoral economy was successful, producing enough surplus to guarantee trade.

The Social Framework

The organisation of villages into individual circular units shows that society had divided up into separate family groups. In smaller sites, one such unit forms the settlement in itself (SRi, BAHi, NABvii, etc.). In this case, we have a village formed at the level of one family. Elsewhere, sites composed of several units (MASi, WYi, RAQi, WTHv, etc.) are indicative of a community at a higher level of social development, with several family units living alongside each other but retaining their individuality and autonomy.

Excavations have shown that these inhabited nuclei consisted of three to four houses arranged around a central communal area, where we find traces of ovens, cooking pits, millstones, etc. Often, one house appears to be more important than the others, displaying specific and distinctive attributes (dominant position, more rooms, grander entrance, etc.). This suggests that there was a system of hierarchy within the community. The ground plans of these units are very interesting. The houses' arrangement in a circle protects the settlement from the outside and, at the same time, creates an independent unit with a focal point for community activities. This focal point is accentuated by the geometric shape of the settlements. The fact that these units always conform to fixed dimensions (circumference about 20-25 metres) and never exceed a certain, limited number of houses, must be examined in relation to the community's social customs, which may have been conditioned by this geometric scheme. In fact, this enclosed, circular, compound plan, while it is a useful shape, cannot grow to absorb an increase in the number of people in the family. So, any increase in population density within a site necessitated not an expansion of the original unit, but the creation of a new unit.

Figure 39
Reconstruction of a model settlement of the Bronze Age (drawn by E. Gatti)

In some of the multiple sites, there are signs of a move away from this rigid adherence to type (at WYi, for example). These villages tend to be arranged in a pattern of opened up and broken circles and seem to be more integrated, unified communities. This may signal the onset of broader social requirements, which are hard to define but may be reflected in architectural details. For example we find structures that stand out on account of their position, shape and size (like L14 at RAQi) which suggest that there were what we might call public activities, that is, those outside the simple family sphere.

The function of some of the rooms has been hypothetically identified in the course of analysing the material from the sites, and may perhaps give us a clue as to specialised activities taking place within the villages. We have found, for example, that room L11 of WYi, which began simply as the annex to L10, was then furnished with the necessary instruments and equipment to become a proper mill, with a far greater production capacity than that needed by the inhabitants of unit A.

Intellectual Life

However, the large room called L14 at RAQi probably did not have an economic function. The room has been identified as a meeting place, on account of its architectural style, which appears to be confirmed by the quantity of bones (often still joined together) which are proof of communal dining. There is no need to hypothesise further about the possible reasons behind these meetings (among the bones were oxen foot bones and a sheep's hock, suggesting sacrifice and confirming that the room had a ritual use); the important thing is that meetings took place here involving more people than the total population of the compound of sector B. This proves that at RAQi, community integration had passed beyond the social autonomy of the single habitation unit.

We can even claim some knowledge, then, of the intellectual life of the community. Even if the function of L14 at RAQi is uncertain, the discovery of a small granite idol at BSUii (Fig. 75) suggests that there was some form of religious feeling. By studying the methods that he used for architecture, animal husbandry, crop farming, the manufacture of pottery and production of stone tools, we indirectly learn a lot about ancient man's mentality and his way of thinking. The sites are almost always positioned in the lee of dykes that dissect the pre-Cambrian rocks, especially in the Al-A'rūsh region, since they contained a convenient supply of building materials (easy to extract as the rock was already fractured, and easy to move down the hill to sites lower down) and also served as defensive features to the rear of the villages. There must have been some advantage in sinking the houses into the ground, although it is difficult to see what that advantage could have been. It does, however, force the builder to devise architecturally more demanding techniques, like placing blocks in horizontal arches to retain the earth around the houses' foundation trenches.

Two things show that agricultural methods and animal husbandry had reached an advanced stage of maturity and complexity. Firstly, as has been deduced from a study of their bones, male goats and sheep were kept until their second or third year and then slaughtered before the winter, in order to achieve the maximum return on the smallest outlay of resources. In similar fashion, farmers would use types of cereals (wheat, barley and sorghum) that allowed them two harvests a year.

The thing that one finds most striking about the mentality of this Bronze Age culture is the way that the people chose the sites for their settlements. After all, it was this choice that essentially guaranteed their continued survival. They learnt to base themselves in places where the particular geological conditions and delicate balance of soil and sediments could guarantee an appropriate and sufficient water supply. This cannot have been a matter of luck and shows that classical Yemen's flair for water management was inherited from a long tradition.

Bronze Age culture does not seem to have been particularly artistically inclined. No representational works have been found, except for the male statuette already mentioned. During the course of our exploration, the rocks around the sites were carefully studied, but no graffiti or figure drawings were ever found. The occasional decorative motif appears on pottery, but these are comparatively rare and vary little.

Everyday Life

Among the activities practised by the inhabitants of our sites were various artisan skills used in the production of tools and pottery. We know that several villages had specific workshops for flint and obsidian, and analysis of ceramic fragments has shown that vases were made locally, which is important as it means that the seed imprints found on some of the fragments were made by local produce. Stone tools, including pestles and mortars and grindstones, must also have been produced locally, to judge by their raw materials. However, it is difficult to say whether these crafts were only carried out by specialists. Pottery, at least, would certainly have been made in a specially designated area, on communal ground and away from individual living quarters.

We can, however, learn something of the activities that took place within the living quarters by studying the distribution of the various types of pottery. For example, excavations at WYi found that the large rooms supported by pillars (L3 and L10) contained most of the large plates, while room L1 contained second-rate ceramic cups and L11 contained vases with no rims or decoration. It therefore seems clear that rooms L3 and L10 were residential. This is where meals would be taken, as in the modern Yemeni *mufraj* (relaxation room). This is confirmed by analysis of the distribution of bones. Meals were communal affairs, to judge from the shapes and dimensions of the plates, which have ethno-archaeological similarities to those of other communities. However, food would be prepared and cooked in the rooms adjoining the houses (L1 and L11). It is possible that the rimless vases found in L11 were used to store food. Meat was cooked in the cooking pits situated in the middle of the communal areas. It is quite probable that a lot of other activities took place here too, including various stages of processing animal and vegetable products (Fig. 39).

Besides the principal cereal crops (wheat, barley, sorghum) and animals (goats, sheep, cattle), other food sources contributed to their diet. We either have direct evidence of these, like the remains of dates, jujube trees, pigs and gazelles; or indirect evidence, like bulbs, rhizomes and fruit. Theirs was obviously a rich and varied diet which incorporated, to some extent, the spoils of hunting and gathering. We are almost certain that they kept cats and dogs, and this somehow makes our picture of the everyday life of this protohistoric community much more balanced and complete.

Chronology

The excavations provided us with some important information on the chronology of the settlements. Radiocarbon tests were carried out on five specimens, from RAQi, MASi and WYi. The results gave us certain absolute dates that, after calibration in the light of the most recent theories, seem totally reliable[8]. On the basis of this information, we can date the Bronze Age culture of Khawlān to the period between 2700 and 2000 BC. This might be stretched to 2900 in one direction and 1800 in the other.

The oldest period is represented by RAQi, where charcoal taken from the hearth in room L8 dates the site's occupation to the first half of the third millennium BC. Charcoal from a hearth in MASi has a slightly later date, around the middle of the third millennium BC. The second sample taken at RAQi, corresponding to the second occupation of the site (room L11), brings us to the second half of the third millennium, while that taken at WYi (L1) dates from 2000, or possibly 1800 BC.

So far, then, it seems that Bronze Age culture in Yemen belongs almost exclusively to the third millennium BC, touching only briefly on the second. This allows us to see the characteristics of the objects found in Yemen in the archaeological context of the Near Eastern old Bronze Age which, as we suspected from the start, is the closest match.

The enormously wide time span covered by these dates, seen alongside the finds from the sites, suggests that this was a remarkably conservative society. Actually, we find hardly any noteworthy changes to the architecture or pottery, even in sites such as RAQi which we know was occupied for the better part of a millennium.

This conservatism means that we cannot use the archaeological evidence as a reliable indicator of dates. However, it is possible that changes in the pottery repertory or the architecture (especially in the sites further south) may be evidence of a phase of the Bronze Age dating from the second millennium BC. As things now stand, it is still difficult to establish whether these variations are due to chronological reasons or simply to local technical/stylistic differences, considering that they were mostly found in sites in the Al-Ḥadā region. Unfortunately we have not been able to excavate that far south, and so no radiocarbon tests have been done; but we still think it possible that the area contains sites in which Bronze Age culture continued to flourish well into the second millennium BC.

I say "continued" because further north, in the Al-A'rūsh area of the Khawlān region, our villages, which were probably not occupied much after the dates attributed to WYi (2000-1800 BC), seem then to have been abandoned at a certain point. One explanation for this is provided by geomorphological and sedimentary analyses, which show the abandonment in the context of a neotectonic movement that slowly changed the tilt of the Yemeni plateau. A sudden increase in gradients, probably combined with increasingly irregular annual rainfall, led to the break-up of the sedimentary equilibrium of the valleys, which had for many centuries guaranteed very comfortable agricultural productivity. The increasing erosive power of the rains ate into the alluvial deposits, destroying the vital alternation of permeable and impermeable strata. In short, the precious deposits of water-bearing sediments were finally washed down the widyān, despite some attempts to hold them back. It seems obvious, therefore, that research on the development of this culture in the second millennium BC will in future need to concentrate on the area south of our explorations, in other words, on the Al-Ḥadā region.

Geographical Distribution

Investigations undertaken for other purposes, until 1987, in the territories surrounding the Bronze Age sites, have demonstrated how altogether localised this culture was. It seems to extend no further east or west than the longitudinal strip which follows the 2000-metre contour line running through the regions of Khawlān and Al-Ḥadā from the Jabal al-Ṭiyāl massif in the north to the volcanic region of Jabal Isbil in the south.

One gets the feeling, however, that Yemen's Bronze Age culture on the inland plateaux cannot be entirely represented by what we have found and studied. The culture of Khawlān and Al-Ḥadā, although geographically localised and therefore apparently complete, appears somehow not to have reached full maturity. The ruins that we explored during these years did not reveal the true centre of this society, which would have boasted the highest level of socio-economic progress. Our research has most probably only scratched the surface of a culture which may have been much more widespread and whose major achievements may have been in areas with far more favourable environments than Khawlān (of which there are many in Yemen). Some aspects of this culture (like hierarchy and specialisation) which we have seen at an initial, formative level, may have reached a more advanced stage of development elsewhere.

The French archaeological mission has recently discovered Bronze Age sites in valleys on the north slope of the Jawf (Wādī Hirāb, Wādī Sabdā)[9]. Yemeni researchers have also recently found a site like ours but much bigger, at Bayt Mujali, near Raydah (1989). These finds show that the culture extended beyond Khawlān, but also show that our conclusions cannot be taken as absolute and final. Future discoveries may well confirm our impression of the marginal status of the culture discussed here.

As a result of these external comparisons we are inclined, for the moment, to believe that this Yemeni culture was essentially autonomous. This does not mean that it has no place within the wider cultural context of the Near East in the third millennium BC, but rather that it is hard to find the same distinctive characteristics as a whole elsewhere.

Many similarities have, however, been found. Similar types of architecture and settlements for example, are found in the south-west and north-west regions of Saudi Arabia, probably right up to the Sinai peninsula. Comparable examples of lithic industry have also been found in these areas and as far away as the deserts of southern Jordan and south-east Iraq. The closest parallels with the pottery are found in early Bronze Age Palestine, though these are much more evolved examples. The decorative motifs pressed into the pottery are reminiscent of the repertories of the prehistoric and protohistoric mesolithic period throughout eastern Africa (Sudan). Objects made from shell opercula have parallels in the third millennium societies of the oases of the United Arab Emirates and Oman. That the culture spread along an east-west axis (from Ethiopia and Sudan to eastern Arabia) is also apparent from palaeo-botanical finds.

These similarities and parallels are undoubtably very isolated and unconnected. We are therefore inclined to believe that this protohistoric Yemeni culture was essentially autonomous. However, if this impression is a result of the fragmentary nature of the evidence so far discovered within Yemen, or indeed that found in the Arabian peninsula in general (which is still rather limited for the period in question), we should simply use it as an incentive to redouble our work and pool initiatives for research.

Footnotes:

1. de Maigret, A. "A Bronze Age for Southern Arabia", *EW* 34 (1984), p. 340-434.
2. de Maigret, A. ed., *The Bronze Age Culture of Hawlan at-Ṭiyāl and Al-Ḥadā* (Republic of Yemen) (Rome: IsMEO, 1990).
3. Marcolongo, B., and Palmieri, A. "Paleoenvironment History of Western Al-A'rus", in de Maigret, A. *The Bronze Age Culture*, p. 137-144.
4. Castiello, B. and Gianni, A. "Grindstone Tools and Hammerstones at Wādī Yana'm, Site 1 (WYi)" in de Maigret, A. *The Bronze Age Culture*, p. 115-128.
5. Constantin, L., "Ecology and Farming of the Protohistoric Communities in the Central Yemen Highlands", in de Maigret, A. *The Bronze Age Culture*, p. 267-289.
6. Fedele, F., "Bronze Age Faunal Collections from North Yemen", in de Maigret, A., *The Bronze Age Culture*, p. 149-186.
7. Francaviglia, V., "Obsidian Sources in Ancient Yemen", in de Maigret, A., *The Bronze Age Culture*, p. 129-136.
8. Fedele, F., "Radiocarbon Dates", in de Maigret, A. The Bronze Age

Culture, p. 205-212.
9. Cleuziou, S., Inizan, M.L., and Marcolongo, B. "Le peuple pré- et protohistorique du système fluviatile fossile du Jawf-Ḥaḍramawt", *Paléorient* 18 (1992), p. 5-29.

VIII

THE PROTOHISTORY OF SOUTH ARABIA

Three Different Chronologies

G. Lankester Harding, an archaeologist and expert in Jordanian antiquities, was asked by the British Colonial Office to oversee a series of reconnaissance missions in the Protectorate of Aden. At the end of his time there in 1964, he concluded that the most interesting aspect of his explorations was the apparent lack of any sign of human occupation between the neolithic period (*c.* 5000 BC) and the eighth or ninth century BC.

The discovery of Bronze Age culture can now start to fill this gap. Unfortunately though, the second millennium BC remains fairly obscure (Table 1). As we are unable, for now, to fill in the gaps by working forwards (perhaps because the finds we studied at Khawlān were rather fragmentary), we must look at the information that we have and find a way to work backwards from the historic period of South Arabia. To do this we must return to the philologists, and their ongoing debate over chronological problems and the origins of the Sabaeans.

The careful, patient study of the inscriptions (many of which were badly made or fragmentary copies) that gradually found their way from southern Arabia into the hands of orientalists was helped by the length of time that passed without exploration or excavation following the American activity at Mārib. This allowed scholars to pinpoint the beginnings of a chronology of South Arabia.

Let us start by saying that the only certain dates we have are those that refer to the latest phases of the South Arabian period. Indeed, inscriptions only started to contain dates, as such, towards the end of this period, and even these were counted forward from the beginning of local tribal eras. Their starting points are now known: 110 BC was the start of the era of Ḥimyar and AD 74 the start of the era of Radmān (a tribe that settled in the area between Radā‘ and Al-Bayḍā in North Yemen).

The earliest inscription that we can date on the basis of this system is an isolated piece dating from 167 of the Ḥimyar period, or AD 57. Unfortunately we have no

8000	sites of the Tihāmah sites of the Khawlān al-Ṭiyāl sites of the Ramlat Sab‘atayn	NEOLITHIC
3000	As-Suhmān sites Al-A‘rūsh sites Jabal al-A‘mās sites Al-Ḥadā sites	BRONZE AGE
1800	*no information*	
1200	South Arabian protohistory	SOUTH ARABIAN PERIOD
700	Period of the *mukarribs* of Saba	
400	Period of the kings of Saba	
0	Period of the kings of Saba and Dhu-Raydan	
300	Period of the Himyarite Empire	
570		

Table 1
Chronological outline of pre-Islamic Yemen

inscriptions referring specifically to the period between this date and the end of the second century AD, but on the basis of the tribal eras, we can date many inscriptions to the following period, from about AD 200 onwards. From then on it is actually fairly easy to fix the dates of historical events in southern Arabia[2].

But how can we date inscriptions made before the third century AD? Throughout the long period between the birth of the South Arabian states and the third century AD the only clues that the inscriptions contain as to chronology are names or eponyms of kings. These give us absolutely no information on the times they lived in, primarily because the inscriptions make almost no reference to the outside world. However, by placing these names in some sort of reasonable order, we can at least use them as reference points, to establish whether one text is earlier or later than another. The problem is that many sovereigns and eponyms had the same names, so it is difficult to know if an inscription relates to one particular king or to his predecessors or successors of the same name.

However, to reconstruct the kingdoms and dynasties, we clearly had to start at the beginning. But this was precisely what fuelled our greatest debates.

Based on Glaser's collection of texts containing lists of sovereigns' names and eponyms, the Russian scholar A.G. Lundin established a theory of dynastic continuity dating back to the eleventh century BC. This was called the *extremely long chronology*[3].

Albert Jamme, the Belgian epigraphist attached to the American mission in Beihan and Mārib, took up Glaser and F. Hommel's classic theory[4]. Jamme, however, believed that the study of the oldest phase of South Arabian epigraphy would benefit enormously from using an important, reliable chronological aid, namely the annals of the Assyrian kings Sargon II (721-705) and Sennacherib (704-681). In these annals we find two Sabaean kings, Ita amar and Karibilu, whose names correspond to the *mukarribs* Yatha''amar Bayyin and Karib'īl Watar of the inscriptions[5]. So the oldest monumental texts of South Arabia (as von Wissmann would later agree) must be dated to the end of the eighth century BC, and not to the sixth, as was widely thought at the time. This theory was termed the *long chronology*.

Jacqueline Pirenne, on the other hand, devised a theory which held that the South Arabian alphabet and arts derived from ancient Greek culture. She maintained that the sovereigns mentioned in the Assyrian texts could not be the same as those in the inscriptions. She referred to the South Arabian custom of frequent and widespread use of the same name, and asserted that the oldest pre-Islamic Yemeni inscriptions could not date back further than the fifth century BC. Her theory became the *short chronology*.

So, everyone agreed that the relative chronology provided by the inscriptions was important. However, in searching for something which would give this chronology some absolute values, Pirenne (who had created a palaeography that was useful to the relative chronology) looked to the Greek world, whereas Jamme looked to the Assyrian world. This was the start of a long controversy between supporters of the *short chronology* and the *long chronology* which, as we shall see, is only now coming to a conclusion with the help of further archaeological studies.

In looking at Biblical extracts, we saw that the Book of Genesis mentions two South Arabian tribes, Saba and Ḥadramawt, and that these citations, going back to the time of Solomon, must date from the tenth century BC. The Bible also relates the story of Solomon's meeting with the Queen of Saba, which *should* belong to the same period. I say "should" because it is widely claimed that the Book of Kings was actually written later – in the sixth century BC – and that in order to boost Solomon's fame, the author associated him with another character who had, admittedly, lived several centuries later, but whose wealth and power had been unrivalled.

We know, however, that according to Pirenne, the first South Arabian inscriptions only appeared in the fifth century BC. How could there have been such a long period of silence? Jamme's theory had at least had the advantage of considerably reducing the length of time devoid of information.

Meanwhile, the supporters of the *short chronology* had another stroke of luck, partly because they maintained that both Biblical and Assyrian references referred not to Sabaeans resident in southern Arabia, but to the semi-nomadic Sabaeans of northern Arabia. These scholars did not believe that the southern Arabian states existed at such

Plate 35
Bronze statue of the Ma'ādī Karib

Plate 36
Grinders and mortars found during the excavation of site 1 in Wādī Yanāʿim (Bronze Age)

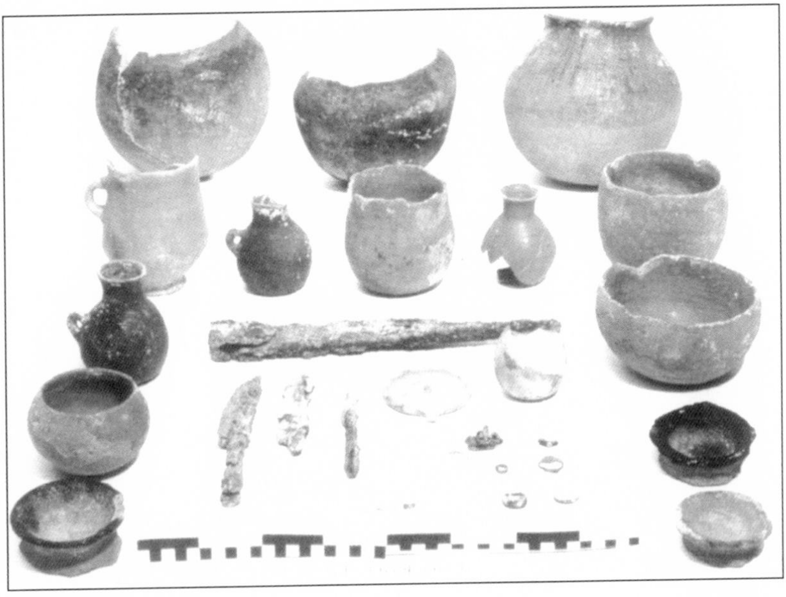

Plate 37
Funerary objects from tomb 2 of Kharibat Al-Ahjar (Dhamār)

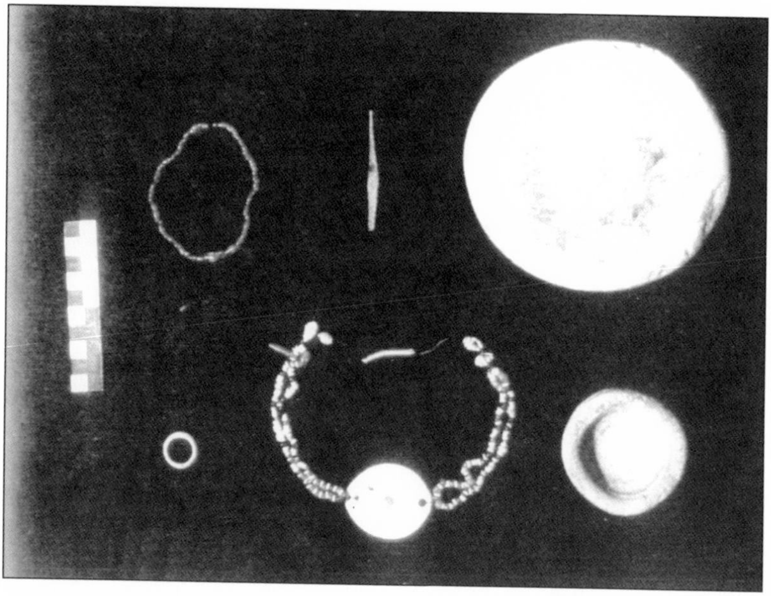

Plate 38
Feminine funerary objects from tomb 13 of Al-Makhdarah (Ṣirwāḥ)

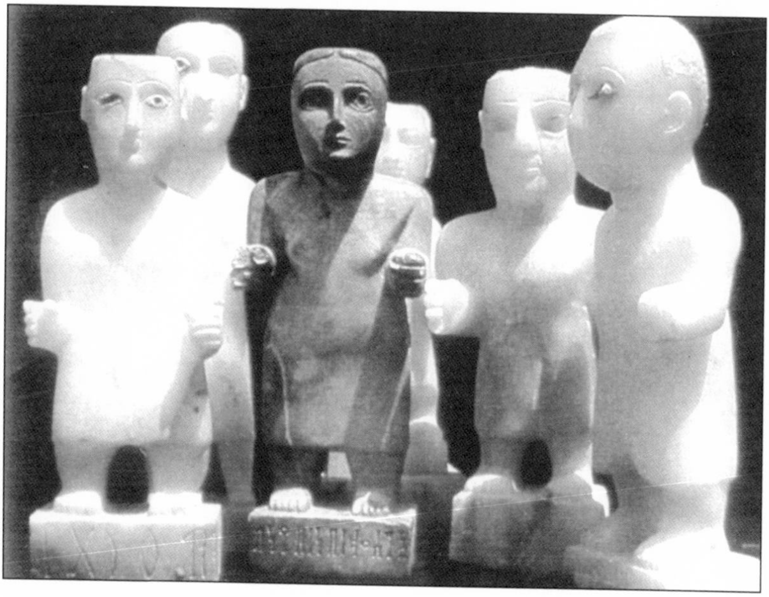

Plate 39
Group of alabaster votive statues held by the Museum of Aden

Plate 40
Female alabaster head of the 1st century BC

an early period. They certainly did not dwell on the fact that the Book of Genesis mentioned Hazarmawet (Ḥaḍramawt) alongside Saba (Genesis 10:26), or on the even more important fact that the American excavations of Hajar Bin Ḥumayd found levels dating back to the seventh century BC at the base of the tell (including Qatabanian or South Arabian pottery).

Pirenne essentially denied the validity of the results of these excavations in a famously aggressive and contentious article in the journal *Syria* which, however, failed to resolve the matter in her favour, and only fuelled her opponents' determination[7]. The intensity of the Belgian scholar's critical review was largely due to the highly inconvenient discovery of some fragments of vases in the lower layers of Hajar Bin Ḥumayd (levels S, P, and Q), which clearly bore South Arabian words in cursive lettering; Sabaean writing could therefore not have derived from Greek.

Charcoal found in layer Q provided the fragments with a very early date: *c.* 850 BC[8]. Unfortunately, though, the Qatabanian site was then the only stratigraphically excavated site, which laid the results rather open to interpretation. Moreover, radiocarbon dating was still at an experimental stage, and the accuracy of these results could be challenged with good, careful criticism. Pirenne was successful: to this day, at least in some circles, her *short chronology* has reigned supreme, and, since that one piece of archaeological data tends to be ignored, the discussion seems destined to remain unresolved.

The chronology debate is also important in that it affects the debate on the origins of the South Arabian peoples. Even if all the scholars agreed to accept that the Sabaeans had foreign origins, the theory would doubtless find more favour with supporters of the short chronology. If they maintained that the South Arabian kingdoms reached their height – and therefore people started to write – in the fifth century BC, while bearing in mind the Assyrian texts and their references to the Sabaeans, this group would be forced to assume that the Assyrians were dealing with the Sabaeans established in the north of the peninsula, who only moved south later to set up their eventual home[9].

This group prefers the theory of a migratory movement

southward, whereas the supporters of the *long chronology*, while not opposed to such an idea, are happier to consider other theories, such as the autonomous (or local) origin of the South Arabians. Whatever their differences on timing and origins, they are all in agreement on one subject: the monuments of the Jawf, Mārib, Ṣirwāḥ and the Beihan (even those thought to be older) already demonstrate advanced and skilled building techniques. The encircling walls, temples and irrigation systems have all been constructed with care and maturity. The written script of the oldest phase, too, is very attractive and elegant.

How can this culture possibly have suddenly appeared at its height, without any formative stages? Could it not be that we have yet to discover these stages and that this very fact has given rise to the *short chronology* theories?

However, if we assume that there was a preparatory period for South Arabian culture, we come back, inevitably, to the question of chronology. In this case, we would probably tend towards the *long chronology*. The formation of a culture takes a long time. South Arabian culture must have evolved over a long period before it was able to produce these huge fortified cities and splendid monuments and turn out such remarkable epigraphy. We need to discover the protohistory of South Arabia. The briefest glance at Mesopotamia or Egypt tells us as much.

If it is true that South Arabian writing derived from the Greek at the start of the fifth century BC, this protohistory was astonishingly short-lived. We could claim that the Greeks only provided the writing, not the encircling walls, temples, irrigation systems and statues. However, South Arabian art and epigraphy do appear to be inextricably linked. It is very hard to look at them separately. It would have taken just as long to develop these inscriptions as it took to develop monumental art (and it must have taken a long time to adapt the Greek alphabet to the South Arabian language).

Seen like this, the advantages of the *long chronology* are quite clear. If we accept that the oldest epigraphy was produced around 700 BC (and therefore discard the idea of Greek origins) there is unlimited potential for a formative period. If we ignore other chronologies (Greek, for example, for supporters of the *short chronology*), we can allow plenty of time for the essential incubation period preceding the appearance of mature period art and architecture and the related monumental epigraphy.

Looking for an Answer on the Ground: Yalā

The Italian mission carried out a systematic reconnaissance of the antiquities of Wādī Yalā in August 1985. The results led us to conclude that the city of Al-Durayb (or Yalā) was particularly well suited to provide answers to questions on South Arabian chronology. We concluded that this Sabaean settlement was abandoned in the seventh to sixth century BC and was not subsequently reoccupied[10].

Some of the structural features of the site convinced me that the greater height of the northern part of the city (the so-called "upper city") was due not to a naturally higher ground level, but to an accumulation of several layers of occupation. This was an important observation. If I was correct in believing that there were several different layers, an excavation would take us who knows how far back in time from the top layers (dating from the seventh to sixth centuries BC). This would give us an opportunity to investigate layers from South Arabian protohistory and perhaps even establish their date.

Luck was on our side, and in December 1987, we were able to open an excavation in the "upper city" of Yalā (Fig. 40). Within the walls, among the mounds of ruins characteristic of the area, we discovered a rubble hillock which was so extensive that we thought it could cover a Sabaean structure of some importance and, at the same time, seemed contained enough to justify a complete investigation, given the limited time at our disposal.

The dig was conducted with the help of 25 workmen from the Al-Ṭāhir tribe (Banī Dabyan) and the assistance of Sabina Antonini and the architects Enzo Labianca and Mario Mascellani. In the end we unearthed about three quarters of the buildings buried within the hillock, and were able to study the basic characteristics of a private Sabaean house (house A, Fig. 9.), whose occupants were clearly of a certain social standing[11].

The building consists of a quadrangular nucleus, with a few rooms opening off the sides, which gives onto the street leading from the main square to the southern sector of the

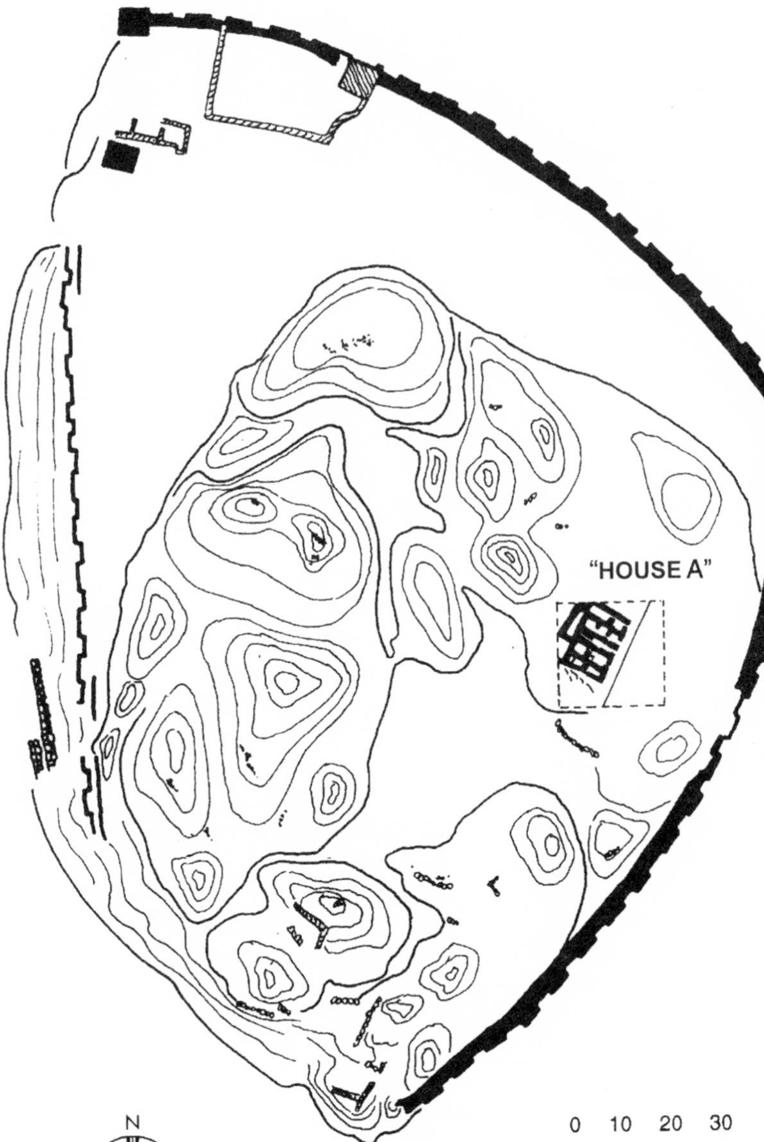

Figure 40
Plan of the city of Yalā/Hafarī

"upper city". The building faces east and has a symmetrical facade, with the main entrance in the middle, flanked by two windows and by the adjoining rooms (Plate 12).

The wide double doors give onto a long narrow room (L1), at the end of which is a flight of stairs leading up to the first floor. The holes in the north wall, designed to hold the beams of the floor above, are still clearly visible.

Halfway down the south wall of L1 a door gives onto a wide, rectangular room (L6), in the south-west corner of which stands a stone basin. The room is lit by a window that gives onto the street to the east. Another window positioned beside a door links L6 to L2, a small adjacent room to the west, whose south-west corner contains another stone basin, this time with a border of granite slabs and crude bricks.

At the top of the first of the two flights of stairs leading up from L1, a door opens onto an irregularly-shaped room called L10; here too there are rectangular holes in the walls which may have supported the floorboards and beams of the upper storey. The west wall of this room leans slightly towards the east, suggesting that the room was built in the space between this house and a neighbouring one.

The entrance room and the northernmost room of the house were only connected by a sort of window (P4) opening off L1 in the very same place that rooms L7 and L12 open onto each other (P12). It seems most likely that this opening, in the north wall of L1, was a door with an exceptionally high threshold, rather than a simple window. This elevated passageway was probably reached by a flight of wooden steps. However, the door connecting L7 and L12 (P12) also has a raised threshold, standing about a metre above the floor level of these two little rooms. L12 has a window looking onto the street to the east of the house and contains a fine stone basin, in the corner by the door. There are no obvious details to be seen on the smooth and well-preserved walls of L7.

The dome-shaped mound of rubble protecting the ruins is the main reason why the structures at the western edge of the excavation are the highest: here the buildings still stand up to a height of five metres. This means that we were able to find many traces of the upper storey in the westernmost rooms. The walls of the little room called L11, for example, not only show signs of flooring (holes

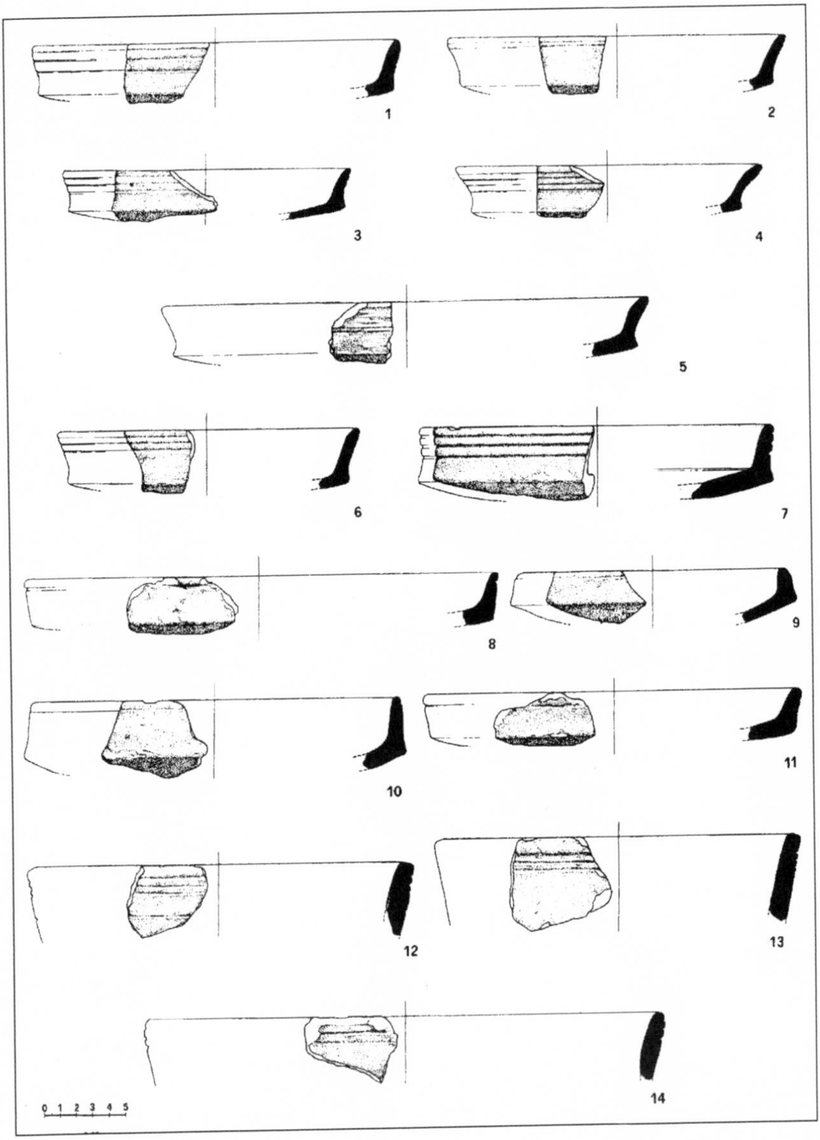

Figure 41
Sabaean ceramics from Yalā/Hafarī

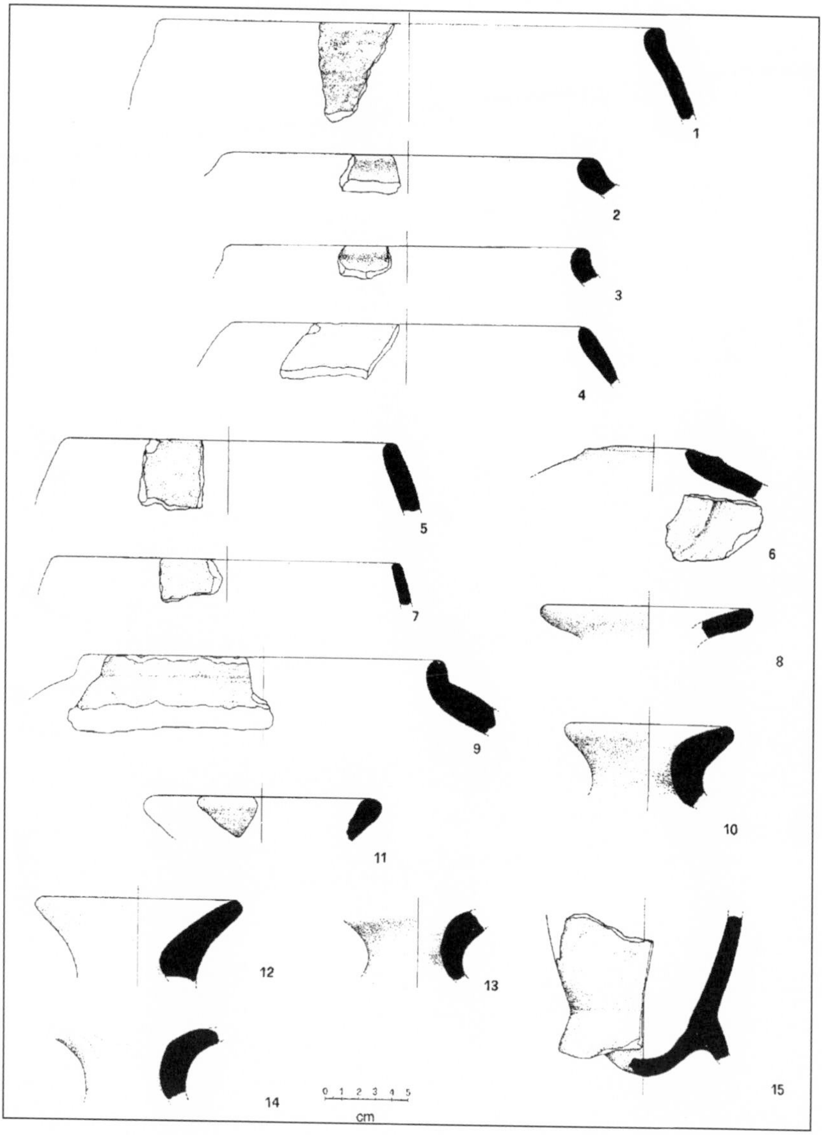

Figure 42
Sabaean certamics from Yalā/Hafarī

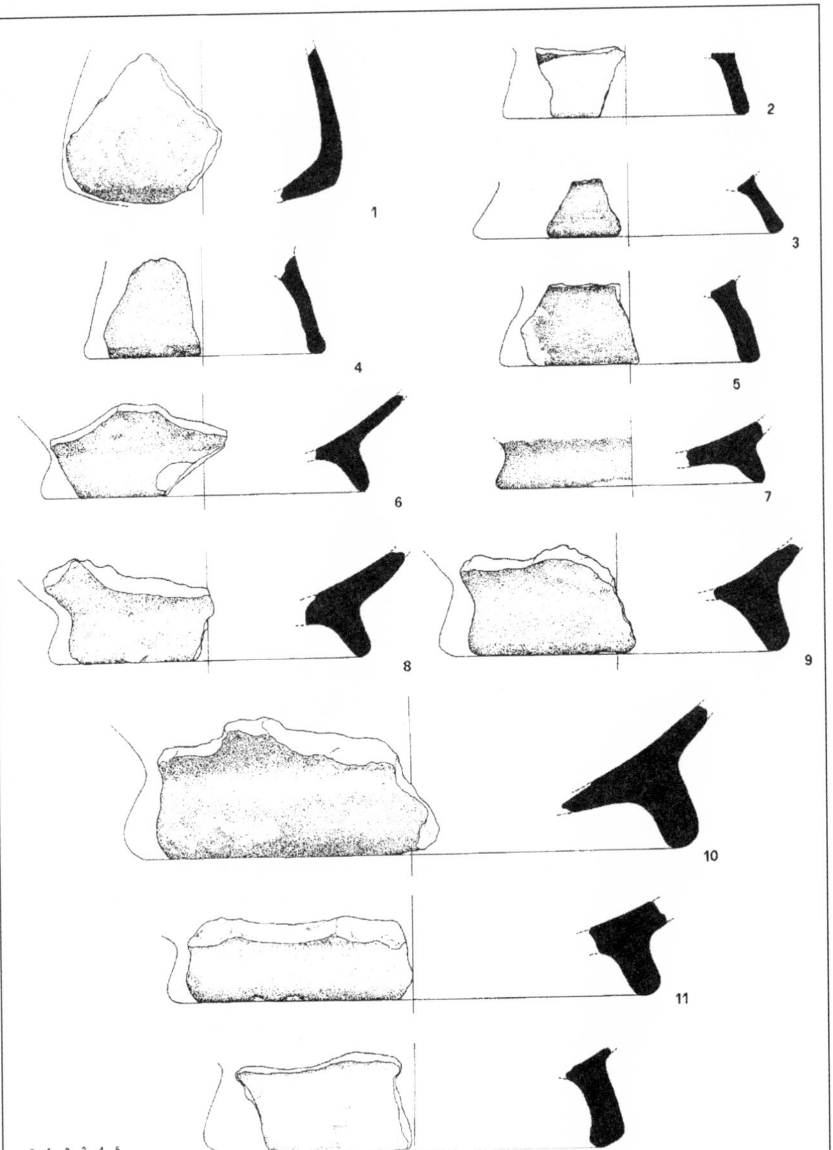

Figure 43
Sabaean ceramics from Yalā/Hafarī

for the beams), but also still contain a window (or possibly a door?) frame (P10) which linked the two first floor rooms directly above L7 and L11.

It seems clear that rooms L3, L4, L5, L8 and L9 were joined onto the side of a pre-existing unit, as they simply lean against this central square nucleus. Room L3 was made out of the space separating this house from a neighbouring house which faced the other way; L5 is a narrow storeroom, possibly lit by a small window in its eastern wall. These two rooms were reached through a door to the south (P2) which led on to door P4 (in L1) which was intended to divide the two rooms. Room L9 is a wide, square space with direct access to the street. Rooms L4 and L8 have not yet been excavated.

The existence of an upper floor has had an appreciable influence on the stratigraphic position of the objects found among the debris within the very well-preserved stone buildings. The excavation first revealed a top level (level 1a) with pottery and other objects, lying about 60-80 centimetres above floor level; then, right on top of the floor (which was mostly made of wooden planks) a second level was discovered (level 1b) containing more artefacts. Clearly, the first level contains things from the upper storey, while the second layer contains ground floor objects.

A great quantity of pottery was recovered (Figs. 41-43). We filled seventy of our standard containers with shards of pottery, which, when reassembled, would form a homogeneous and complete set of Sabaean pottery. Apart from a fired clay religious panel (Plate 13) which shows interesting and unusual designs[12], the other finds were not of great artistic value (grinders, pestles, mortars, fragments of bronze and iron, bits of alabaster vases, shells, animal bones, seeds, etc.); but a comparative study of the types of object found, associated with a functional study of the architecture, was very interesting, giving us a sense of everyday life in a southern Arabian community in the archaic period.

An Archaic Sabaean Stratigraphy

Once excavations had reached the floor of house A, we decided to dig on down to prove our hypothesis that there were further levels of occupation underneath. So we continued to excavate at a point where certain structural anomalies in the house's construction suggested the likely presence of objects and accumulations of material underneath. Three trial stratigraphic pits were dug beneath the floors of rooms L2, L5, and L6, which greatly enriched the results of that first excavation.

A few dozen centimetres were all it took to reveal some older construction, orientated the same way as the building above, but demonstrating a different internal layout. An analysis of the architecture and stratigraphy showed that these walls belonged to two separate periods: the later period represented by constructions that were reused as foundations for the private house already excavated; and an earlier period represented by two parallel walls, a fair distance apart, which were not used by later builders.

To record the sequence of buildings and levels we made detailed drawings and took photographs of the two deepest probes (those of L5 and L6). The material found in the various levels was identified and catalogued, and charcoal samples were taken from the thick burnt levels covering the floor of house A and from the cross-sections exposed (Fig. 10).

The section drawings show that level A, the top level relating to the construction of house A, was preceded by at least three other phases of occupation. In descending order these are: level B, characterised by layers of pale beige earth containing a lot of pottery and bones (level 2a), then a thick layer of ash and charcoal; level C, marked by a back filling of compacted hazelnut-coloured earth mixed with granules of gypsum and ceramic fragments (level 3a), and finally a burnt layer containing wood and charcoal (level 3c); and level D, which, although devoid of construction (which we probably did not find on account of the very small area of the probe) was clearly inhabited, as ceramic fragments and widespread ashes were found there.

The pottery found in the various layers, while differing greatly in its state of preservation (that found in level D, for example, was in a much more fragmentary state than the pieces found at higher levels), was stylistically the same, staying within the usual repertory of Sabaean earthenware. At the bottom of level D, in the south-east corner of the L6 probe, we came across a layer of granite sand of alluvial origin (level 4d), which presumably indicates the end of occupied layers at ground level (the *wādī* bed), where the first settlers (Sabaeans) of Yalā/Al-Durayb would have established themselves.

New Dating Methods

On 27 January 1989, just over a year after we had finished excavating house A in Yalā/Al-Durayb, we received the results of the C14 analyses carried out by the Physics Department of the "La Sapienza" University of Rome on five selected samples taken from the excavated area. Seen in conjunction with the stratigraphic sequences provided by our probes, these results provided the facts we needed to define the chronological sequence of the principal phases of settlement at Yalā (Table 9).

Samples 1 and 2, taken from burnt beams that had fallen to the floor in rooms L1 and L10 respectively of house A, date from the destruction of level A. They provided the following information: the fire in L1 occurred between 850-650 BC, and that in L10 occurred between 825-585 BC.

Samples 3, 4 and 5 were taken from the probe under the floor of L6. Specifically, sample 3 was taken from charcoal layer 2d when it first appeared on the excavated surface; sample 4 was from the same layer, but taken directly from the side of the trench at the end of the excavation (east wall); sample 5, on the other hand, was taken from the

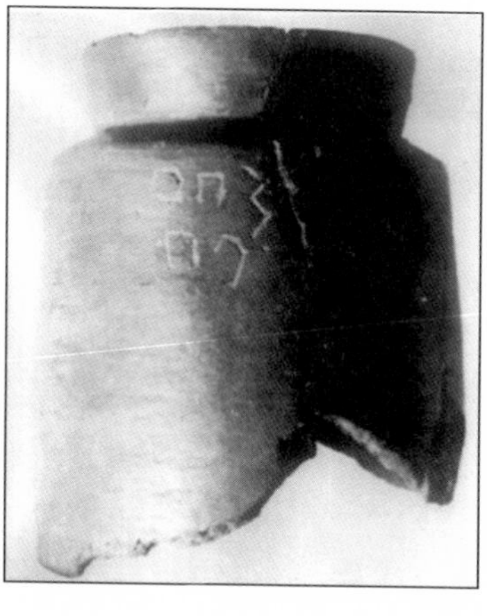

Plate 41
Inscribed fragment of a vase from the excavations of house A of Yalā/Al-Durayb

Plate 42
Inscription Y.85.Y/3b from Yalā/Al-Durayb (c. seventh century BC)

lowest level of wood and charcoal, 3c, and, like sample 4 was taken directly from the stratigraphic section (west wall) at the end of the excavation. These charcoal samples therefore dated from the destruction of level B (samples 3 and 4) and that of level C (sample 5). The dates are: sample 3: 1100-795 BC; sample 4: 1240-830 BC, sample 5: 1395-920 BC.

These dates were expressed in calibrated values, meaning that the absolute values obtained in the laboratory were corrected to take into account solar radiation, the earth's magnetic field and so on, based on information from the most recent dendro-chronological observations. The point should be made that the dates refer to the death of the plants rather than the carbonisation of the wood.

Clearly, the dates are contained within a very broad time span, but this enabled us to be almost completely sure that the true dates definitely fall somewhere within this period.

The periods to which these dates referred did not seem to clash, from an archaeological point of view, with the chronology we had established for the antiquities of Wādī Yalā or with the results of the American excavations at Hajar Bin Ḥumayd in Wādī Beihan and at Hajar al-Tamrah in Wādī al-Jubah. But for philologist-historians who supported a short chronology for the origins of southern Arabian writing, these dates obviously presented a serious threat to their theory.

In fact, even if we had taken the latest dates in the time spans provided by the calibrations, we would have come up with dates that were too early: 585 BC for the carbonised beams found on the floor of L10; 650 BC for those found in L1; 795 BC and 830 BC for the charcoal taken from level 2d;

and 920 BC for the charcoal from level 3c, of the trench under L6.

As we have already said, these dates refer to the death of the plants, rather than the date when the wooden parts of the building were burnt. But even if we had been able to calculate that these wooden floors and ceilings had been in use for an average of 50 years, and therefore considered 535 BC (end of L10), 600 BC (end of L1), 755 BC (end of level B) and 870 BC (end of level C) as the definitive dates for the destruction of these rooms and buildings, these dates would still have posed a serious problem for those who see the first half of the fifth century BC as the beginning of South Arabian writing.

The reference to writing is not casual. In fact, the excavation turned up numerous inscriptions on ceramic shards (Plate 28), not only from level A, but from level B too[13]. The latter must predate 755 BC, at least. One brief inscription was found stamped onto the top of the clay religious tablet mentioned above. Having considered the latest possible dates for the ends of the three phases of occupation of Yalā, there remained a very good possibility that they were in fact much earlier, and might belong to a date much further back along the time spans provided by the calibrated calculations. So, fixing the destruction of house A (and therefore also the destruction of Yalā/Al-Durayb) at 535 BC, on the one hand simply meant that this was the latest possible date, but on the other meant that there was a strong likelihood that the real date was actually much earlier. It could in fact be as far back as 825 BC, in other words, corresponding to the oldest calibrated date obtained for sample 2 of the floor of L10. The same is true, of course, for the other samples. It would be equally possible, for example, for the date of level C's destruction to be placed at the oldest extreme (around 1395 BC) of the calibrated time span which contained sample 5 taken from level 3c.

Whatever the answer, the inscriptions on pottery found at Yalā/Al-Durayb showed us firstly that Sabaean writing had existed at a remarkably early date, and secondly, that it was popular and widely used, which presupposes a much older tradition. (This was shown by the fact that these inscriptions were found in a domestic environment.)

However, the results were not limited to what we might

call utilitarian inscriptions. A monumental inscription (Plate 42) that had been built into the only modern building currently standing within the walls (according to the local inhabitants it came from the exterior western wall of the site), bears a dedication from a "friend" of the two Sabaean sovereigns, Yada'īl and Yatha''amar, commemorating other buildings "on the boundary of HFRY"[14]. This was important because it revealed the ancient name of Yalā and also because it showed that the style of writing that Pirenne called B4 (and which she attributed to about 380 BC) was actually employed *at least* before 535 BC.

The lovely classical script created by Karib'īl Watar the Great, which we came across in the rock carvings at the nearby site of Shi'b al-'Aql and which seems to be several generations earlier cannot therefore be any later than the end of the seventh century BC. This seems to justify us in identifying this king with Karibilu, mentioned in the Assyrian texts, and gives weight to the theories behind the *long chronology*.

A Theory Regarding the Problem of Origins

The excavation at Yalā proved the validity of the Hajar Bin Ḥumayd stratigraphies and the time values that Gus van Beek attributed to them many years ago. New excavations are gradually confirming the Yalā results, for example the Russian work on the south-west part of the ruin of Raybūn in the Ḥaḍramawt[15].

South Arabian culture (certainly the objects, but, as we have seen, perhaps also the script) seems then to be firmly rooted in the second millennium BC (fourteenth to thirteenth centuries BC, or even earlier). The time lapse since the Bronze Age seems to be considerably reduced by this new archaeological evidence, and a meeting of the two cultures starts to seem increasingly natural and reasonable. If the interval between them gets shorter, but the strong differences that distinguish them persist, then we must assume that we are dealing with two separate cultures. The differences between the two are great, and equally as visible in the structure and design of the architecture as in the types and methods of ceramic production. It is particularly hard to see a possible derivation from Bronze Age culture in the finds of the deepest levels of Hajar Bin Ḥumayd, Yalā or Raybūn, even allowing for the time gap which still today remains blank between the two known cultures.

Archaeology can therefore provide us with more than just chronological information: namely that the culture of the peoples who settled in Yemen in the third, and the first half of the second millennium BC, those we have called Bronze Age, turns out to be distinctly different from that which we found to be widespread among the other southern Arabian populations.

If the chronological information is true, i.e. if it is true that the bearers of South Arabian culture settled in Yemen from the second half of the second millennium BC, we must assume that they could not put down ethnic and cultural roots in the same part of Yemen as the Bronze Age culture covered. At this point, we must opt for an external origin for the South Arabians[16].

Further north, in Mesopotamia, Syria and Palestine, we find that new populations arriving with quite different material cultures were commonplace and were, we might say, the rule. This was almost always due to the waves of nomads who settled along the semi-desert edges of the Arabian Peninsula, and who gradually gained the upper hand in terms of culture, politics and economy over the neighbouring agricultural cultures. The fertile areas of southern Arabia lie essentially along the edge of the same desert, and it would not be too far-fetched to think of the South Arabians as a nomadic people who gradually established themselves in the lee of the Yemeni mountains. The locations of their settlements seems to confirm this theory.

This makes it much easier to explain many tricky aspects of this culture. I refer to the Mesopotamian influences (sometimes dating as far back as the third millennium BC) that can be seen in the oldest examples of South Arabian art, and also in the pantheon; I refer to their writing, whose origins are being linked increasingly with the Palestinian world of the late Bronze Age[17]; and I refer especially to the same material culture that is undoubtably linked (for example in its defensive architecture and pottery) to Syrian-Palestinian cultures of the Iron Age. These are testimonies, traditions and reminiscences drawn from repeated fleeting contact with the settled inhabitants of the Fertile Crescent, by a people who must have wandered for many centuries on the borders of the Syrian Arab desert.

Excavations suggest that the South Arabians were already established in Yemen by the late second millennium BC. (This is linked to the great ethnic and political movements throughout the Near East around 1200 BC.) It seems quite natural, then, that a few centuries later, being particularly well placed to intercept the caravan commerce, the name of Saba and the Sabaeans should appear next to that of Solomon and, a little later again, next to the names of sovereigns of the neo-Assyrian empire. Nor is it surprising that these populations had a written language, even at this early date. As we have seen, South Arabian letters appear at the deepest levels of Hajar Bin Ḥumayd, Yalā and Raybūn.

I realise that, by lengthening the chronology, the few facts that historians possess on the most problematic periods of southern Arabian history, like the periods of the *mukarribs* and the kings of Saba, will be diluted in a sea of time. But then, this may be due to the profound lack of information available on these periods. Just as a mass of new information filled in many of the gaps that existed in the later obscure periods when the texts were discovered in the Maḥrām Bilqīs at Mārib, so, hopefully, our understanding of the earlier obscure periods will be filled out with new information as soon as we can research the archaic cities extensively. Continued excavations at Yalā and Raybūn, and the promising new initiatives in centres such as Mārib and the sites in Wādī Raghwān, for example, should provide invaluable information on the early days of the South Arabian kingdoms.

Footnotes:

1. Harding, G.L., *Archaeology in the Aden Protectorates* (London: H.M. Stationery Off., 1964), p. 5.
2. Robin, C., "La civilisation de l'Arabie méridionale avant l'Islam", in J. Chelhod (ed.), *L'Arabie du Sud: histoire et civilisation: 1. Le peuple yéménite et ses racines* (Paris: G.-P. Maisonneuve et Larose, 1984), p. 195-223.

3. Garbini, G., "Un nuovo documento per la storia dell'antico Yemen", *OA* 12 (1973), p. 148.4.
4. Hommel, F., "Geschichte Südarabien in Umriss", in D. Nielsen (ed.), *Handbuch der altarabischen Altertumskunde, I. Band: die altarabische Kulture* (Copenhagen: A. Busck, 1927), p. 86.
5. Jamme, A., *Sabaean Inscriptions from Maḥrām Bilqīs* (Mārib) (Baltimore: Johns Hopkins Press, 1962), p. 389.
6. Pirenne, J., *Paléographie des inscriptions sud-arabes. Contribution à la chronologie et à l'histoire de l'Arabie du Sud antique. Vol I: Des origines à l'époque himyarite* (Brussels: Paleis der Academien, 1956).
7. Pirenne, J. "Notes d'archéologie sud-arabe, IX: Hajar bin Humeid", *Syria* 51 (1974), p. 137-170.
8. van Beek, G., *Hajar Bin Humeid. Investigations at a Pre-Islamic Site in South Arabia* (Baltimore: Johns Hopkins Press, 1969), p. 355.
9. Pirenne, J. *La Grèce et Saba. Un nouvelle base pour la chronologie sud-arabe* (Paris: Imprimerie nationale, 1955), p. 105. 10. de Maigret, A. (ed.), *The Sabaean Archaeological Complex in the Wādī Yalā (Eastern Hawlan at-Ṭiyāl - Yemen Arab Republic)* (Rome: IsMEO, 1988), p. 13.
11. de Maigret, A. and Robin, C. "Les fouilles italiennes de Yalā (Yémen du Nord): nouvelles données sur la chronologie de l'Arabie du Sud préislamiques", *CRAIBL* 1989, p. 255-291.
12. Antonini, S., "Oggetti d'importazione dalle tombe di Kharabat al-Ahjār (Dhamār)", *Yemen* 1 (1996), p. 3-12.
13. Garbini, G., "Le iscrizioni su ceramica da ad-Durayb-Yalā", *Yemen* 1 (1992), p. 79-92.
14.Garbini, A. "The Inscriptions of Shi'b al-'Aql, Al-Jafnah and Yalā/Ad-Durayb", in de Maigret, A. (ed.), *The Sabaean Archaeological Complex*, p. 38.
15. Sedov, A., "On the Origin of the Agricultural Settlements in Ḥaḍramawt", in Robin, C. (ed.), *Arabia Antiqua. Early Origins of the South Arabian States* (Rome: IsMEO, 1996), p. 67-86.
16. de Maigret, A. "I dati degli scavi yemeniti per un'ipotesi sull'origine della cultura sudarabica", in Robin, C. (ed.), *Arabia Antiqua*, p. 111-119.
17. Lundin, A.G., "L'abécécedaire de Beth Shemesh", *Le Muséon 100* (1987), p. 243-250.

PART THREE

The Kingdoms of Arabia Felix

IX

SOUTH ARABIAN HISTORY

The Inscriptions

We are now in a position to deal with the actual history of South Arabia. Traditionally, this period starts with the appearance of monumental writing, in around the eighth century BC.

Firstly, we have incredibly little information to fill the long centuries that make up this period. This means that, when we try to link up these few bits of information, we form hypothetical reconstructions which vary greatly, often on account of bitter disagreements between scholars. But of course it is very hard to resist the temptation to sketch out a picture, even if only to verify which are its weakest points. Our principal aim in doing this was to be able to reinforce the background which is essential to our picture. As investigators of antiquity, it is our job to try to do this.

Having said all this, it is clear that the amount of information that we have on South Arabian history is certainly not as comprehensive as the amount available for other ancient civilisations. This is a pity, but we must now start to prepare some sort of similar framework, if only to give ourselves something to build on in the future. Since the majority of our knowledge is now based on direct evidence, it is essential to examine the epigraphy that we have more closely.

Christian Robin, head of a French research mission in Yemen in 1978 (and epigraphist with our own mission

Plate 43
Christian Julien Robin

since 1988), published an article in 1984 in which he divided the 8,000 texts so far discovered into four principal categories, according to their subject matter[1].

The first category of texts are called *prescriptive texts*. These are mostly decrees issued by rulers, a tribal assembly or a temple. These documents are very important to us, as they touch on many aspects of life and society, and give us a better insight into everyday life in a South Arabian community than any other source. Here we find rules for regulating commerce, for dividing up land, for regulating irrigation, for formal temple visits, etc. Unfortunately, this is also the smallest category.

The second group is composed of *religious texts*. These are the most numerous and include dedicatory inscriptions, public confessions and documents testifying to particular ceremonies or ritual acts (sacrifices, ritual hunts and banquets, pacts of tribal alliance, etc.). Dedicatory inscriptions are the most common, and are extremely repetitive. Besides the propitiatory formulae and gifts to the various gods, we often find a list of the reasons why the donor was presenting the gift (dangers escaped in battle, recoveries, absolution granted in trials), and we gain a lot of information on the society, institutions and events of those days from the details that accompany the main reason for the inscription. In the late period especially (third century AD), the explicit part of the text becomes particularly redundant. The gift almost ends up being an excuse to list and immortalise the donor's exploits.

The third group is characterised by *property claims*. These are inscriptions that deal with building houses, monuments and irrigation systems, that lay down the worth of a building and that claim a family's or tribe's right of ownership. This group also contains inscriptions that define boundaries or access rights to fields, cultivation and so on.

The fourth and final category deals with *commemorative texts*. Unfortunately there are not many of these, but they are particularly important because they refer to military campaigns and great construction works (e.g., the Mārib dam), and as such they are the only truly historical texts. In the early period, these do not differ much from the dedicatory inscriptions, but later (particularly in the fifth to sixth centuries AD) they take on a distinctive new form, becoming the means of glorifying the kings and eminent figures of the Himyarite kingdom.

The Written Word

The majority of these texts are engraved in stone, but there is also a fair amount of epigraphy cast in bronze, drawn onto pottery and carved in wood. The language used is South Arabian, a Semitic language linked to Arabic and Ethiopian. The dialect varies a little, according to the regions of southern Arabia where it was used, and so we can use the terms Sabaean, Minaean, Qatabanian and Hadrami. Although this language was mostly replaced by Arabic with the advent of Islam, there are parts of southern Arabia where a derivative of it is still spoken today (the island of Socotra, and the borders of Yemen and Oman).

The South Arabian script is based on an alphabet of 29 consonants (Table 2). It is the richest of all Semitic languages and its origins are the subject of much discussion. We know that in the second millennium BC in Ugarit (coastal Syria), a system of writing in which every consonant corresponded to a symbol was developed for the first time. This system (the alphabet) greatly simplified previous systems (especially the Egyptian hieroglyphics and the Mesopotamian cuneiform) which used innumerable symbols to express the various phonetic values of the syllables and, traditionally, many symbols denoting ideas or things (ideograms). With the start of the Iron Age (c. 1200 BC), the Ugaritic alphabet was taken and adapted by Phoenicians, Jews, Aramaeans and Greeks. The problem lies with the alphabets used in ancient Arabia, which are not obviously derived from any of these systems[2].

It is difficult to establish with certainty when these alphabets first appeared in Arabia, and we shall see that the subject is highly controversial. We have here evidence of four principal alphabets, dating from about the sixth century; Lihyanite-Dedanite, South Arabian, Safaitic and Thamudic. All of these have written similarities to Phoenician (which indicate their origin in this language), but also enough differences to exclude any direct derivation. The most likely answer is that the Arabian alphabets are very ancient in origin and derived, along with Ugaritic and Phoenician, from a common root unknown to us and then developed parallel to

			ص	𐩮	ṣ
ا	𐩱	'	ض	𐩳	ḍ
ب	𐩨	b	ط	𐩷	ṭ
ت	𐩩	t	ظ	𐩼	ẓ
ث	𐩻	th	ع	𐩲	'
ج	𐩴	g	غ	𐩶	gh
ح	𐩢	ḥ	ف	𐩰	f
خ	𐩭	kh	ق	𐩤	q
د	𐩵	d	ك	𐩫	k
ذ	𐩹	dh	ل	𐩡	l
ر	𐩧	r	م	𐩣	m
ز	𐩸	z	ن	𐩬	n
س	𐩯	s	ه	𐩠	h
ش	𐩦	sh	و	𐩥	w
	𐩪	ś	ى	𐩺	y

Table 2
The South Arabian alphabet and the corresponding Arabic and Latin characters

each other. To prove this, however, we would need to find evidence that local alphabets had a more ancient origin than we thought. As we will see, recent archaeological research is helping to provide this proof.

To date, the oldest recognised Arabian alphabets are the Lihyanite-Dedanite employed in the oases of Al-'Ulā and Madāin Sālih in northern Ḥijāz, and the South Arabian used in southern Arabia and, less often, in the Al-Ḥasā region of the Persian Gulf (as well as a few oases in central Arabia). Besides these, there are two alphabets which appear to have been used primarily by nomads. These are the Safaitic, typical of northern Arabia, Jordan and Syria, and the Thamudic, characteristic of central and northern Arabia.

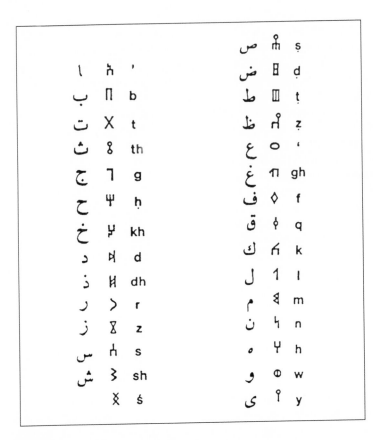

In written South Arabian, the words are always separated from each other by vertical strokes, and are made up of clearly defined letters (Plate 44). The letters are also used as decorative motifs. Proportions of height and width are carefully maintained, the strokes are finished with decorative flourishes, and the aesthetic value of curves and circles is preserved, proving the existence of strict and precise artistic canons (Plates 45 and 46) By studying these canons and their variations, scholars like Pirenne have managed to develop relative chronologies for the various groups of inscriptions.

We should bear in mind that, besides the kind of writing we find on monumental inscriptions, there was also cursive writing, which is much more flowing (and problematic), and was usually written on less durable materials than stone or bronze, such as ceramics, wooden blocks, etc[3]. The study of these texts is still preliminary, but looks promising, precisely because these are the only inscriptions that were not commemorative in purpose, and that can therefore throw some light on the economy and everyday life of the ancient South Arabians.

Periods of History

The history of South Arabia covers nearly sixteen centuries, from the time of the Queen of Sheba's trip to

Plate 44
Inscription on the walls of Kharibat Sa'ud/Kutal (c. seventh century BC)

Israel to visit king Solomon, up to the Persian (Sassanian) conquest of South Arabia in about AD 570 (Table 1).

This long period can basically be divided into two phases. The first phase lasts for the whole of the first millennium BC, more or less until the time of Christ, and covers the history of the kingdoms established in the interior of Yemen, in the great alluvial valleys that run from the mountains to the Ramlat Sab'atayn desert (which Islamic writers called the Ṣayhad desert). These kingdoms (Saba, Awsān, Ḥaḍramawt, Ma'īn, Qatabān) were locked in a perpetual struggle over the control and exploitation of the caravan routes which carried spices, incense and other exotic produce from the shores of the Erythrean Sea and Indian Ocean to the Mediterranean basin and the northern Persian Gulf.

Their political interests, in this sense, basically revolved around the desert, while the mountains at their backs remained of secondary importance. So, we can call this the *period of the caravan kingdoms.* This combines the two classic periods – the *period of the Sabaean mukarribs* and the *period of the Sabaean kings* – differentiated by scholars according to the different titles employed by the Sabaean sovereigns over the course of time (Table 1).

The second phase, from the first century BC to the sixth century AD saw a shift in the kingdoms' political and economic interest towards the highlands and, therefore, the sea. By now the old caravan routes had lost their importance, and maritime trade had taken over. The people of Ḥimyar, having broken away from the kingdom of Qatabān, gathered mountain tribes around them and declared their independence. Their power grew with time, until they had become an independent state dominating the whole of southern Arabia.

This phase could well be called *the period of the commercial maritime kingdoms,* or *the period of the mountain kingdoms.* Scholars generally divide the period into two, based on the sovereigns' new titles: the *period of the kings of Saba and Dhū-Raydān,* from the first century BC to the end of the third century AD; and the *monotheistic period* (based on the Himyarite sovereigns' conversion to monotheism) from the fourth to the sixth century AD. The monotheistic period, though, could be more appropriately called the *period of the Himyarite Empire,* given that the other kingdoms no longer existed by the beginning of the fourth century, and the sovereigns of Ḥimyar were the only undisputed rulers of the whole of southern Arabia.

Footnotes:

1. Robin, C., "La civilisation de l'Arabie méridionale avant l'Islam", in J. Chelhod (ed.), *L'Arabie du Sud: histoire et civilisation: 1. Le peuple yéménite et ses racines* (Paris G.-P. Maisonneuve et Larose, 1984), p. 195-223.
2. Robin, C. "Langue et écriture sudarabiques", *DA* 33, Mar/April (1979), p. 62-67.
3. Ryckmans, J., "Une écriture minuscule sud-arabe antique récemment découverte", in H. Vanstiphou et al (eds.), *Scripta Signa Vocis.* Studies presented to J.H. Hospers (Groningen: E. Forsten, 1986), p. 185-197. See also Ryckmans, J. Müller, W.W. and Abdullah, Y.M. *Textes du Yémen antique incrits sur bois* (Louvain-la-Neuve: Universite catholique de Louvain, 1994).

X

THE CARAVAN KINGDOMS AND THE *MUKARRIBS* OF SABA

The Sovereigns' Names

The first, oldest phase of South Arabian history is known as the period of the *mukarribs* because this was the title that preceded the sovereigns' names for a certain time. The meaning of the title "mkrb" is unclear (although many people have attributed a religious meaning to it, without providing any real proof), as is the pronunciation of the word. There are many Sabaean inscriptions bearing the names of people with this title, but there is not much variation in the names themselves, so we assume that sovereigns of this period were often given the same name. However, the name of the mukarrib is almost always accompanied by an epithet, and is often also a patronymic.

Only six names have come down to us: Dhamār'ali, Karib'īl, Sumhu'alī, Yada'īl, Yakrubmalik, Yatha''amar; and there are only four epithets: Bayyin, Dhariḥ, Watar and Yanūf. These limitations make it extremely difficult to positively identify the sovereigns, and even with the use of the patronymic to distinguish them and with palaeographic indications, we have not yet managed to establish the exact number of *mukarribs* who ruled Mārib. Besides, it is quite hard to lay down the precise order of succession between these names, partly because it is all complicated by the possibility of co-rulers and adoptions. As a result, the number of rulers seems quite small considering how many centuries this title was used in Saba.

So, if we favour an intermediate chronology (somewhere between Lundin's very long and Pirenne's short chronologies), we can place the first known *mukarribs* (Yatha''amar, Bayyin, son of Sumhu'alī; and Karib'īl Watar, son of Dhamār'ali, identified respectively in the Annals of Sargon II and Sennacherib as Ita'amar and Karibilu) somewhere between 715 and 685 BC. However, it is likely that other *mukarribs* reigned before this date, during the two and a half centuries that followed the Queen of Saba's famous reign. Unfortunately, however, we know absolutely nothing about that period, and we are forced to turn

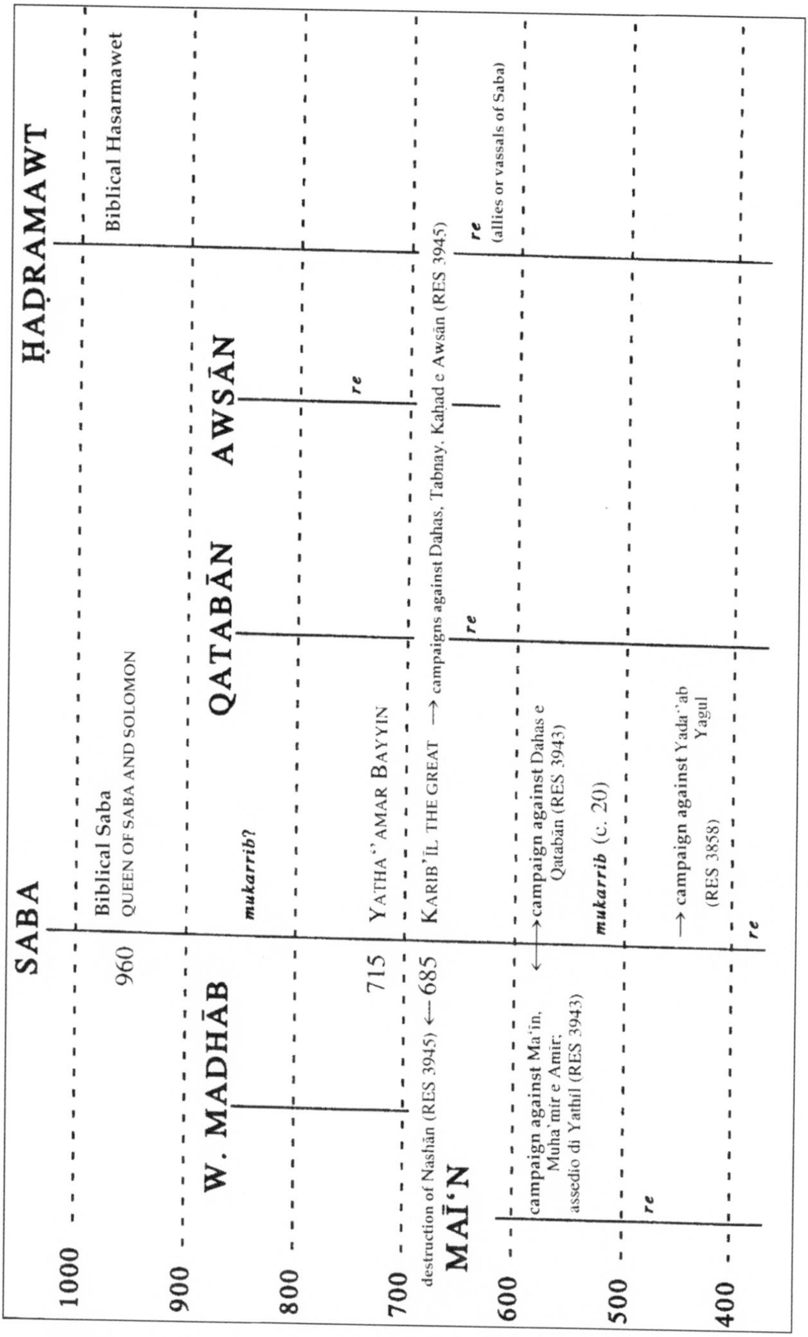

Table 3:
The caravan kingdoms in the period of the *mukarribs* of Saba

to later dates, stating that the title of *mukarrib* continued in use in Saba until approximately the end of the fifth century BC, when it was replaced with the title *malik*. Table 4 shows the names of the *mukarribs* in the order laid down by von Wissmann, although of course this is not definitive, and we lack the epithets and patronymics for many rulers. This shows how uncertain and difficult it is to reconstruct dynasties, as do the dates in parentheses.

Malik and Mukarrib

We know very little about these three centuries of South Arabian history. Information from reconnaissance missions and inscriptions show a country populated by farmers, taking advantage of the fertile earth carried down by the *widyān* to the edge of the desert, and mountain dwellers who essentially lived as shepherds.

Society was divided into village (*bayt*) communities which were held together, not so much by family ties as by the attachment of the people to their land. Several village communities formed one tribe (*sha'b*). This was not a nomadic tribe of the bedouin type, held together by blood ties, but rather an agricultural tribe, with socio-economic interests in common. This kind of tribe settled mostly on high ground, while in the pre-desert regions they tended to be more closely linked to the big inhabited centres (cities/tribes of the Jawf).

With the evolution of South Arabian culture, for reasons unknown to us, one tribe gained superiority over its neighbours and formed a third level of regrouping, of a socio-political type, that we might call a confederation. These confederations were named after the dominant tribe within the group, hence Saba, Qatabān, Awsān and Ḥaḍramawt.

Alfred Beeston, an English scholar to whom we are greatly indebted for his accurate and balanced interpretation of the sometimes indirect information from southern Arabian sources, has written that the Sabaeans, Minaeans, Qatabanians and Hadramis mentioned in classical texts corresponded to the four principal dialects that we recognise today in southern Arabia, and were therefore populations distinguished from each other by means of language, rather than geography[1]. We do not know if, from a political point of view, the great confederations like that of Saba or Qatabān had territorial borders that corresponded exactly with the borders of their languages.

Classical sources tell us, for example, that Qatabanian territory stretched to the shores of the Red Sea and the Indian Ocean. Indeed Wādī Tuban (Lahej) is mentioned in several Qatabanian texts. This is not enough, however, to establish whether the references are to the ethnic habitat of the Qatabanians or to their political sphere of influence.

It is also interesting that the Minaeans, despite their fame, never achieved socio-political organisation on the scale of a confederation. Their community was in fact always limited to a simple tribe system (*sha'b*). The Minaean dialect is only documented in a few cities of the Jawf (Ma'īn, Barāqish, Al-Sawdā).

Inscriptions from this time tell us that the head of a Sabaean *sha'b* was known as a *malik* (king). The king of the dominant tribe was also the king of the confederation of tribes. But in this superior role he assumed the title *mkrb* (*mukarrib*). The initial assumption that this title had some sort of religious connotation led to the idea that the confederation of tribes was organised along theocratic lines[3].

Today we can disprove this theory. The title of *mukarrib* was effectively taken on by the king of the dominant tribe only when acting as the king and head of the confederation. This does not mean that he could not also have been *malik* of his tribe at the same time. We are inclined to think that the term *mukarrib* was coined to avoid confusion with the title *malik.*

Royalty had no absolute value in southern Arabia, at least in this ancient period. Inscriptions often repeat the following formula regarding a *mukarrib:* "...when he established the whole community of gods, patron, alliances and the federation".

Obviously the *malik* (like the *mukarrib*) was only one member of the legislative authority in a tribe or federation and, on official occasions, needed to recall the federation's formula on the basis of which he had been given his role[4]. Indeed, on decrees and laws, his name is always followed by those of other functionaries. Rather than legally authorising the various initiatives, the *mukarrib* would promote them and take initiatives; rather than making the decisions, he would make sure that what had been decided had been carried out.

As the executive leader, whose job was to implement the decisions of a committee that he also participated in, it was natural that he should also as the head of the confederation be the supreme commander in military operations.

Around 400 BC (some say earlier, some later), the title *mukarrib* fell out of use in Saba, and was replaced by the exclusive use of *malik.* This probably coincided with a form of social transformation within the Sabaean community. It is possible, for example, that the king of the confederation, whose power had previously focused on the social unit, transferred his attention gradually to territory; and therefore, the sovereign's power as head of the group declined, while his power as ruler of a territory grew. As a result, the title of *malik* of the *sha'b* declined in importance, and from then on was used for the head of the confederation[5].

Building Activity

On the whole, the inscriptions only mention some aspects of the *mukarrib's* work. Most commonly mentioned are building works, religious activities, political activities and military operations. As epigraphy tends to be commemorative we have no information on the economy, society and everyday life. We have already seen how difficult it is to distinguish individuals from the names of the *mukarribs,* and how it is therefore impossible to establish correct dynastic profiles and a diachronic picture. Unfortunately this means that we have no clearly defined framework for the information that we have gathered, some of which is historically important, and any attempt to catalogue this information would be a bit of a stab in the dark.

The defensive walls that the *mukarribs* built around the important cities of the Jawf are among the most important works. Yatha''amar Bayyin, son of Sumhu'alī, had walls built around 'Ararat (Al-Asāḥil); Karib'īl Watar had walls built around Kutal (Kharībat Sa'ūd), Nashq (Al-Bayḍā), Yathil (Barāqish) and again around 'Ararat and Kutal; and Yada'īl Bayyin later refortified Nashq. In the eighth to seventh centuries BC, Ma'īn did not exist as an autonomous kingdom. Saba seems to have had widespread power in the territory of the Jawf, at least in the south. However, in this period, the cities along the north of the Wādī Madhāh valley (Haram, Kaminahū, Nashan and Inabbah) seem to have preserved a certain degree of independence and can therefore be called Madhabite city-states[6].

Karib'īl Watar, son of Dhamār'ali (better known as Karib'īl the Great, on account of his fame), also finished building the royal palace of Mārib (probably the famous Salhin or Salhim) and completed extensive irrigation works in the two oases. A later *mukarrib* probably intervened in the Mārib works, rebuilding and renovating two of the city gates. He was also responsible for several water-management schemes in Wādī Dhanah, which improved the irrigation of the capital's territory. Other *mukarribs* are linked to projects of less import. Yada'īl Dhariḥ, Sumhu'alī Yanūf, Karib'īl Bayyin bin Yatha''amar, and Dhamār'ali Watar bin Karib'īl are all mentioned in connection with building houses, towers, walls and cisterns.

The *mukarribs* also built temples in stone. Yada'īl Dhariḥ, son of Sumhu'alī, for example, built the Ma'rab temple in honour of the god Almaqah at Al-Masājid (a few kilometres north-east of Yalā) and the walls around the Awwam temple at Mārib and the Almaqah temple at Ṣirwāh[7]. These works were often accompanied by sacrifices. The *mukarrib* would offer stelae and altars to the gods, and would dress their statues with new clothes and gold ornaments[8].

There is an interesting inscription on a stela dedicated by Yatha''amar Bayyin son of Sumhu'alī, in which he celebrates a ritual hunt (RES 4177). Likewise, Karib'īl the Great gave a sacrifice and organised a ritual hunt to celebrate his conquest of cities and land in Najrān and the Jawf, as the famous Ṣirwāḥ inscription relates. The sacred hunt was evidently a particularly fashionable rite at the time of these two sovereigns. This idea is reinforced by some inscriptions that we found on rocks in the Shi'b al-'Aql, near Yalā.

Politics

The word *gn'*, meaning "he surrounded by walls", appears in many inscriptions and clearly refers to the *mukarribs'* great works of fortification around many cities. Some scholars believe that it may also refer to the boundaries which the victor would impose on a conquered territory, before plundering the land in the name of Saba. In this sense, the *mukarrib* was probably constructing political boundaries rather than physical walls. Indeed, all the texts referring to conquests of cities describe the victor's eagerness to make use of his new lands, often by enlarging his territory, and giving his new subjects precise agricultural duties. Territories thus conquered and reorganised were then officially annexed by the *mukarrib*, and transferred to the Sabaean state, referred to as "Almaqah and Saba"[10].

Except for some later documents which relate how, having conquered Nashq, the *mukarrib* Karib'īl Bayyin Yatha''amar and his son Dhamār'ali Watar, expanded and divided up the territory (CIS 610 and CIS 637), the most important acts of annexation were made by Karib'īl the Great following his successful campaigns against territories to the north and south of Saba. These decrees always follow the same lines. They start with an official formula justifying the annexation, followed by a list of the religious ceremonies and the monuments built to celebrate the event, and they end with a description of the military operations and a list of the conquered territories.

Annexation was never a simple matter. It could take the form of a confiscation, a direct transfer within the Sabaean state, a colonisation, or a lease arranged with allies, the result of a feud or a peaceful takeover. The state pursued its policy of territorial expansion in many different ways, and did not always have to resort to battle. It is more than likely, though, that at the time of Karib'īl Watar, Saba held the surrounding territories in a state of fearful submission, and it cannot have been hard to then employ alternative methods of expropriation, possibly accompanied by appropriate acts of compensation[11].

All this suggests that fairly complex bureaucratic and diplomatic systems existed within the Sabaean state at this early period. The *mukarrib* had a new role as executive leader at the heart of this intricate and complicated series of interests; he seems to have had more to do with the administration of power than with the purely political side. This confirms that the *mukarrib* was not the arbiter of the original ideas so much as their executor.

Dynastic Succession

In the historic inscription of Ṣirwāḥ (RES 3945), Karib'īl the Great lays down his formula of annexation thus: "This has been acquired by Karib'īl Watar, son of Dhamār'ali, *mukarrib* of Saba, *bmlkhw*, on behalf of Almaqah and Saba".

It is amazing to think that our understanding of the period of the *mukarribs* has depended for years on the interpretation of the (unvowelled) word "bmlkhw". In 1927, the Austrian scholar Nikolaus Rhodokanakis claimed that the word meant "when he became king", and this interpretation was universally accepted and believed, despite alternative ideas from other scholars[12]. Rhodokanakis' interpretation of the word actually imposed some order on the oldest period of South Arabian history.

So, at a certain point the *mukarrib* Karib'īl Watar, son of Dhamār'ali became a *malik*. Since we know from the inscriptions that in the kingdom of Saba the dynasty of the *mukarrib* was followed by a dynasty of kings, it is clear that Karib'īl the Great was the last *mukarrib* and the first king[13]. We can therefore place his reign at around 400 BC, and his achievements must be considered as later than those of the other *mukarribs*.

Thus the entire history of the period was seen as a progressive political evolution of the Sabaean state, culminating in the establishment of a true empire under Karib'īl Watar. This would also have provided an adequate reason for the change in title. Thanks to the constant expansion of the Sabaean kingdom's territories, Karib'īl was well placed to extend his conventional sphere of power. From being simply a *mukarrib*, with administrative duties, he became the *malik*, or king, head of the state, making as well as executing decisions.

This all seemed perfectly clear and reasonable. Jacques Ryckmans arranged the two known phases of military campaigns that characterise the period of the *mukarribs* like this: 1) wars fought by the various *mukarribs* against Qatabān and their allies, and against Ma'īn for territorial expansion or defence; 2) decisive stage of victory in Karib'īl Watar's campaigns against Awsān in the south and Nashan, the Madhabite cities of the Jawf, and Najrān in the north[14].

Shortly afterwards, in 1956, Jacqueline Pirenne

published a brilliant study on the palaeography of the inscriptions clearly proving that the word "bmlkhw" must have had another meaning, and – although the exact meaning of the word is still unclear – her work showed beyond a shadow of a doubt that Karib'īl Watar was not the last, but the first *mukarrib* of the dynasty[15].

It is quite paradoxical that Pirenne was the one to establish this change in position during the reign of Karib'īl Watar. In acknowledging the existence of such a huge and powerful kingdom of Saba at the start of the dynasty (and of writing), she makes her *low chronology* theory somehow less plausible. The new factual evidence undoubtably presupposed a long formative period for Saba before the reign of Karib'īl Watar, which hardly ties in with her theory that the culture "des grands *mukarribs*" of the fifth century BC appeared as a sort of sudden revelation.

Notably, too, Pirenne dated Karib'īl Watar's inscription, RES 3945, to 430 BC. As a result, all the other known *mukarribs* (twenty-two in all) must be fitted into just over a century (Pirenne dated the end of the *mukarrib* period to about 300 BC). This is why she decided that several *mukarrib*s must have ruled at the same time, and that there were many parallel lines of descent from the same royal clan.

Her work is, however, extraordinarily valuable. Thanks to her painstaking analysis of the palaeography of the letters in the inscriptions, we have the first reliable relative chronology, not just for the Sabaean sovereigns throughout the ages, but also for sovereigns of other kingdoms. In many ways her studies remain completely valid.

The sequence of the *mukarribs*, with Karib'īl at the head of the dynasty, provides a much more coherent framework for the history and culture of the period (Table 3). This is especially true if we combine Pirenne's results with those of Hermann von Wissmann, who gave an earlier date for Karib'īl the Great and his predecessor Yatha''amar Bayyin bin Sumhu'alī, allowing a much longer period for the historical development of the *mukarribs*, and a better framework of reference for archaeologists[16].

We still have a lot of work to do before we understand the exact meaning of the word "bmlkhw" in Karib'īl Watar's inscription, but in the meantime many things begin to make more sense if we take an earlier date for the period of his reign. It now makes sense that the names of Karib'īl and Yatha''amar Bayyin bin Sumhu'alī (who, as we shall see, was probably his predecessor) appear on the walls of cities and monuments that archaeologists and art historians have classified amongst the oldest. We can now also understand why there was no mention of the kingdom of Ma'īn during the reign of Karib'īl, despite his frequent excursions in the Jawf. Besides, as we have already said, it is easier to reconcile archaeological evidence with an earlier date for Karib'īl Watar.

We shall say more on this subject further on. For now we should remember that our archaeological mission in the Sabaean city of Yalā uncovered a monumental inscription that apparently dates from just after Karib'īl Watar's inscription. Since we know that Yalā existed no later than 585 BC (the latest possible date, from the radiocarbon dating analyses), we have to conclude that the great Sabaean sovereign reigned before the destruction of Yalā.

As regards the chronology of the *mukarrib* period, I believe that Pirenne was correct in a relative sense, and von Wissmann in an absolute sense. I would also not hesitate in agreeing with the German scholar when he identifies Yatha''amar Bayyin son of Sumhu'alī and Karib'īl Watar son of Dhamār'ali with their two namesakes mentioned by the Assyrian Annals. This is why we have chosen von Wissmann's dynastic sequence of the *mukarrib*s (Table 4) over the many others available.

Karib'īl Watar the Great

Karib'īl Watar's military campaigns have been mentioned several times. We will now look at them in more detail with a summary (by Christian Robin) of the exact wording of the large inscription of Ṣirwāḥ, RES 3945.

The first campaign was conducted against cities in the Ma'afir region, in the south of North Yemen. Three thousand men were killed in the battle, and a further eight thousand captured. The second campaign, against the kingdom of Awsān in Wādī Markhah, resulted in 16,000 dead and 40,000 prisoners. The third, against Dahas and Tabnay, north and north-east of Aden, produced 2000 dead and 5000 prisoners, while the fourth, against Kahad dhu-Sawt in the same region, resulted in 500 and 1000 respectively. We can leave the fifth and sixth campaigns, against Nashan in the Jawf until later. We do not know the results of the seventh campaign, which was conducted against an unidentified enemy area, probably in the Tihāmah or even on the other side of the Red Sea. The eighth and final war was waged against cities and tribes of unknown identity; but the Sabaeans killed every king and up to 3000 people, taking 5000 prisoners and 150,000 head of livestock. The Muha'mir and Amir tribes (from Najrān, and between Najrān and the Jawf respectively) were also seriously affected by this war, losing 5000 men, 12,000 prisoners and 200,000 head of livestock.

These are impressive – and maybe exaggerated – figures, but even so they show that these regions were fairly densely populated. The Awsān campaign involved 57,000 people, and that against Muha mir and Amir 17,000, although these territories have a rather limited agricultural value. The prisoners probably became slaves, and were forced to work on the Sabaean *mukarrib*'s great building projects (construction and hydraulic projects). All this clearly involved the relocation of huge numbers of people.

Karib'īl Watar's campaigns against Nashan (current site of As-Sawdā) are particularly interesting for us, since we are working with an archaeological mission in the Jawf. Most of our information on the conflict between Saba and Nashan comes from the inscription RES 3945. Here is Robin's translation of the summary of Karib'īl's fifth and sixth campaigns:

> (14) "...When he [Karib'īl Watar] attacked Nashan, he set fire to the cities, and destroyed Ashr, Bayḥan and all the valleys in one sole campaign. When he launched his second campaign, he built a wall around Nashan and Nashq and, enjoining the help of 'Athtar for three years, he made himself ruler of Nashq and the territories, in the name of Saba and Almaqah, he massacred 1000 Nashanites, devastated Sumhuyafa' and Nashan, and gave the territories, which
>
> (15) had been given to him [Sumhuyafa'] by the king of Saba, to Saba and Almaqah, took control of the cities of Qawm, Jaw'al, Dawr, Fadhm, Shibām and all the cities of Ayk, and everything that

> belonged to Sumhuyafa' and Nashan in Ayk, took possession of his territory until he reached the border of Manhiyat, for Saba and Almaqah, took the Zalam dam and the Hurmat dam, and took control of the network of water channels belonging to the king of Nashan, [fed by] the waters of Madhāh, and he attacked the wall around Nashan until
>
> (16) he had destroyed it, just as he had done to Nashan, destroying it with fire, he destroyed his palace 'Afraw and his city Nashan, he imposed a tax on Nashan [regarding] the priests, forbade Nashan to renege on his promise that his citizens would turn to the gods [or else] they would be massacred, he forced Sumhuyafa' and Nashan to accept that Saba would be established within the city of Nashan and that Sumhuyafa' and Nashan would build the temple of Almaqah in the centre of Nashan city, he took the waters of dhu-Qaf'an away from
>
> (17) Sumhuyafa' and Nashan and gave them to Yadhmurmalik, king of Haram, he took away the canals of dhat-Malikwaqih from Sumhuyafa' and Nashan and gave them to Nabaṭ'ali, king of Kaminahū, as well as the dhat-Malikwaqih canals lying outside the borders that Karib'īl had established, he built a fortifying wall around Nashq and populated the city with Sabaeans in the name of Saba and Almaqah...."

In inscription CIS 516, which Halévy copied at Haram (Kharībat Hamdān), there is an allusion to the first of the two campaigns waged against Nashan, and an important citizen of Haram recalls his role as governor of the city for two years, until he was forced to hand it over to Karib'īl.

The importance of Karib'īl Watar's military campaigns is proved by numerous references in other texts (mostly fragmentary). These testify, in effect, to a considerable growth in Sabaean power in South Arabia. The kingdom of Awsān was destroyed, and Sabaean territory expanded southward as far as the borders of Ḥaḍramawt (which must by then have been reduced to a subordinate position), and northward as far as Najrān.

Despite resistance by Nashan and Haram, the cities of the Jawf eventually capitulated, and became part of what Karib'īl

Watar had managed to transform into a proper empire, whose influence, we remember, spread as far as the highlands in the north of Yemen and the far shores of the Red Sea. The South Arabian inscriptions found in pre-Aksumite Ethiopia, along with magnificent examples of art and architecture, bear witness to direct Sabaean influence, and can be dated to the period starting with Karib'īl Watar[17].

Compared to what we know about Karib'īl Watar, our knowledge of his successors is poor indeed, especially as regards their military campaigns. At any rate, Saba seems to have remained the principal force in the region for a long time, and its sovereigns certainly took steps to keep it that way. There does seem to have been internal trouble with some tribes and confederations, however, and the Sabaeans were forced to restore order in Qatabān and the Jawf, where, in the meantime, the name of Ma'īn was steadily growing[18].

The first mention of Ma'īn is in the Sabaean inscription RES 3943. (We do not know the author's name, but its palaeography suggests that it is at least a few generations later than Karib'īl Watar.) It records a Sabaean invasion, moving first south, against Qatabān and the people of Dahas, and then north, against Ma'īn and the Muha'mir and Amir tribes. Rajmat, the capital of Muha'mir, was destroyed, as were other cities in the Najrān area, and the city of Yathil (which Karib'īl Watar had previously provided with encircling walls) was attacked and its irrigation area sacked.

Another document, Qatabanian this time (RES 3858), and probably dating from about the end of the *mukarrib* period in Saba, tells of a war conducted by three different Sabaean sovereigns against Yada''ab Yagul, king of Qatabān. This was clearly a long and difficult war, and seems to be an indication of the increasing autonomy that the other South Arabian kingdoms sought from Saba from about 400 BC onwards.

Footnotes:

1. Beeston, A., "Kingship in Ancient South Arabia", *JESHO* 15 (1972), p. 256-268.

2. Hommel, F. "Geschichte Südarabiens im Umriss", in D. Nielsen (ed.), *Handbuch der altarabischen Altertumskunde, I. Band: Die altarabische Kultur* (Copenhagen: A. Busck, 1927), p. 56-108.
3. Beeston, A., "Kingship in Ancient South Arabia", p. 264.
4. Garbini, G., "Un nuovo documento per la storia dell'antico Yemen", *OA* 12 (1973), p. 147-48.
5. Beeston, A., "Kingship in South Arabia", p. 265.
6. de Maigret, A. and Robin, C. "Les fouilles italiennes de Yalā (Yémen du Nord): nouvelles données sur la chronologie de l'Arabe du Sud préislamique", *CRAIBL* (1989), p. 267.
7. Lundin, A.G., *Gosudarstvo mukarribov Saba* (Moscow: Nauka, Glavnaia rudaktsiia vostochnoi literatury, 1971).
8. Ryckmans, J., *L'institution monarchique en Arabie méridionale avant l'Islam (Ma'īn et Saba)* (Louvain: Pulications universitaires, 1951), p. 64.
9. Beeston, A., "The Ritual Hunt, A Study in Old South Arabian Religious Practice", *Le Muséon* 61 (1948), p. 183-196. See also Serjeant, R.B., *South Arabian Hunt* (London: Luzac, 1976); and Ryckmans, J., "La chasse rituelle dans l'Arabie du Sud ancienne", in *Al-Bahit, Festchrift Joseph Henninger* (Bonn: 1976), p. 259-308.
10. Ryckmans, J., *L'institution monarchique en Arabie*, p. 72.
11. Ibid, p. 71.
12. Rhodokanakis, N., *Altsabäische Texte I* (Wien: 1927), p. 38.
13. Beeston, A., "Problems of Sabaean Chronology", *BSOAS* 16 (1972), p. 42.
14. Ryckmans, J. *L'institution monarchique en Arabie*, p. 75.
15. Pirenne, J., *Paléographie des inscriptions sud-arabes. Contribution à la chronologie et à l'histoire de l'Arabie du Sud antique. Vol I: Des origines à l'époque himyarite* (Brussels: Paleis der Academien, 1956), p. 157.
16. von Wissman, H., *Zur Geschichte und Landeskunde von Alt-Südarabien* (Wien: H. Bohlaus Nachf, 1964); and *Die Geschichte von Saba II: Das Grossreich der Sabäer bis zu seinem Ende im frühen 4* (Wien:Verl. D. Osterr. Akad d. Wiss., 1982).
17. Pirenne, J., "Sabea d'Etiopia, arte", *Enciclopedia dell'Arte Antica Classica e Orientale vol. VI*, (1965), p. 1044-48.
18. Robin, C., "La civilisation de l'Arabe méridionale avant l'Islam" in Chelhod, (ed.), *L'Arabie du Sud: histoire et civilisation: 1. Le peuple yéménite et ses racines* (Paris: G.-P. Maisoneuve et Larose, 1984), p. 210.

Karib'īl	(775)
Yada''īl Yanūf bin Karib'īl	(755)
Sumhu'alī Dharīḥ bin Yada''īl	(735)
Yatha''amar Bayyin bin Sumhu'alī	*715*
Dhamar'alī	(695)
Karib'īl Watar bin Dhamar'alī	*685*
Sumhu'alī	(675)
Yada''īl Dharīḥ bin Sumhu'alī	(665)
Sumhu'alī Yanūf bin Yada''īl Dharīḥ	(645)
Dhamar'alī Dharīḥ bin Yada''īl	(625)
Karib'īl	
Yakrubmalik	
Sumhu'alī	
Dhamar'alī	
Yatha''amar	(605)
Yada''īl Bayyin bin Yatha''amar Watar	(590)
Karib'īl Bayyin bin Yatha''amar	(580)
Dhamar'alī Watar bin Karib'īl	(560)
Sumhu'alī Yanūf bin Dhamar'alī	(545)
Yatha''amar Bayyin bin Sumhu'alī Yanūf	(525)
Karib'īl	(495)
Yada''īl	(475)
Yatha''amar	(470)
Sumhu'alī	(430)
Yatha''amar Watar	(420)
Yada''īl Bayyin bin Yatha''amar Watar	(415)

Table 4
The *mukarribs* of Saba

XI

THE CARAVAN KINGDOMS AND THE KINGS OF SABA

The Dynasty of the Kings of Saba

At a certain point in their history, the *mukarribs* of Saba stopped using the title *mukarrib*, and instead began to refer to themselves as *mlk sb*' (king of Saba). Two things make it certain that the change in title happened this way round, rather than vice versa. Firstly, as we have already seen, palaeographic evidence supports this, and secondly, while in the *mukarrib* period writing ran from left to right, and right to left alternately, in the era of the kings it became stricter, only running from right to left.

We cannot be sure of the date of transition between these two periods. It fluctuates between around 400 BC, according to F. Hommel and his followers[1], who established the date on the basis of the presumed length of *mukarribs*' reigns; 450 BC according to W. F. Albright[2]; and around 300 BC according to Pirenne and Beeston, who calculated the length of the reigns by working back from the beginning of the following period (the Sabaean era or rather, the Himyarite era, 110 BC)[3]. Therefore the duration of the period of the kings of Saba, which must have ceased around the end of the first century BC, varies between 450 and 300 years.

From the sovereigns' names that we know from the inscriptions, we can identify around twenty kings who ruled Saba between the *mukarrib* period and the period of the kings of Saba and Dhū-Raydān. This is a familiar roll-call: all these kings' names, as well as their epithets, are contained within the limited list of names used by the *mukarribs* before them. Table 5 gives von Wissmann's hypothetical reconstruction of the dynastic succession.

Von Wissmann's reconstruction is indeed theoretical, and neither the sequence of monarchs nor their number can be considered exact. We now have a list of seventeen kings, when in the 1950s we had only eleven, according to Beeston or fourteen according to Ryckmans[5]. Clearly, this number will slowly increase with the discovery of new texts, and we are still far from completing the list.

Sumhu'alī Yanūf	c.410 B.C.
Yatha''amar Watar	
Yakrubmalik Dharīḥ	
Sumhu'alī Yanūf	
Yada''il Bayyin I	
Yakrubmalik Watar I	
Yatha''amar Bayyin I	
Karib'īl Watar	
Yada''īl Bayyin II	
Yakrubmalik Watar II	
Yatha''amar Bayyin II	
Sumhu'alī Dharīḥ	
Karib'īl Bayyin	
Yada''īl	
Sumhu'alī Yanūf	c. 110 B.C.
Yada''īl Watar	
Dhamar'alī Bayyin	c.60 B.C.

Table 5
The kings of Saba

It is worth noting, though, that it is easier to follow how one king succeeded another in this list than in the list of the *mukarribs*. Here, the relationship between one king and the next (son, brother) is recorded more often, which makes it easier to be certain about at least some of the sequence. There are, however, some breaks in the chain. The fact that we do not know the length of these gaps means that we cannot rely on this chronology.

Apart from the names of the kings of Saba, we know very little about this period. Our best sources of information are dedications made by the kings on statues and monuments and, especially, a series of royal decrees, which are highly important as they provide insight into their political activities.

The Political Power and Behaviour of the Kings

Text CIS 601 is a report of a decree made by Yada'īl Bayyin, son of Karib'īl Watar, in which he declares that the

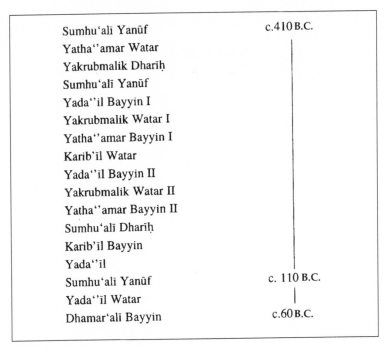

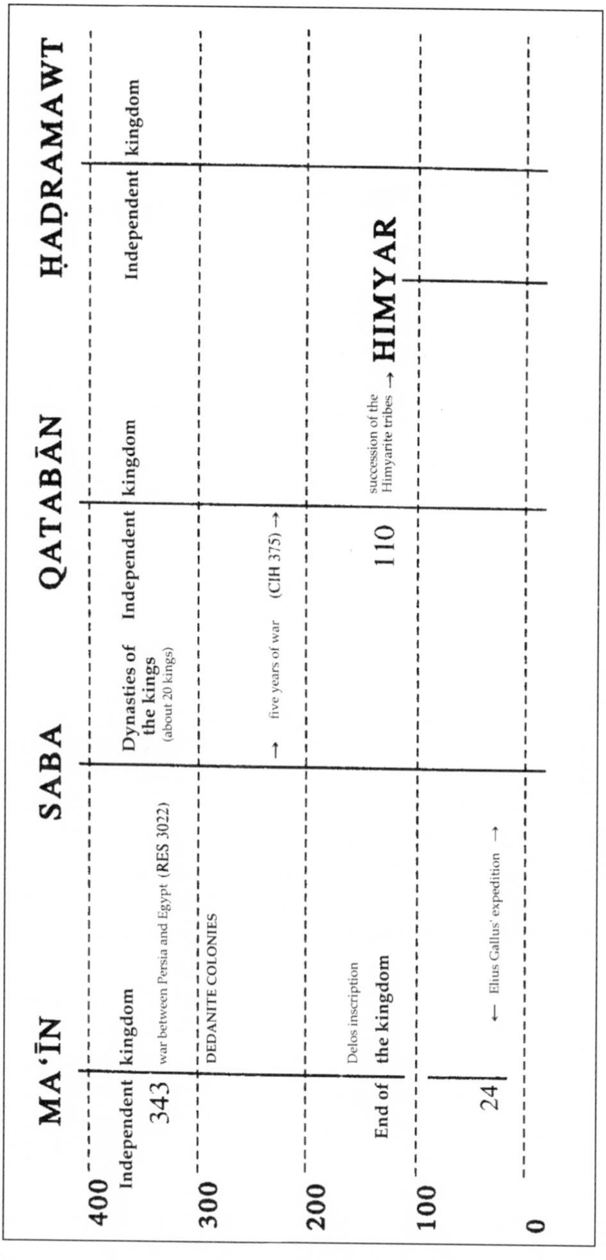

Table 6
The caravan kingdoms in the period of the kings of Saba

tribes of Saba and Yuhabliḥ are to become colonies of the state of Ṣirwāḥ. The colonies would then be duty-bound to sell their harvests to the state every year, after an evaluation. They would thus redeem the price of their land and the value of the produce at the same time. This annual "sale" was obviously meant to cover the taxes that the colonies owed to the state and was therefore intended as a favour, to encourage the colonies' exploitation of the land for the benefit of the state.

However, with Yada'īl Bayyin's son, Yakrubmalik Watar, the state's demands became increasingly excessive. In the same inscription, CIS 601, Yakrubmalik establishes that certain dues, such as military taxes, can no longer be covered by the annual sale of produce. Saba and Yuhabliḥ therefore will no longer benefit from their position of favour under Yada'īl.

In another decree referring to Ṣirwāḥ and Yuhabliḥ, RES 3951, Karib'īl Watar, son of Yatha'amar, increases fiscal pressure on the two tribes, declaring that Ṣirwāḥ must, in addition, pay all present and future military expenses. The tribe of Yuhabliḥ is incorporated into the city-based tribe of Ṣirwāḥ, under the authority of a prefect (*kabīr*), and included in a precise fiscal system. Here is how Karib'īl Watar expresses his commands:

> This has been decided and ordered by Karib'īl Watar, son of Yatha''amar and king of Saba, along with the Sabaean landowners and they have agreed to everything that he has proclaimed and ordered, in perpetuity and Nazaḥat and the leaders of Fayshān and Arba'ān and the executors of [M...], to Yatha'Karib, prefect [*kabīr*] of Ṣirwāḥ and their sons and servants....

Ryckmans' dynastic sequence did not include the three kings Yada'īl Bayyin II, Yakrubmalik II and Yatha''amar Bayyin II, who we find in the list compiled by von Wissmann. As a result, the decrees contained in CIS 601, made by Yada'īl Bayyin and his son Yakrubmalik, were thought to precede that made by Karib'īl Watar. On this basis, Ryckmans thought he would find gradual steps towards the centralisation of power within the Sabaean state in the hands of the kings and increasing confirmation of the central authority of the state[6].

In fact, it now seems that the decree made by Karib'īl Watar, son of Yatha''amar Bayyin, precedes, rather than follows, that made by Yada'īl Bayyin and his son Yakrubmalik (shown on von Wissman's list distinguished by the word "second"), and we therefore have no proof of the progressive growth of authority in that period. Indeed, the very opposite seems true, although the precise reasons for this remain obscure, and will for some time.

These decrees do, at least, provide us with some useful information on the power of the kings. Legislation was initiated by the king and approved by representatives of the population. The latter would then help the king to spread the word. The king was assisted by a sort of assembly, made up of the most important landowners and representatives of the tribes. We have proof of the existence of a proper council of ministers in an inscription (Gl 1533) which refers to a council of six *qyn* (administrators). The task of carrying out the decrees (for example at Ṣirwāḥ) was given to the highest ranking functionary (*kabīr*) and the leaders of the tribes (*mswd's*). Clearly, then, this is a considerable change from the *mukarribs*' powers. Legislative power now appears to be separate from executive power, and the sovereign increasingly tends to take the decisions, delegating administrative tasks to others.

We also have some epigraphy relating to military operations dating from this period. These are mostly texts that document the continuing battles against Qatabān, started by the *mukarribs*. The most important (CIS 375) is a document in which an officer under the kings Yada'īl Bayyin, Yakrubmalik Watar and Yatha''amar Bayyin records his role as commander in chief during five years of war between Saba and Qatabān, and his attempts to restore peace. Unfortunately, we have almost nothing on the final period of the dynasty.

In general, the kingdom of Saba during the period of the kings seems very different to the strong state ruled by the *mukarribs*. The Sabaeans had, at first, been the unquestioned rulers. Ma'īn and Qataban's appearance on the political scene had been easily controlled. The distant tribes of the Ḥaḍramawt had at that time been quiet allies, or perhaps subjects, who presented no threat. The only danger, in the form of the kingdom of Awsān, had been destroyed. The fame of Saba had spread across the northern desert and had reached first Solomon, and then the neo-Assyrian kings; and across the Red Sea, stable and lasting commercial colonies had been established in the Ethiopian highlands.

Now, with the period of the kings, everything appears to be redefined. Saba no longer takes the initiative, but follows others, repelling attacks by Qatabān, and accepting the newly important commercial position of Ma'īn in the Jawf. Outside South Arabia, Saba is no longer seen as an important political force (see for example Herodotus, Theophrastus, Eratostenes). The fame of Karib'īl the Great was fading fast and the kingdom was no longer an empire, but a local political force.

So, while Saba saw a succession of royal dynasties, three new protagonists were making a dramatic impact on ancient Yemen's political and economic scene: Qatabān, Ma'īn and Ḥaḍramawt. These three cultivated a fame which for a time surpassed that of Saba (Table 6). Was their political growth of their own doing, or did it depend on a gradual reduction in Sabaean hegemony? As far as we can tell, Ma'īn owed its success partly to the fact that it focused on commerce, an area that was not particularly important to Saba. The Mārib confederation was mainly composed of warrior tribes, and they may have welcomed and encouraged the fact that a tribe like the Mineans, which was entirely dedicated to commerce, was flourishing nearby.

The Kingdom of Qatabān

Although American archaeologists digging in Wādī Beihan dated the period of the kingdom of Qatabān to between the sixth and first centuries BC[7], we can now confidently extend this period to include the seventh century BC at one end, and the whole of the second century AD at the other.

The confederation as such emerged shortly after the collapse of the kingdom of Awsān, which was demolished by Karib'īl Watar. We know that Awsān occupied land (Wādī Markhah) which later belonged to Qatabān, and we can therefore assume that at the start, Awsān was simply the dominant tribe of the future confederation of Qatabān. But this is not absolutely certain, as the name Awsān crops up later, alongside the name of Qatabān.

The land occupied by the confederation of tribes with Qatabān at their head extended beyond the *wādī* that now bears the same name, into Wādī Ḥarib to the west and probably into Wādī Markhah itself to the east, as far as what is now the centre of Niṣāb. Classical authors believed that Qatabān extended as far as the Indian Ocean to the south and the Red Sea to the south-west. This theory was disputed by scholars until fairly recently[8]. Since there were no surviving inscriptions from the area to prove Qatabān's political supremacy, one was more inclined to think that the classical authors were referring to the Qatabanians' linguistic and ethnic origins, rather than the land under their political control. However, inscriptions mention the presence of Qatabanians in Wādī Tuban (an area north of Aden) and we cannot rule out the possibility that Qatabān-controlled land reached as far as the two coasts of southern Arabia, just as the kingdom of Ḥimyar would later on.

As we have seen, the American excavations at Timnaʿ revealed the splendour and wealth of the kingdom's famous capital. However, the nearby site of Hajar Bin Ḥumayd contained older layers, and so it is possible that the capital was based here, before being transferred to Timnaʿ. Qatabān's importance to the caravan trade in spices and perfumes has been proven by the discovery of ancient, well-made roads cut out of solid rock that cross the mountain ranges between the valleys of Markhah, Beihan, Ḥarib and Jubah. The Qatabanian administration obviously invested great sums of money in ensuring that they could trade with the caravans, which could now travel safely, rather than having to skirt the mountains along the edge of the desert, where they were open to attack by nomads. Irrigation works and agricultural plots were also exceptionally well tended, and show the degree of central organisation present in Timnaʿ at its height, around the third century BC. The sovereigns disposed of the title *mukarrib*, and the state became internationally renowned; coins started to bear an owl motif typical of Athenian currency and an inscription tells of a "kabīr of the Minaeans of Timnaʿ". We also find a strong Greek influence in the arts, especially in the later period.

Here, as in Saba, the head of the tribe was a *malik*, or king, and the head of the confederation was a *mukarrib*, who still remained *malik* of his own tribe (the dominant tribe). The few sovereigns' names that we have cannot be put into any precise order on account of chronological uncertainties, but we know that the *mukarribs*' power was consolidated by an assembly – like at Saba – which discussed the issues before a decision was taken. So the sovereign was not the legislator, but the head of the executive body. This is further proved by the variety of titles that the *mukarrib* assumed for his different roles. Thus he would be called *qẓr* when he was collecting taxes, *qyn* when he was running the administration and *bkr*, meaning literally "the first born (of two gods)", when he had to preside over religious events[9].

We can reconstruct the Qatabanian pantheon to a certain extent from the gods that appear in order of importance in the inscription RES 3881 on the southern gateway of Timnaʿ. These are ʿAthtar, ʿAmm (all Qatabanians considered themselves his "sons"), Anbay, Ḥawkum and the goddesses Dhāt-Ṣantim and Dhāt-Zahrān. We will look at religion in greater depth further on, but for now let us assume that ʿAthtar was their supreme god, possibly more easily identified with the sky in general than – as has often been claimed – with the planet Venus. He is the equivalent of the Mesopotamian goddess Ishtar and the Phoenician goddess Astarte, but assumes a male form throughout southern Arabia. Beeston finds that the Qatabanian inscriptions are characteristically more pagan than the Sabaean ones, but that may be due to his choice of texts[10]. Were this true, we could deduce that Qatabān fostered a more pragmatic mentality, concentrating essentially on commercial affairs. On this subject, we should bear in mind the stela found in the centre of Timnaʿ, recording the meticulous organisation of the market.

These inscriptions differ from the Sabaean ones in their distinctive style of writing, which is beautiful and highly decorative. Even the language is different, as far as we can tell: third person pronouns, both independent and suffixes, are expressed using the sibilant (Sabaean uses the "*h*"), and the imperfect indicative has the prefix "*b*". But there were probably many other differences in the pronunciation of the words, which are obviously not discernible from the inscriptions.

Finally, it is interesting that Arab writers do not mention Qatabān as a social entity, although they call the region by this name. In fact we have no Qatabanian inscriptions later than the fourth century AD, and we are probably justified in supposing that the kingdom of Beihan had disappeared by then. It therefore makes sense that Islamic historians were unaware of its existence, since those who concerned themselves with the events of the *jahiliyyah* rarely looked further into the past than, say, a couple of centuries.

Further on we will try to identify the possible reasons behind the kingdom's gradual disintegration, and eventual collapse. During our period, we know that Qatabān hit a profound crisis when, towards the end of the first century BC, the provinces of the southern Yemeni highlands, under the control of the Ḥimyar tribe, separated from the kingdom to form an independent political entity. This does not seem to have had an immediate affect on Saba, where the royal dynasties continued to rule, but gradually the new Himyarite kingdom gathered force and became increasingly important, economically and politically, until it constituted a serious, lasting threat for Saba, Ḥaḍramawt and Qatabān itself.

The Kingdom of Ma'īn

As we have seen, Karib'īl Watar, son of Dhamār'ali, made no mention of the kingdom of Ma'īn in his historic inscription (RES 3945). And this despite his conducting long and hard battles in the Jawf. We must therefore conclude that Ma'īn had not yet reached a stage of true political unity at the time of his reign. Yet if we support the validity of the relative chronology established by Pirenne, we must believe that Ma'īn appeared on the scene not long after the reign of Karib'īl Watar, since text RES 3943 records an expedition against the kingdom of Jawf, which probably occurred about two or three generations after Karib'īl Watar.

The written style that characterises the oldest known Minaean inscriptions (those found at Barāqish) was classified by Pirenne as type B3, while those made by Karib'īl Watar, which are a little earlier, are called B1. There are, in fact, older inscriptions in the Minaean language, but – as we have already mentioned – these refer to divinities that were not truly Minaean, as they belonged to city-states that constituted self-contained kingdoms (Nashan, Kaminahū, Haram, Innabah). They therefore belong to a different historical context and are rightly distinguished by Robin, who calls them "Madhabite" on account of their geographical position (on the water course that flows from Wādī Madhāh down the length of the northern Jawf).

The kingdom of Ma'īn itself ruled over a rather restricted area, containing Qarnāw, the capital, Yathil (modern-day Barāqish) and later Nashan (Al-Sawdā). It never reached the level of political integration enjoyed by Saba, Qatabān or Ḥaḍramawt, remaining simply at tribal level and never becoming a confederation of tribes. This is why we find that Ma'īn was always ruled by a *malik* and never by a *mukarrib*.

Nonetheless, the fame of the Minaeans spread far and wide, principally because they controlled the perfume trade between South Arabia and the Mediterranean[12]. Eratostenes lists the Minaeans among the four main peoples of the region, and Pliny credits them with starting the incense trade.

Their great capacity for trade is shown by their emporiums established in the northern Ḥijāz at Dedan (now called Al-'Ulā), and at Timna'. It is also documented in various inscriptions, discovered in Egypt (an epitaph on a sarcophagus dating from the Ptolemaic era) and in the Mediterranean Levant (a dedication on an altar on the island of Delos). Further inscriptions, known as "lists of hierodules", testify to Ma'īn's international status, describing how foreign women were made citizens by the Minaeans; these brides came from Gaza, north-west Arabia and Egypt.

These texts testify to the great expansion of Minaean commerce, and show that this must have occurred at a fairly late date. It would therefore be reasonable to conclude that the kingdom of Ma'īn's finest hour coincided with the height of the Hellenistic period.

The date must however be slightly altered, on account of an inscription on the facade of the south wall of Barāqish. This document (RES 3022) was written by some Minaeans to commemorate the building of one of the city's bastions, expressing their gratitude to the gods 'Athtar, Wadd and Nakraḥ who delivered them from danger in Egypt "during the revolt between *Mdhy* and Egypt".

The Minaeans used the term *Mdhy* (the Medes) to refer to the Persians, and thus in the Barāqish inscription we have an explicit reference to a war between Egypt and Persia in the Achaemenid period (sixth to fourth centuries BC). The question has been discussed at length, and several scholars agree that this battle is recognisable as one that took place, in 343 BC and resulted in the Persian Artaxerxes Ochus' domination of Egypt[13]. If this were true, we would need to place the Minaean kingdom and its long-distance trade a little further back in time than the Hellenistic period. This seems to be backed up by the current excavations of the Italian mission at Barāqish, which we shall look at later. It seems unlikely, though, that Maʻīn is as ancient as Saba, since, as Robin has pointed out, there is no explicit reference to the Minaeans in the Bible[15].

Maʻīn was mentioned by Pliny the Elder (first century AD) and Claudius Ptolemy (second century AD), although it was already weakening in the second century BC, possibly due to the growth of Sabaean power in northern Yemen in opposition to the rising star of Ḥimyar. This great commercial kingdom must have collapsed around the beginning of the first century BC. The last inscriptions in the Maʻīn area date from around 100 BC, and the last mention of Maʻīn, together with Yathil, is in a Sabaean inscription from Ṣanʻā (CIS 609) dating from approximately AD 50. From then on, the various peoples that made up the Minaean tribe lost their political cohesion, and the cities were gradually abandoned. When Aelius Gallus took Yathrula (Yathil) in 24 BC without a struggle, the town was probably occupied by more Arabs than Minaeans[16].

The Kingdom of Ḥaḍramawt

The Hadrami sites that have been identified so far have proved rather poor sources of information. They do, however, mark the boundaries of the kingdom of Ḥaḍramawt on the map, by documenting a dialect that differs in some grammatical respects from Qatabanian, Minaean and Sabaic. The kingdom was not contained within the *wādī* that now bears the same name. It once stretched as far as the Indian Ocean to the south, the Ramlat Sabʻatayn desert to the west (site of the capital, Shabwat), and the commercial outpost of Samhar (now called Khawr Rūrī) to the east.

We do not yet know a great deal about the ancient centres of the Ḥaḍramawt. So far only a few sites have been discovered – Al-Barīrah, and Al-Binā in Wādī Jirdān[17]; Naqīb al-Hajar in Wādī Mayfaʻah[18]; the port of Qana, near Bīr Ali – and still fewer have been excavated (Ḥurayḍah and Khawr Rūrī). Other sites cannot be excavated, since they are now occupied by major modern centres, like Tarīm and Shibām. However, the excavations at Raybūn, the sites in Wādī Du'ān, Qana and Shabwat have recently been completed with interesting results.

Most of the information that our primary sources give us about this ancient incense kingdom concerns relatively late periods. For information on earlier periods we have to look to secondary, i.e. Sabaean sources, as well as Biblical and classical sources.

The fact that the Bible mentions Saba alongside Hasarmawet in Genesis shows that the origins of Ḥadramawt lie deep in the mists of time (early first millennium BC). The kingdom is mentioned in Sabeaean texts of the *mukarrib* period, and it probably fell into Mārib's political sphere of influence. Later, during the time of the kings of Saba, the kingdom gained independence, along with Ma'īn and Qatabān. The name of a king of Ḥadramawt appears on a tower near the eastern gate of Ma'īn (RES 2775).

Although later Sabaean texts bear the names of many Hadrami sovereigns, it has so far been impossible to establish a precise order of succession. What we do know for certain, though, is that the capital Shabwat was conquered by Saba at some point between AD 225 and 235. Shortly afterwards, towards the end of the third century AD, the kingdom lost its autonomy, and eventually gravitated towards the political sphere of the Himyarite kingdom of Saba and Dhū-Raydān.

As an independent kingdom, the Ḥadramawt alternated between wars and alliances with the various other South Arabian states. Its interests were essentially commercial, and the fact that the capital was placed at the westernmost edge of its territory tells us that the Ramlat Sab'atayn basin was the focal point for commerce at the time, partly because it lay on the trade route for the incense produced in the eastern regions of Mahrah and Dhofār.

We know that, besides being an important commercial centre, Shabwat was also a fairly major religious centre (Pliny claimed that there were sixty temples within the walls). These two things were closely related, and Pliny informs us that all the transactions and procedures regarding incense were governed by precise and meticulous religious rules.

The Periplus of the Erythraean Sea (first century AD) further testifies to the importance of Shabwat in the incense trade, and clarifies the role played by the two ports of Ḥaḍramawt, Qana and Moscha (Samhar) in transporting the resin towards the capital.

About 15 kilometres west of Shabwat, an isolated spur of rock encroaches on the desert sands. The Arabs call this rock Al-'Uqlah; it was discovered by Philby in the 1930s when he travelled down from Saudi Arabia to explore Yemen[19]. Some ruined buildings at its base and on its summit, along with numerous inscriptions carved into the rock side, bear witness to the importance of the site in antiquity. This epigraphy is invaluable, as it allows us to reconstruct the only definite, albeit short, sequence of the sovereigns of the independent kingdom of Ḥaḍramawt[20].

A rite called "the incantation of the names" was repeatedly celebrated here by king Il'azz Yaluṭ son of Amdhakhar, his successor Yada'īl Bayyin son of Rabshams, and by his successor Ilriyam Yadum son of Yada'īl Bayyin, and his brother Rabshams.

We do not know the exact details of this rite, but we know that it was very high profile, since the inscriptions show that besides the sovereign, a host of important people in the Hadrami court were invited to attend, along with various foreign guests who were probably ambassadors (Himyarites, Palmyrans, Chaldeans and Indians).

The inscriptions on the rock at Al-'Uqlah date back to the third century AD. The information that they provide can be added to that provided by all the Sabaean and Himyarite texṭs that we have from this period, some of which are even dated. As we shall see in the next chapter, this gives us the opportunity to investigate a period of history in which the events that shaped the ancient kingdoms of Arabia finally start to take on a more satisfying, possibly more human, character.

Footnotes:

1. Mlaker, K., *Die Hierodulenlisten von Ma'īn, nebst Untersuchungen zur alts Ädarabischen Rechtsgeschichte und Chronologie* (Leipzig: Harrassowitz, 1943), p. 84.

2. Albright, W.F., "Recensione à J. Ryckmans 1951", *JAOS* 73 (1953), p. 40.
3. Beeston, A., "Problems in Sabaean Chronology", *BSOAS* 16 (1954), p. 42.
4. Ibid, p. 50-51.
5. Ryckmans, J., *L'institution monarchique en Arabie méridionale avant l'Islam* (Louvain: Publications universitaires, 1951), p. 337.
6. Ibid, p. 127.
7. Albright, W.F., "The Chronology of Ancient South Arabia in the Light of the First Campaign of Excavation in Qatabān", *BASOR* 119 (1950), p. 5-15.
8. Beeston, A., "Kataban", in *Encyclopédie de l'Islam, Nuova Series, vol. VI* (1976), p. 776.
9. Ibid, p. 778.
10. Ibid, p. 777.
11. de Maigret, A. and Robin, C., "Les fouilles italiennes de Yalā (Yémen du Nord): nouvelles données sur la chronologie de l'Arabie du Sud préislamiques", *CRAIBL* (1989), p. 267.
12. Beeston, A., "Ma'īn", *Encyclopédie de l'Islam, Nuova Serie, vol. VI*, p. 86.
13. de Maigret, A., and Robin, C., "Les fouilles italiennes de Yalā", p. 270.
14. Gnoli, G., "Il sincronismo mineo-persiano", in Robin (ed.), *Arabia Antiqua. Early Origins of the South Arabian States* (Rome: IsMEO, 1996), p. 23-34.
15. de Maigret, A. and Robin C., "Les fouilles italiennes de Yalā", p. 268.
16. Robin, C., *L'Arabie antique de Karib'īl à Mahomet. Nouvelles données sur l'histoire des Arabes grace aux inscriptions* (Aix-en-Provence: 1991-93), p. 63, 77.
17. von Wissman, H., "Al-Barira in Girdan im Vergleich mit anderen Stadtfestungen Alt-Südarabiens", *Le Muséon* 75 (1962), p. 177-209.
18. Doe, B. *Monuments of South Arabia* (Naples: Falcon, 1983), p. 142-44.
19. Philby, H., *Sheba's Daughters, Being a Record of Travel in Southern Arabia* (London: Methuen & Co., 1939), p. 313.
20. Jamme, A. *The Al-'Uqlah Texts* (Washington: Catholic University of America Press, 1963).

XII

THE MOUNTAIN KINGDOMS AND THE KINGS OF SABA AND DHŪ-RAYDĀN

The Question of Royal Titles

As we have seen, we have very few dates for the period of the kings of Saba and for the earlier period of the *mukarribs*. Even the dates we do have are subject to opinion and alternative interpretations. Dividing history into periods according to the title of the sovereign is a completely arbitrary method, and we risk making serious mistakes. Let us illustrate this by looking at one revealing example.

In his authoritative work, "L'institution monarchique en Arabie méridionale avant l'Islam"(1951), Jacques Ryckmans bases his arguments on the title *mlk sb'* (king of Saba) and adds an extra king, Nasha' Karib Yuha'min, to the "traditional" Sabaean dynasty, thereby making it end in 115 BC (whereas we would now say 110 BC). According to his reconstruction, the dynasty of the kings of Saba continued, absorbing sovereigns from other tribal dynasties (Hamdān, Hashid and Bakil), until 25 BC when Ilsharaḥ Yaḥḍub (identifiable as Ilasaros, the king who, according to Strabo, governed Mārib at the time of Aelius Gallus' siege) became the first sovereign to use the title "king of Saba and Dhū-Raydān". This new dynasty comprised 21 sovereigns, ending with King Shamir Yuhar'ish towards AD 300.

In 1956 Jacqueline Pirenne caused an uproar with her comments on an inscription that had been published by Gonzague Ryckmans (Ry 535)[1]. The palaeography showed, beyond a shadow of a doubt, that king Ilsharaḥ Yaḥḍub was a contemporary of king Shamir Yuhar''ish[2]. There was good reason to be surprised. The first sovereign of the dynasty of the kings of Saba and Dhū-Raydān, which lasted approximately four centuries, seemed to be contemporary with the last! The whole chronology, which had been so painstakingly pieced together, crumbled away. The process had to start all over again, and it was not going to be easy.

As Pirenne herself observed, the main reason for this error was that scholars' understandable desire for order had meant that the various titles of the Sabaean rulers had always been seen as a sequence. Thus the *mukarribs* of Saba would be succeeded by the kings of Saba, who would in turn be succeeded by the kings of Saba and Dhū-Raydān, and finally the kings of Saba and Dhū-Raydān, Ḥaḍramawt and Yamanat. As a promoter of the *short chronology*, Pirenne naturally blamed this on those who searched too hard within the various dynasties for names to fill in the empty centuries.

In the same year, Pirenne published her famous *Paléographie des Inscriptions Sud-Arabes*, giving herself another chance to prove that the historical revolution which she was proposing was entirely backed up by the sequence of the South Arabian sovereigns established by the palaeographic study of the inscriptions. Never had Europe been so unanimously in favour of the *short chronology*.

Jacques Ryckmans, meanwhile, began to revise his chronology in the light of the new Mārib texts. He tried to use different criteria to reorganise the dynastic succession of the kings of Saba (the ones that he called the Hamdānī dynasties, successors to the traditional dynasty) and the kings of Saba and Dhū-Raydān[3].

In 1962 Albert Jamme published the great cache of inscriptions discovered during the excavation of Maḥrām Bilqīs at Mārib[4], greatly increasing the number of sovereigns known to us. This clearly showed that the dynastic situation after 110 BC – the conventional date for the start of the period of the kings of Saba and Dhū-Raydān – was a lot more complicated than people had assumed a few years earlier.

This now extensive list of sovereigns' names, together with the shortening of the chronology, convinced J. Ryckmans not only that the kings of Saba were contemporary with the kings of Saba and Dhū-Raydān, but also that several parallel lineages existed alongside each other, each headed by its own ruler. This was the basis for his important work of 1964, in which he outlined the multitude of contemporary royal lines[5].

However, that same year scholars like von Wissmann embarked on the difficult task of reducing the number of dynasties[6], maybe because they saw that it was absurd to have several branches reigning at the same time. It was becoming clear that – contrary to Jamme's assertions – the title of "king

	SABA	ḤIMYAR	ḤAḌRAMAWT	QATABĀN
		110 Start of the dynasty		
24	Elius Gallus' expedition			
	Dhamar'ali Watar Yuhan'im Dhamar'alī Bayyin Karib'il Watar Yuhan'im I (Charibael?) Dhamar'alī Dharih Karib'il Bayyin (Charibael?) Nasha'karib Yuha'min 'Amdan Bayyin Yuhaqbiḍ	Sabaean sovereignty Independent kingdom	Yada''il Il'azz Yaluṭ (Eleazos)	
153	Ilsharaḥ Yaḥḍub I Watar Yuha'min Sa'dshams Asra' Marthad Yuhaḥmid Wahab'īl Yaḥūz Anmar Yuha'min Karib'il Watar Yuhan'im II Yarim Ayman	Yāsir Yuhaṣdiq Shamir Dhamar'ali Yuhabirr	Yada''īl	Nabaṭ End of **Qatabān**
Suwa'rān: 222 …-Ḥurma: 253	'Alhān Nahfān Sha'r Awtar Laḥay'athat Yarkham Fari' Yanhub Ilsharaḥ Yaḥḍub II Yazil Bayyin Nasha'karib Yuha'min Yuharhib	Tha'rān Ya'ub Yuha'min Li'azz Yuhanif Yuhaṣdiq Shamir Yuhaḥmid Karib'il Ayfa' Yasir Yuhan'im Shamir Yuhar'ish	Yada''ab Ghaylān Yada''il Il'azz Yaluṭ *(fall of Shabwa)* Yada''īl Bayyin Ilriyam Yadum	
End	of **Saba**	End of the **Ḥaḍramawt**		

Table 7

The mountain kingdoms in the period of the kings of Saba and Dhū-Raydān

of Saba and Dhū-Raydān" was not used exclusively by sovereigns of the highlands of Yemen, but also by those further north, who ruled Saba. Both rulers would claim the right to use the double title on accession to the throne of their kingdom, in a transparent attempt to gain control over the other. The difficulty now was to decipher which of these reigned at Mārib (Saba) and which at Ẓafār (Ḥimyar), and to establish the exact order of their dynasties.

However, the information provided by the various inscriptions for these later periods, which referred to particular eras, had still not been given definitive values. Alongside a long timescale, known as the Mabḥuḍ ibn Abḥaḍ, or Himyarite chronology (which probably started around 110 BC), we also had a shorter scale called the Ab'ali, or Hadrami chronology, whose origins are uncertain and controversial[7]. For a couple of decades the whole affair was clouded by confusion and uncertainty, until an important discovery in 1980 cleared up a lot of the problems.

The French epigraphist Christian Robin, probably aware of the strong differences that characterise written evidence in South Arabia (mostly found in Sabaean territory), set out in 1978 to explore the province of Al-Bayḍā in the south-east of North Yemen, seeking direct testimonies from the people of Ḥimyar. In 1980, near the ancient city of Wa'lan (now occupied by Al-Mi'sāl), he found what he was looking for.

On one of the sides of a rocky outcrop, whose summit held an ancient temple dedicated to the sun goddess Shams, Robin made out some inscriptions which, as he would declare during a 1981 conference at the Académie des Inscriptions et Belles-Lettres in Paris, turned out to be critically important for the chronology and history of South Arabia.

To start with, one of these inscriptions provided the first ever double date: "79 of the Ab'ali era, which in the calculation of Ḥimyar corresponds to 363 of the Mabḥuḍ era...[8]." In this year, a certain Laḥay'at Awkan, *qayl* (or prince) of the Himyarite tribe Radmān and Khawlān, gave thanks to Shams for his safe return from a battle between Karib'īl Ayfa', king of Saba and Dhū-Raydān; and Ilsharaḥ Yaḥḍub, king of Saba.

If the Himyarite era began in 110 BC, this year must have been AD 253, and the Ab'ali era (which, from the time the inscriptions were discovered, would be called the Radmanite era rather than the "Hadrami era") must, without a doubt, have begun in AD 74[9].

The amazing thing was that, besides giving these absolute dates, the Al-Mi'sāl inscriptions also provided a complete sequence of three Himyarite sovereigns, and their contemporaneity with three kings of Ḥaḍramawt and a king of Saba. Although these are ruling dynasties of a fairly late period (third century AD), we finally had a series of definitively dated events in the history of South Arabia (Table 7).

Moreover, these texts bore the full names of each Himyarite sovereign. The Mārib inscriptions, which provided the names of the Sabaean sovereigns in full, actually abbreviated names and titles when referring to enemies. So the references to "Karib'īl Dhū-Raydān" or

"Shamir Dhū-Raydān", which were associated with the most varied epithets until the Al-Mi'sāl discovery, and therefore referred to different people, came to take on precise, undeniable significance: Karib'īl was identified with certainty as Karib'īl Ayfa', the king who fought the Dhū Hurma battle against Ilsharaḥ Yaḥḍub of Saba at the time of Yada'īl Bayyin king of Ḥaḍramawt; and Shamir became recognised as Shamir Yuhaḥmid, the predecessor of Karib'īl Ayfa'. It is worth noting that until that point, Shamir had always been thought of as Shamir Yuhar'ish, the sovereign who ruled later, at the start of the period of the Himyarite Empire[10].

Furthermore, the Al-Mi'sāl texts provided useful information on the kingdom of the Ḥaḍramawt. In one of them (MAFRAY-al-Mi'sāl 4), a certain Naṣir Yuhaḥmid, *qayl* of Radmān and Khawlān, thanks the sun goddess for having helped him and favoured him when he took 1500 warriors, 20 cavaliers and 800 cameleers to the aid of Il'azz Yaluṭ king of the Ḥaḍramawt to suppress a revolt by the Yuhab'ir tribe. Having reached Shabwat and joined forces with other allies of the king (including Qatabān), Naṣir defeated the rebels at the battle of Suwa'ran and returned home in glory. This was in the year 148, although we are not sure of which era. It would, however, be logical to assume that it was the era of Ab'ali, in other words, the victory occurred in AD 222. As a result, the Hadrami dynasty documented by the Al'-Uqlah texts could now be based on a solid date, and besides, the basic elements were now in place to establish the precise order of succession of this kingdom's sovereigns (Il'azz Yaluṭ, Yada'īl Bayyin, Ilriyam Yadum)[11].

This opportunity to reconstruct the genealogy of the sovereigns of Ḥimyar and Ḥaḍramawt also made it possible to establish the sequence of the kings of Saba of this period, which had been disputed for years without anyone ever reaching any definitive conclusions. Kings like 'Alhān Nahfān, Sha'r Awtar, Fari' Yanhub, and Ilsharaḥ Yaḥḍub himself, who had all either been allotted random dates or been lumped together until this point, were finally given their fixed position in history (Table 7).

It was beginning to seem possible that we could reduce the length of time which encompassed two very important events: the end of the kingdom of Qatabān (which Robin places between AD 160 and 210, much later than the date given by the American archaeologists at Timna‘); and the end of the kingdom of Saba (which Robin places between AD 270 and 280). Even the famous attack on Shabwat, waged by the Sabaean king Sha‘r Awtar against king Il‘azz Yaluṭ, which resulted in the destruction of the Hadrami army, the burning of the city, the king's capture and the massacre of his sons and dignitaries, could finally be dated, with some certainty, to around AD 225[12].

Thanks to the Mārib texts, the third century AD was the most thoroughly documented period of the history of South Arabia. While the key events of this period had begun to take shape, other (especially earlier) events still had to be discovered.

It must be said, too, that the Al-Mi‘sāl experience had taught us an invaluable lesson about methodology. We had fallen into the trap of limiting ourselves to royal inscriptions in our attempt to establish dynastic succession. Now we could prove that, by examining inscriptions made by lesser citizens like the Himyarite *qayls*, we would be able to reconstruct the dynastic succession of princes and tribal leaders. These inscriptions, thanks to their historical references to sovereigns and especially to their dates, actually constituted invaluable, parallel historical frameworks which could be used to challenge earlier, controversial theories regarding the royal dynasties.

The *qayls* of Radmān and Khawlān helped to clarify the history of the third century AD, with their meticulous records of the dates of their enterprises. They had, it appears, always had this desire for precision. Indeed, Robin was delighted to find an inscription among the ruins of a building which was being dismantled by the inhabitants of a village called "Irq Sāri‘", not far from Al-Mi‘sāl. In this brief inscription, Wahab‘īl Yahuz, *qayl* of the tribes of Radmān and Khawlān, is said to have dug a well in the arzea in the year 72[13]. This must have been the era of Ab‘alaī, which was the era used by the Radmān tribe, and so Wahab‘īl must have lived in about AD 146.

Despite lacking any references to sovereigns, this inscription turned out to be of vital importance, as it was the oldest dated inscription ever found in southern Arabia. Wahab‘īl Yahuz was not an entirely unknown character. Other inscriptions had placed him alongside the Sabaean sovereigns Sa'dshams Asra' and Marthad Yuhaḥmid, who had not previously been given any firm dates. So, we now also had some initial points of reference for the second century AD.

The Title of "King of Saba and Dhū-Raydān"

In an attempt to penetrate further back in time and so get closer to the start of the kingdom of Saba and Dhū-Raydān, Robin spent these years continuing his search for the missing inscriptions of Yemen. In 1981, together with the archaeologist Jean-Francois Breton, he investigated an important site on Jabal al-Lawdh, the mountain that dominates the entrance to the Jawf valley from the north[14]. Their study of the ruins and the mass of epigraphy proved that this was an ancient sanctuary which had been used by several *mukarribs* (among them Karib'īl Watar) to celebrate two particular ceremonies: the ritual banquet and the federation pact. The place had then fallen into disuse for many centuries, until Dhamār'ali Watar Yuhani'm, king of Saba and Dhū-Raydān, a hitherto almost unknown sovereign, returned there to practise the same rites.

A study of the palaeography of the many texts produced by this king that were found within the sanctuary proved beyond a doubt that he is the earliest known king of Saba and Dhu-Raydān. He must have ruled during the first decades of the 'decadent era'.

Dhamār'ali Watar Yuhan'im's return to the Jabal al-Lawdh sanctuary must be seen in the context of the rites celebrated there by his forefathers, the *mukarribs* of Saba. The ritual banquet and the federation pact were intended to seal political unity between tribes in the sight of the gods. These rites were the basis of Karib'īl Watar's powerful empire and the great *mukarrib* celebrated them here, in this sanctuary. Dhamār'ali Watar Yuhan'im, a Sabaean with a typically Sabaean first name and epithet, adopted a second epithet from Qatabanian tradition, which later became common to Ḥimyar. In so doing, he demonstrated his intention to unite the lands of the north and south. He reinstated his ancestors' rites and travelled to the sanctuary at Jabal al-Lawdh to legitimise his ambitious, daring investiture in the most authoritative way imaginable[15].

Here we have a glimpse of the origins of the kingdom of

Saba and Dhū-Raydān. After a period of obscurity – of which we know almost nothing – a Sabaean king (probably Dhamār'ali Watar Yuhan'im himself) attempted to restore what had once been the empire of the *mukarribs*. But as is obvious from the double title (Saba and Dhū-Raydān), the empire was destined to stay divided for some time to come. Ironically, the Himyarite king Shamir Yuhar'ish, an enemy of Saba, was actually the first to achieve uncontested hegemony over the whole of Yemen, at the end of the third century AD.

We have already seen that the Himyarite dynasty began in 110 BC. Although the date is still contested[16], it resulted from a study of three long rock carvings found in 1951, just north of Najrān in Saudi Arabia, by the Lippens-Philby-Ryckmans expedition. Two of these inscriptions (Ry 507 and Ry 508) were found at Bīr Hima and Jabal Kawkab[17], and a third, also from Bīr Hima (Ja 1028), was later published by Jamme[18]. The inscriptions refer to military operations carried out in the region by the Himyarite king Yusuf As'ar Yath'ar (more commonly known as Dhū-Nuwās) and all carry the date 633 of the Himyarite era. Since we know that these events occurred in the same year that Dhū-Nuwās launched his terrible persecution of the Christians of Najrān and that the latter took place in AD 523, we can fix the first year of the Himyarite era at 110 BC (633-523=110).

But we cannot possibly go back through the ages and reconstruct a definitive Himyarite dynasty ending in 110 BC. By the time the Ḥimyar clan decided to measure the years in this way, the era must have been well advanced. (The earliest date given for the Mabḥuḍ ibn Abḥaḍ, or Himyarite era dates to AD 253, in other words, a good 363 years after its start.) In fact, the starting point for the era was probably a date chosen precisely on account of its established and authoritative antiquity.

So, later genealogical reconstructions, based on memory, pushed the origins of the Himyarite era as far back into the mists of time as possible, in order to lend it an aura of unquestionable legitimacy. Moreover, even if this is the correct family tree and began around 110 BC, we cannot be sure that the founding members were important enough people to leave their names carved in stone. It seems pointless, therefore, to search for the ancestors of the kings of Saba and Dhū-Raydān that far back in time.

The First Century AD *and Ḥimyar's Political Independence*

At this point it seems reasonable to ask two questions. Firstly, who were these kings of Saba and Dhū-Raydān? And secondly, who were the Himyarites? In answer to the first question, we should bear in mind that "king of Saba and Dhū-Raydān" was only a royal title and had no precise ethno-social connotations. We know that the title was used by both the Sabaean and the Himyarite kings, and that they used it to claim governance over the two socio-political entities that made up the country. As we have seen, the first sovereign documented as using the title was Dhamār'ali Watar Yuhan'im. Both the name and epithet are traditional, and we would probably not be wrong in classifying him as one of the last kings of Saba. But it is clear that the country was fearfully divided at this time (as we see in the feeble resistance offered to Aelius Gallus' expedition in the Jawf in 24 BC). The tribes gravitated towards two principal political centres, one in the region of the old kingdom of Saba and the other in the southern highlands of Yemen. Dhamār'ali Watar added to his title of "king of Saba" that of "king of Dhū-Raydān" (and was he really the first?) in an attempt to reunite the whole country under his control. His choice of Yuhan'im as his second epithet seemed to legitimise his claim, as the name (which had never before appeared in the history of Saba) was of southern origin[19].

It appears, then, that Himyarite kings never governed the whole country, or at least, that they never tried to gain control over the whole country by using, or usurping, the title of "king of Saba and Dhū-Raydān" already used by Sabaean kings. Indeed there is no reason to believe that there were any Himyarites among the Sabaean rulers of the first century AD: Dhamār'ali Watar Yuhan'im, Dhamār, Karib'īl Watar Yuhan'im I (the founder of Ṣan'ā and probably the Charibael of *Periplus of the Erythraean Sea*), Dhamār'ali Dhariḥ, Karib'īl Bayyin and Nasha'Karib Yuha'min.

So who exactly were the Himyarites? Alfred Beeston was amazed to find no mention of a "king of the Himyarites" in the inscriptions, at least not in those of the first three centuries of our era[20]. Locally, the references are always to the "*qayl* and the tribes of Ḥimyar", and never to a sovereign of the Himyarites. This was clearly a collective term to denote a group of tribes that occupied the south-east highlands of Yemen of which Ḥimyar was the most prominent. Most scholars agree that as a political entity, Ḥimyar probably came into existence during the first century BC after breaking away from the kingdom of Qatabān. It is no coincidence that the second epithet used by the Sabaean kings to vindicate their hegemonic control over the Himyarite tribes was of Qatabanian origin and that the cult of the god 'Amm was equally popular in Qatabān and Ḥimyar. It probably took some time for tribes with strong and powerful *qayls* to set up a unified government and, while they defined themselves as "Himyarites" as a whole, it probably wasn't until they were threatened by the expansionism of the kings of Saba that they achieved real political unity.

A further point of interest is that while this kind of political unity had previously been expressed in the name of a deity, it is now made explicit by using the name of the palace. In fact, the palace of Raydān at Ẓafār was the symbol of power that was recognised by all the tribes[21].

The Himyarites must have reached this level of political unity by the time that classical authors began to write of a Himyarite nation. Pliny the Elder uses the expression, as does the anonymous author of the *Periplus of the Erythraean Sea* – which probably dates from the first century AD – and speaks of a "Charibael, legitimate king of the two nations (*ethne*), the Himyarites and their neighbours, who are called Sabaeans"[22]. However, if we are right in thinking that the kings of the first century AD all belonged to a Sabaean dynasty, it means that the tribes of the southern highlands were still under the hegemony of the sovereigns of Mārib. This situation did not last for long.

After Nasha'Karib Yuha'min, the last king of the Sabaean dynasty, the throne of Saba and Dhū-Raydān was taken by 'Amdan Bayyin Yuhaqbiḍ, the first sovereign to omit his father's name in epigraphy[23]. This fact (which was until very recently a serious hindrance to those trying to establish his place within the dynastic sequence), along with his unusual name ('Amdan), which represented a dramatic break with the onomastic tradition observed since the beginnings of the Sabaean state, seems to indicate that 'Amdan was not in fact Sabaean. The fact that his rule was accepted by the south, and that he had various coins made bearing the name "Raydān" on the reverse actually leads us to assume that he was of Himyarite descent.

A king from the highlands was now on the throne, marking a sudden break in tradition. This was the end of the first century AD and after the reign of ‘Amdan Bayyin Yuhaqbiḍ, Ḥimyar gained a certain political independence from Saba. Texts from this time onwards bear the names of kings belonging to two parallel dynasties who, on account of their bitter antagonism and constant desire for retaliation, both vociferously laid claim to the double title of “king of Saba and Dhū-Raydān”.

We can therefore classify the period of the kings of Saba and Dhū-Raydān up to and including the reign of ‘Amdan Bayyin Yuhaqbiḍ, i.e. until AD 100-120, as a monarchy united first under the sovereigns of Mārib and then under a sovereign of Ḥimyar.

South Arabia entered a period of crisis in the first century BC. This appears to be proven by three things: the end of the kingdom of Ma‘īn, the Himyarite tribes' breakaway from the kingdom of Qatabān and the Roman invasion of the Jawf. However, the period immediately after this saw a resurgence in Sabaean power and a steady increase in their influence in the western highlands (the foundation of Ṣan‘ā), alongside a gradual increase in Ḥimyar's political power. The first century AD was a time of prosperity in Yemen under this united monarchy of the kings of Saba and Dhū-Raydān, as is shown by the quantity of coins minted by Karib'īl Watar Yuhan‘im and ‘Amdan Bayyin Yuhaqbiḍ, and by the great water works that covered every corner of the southern highlands. The highlands and the coast became the focal points for politics and economics, which had previously centred on the desert. The old caravan route inland was no longer the main commercial route between the Erythrean Sea and the Mediterranean Sea. This is most clearly demonstrated by the crisis that hit Ma‘īn and Qatabān[24].

On the other hand, we know that in this period Ḥimyar's sphere of influence spread south and south-west as far as the shores of the Indian Ocean and the Red Sea, which was also by now the centre for the incense trade. The anonymous author of the *Periplus of the Erythrean Sea* informs us that Ḥimyar controlled Eudaemon Arabia (Aden), as well as the province of Ma'afaritide (southern

Tihāmah) and its important port, Mawza'. There must have been bitter political struggles with the old enemy, the kingdom of the Ḥaḍramawt, for control over Qana, the main port on the south coast of the Arabian Peninsula.

Saba was the only state with no commercial outlet on the coast. But it managed to keep afloat, possibly thanks to its increased hegemony in the highlands of Ṣan'ā and its fragile political alliances with the Himyarite tribes in the south, and so was able to directly influence the new directors of maritime commerce. But as time passed, Saba had an increasingly high price to pay for its diplomatic alliances. 'Amdan Bayyin's accession to the throne probably spelled the end of Saba's upper hand in its political coalition with Ḥimyar, which the Mārib dynasties had preserved on account of their great tradition, but which actually lacked the economic stability that was increasingly becoming Ḥimyar's strong point. There was only a short gap between the end of this political hegemony and the start of Ḥimyar's independence.

Parallel Kingdoms: Saba and Ḥimyar During the Second Century AD

At the start of the second century AD, two separate kingdoms were in violent opposition; Mārib was the capital of one and Ẓafār was capital of the other. Texts from Mārib enable us to reconstruct the royal Sabaean dynasty up to the beginning of the third century: Ilsharaḥ Yaḥḍub I, Watar Yuha'min, Sa'dshams Asra', Marthad Yuhaḥmid, Wahab'īl Yahuz, Anmar Yuha'min, Karib'īl Watar Yuhan'im II and Yarīm Ayman. Meanwhile, texts found in Himyarite territory give us the names of the contemporary governors of Ẓafār: Yāsir Yuhasdiq, Shamir, Dhamār'ali Yuhabirr, and Tha'ran Ya'ub Yuha'min. As we have already seen, both of these dynasties claimed the title "king of Saba and Dhū-Raydān", even if some claimants to the throne of Saba still used the title "king of Saba", which made it so difficult to reconstruct the two dynasties. There are significantly fewer texts for the Himyarite line, though, which may mean that it is not complete.

We know very little about the second century AD, but

there seems to have been no single dominant force and bitter, bloody battles were fought between the various pretenders (Saba, Ḥimyar, Ḥaḍramawt and Qatabān). A lengthy inscription by the Awwam temple in Mārib reports a battle fought near Wa'lān by the Sabaean king Sa'dshams Asra' and his son Marthad Yuhaḥmid against a coalition of Himyarite tribes (Ma'ahir, Khawlān, Radmān, Mudhay), Ḥaḍramawt (with king Yada'īl) and Qatabān (with king Nabaṭ). We can probably date this battle, which ended in a victory for the Sabaeans, by considering the name of the *qayl* at the head of the Himyarite tribes, namely Wahab'īl. If he is in fact the same Wahab'īl Yahuz mentioned in the inscription that Robin found in the village of Al-Irq, near Wa'lan, the battle cannot have happened much before (or much after) AD 146[25].

These wars for supremacy were never decisive, though, maybe due to the internal political weakness of the two main rivals. Besides, we know that at this time some tribes in the Yemeni highlands were trying to assert their authority against that of Saba and Ḥimyar: the Banū Bata of Hāz, the Hamdānīdi of Na'it, the Marthad of 'Amrān, and the Giuratidi of Jabal Kanin (Na'd)[26].

In the meantime, the kingdom of Ḥaḍramawt was gaining strength, and enjoying its position of power over the principal caravan routes. We know that in the first century AD, it had successfully challenged Ḥimyar's growing power on the coast, building the barrier known as Qalat (RES 2687) – modern-day Al-Binā – to protect its own monopoly of the port of Qana, as well as delivering a serious blow to Qatabān by destroying the capital Timna'. King Il'azz Yaluṭ (probably Eleazos of the *Periplus*) had consolidated his power over Sa'kalan (now Dhofār) and founded the fortified city of Samhar (Khawr Rūrī), guaranteeing his kingdom control over the incense trade right from its sources. Then, at the end of the second century AD, Ḥaḍramawt delivered the final blow to Qatabān and this great South Arabian kingdom was never again mentioned in inscriptions. Its annexation by Ḥaḍramawt was a definitive victory for the "kingdom of incense" which, along with Saba and Ḥimyar, played an important part in the best-known period of South Arabian history, the third century AD.

The First Ethiopian Invasion and Events of the Third Century AD

The endless conflicts that characterised the second century AD in Yemen had obviously weakened the power of Saba and Ḥimyar. In fact, the start of the third century found western Yemen (Tihāmah) under Ethiopian rule. An inscription from this period (CIS 308) records a pact of alliance made between ʻAlhān Nahfān, king of Saba, and Gadūrat king of Abyssinia and Aksum, finally spelling the end of a long conflict (Plate 45). African expansionism

Plate 45
The Sabaean inscription CIS 308 from Riyām

surely posed a serious threat and so Sha'r Awtar, son of 'Alfan Nahfān, annulled the pact and declared war again[28].

But just before this, Sha'r Awtar had had to confront the other great power of the time, the kingdom of Ḥaḍramawt. He mounted a sudden expedition in about AD 225 against the Hadrami king Il'azz Yaluṭ, fighting him at the battle of Dhat-Ghayl (in ex-Qatabanian territory), capturing him and taking him to Mārib as hostage. His son was killed, and Shabwat was taken, and razed to the ground[29].

This expedition may well have been revenge for Ḥimyar's diplomatic/military policies which, a few years previously (in AD 222) had helped the Hadrami king Il'azz Yaluṭ to repress a revolt of Himyarite tribes headed by the Yuhab'ir tribe. We have already looked at the battle of Suwa'ran, during which the Himyarites and Qatabanians (this is the last mention of Qatabān in the inscriptions) helped the king of the Ḥaḍramawt at a difficult moment for his internal politics, ensuring a solid alliance. So, a few years later, Saba clearly intervened in order to balance out the forces. Il'azz Yaluṭ's capture by Sha'r Awtar effectively put an end to the unstable political alliance created between Shabwat and Ẓafār and to guarantee this, the Sabaean king placed Yada'īl Bayyin of the Yuhab'iridi tribe, which had led the revolt against Il'azz Yaluṭ, on the throne of Ḥaḍramawt.

Sha'r Awtar was a powerful and warlike king. Besides Ethiopia and Ḥaḍramawt, he fought the Arab tribes of central Arabia, who had started to gather threateningly close to the foothills of the Yemeni mountains. One inscription (Ja 635) testifies to a battle at Qaryat dhāt- Kāhilim (now the site of Qaryat al-Fāw) between the Sabaean king and the king of Kinda and Qaḥṭān[30].

The fact that Sha'r Awtar was able to throw himself into all these different important battles shows that his greatest enemy, the kingdom of Ḥimyar, did not pose an immediate threat at this point. At this time, the Dhū-Raydān tribes were actually mainly occupied in defending their territory against Ethiopian invasions, which crept upwards from the Tihāmah, advancing on the highlands and menacing the very existence of their capital. We know that around AD 240 the Abyssinians, led by Bayga, son of the Ethiopian ruler 'Adheba, occupied Ẓafār, and that from then on the Himyarites were bound to Ethiopia by a pact of alliance.

This was a time of profound weakness for Ẓafār's government, and the Ethiopians may well have managed to put a king on the throne of Ḥimyar who was favourable to them. Political relations with Aksum changed when Karib'īl Ayfa' came to the throne, and the hostilities between Himyarites and Abyssinians restarted. The Ẓafār area was occupied on several further occasions and there were more confrontations with Yāsir Yuhan'im, the successor to Karib'īl Ayfa'.

Shortly after this, Saba undertook some successful military campaigns against king Ilsharaḥ Yaḥḍub II, son of Fari' Yahnub, who reigned together with his brother Yazil Bayyin over a long period. This success may have been partly due to the crisis inflicted on Ḥimyar by the Abyssinians.

Some lengthy inscriptions discovered at Mārib (Ja 574, 576, 577 and 600) tell us that Ilsharaḥ Yaḥḍub and his brother were helped by the god Almaqah to defeat "all the armies and tribes that rose in battle against them, tribes from the north and south, from sea and land". They also led a campaign against Najrān, chasing out the Abyssinians, and we know that they sent envoys to the volatile desert Arabs. It was at this point that the Ethiopian king 'Adheba gained control of the Himyarites and it was probably he who put Shamir Yuhaḥmid, then king of Ẓafār, on the throne.

With the defeat of Ḥimyar and Karib'īl Ayfa's accession to the throne, Ilsharaḥ Yaḥḍub turned to the south and met the new sovereign at the battle of Dhū-Hurma (AD 253). This encounter did not have a decisive outcome, as is obvious from the different accounts of it written by the two sides. The Sabaeans said: "Karib'īl Dhū-Raydān was expelled from the citadel of Usi and from Qarnanahan along with his tribes and his army and made for 'Arawshat, Ẓalman and Hakir." (Ja 578)

The Himyarites said: "After the battle, the king of Saba, along with his army, returned three times and then went back home; while lord Karib'īl Ayfa' and his army, the forces of Ḥimyar, stayed there as long as it pleased them, and then returned to the city of Hakir bearing trophies, men and horses both dead and alive[31]."

Ilsharaḥ Yaḥḍub was fighting a battle over an extensive area. Not even the Ḥaḍramawt, home of kings

Yada'īl Bayyin and Ilriyam Yadum, was safe. While on the one hand this apparently increased his fame as a warrior and last great sovereign of Saba, on the other it marked a period of profound crisis for the Sabaean kingdom. Admittedly, the war against Ḥimyar was set to continue for several decades more, but Īlsharaḥ Yaḥḍub's successor, Nasha'Karib Yuha'min Yuharhib, could do very little against the aggressive descendants of Karib'īl Ayfa': Yāsir Yuhan'im and Shamir Yuhar'ish.

The End of Saba

The kingdom of Saba was now suffering badly as a result of the decline of the caravan trade. While the Himyarite economy was gathering strength all the time thanks to the flourishing commercial activity of its ports (especially trade with the Roman Empire), the Sabaean economy was becoming gradually weaker. Ilsharaḥ Yaḥḍub's campaigns were simply a last-ditch attempt by the glorious Sabaean kingdom to save itself from the clutches of its enemies who were closing in on every side: Abyssinia to the west, Ḥimyar to the south, Ḥaḍramawt to the east and the Arab kingdoms of central Arabia to the north.

Nomads encroaching on Sabaean territory must have posed a particularly serious problem. We know that bedouin tribes had always lived in the Ṣayhad desert, but since they too made a profit from the steady stream of caravans (although we don't know if this was direct or via the kingdoms), they had never before given the settled southern Arabs any cause for alarm. When this commerce dried up, and along with it their livelihood, the nomads of the north-eastern deserts began to converge menacingly in the valleys at the foot of the Yemeni mountains, encroaching on Sabaean territory (and possibly also Hadrami territory). A report from this time tells of Arab mercenaries joining the South Arabian armies. Their gradual infiltration may have caused the social breakdown that occurred in the internal organisation of the tribes and tribal confederations, shown, for example, by the end of the traditional cults that were common to each tribal group[32].

Interestingly, the third century AD also saw the

development of new military techniques. The previous century had seen the widespread diffusion of horses throughout South Arabia and armies now had the advantage of a cavalry which, although not very large, could be the deciding factor in a battle. The horses were a result of maritime commerce and clearly the people most likely to benefit from this precious resource were the Himyarites.

Around AD 270-280, however, the kingdom of Saba collapsed, and was annexed to the kingdom of Ḥimyar by Yāsir Yuhan'im and Shamir Yuhar'ish, who were co-rulers at the time. Shortly afterwards (between AD 280 and 295), Shamir Yuhar'ish took the kingdom of Ḥaḍramawt and gave himself the pompous title of "king of Saba and Dhū-Raydān, Ḥaḍramawt and Yamanat", boasting that he had total control over an area that had not been united since the days of the Sabaean *mukarribs*.

Footnotes:

1. Ryckmans, G., "Inscriptions sud-arabes, treiziéme série", *Le Muséon* 69 (1956), p. 139-163.
2. Pirenne, J., "L'inscription 'Ryckmans 535' et la chronologie sud-arabe", *Le Muséon* 69 (1956), p. 165-181.
3. Ryckmans, J., "Chronologie des rois de Saba et Dhu Raydān", *OA* 3 (1964), 67-90; and *La chronologie des rois de Saba et Dhu Raydān* (Istanbul: Nederlands Historisch-Archaeologisch Instituut, 1964).
4. Jamme, A., *Sabaean Inscriptions from Maḥrām Bilqīs* (Mārib) (Baltimore: Johns Hopkins Press, 1962).
5. Ryckmans, J., *La chronologie des rois de Saba et Dhu Raydān*, tables I-II.
6. von Wissman, H., *Zur Geschichte und Landeskunde von Alt-Südarabien* (Wien: H. Bohlaus Nachf, 1964).
7. Beeston, A., *Epigraphic South Arabian Calendars and Dating* (London: Luzac, 1956), p. 35.
8. Robin, C., "Les inscriptions d'al-Mi'sāl et la chronologie de l'Arabie méridionale au III siècle de l'ère chrétienne", *CRAIBL* (1981), p. 323.
9. Ibid. p. 331-332.

10. Pirenne, "L'inscription 'Ryckmans 535'", p. 179.
11. Robin, C., "Les inscriptions d'al-Mi'sāl", p. 326, 334.
12. Ibid, p. 332.
13. Robin, C. and Bafaqīh, M., "Deux nouvelles inscriptions de Radmān datant du deuxième siécle de l'ère chrétienne", *Raydān* 4 (1981), p. 67-90.
14. Robin, C. and Breton, J.F., "Le sanctuaire préislamique du Jabal al-Lawd (Nord Yemen)", *CRAIBL* (1982), p. 590-629.
15. Ibid, p. 619-620.
16. de Blois, F., "The Date of the 'Martyrs of Nagran'", *AAE* 1 (1990), p. 119.
17. Ryckmans, G., "Inscriptions sud-arabes, dizième série", *Le Muséon* 69 (1953), p. 285-7 and 296-7.
18. Jamme, A., *Sabaean and Hasaean Inscriptions from Saudi Arabia* (Rome: Istituto di studi del Vicino Oriente, Universita di Roma, 1966), p. 39.
19. Robin, C., and Breton, J.F., "Le sanctuaire préislamique du Jabal al-Lawd (Nord Yemen)", p. 619-620.
20. Beeston, A., "The Himyarite Problem", *PSAS* 5 (1975), p. 2.
21. Avanzini, A., "Appunti di storia sudarabica" *EVO* 8 (1985), p. 155-165.
22. Schoff, W.H. (ed.), *The Periplus of the Erythrean Sea. Travel and Trade in the Indian Ocean by a Merchant of the First Century* (New York: Longmans, Green & Co., 1912), p. 30.
23. Robin, C., "Amdan Bayyin Yuhaqbiḍ, roi de Saba' et du-Raydān" in *Etudes sud-arabes. Recueil offert à Jacques Ryckmans* (Louvain-La-Neuve: Universite catholique de Louvain, 1991), p. 167-205.
24. Robin, C., "La civilisation de l'Arabie méridionale avant l'Islam" in Chelhod (ed.), *L'Arabie du Sud: histoire et civilisation* (Paris: G.-P. Maisonneuve et Larose, 1984), p. 212.
25. Robin. C., and Bafaqīh, M., "Deux nouvelles inscriptions de Radmān" p. 67-90.
26. Müller, W.W., "Survey of the History of the Arabian Peninsula from the First Century AD to the Rise of Islam", in *Studies in the History of Arabia, Vol. II: The Pre-Islamic Arabia* (Riyadh: 1984), p. 125.
27. von Wissman, H., "Ḥimyar, Ancient History", *Le Muséon* 77 (1964), p. 444.
28. Robin, C., "La première intervention abyssine en Arabie mérid ionale" in T. Beyene (ed.), *Proceedings of the Eighth International Conference of Ethiopian Studies, University of Addis-Adeba,* 1984, vol. 2 (Addis Adaba: Institute of Ethiopian Studies, 1989), p. 147-162.

29. Iryani, M.A., *Fi tarik al-Yaman* (Ṣan'ā: Markaaz al-Dirasat al-Yamaniyah, 1973), p. 13.
30. Müller, W.W., "Survey of the History of the Arabian Peninsula", p. 126.
31. Robin, "Les inscriptions d'al-Mi'sāl et la chronologie de l'Arabie méridionale..." p. 323, 339.
32. Robin, C., "La civilisation de l'Arabie méridionale avant l'Islam", p. 213.

XIII

THE EMPIRE OF ḤIMYAR

The Fourth Century AD and the Advent of Monotheism

By the beginning of the fourth century AD, South Arabia was unified under the Himyarite dynasty (except for the Red Sea coastline, which remained under Ethiopian control), forming a vast empire that stretched from Najrān to Dhofār. South Arabia would remain united until towards the end of the sixth century AD, when it was incorporated into the domain of Sassanid Persia.

Later, Arab historians would use this period as the basis for their work on the "time of ignorance", or the pre-Islamic era, known in Arabic as the *jahiliyyah* and this is why they, and the Arab world in general, used "Ḥimyar" as a synonym for "Arabia Felix".

Shamir Yuhar'ish probably reigned until the end of the third decade of the fourth century AD. In an inscription found at Al-Namarah in southern Syria dated AD 328 (RES 483), the Arab king Imru al-Qays claims to have fought Shamir at Najrān. The Himyarite king's power was felt beyond the borders of southern Arabia. For example, we know that he sent envoys to the king of Al-Azd in Northern Arabia and to Seleucia and Ctesiphon, the twin capitals of the Sassanians on the banks of the Tigris[1].

However, there were probably uprisings in Ḥaḍramawt during his reign, as there certainly were under his successors Yāsir Yuhan'im and his son Dhamār'ali Yuhabirr (Table 8). But the Ḥaḍramawt was now on its last legs, and these final, sporadic bids for independence by the great eastern kingdom were doomed to failure; Shabwat sank into oblivion. Despite losing its political importance, Mārib managed to stay afloat, if only as a famous cult centre. From the religious point of view, however, everything underwent dramatic changes in the second half of the fourth century AD.

An inscription that records the first time the Mārib dam burst (Ja 671), at the time of king Tha'ran Yuha'min and his son Malik-Karib Yuha'min, is the first one dedicated not to Almaqah, but to Rahmanan, Lord of Heaven and Earth. This is the first sign of South Arabia's rapid conversion to monotheism. Two further inscriptions – both

		ḤIMYAR
300		
		Shamir Yuhar'ish
	Bishop Theophilus, c. 340	Yasir Yuhan'im
		Dhamar'alī Yuhabirr
	the first bursting of the Mārib dam	Tha'rān Yuha'min
	building of the palaces of Ẓafar, 383	Malikkarib Yuha'min
		Dhara''amar Ayman
400		*Mārib*
		Abūkarib As'ad
	second bursting of the Mārib dam, 455	Sharaḥbi'īl Ya'fur
	Christian communities in Najran, 472	Sharaḥbi'īl Yakkaf
500		
	Ethiopians build in Ẓafar, 509	Marthad'ilān Yanūf
	expeditions against the bedouin, 516	Ma'dīkarib Ya'fur
	massacre of Najran, 523	Yūsuf As'ar Yath'ar (dhu-Nuwās)
	Abyssinian conquest of Yemen, 528	Sumyafa'
	third bursting of the Mārib dam, 547	Abrāhā (547-558)
	last dated inscription, 559	
	Persian conquest of Yemen, c. 570	
600		
	fourth and final bursting of the Mārib dam, c. 600	
	conversion to Islam, 628	

Table 8
Key events and the dynastic successin of the period of the Himyarite Empire

from Ẓafār and a little later than Ja 671 – that commemorate the dedication of two palaces by the king Malik-Karib Yuha'min, who ruled alongside his two sons Abu-Karib As'ad and Dhara''amar Ayman, allow us to put an exact date of AD 383 on this event.

It is not entirely clear whether this new god, who replaced the whole pantheon of divinities that had been worshipped in southern Arabia for centuries, was the Christian or Jewish God. But the fact remains that this conversion, and the abandonment of pagan temples, put an end to the lengthy inscriptions of dedication, which constituted our primary source of information until this point. Epigraphy was now confined to the occasional grand commemorative text, mostly in stone, which only related important events[2].

Christianity made its first appearance in South Arabia during the early years of the rule of the Roman Emperor Constantine II (AD 337-361), when, as the Greek ecclesiastical historian Philostorgius tells us, a certain bishop Theophilus was sent from the island of Socotra to the Himyarite court. Churches were built in Yemen from then onwards, and many Christian communities were founded[3].

Judaism probably appeared at about the same time, and was probably more popular with the Himyarite sovereigns than Christianity, if only because it did not conform to Christian Ethiopia which was allied to Rome. The oldest reliable written evidence of the presence of Jews in Yemen dates from the last quarter of the fourth century AD, in other words from the reign of Dhara''amar Ayman. This evidence rests in an inscription found at Bayt al-Ashwal (the modern village near Ẓafār, whose houses were built reusing large quantities of material from the ancient capital). It was written by a Himyarite who had been converted to Moses' faith[4].

The conversion to monotheism was an important move, especially from a political point of view. The history of the Himyarite Empire from this point on unfolded with a hitherto unknown degree of internationalism. Rome still held the monopoly on trade in the Red Sea and the Indian Ocean, and used its alliance with the powerful Christian Ethiopia to protect its interests in these far-flung lands. As we shall see, the

Himyarites were forced to react to this Christian movement by adopting Judaism as their religious (and political) vessel, in whose name alone they could alter the state of affairs that was suffocating its ports and that could even have constituted a threat to its territory.

It is partly because of the political importance of the new religion that these last two and a half centuries of South Arabian history are usually called the monotheistic period.

The Second Ethiopian Invasion and the Fifth and Sixth Centuries AD

We know very little about the fifth century AD, in terms of historical fact. What follows are the key events as laid down by Walter Müller[5].

In the first third of the fifth century, there reigned one of the greatest sovereigns in the history of South Arabia: Abu-Karib As'ad. Under him, the empire reached its greatest extent, and his fame has survived to the present day. He led military campaigns as far afield as central Arabia, and he is thought to have reached Yathrib (Medina). He eventually assumed the title "king of Saba and Dhū-Raydān and Ḥadramawt and Yamanat and (king) of the Arabs of the Highlands and of the Coast".

In AD 455 his son Sharahbi'il Ya'fur was busy repairing the damage done to the Mārib dam by the heavy summer

Plate 46
The Himyarite inscription CIS 325 (ad 559)

rains. This is the second time that we hear of this impressive structure being damaged. The city was clearly still occupied. We know that Sharahbi'il Ya'fur was still ruling in AD 462 because he embellished the capital, Ẓafār, by building a lavish new palace[6].

Few inscriptions survive from the period AD 462 to 523. We do, however, know that in this period (probably starting with the reign of Sharahbi'il Yakkaf, mentioned in an inscription of AD 472) a large Christian community was founded in Najrān (CIS 537 and RES 4919). This may have been a result of the increasingly strong Ethiopian influence; an inscription dated AD 509 written by some Ethiopian envoys records that they built a house in Ẓafār during the reign of Marthad'ilan Yanūf. In AD 516, king Ma'di-Karib Ya'fur led an expedition into central Arabia, stopping a few kilometres west of Riyadh, to suppress a bedouin revolt (Ry 510).

In AD 523 the situation changed dramatically. A sovereign named Yusuf As'ar Yath'ar (known in Islamic tradition as Dhū-Nuwās) came to the throne, possibly as a usurper. He loudly proclaimed his Judaism and declared war on the Abyssinians of southern Arabia and on their Christian allies. Ethiopian residents of Ẓafār were slaughtered, their highland fortresses destroyed and their churches burnt. The coastal regions were reoccupied.

Yusuf was particularly merciless towards the Christian stronghold of Najrān. The city was surrounded and forced to surrender hostages. Eventually, towards the end of 523, Najrān capitulated and Yusuf executed many members of the Christian community. (Ry 507, 508; Ja 1028). The martyrdom of these Himyarite Christians caused outrage among the Christian communities of the East, and Ethiopia reacted with force, probably encouraged by Rome which feared for its commercial interests. In ad 528 the Abyssinian king Caleb landed in Arabia, defeated the Himyarite army and conquered the whole of Yemen. Arab tradition has it that Dhū-Nuwās committed suicide by riding his horse into the sea. However, if the events reported by the Ḥuṣn al-Ghurāb inscription (CIS 621) refer to him, it would seem that he was actually killed by the Abyssinians.

South Arabia was a vassal kingdom under Abyssinian rule for many years. A certain Sumyafa', a Himyarite

Christian, was the first to be put on the throne, but shortly afterwards an Abyssinian general, Abrāhā, took direct control and remained on the throne from AD 547 to 558. In fact, in an inscription of AD 547 which records the third time the Mārib dam broke (CIS 541), Abrāhā is still referred to as the viceroy of the Abyssinian negus. He must have assumed total control shortly after this though, since we know that he received envoys from the king of Abyssinia and the Eastern Roman Emperor, a delegation from Persia and a few emissaries from northern and central Arabian rulers. It is clear from an inscription dated AD 553 (Ry 506) that Abrāhā considered himself a rightful and proper king. However he was probably no longer on the throne in AD 559 since there is no mention of him in the last dated inscription of the Himyarite era (CIS 325: the year 669 of the Himyarite era) (Plate 46).

This text is the last direct source of information on pre-Islamic South Arabia. The following period, leading up to the Persian conquest of Yemen in around 570, remains obscure, but probably saw the definitive decline of the Himyarite Empire. Possible reasons for this decline, as enumerated by Müller, are: social tensions, feudalism among the powerful aristocratic clans, the decline of central authority leading to an increase in foreign power, an increasingly influential bedouin element due to infiltration of the cavalry and North Arabian tribes, the decline of agriculture due to abandoned irrigation systems, the disintegration of a well-organised society, a drop in demand for the incense of South Arabia, and a dramatic decline in the ancient caravan trade[7].

The events of the late sixth and early seventh centuries are rather confused. Towards the end of his reign, Abrāhā tried to conquer Mecca, but failed. The episode has stuck in Arab literature because on this occasion Abrāhā used several elephants. Around AD 570, the Himyarites requested help – via the kings of North Arabia (Al-Hirah) – from the king of Persia, who helped the Yemenis expel the Abyssinians from their land at last. From then on, South Arabia became a vassal state, and subsequently a satrap of the Sassanid Empire.

The Mārib dam broke for the fourth and final time in around AD 600, leading – as is reported in the Qur'an – to the definitive destruction of the ancient capital of Saba.

Badhan, the Persian governor of South Arabia, converted to Islam in AD 628, and from this date the whole of Yemen followed the new religion.

Footnotes:

1. Müller, W.W., "Outline of the History of Ancient Southern Arabia", in Daum (ed.), *Yemen: 3000 Years of Art and Civilization in Arabia Felix* (Innsbruck/Frankfurt: Umschau-Verlage, 1987), p. 52.
2. Robin, C., "La civilisation de l'Arabie méridionale avant l'Islam", in Chelhod (ed.), *L'Arabie du Sud: histoire et civilisation* (Paris: G.-P. Maisonneuve et Larose, 1984), p. 214.
3. Beeston, A.F.L., "Judaism and Christianity in Pre-Islamic Yemen", in Chelhod (ed.), *L'Arabie du Sud*, p. 271-278.
4. Garbini, G., "Una bilingue sabeo-ebraica da Ẓafār", *AION* 30 (1970), p. 154-160.
5. Müller, W.W., "Outline of the History of Ancient Southern Arabia", p. 52-53.
6. Garbini, "Una nuova iscrizione di Sharahbi'il Ya'fur", *AION* 29 (1969), p. 560.
7. Müller, "Outline of the History of Ancient South Arabia", p. 53.

PART FOUR

Religion and Material Culture

XIV

RELIGION

The Sources

By studying inscriptions we have managed to reconstruct, at least in general terms, the various political events that affected the southern Arabian kingdoms throughout their long history. Occasionally we have been given a deeper insight into some of these events, allowing us to appreciate their human side. But clearly this is not so much a proper history as a kind of chronicle of events, within which the real missing links are the people. It is difficult to get a sense of the personalities behind the complicated names of the kings, and impossible to look beyond the kings and princes and discern the characters of the ordinary people. Our reconstruction so far is a rather soulless history, which shows how unwise it is to rely on theory to explain the real reasons behind historical events.

We might then ask ourselves whether, or to what extent, we might be able to piece together the mentality, the way of thinking, and the personalities of the sovereigns and subjects of the South Arabian kingdoms. Since our written sources lack the kind of literary texts that were so helpful in reconstructing the religions of other ancient civilisations like Egypt and Mesopotamia, here we will have to make do with other types of epigraphy produced, for example, for offerings and commemorations. The best way to interpret this indirect information is by looking at other kinds of evidence, even if it is not written, which sometimes gives us a better insight than inscriptions can into the mentality of ancient South Arabia. We shall therefore be looking at the arts.

Starting with religious feeling, we will then turn to material culture, architecture and other art forms, as we believe that the best indication of a community's profoundest beliefs can be found in the expression of its arts.

The first thing we should say is that no external sources can help us decipher the religion of southern Arabia. Classical authors' comments are rather fleeting and vague, and those by Arab historians and geographers are generally unreliable and imprecise, mostly because they were all written too late. While the latter often digressed into discussions of Arab paganism, due to the Qur'an's interest in the idols and practices of the time of ignorance, we also find that works like Ibn Al-Kalbī's *Book of Idols* (late eight century), rather than objectively examining pre-Islamic religion and gods, tend to be swamped by a rather biased attempt to prove that the polytheistic idolatry of the *jahiliyyah* was merely a corrupt interlude between the monotheism of Abraham and Ishmael and that of Islam.

Therefore, South Arabian inscriptions, whether votive or commemorative, can provide us with a religious framework which differs between the various ethno-political groups, but that shows clear conceptual traits common to all. This is evident in both types of information provided by the texts; firstly, the roll-call of divinities, or pantheon; and secondly religious practices and sentiments.

The Beliefs

We can reconstruct the South Arabian pantheon on the basis of the "final appeals" that end dedications of objects, people or buildings to a god[1]. These appeals place the object of the dedication under the protection of a series of gods, listed in hierarchical order. The name that appears consistently at the head of these lists is that of the god 'Athtar. The names of subsequent gods vary according to the dialect that the epigraph is written in, and therefore, according to the socio-political environment. 'Athtar, then, was the supreme god and was universally recognised.

As always with the South Arabian pantheon, it is difficult to make out 'Athtar's characteristics. His name is identical to that of the male counterpart of the Ugaritic and Phoenician goddess Astarte, but is also similar to that of the Mesopotamian goddess Ishtar. This similarity was actually the reason that scholars tried from the start to link 'Athtar to the planet Venus. This marked the beginning of astral interpretations of South Arabian religion[2]. Among the gods who follow 'Athtar in the Hadrami lists, we find Sin (or Sayyin), well-known in Mesopotamia as the moon god (and we remember that the English mission gave the name "Moon Temple" to a temple of Sin excavated at Ḥurayḍah). A lunar character can also be ascribed to various other divinities that followed 'Athtar in the final appeals of Sabaean, Minaean and Qatabanian texts. On the other hand, the goddesses who came at the bottom of the lists can be linked to the sun. Out of this was born the notion that the whole South Arabian pantheon could be reduced to a primitive astral triad.

The Danish scholar Ditlef Nielsen even managed to discern a family trio, comprising a father-moon, a mother-sun and a son-Venus[3].

The idea of an astral type of religion in South Arabia proved very popular, and is still widely believed. In my opinion, its success depends on the romantic concept of the ancient Arabs wandering alone in the desert with the immense, mysterious canopy of stars above them. The other theory, which organised the pantheon into a precise family triad, also proved very popular. This was so for a different reason; it was a way to overcome one of the biggest problems in southern Arabian religion, the almost total lack of information on theogony and mythology.

However, it gradually became clear that both of these theories were groundless and that although they were convenient, they had stopped us getting to the heart of religious thinking in South Arabia for decades. We can sense a particular kind of religious feeling in the disorder, incongruities and disorganisation of South Arabian religious thinking. In ancient Egypt, Mesopotamia and Greece, divinities inhabited an independent and distinct world of their own, whereas in South Arabia (and, I imagine, throughout the Arabian Peninsula in the pre-Islamic era) religion took on a much more subjective form. Here, religious feeling was a personal, intimate concept, confined to the individual's relationship with his god and leaving no room for a separate world for the gods. As André Caquot explains in an excellent, recent summary of pre-Islamic Arabic religion, the Arabs seemed "more interested in the relationships between men and gods than the relationships between the gods. They had a well-populated pantheon, but we have no clear idea of its organisation. The Arabs themselves probably saw it as loosely structured: this culture did not produce much in the way of theology or myths but this does not rule out a fervent religiosity."[4]

This exclusive relationship between the individual and the gods must have led to the proliferation of parallel gods, with different names but identical attributes (lunar gods for example), which has rather hindered the various attempts to define their roles and functions. For the same reason, we remain in the dark about most of the gods' exact identities: communion with a god was so intimate and direct that they could easily have avoided referring to the god by his usual proper name. Apart from ʿAthtar and a couple of others, the members of the South Arabian pantheon are often concealed behind a title, an abstract name (Almaqah means "powerful god", Wadd means "love", etc.), or a topical designation (many gods' names start with *dhū*, "he of", or *dhat*, "she of").

The people of South Arabia were consistently dependent on their gods. This much is evident in the inscriptions. The faithful are portrayed as humble supplicants, offering prayers of thanks and propitiation and seeking a positive outcome for themselves, their families and communities. At the same time, the supplicants devoutly give thanks for favours received. If they had sinned against divine or human law (which was also laid down by the gods), they expiated themselves with a public confession and paid a fine[5].

However, the fact that they had such an intrinsic feeling for the divine does not mean that there were no barriers between man and god. Man is mortal and cannot alter the fact, however important he is. The gods have their own transcendental sphere, and man cannot tangibly feel their presence, but only sense it through the spirit.

The scarcity of exact representations of the gods, along with the profusion of symbols which refer to them in South Arabian art (animals, objects, characters etc.) proves that the gods were seen as supernatural. Scholars have often studied these symbols[6], but have never been able to establish the precise nature of the various gods on this basis. If South Arabian religion was indeed as we have described it, this was bound to be the case.

Having said this, we can see why even the highest-ranking person, the king, could not benefit from a special relationship with the gods. An inscription from Barāqish finds king ʿAmmyatha Nabit doing penance before ʿAthtar because some documents had gone missing from the temples of Yathil (RES 2980). The king was, of course, not responsible for the theft, but as the people's representative before the gods, this was his duty. This is the only sacred aspect of South Arabian rulers; the fact that the king was the representative of his subjects in the eyes of the gods.

This is why he is called, in Qatabān for example, “the first born” of a couple of gods, or in Ma‘īn, “son of Wadd”.

Nevertheless, the king was still dependent on the gods like any normal person, and expected them to grant him protection and favour for his people. Besides, both the Qatabanians and Minaeans considered themselves “sons” of their gods, and neither more nor less so than the king himself.

Since it was so direct, the relationship between man and god tended to rule out the need for a clergy to be ministers of the soul in ancient South Arabia. The king remained the only intermediary, purely on account of his role as a representative of the state. In this guise, he would preside over communal rites (sacred hunts, ritual banquets, sacrifices etc.) and the building of temples.

In this we can see the temporal side of South Arabian religion and the thing that differentiates it from other cults in the Arabian Peninsula, which derives from the position of complex societies within South Arabian culture. The divine kept its transcendental value on a personal level, but took on a distinctly earthly form at community level, becoming a solid political tool. We have already discussed the pacts of alliance between tribes undertaken since the time of the *mukarribs* of Saba. On these occasions, various gods would be “used” to guarantee a lasting and solid political alliance between the tribes. The temples themselves are tangible proof of the temporality assumed by religion on a socio-political level. Temples were maintained by donations, and could receive taxes. They also owned land and slaves. This accumulation of wealth must have afforded a temple an important role in the economy of the society. The completely different kind of religious sentiment assumed in this case is proven in exemplary fashion, we think, by the presence within a sanctuary of a complex, hierarchical clerical organisation.

‘Athtar, the Supreme God

We come now to the pantheon itself. The first thing to note is that most of the important South Arabian gods were venerated in their capacity as rain-bearers and guarantors of the irrigation system. They were essentially fertility gods[8].

As we have seen, ‘Athtar was the supreme, universally

recognised god. But in more ancient times, the most important god was probably Il. Although he is hardly ever mentioned, this supreme god of the Semites is actually found in personal theophoric names (Karib'īl, Yada'īl etc). 'Athtar, whose symbols were the antelope and a horizontal crescent moon with a small disc in its centre, must have been the god of the thunderstorm and provider of rain. He was the most important god of the Minaeans, who gave him the title "dhū-Qabd". He had numerous other names, among them Sharqan ("the eastern"), dhū-Yahriq, and dhū-Dhiban ("he of the waters"[9]). The sacred hunt, which had been practised since the time of the *mukarrib*s of Saba, was dedicated to him, and to Kurum, who also had the antelope as his symbol[10].

Müller finds an interesting parallel for 'Athtar and Kurum in the idol Atarquruma, which Sennacherib (704-681 BC) took as a spoil of war from the north Arabian city of Adumatum, as the Assyrian king Asarhaddon relates in his Annals[11]. This tells us that there were clearly links between the Assyrian world and the contemporary, earliest sovereigns of Saba in the historic period.

In Sabaean texts, 'Athtar is often identified with a god of unknown gender called Hawbas, who seems to have been mostly venerated slightly south of Mārib[12]. The identification of this god with 'Athtar, based on a simple association of the names and hieroglyphs of 'Athtar and a priestess, related by a Minaean text (RES 3306A), remains a matter of opinion[13].

'Athtar was therefore considered the supreme god, not only in the *mukarrib* period, but also later, as we find the formula of federation at Jabal al-Lawdh. Gradually, though, while 'Athtar retained his position at the head of the list, the local cults of patron gods (*shim*) began to gather strength.

The Patron Gods

Almaqah was the national god of Saba. Sovereigns dedicated their conquests to him and to Saba. The Sabaeans considered themselves "progeny of Almaqah". The great temples of Mārib and Ṣirwāḥ were dedicated to him, and he was the subject of great annual pilgrimages to Mārib. It was quite natural that he should become a god of irrigation and agriculture, given the area of his cult. But his identification as moon god is unsubstantiated; indeed, his symbols and attributes (bull, vine shoots, etc.) seem to link him more to the sun and Dionysiac cults[15]. If this were the case, Almaqah could be considered the male counterpart to the sun goddess Shams, worshipped in Saba and later in Ḥimyar. Some rather adventurous etymological interpretations have claimed to see a solar aspect in the epithets of other Sabaean divinities, like dhāt-Ḥimyam ("she of the heat") and dhat-Ba'dan ("she of the distancing [of the winter sun]"). However, as we said at the beginning, we are still in the dark as regards the identification of the South Arabian gods.

The Sabaean divinity of the highland regions around Ṣan'ā was Ta'lab Riyām, patron of the great tribal confederation of Sum'ay. His symbol was the ibex, and he was considered to be a rain-bearer and a protector of flocks. The temple at Ḥuqqah was dedicated to him.

Wadd, on the other hand, was certainly a lunar god. It has always been claimed that he was the national god of Ma'īn, but this is not certain. It is not sufficient to rely on the formula Wadd-Ab ("Wadd is the father") which we often find inscribed on amulets and buildings. Instead, we can now confirm that the most important god of Ma'īn was 'Athtar dhū-Qabd, although his specific characteristics are still uncertain. However, as far as Wadd is concerned, we know that his animal attribute was the serpent, and that he was therefore associated with fertility of the earth, humans and animals.

Another important Minaean god was Nakraḥ. He was the patron god of Yathil, and important sanctuaries dedicated to him have been found both inside the city (the temple thought to be dedicated to 'Athtar before the Italian excavations) and outside (on the hill of Darb as- Sabi)[16]. He was a warrior god, and as such had the power to absolve sins. He was therefore sought out by the sick, the dying and women in childbirth. Public confessions were also addressed to him. A logical conclusion is that the Minaeans saw physical illness as a symptom of moral decay.

In the northern territory of Ma'īn, home to the caravan tribe of Amir, the god-patron dhū-Samawi ("he of the sky") was worshipped instead, and his cult spread as far as central Arabia. Statuettes of camels were dedicated to him and, like

Nakraḥ, he was the recipient of public confessions.

The patron deity of Qatabān was ʻAmm ("the paternal uncle"). We do not know if the epithet refers to his place in the pantheon, or to his rapport with the faithful. The latter seems more likely, partly because the Qatabanians considered themselves "progeny of ʻAmm" and their sovereigns, as we have seen, were the first born of ʻAmm and another god.

His animal attribute was the bull, which makes his identification as a lunar god rather doubtful. A god often associated with ʻAmm is Anbay, who must have been of considerable stature, considering that for example, the concept of state was expressed by the formula ʻAmm and Anbay. Since Anbay is sometimes called "patron", this formula probably reflects the merging within a confederation of two important tribes of different origins. Or, if the etymology of the name does indeed mean "he who declares [the law]", it could be that Anbay's support of ʻAmm somehow renders legitimate Qatabān's claim to be a state. Further proof that Anbay had legal characteristics is his frequent appearance alongside Ḥawkum. They are given a common epithet which is translatable as "ḥe who orders and (he) who decides"[17].

The national god of Ḥaḍramawt was Sayyin. We have already mentioned his identification with the Mesopotamian lunar god Sin, but Sayyin was probably a local god who had nothing to do with Mesopotamia. He appears on Hadrami coins wearing a crown with rays emerging from it, and with the eagle as his symbol. He was undoubtably a solar god. Besides, Alfred Beeston has proven that there are no real phonetic similarities between Sayyin and Sin. We should also bear in mind that Pliny, when referring to the god of Shabwat in *Historia Naturalis*, called him Sabin; and that Theophrastus clearly states in *De Historia Pantarum* that he was a sun god. The Hadramis considered themselves "progeny of Sayyin", but the state was expressed in a formula which placed Sayyin alongside another god, Hawl, and this may be an indication that Ḥaḍramawt was a confederation.

These, then, are the gods that make up the South Arabian pantheon. As we said at the beginning, if taken individually they never seem to have a clearly defined form. The gods of South Arabia are only fully realised in their relationships with men. This is when we see the lords that a man prays to, who grant him their blessing, along with prosperity, abundance, victory and recovery. They are intimately involved in the lives of men as providers and benefactors. As André Caquot rightly pointed out, the South Arabian gods are the true patrons of human societies. This is the fundamental element behind a set of beliefs, which takes us back to Semitic cultures as a whole.

Footnotes:

1. Ryckmans, J., "Le panthéon de l'Arabie du Sud préislamique", *RHR* 206 (1987), p. 151-169.
2. Nielsen, D., "Zur altarabischen Religion" in D. Nielsen (ed.), *Handbuch der Altarabischen Altertumskunde, I. Band: Die altarabische Kultur* (Copenhagen: A. Busck, 1927), p. 177-250.
3. Ibid, p. 206.
4. Caquot, A., "Les religions des Sémites occidentaux; Les Arabes du Sud", in *Histoires des religions* (1970), p. 348-355.
5. Ryckmans, G., "Rites et croyances préislamiques en Arabie méridionale", *Le Muséon* 55 (1942), p. 175.
6. See, for example, Grohmann, A., *Göttersymbole und Symboltiere auf Südarabischen Denkmälern* (Wien: Alfred Holder, 1914).
7. Caquot, A., "Les religions des Sémites occidentaux; Les Arabes du Sud", p. 353.
8. Ryckmans, J., "Le panthéon de l'Arabie du Sud préislamiques", *RHR* 206 (1987), p. 159.
9. Höfner, M., "Die vorislamischen Religionen Arabiens", in H. Gese, M. Höfner, and K. Rudolph (eds.), *Die Religionen Altsyriens, Altarabiens und der Mandäer* (Stuttgart: W. Kohlhammer, 1970), p. 244, 269.
10. Garbini, G., "The Inscriptions of Si'b al-'Aql, Al-Jafnah and Yalā/Ad-Durayb" in de Maigret, A., *The Sabaean Archaeological Complex in the Wādī Yalā* (Rome: IsMEO, 1988), p. 26.
11. Müller, W.W., "KRWM in Lichte einer neuentdeckten sabäischen Jagdinschrift aus der Oase von Mārib", *ABADY* III (1986), p. 106.
12. Gnoli, G., "South Arabian Notes", *EW* 37 (1987), p. 450.
13. Ryckmans, J., "Le panthéon de l'Arabie du Sud préislamique", p. 161.
14. Robin, C. and Breton, J.F., "Le sanctuaire préislamique du Jabal al-Lawd", *CRAIBL* (1982), p. 621.

15. Ryckmans, J., "Le panthéon de l'Arabie du Sud préislamique", p. 163.
16. Robin, C. and Ryckmans, J., "Le santuaire Minéen de NKRH à Darb as-Sabi (environs de Barāqish). Rapport préliminaire (Seconde partie): Étude des inscriptions", *Raydān* 5 (1988), p. 91-159.
17. Ryckmans, J., "Le panthéon de l'Arabie du Sud préislamique", p. 164.
18. Beeston, A., "The Religions of Pre-Islamic Yemen", in Chelhod, *L'Arabie du Sud*, p. 263.

XV

THE CITY

Fortified Cities and Their Evolution

The picture that we have built up so far of South Arabian civilisation has been primarily determined by epigraphic evidence. We can construct an overall picture of these ancient societies by looking at their political development, the organisation of the institutions and their feeling for the divine, even if all of these are expressed in rather vague terms.

To make the picture more complete and consistent, we now need to add the detail and colour which we can only get from purely archaeological evidence. Let us turn, then, to those categories of South Arabian material culture like the cities, temples, tombs and objects which have come down to us in a much less self-conscious form than the epigraphy and which should therefore help us form a more rounded history of South Arabia. We shall start with the

Plate 47
View of the walls of Kharibat Sa'ud/Kutal

Plate 48
View of the walls of the city of Yalā/Al-Durayb, ancient Hafarī

most striking and characteristic manifestation of this culture; the cities. It is impossible to establish exactly when or why South Arabian settlements started to surround themselves with fortified walls. Until a few years ago, since all the walls of South Arabian cities contained inscriptions, it was assumed that the earliest fortifications could not have preceded the beginning of monumental epigraphy[1]. Given that the oldest inscriptions were those of the *mukarrib*s Yatha‘’amar Bayyin and Karib’īl Watar, built into the walls of cities in Wādī Raghwān, the accepted view was that Al-Asāḥil and Kharībat Sa‘ūd were the oldest fortified cities of Yemen.

However, this theory had to be modified with the discovery of cities like Hajar Abū Zayd in Wādī Markhah and Yalā/Al-Durayb. These cities’ walls were built in a relatively archaic style and do not bear any inscriptions, which indicates that the fortifications must have predated the earliest monumental inscriptions. This was confirmed by the excavation of Yalā and the relative chronology.

However, if we want to establish the evolution of the South Arabian city, then before considering the inscriptions we need to bear two other technical/stylistic variables in mind: 1) the regularity of the perimeter walls in their plan, or rather, how much rhythmic alternation of bastions and indentations exists; and 2) to what extent the walls have been finished, or to what extent the blocks of stone have been well-cut, accurately connected and decorated on their visible surfaces. We could then add another consideration: 3) the extent or existence of inscriptions on the outer face of the walls.

We only find evenly alternating walls in what we might term mature cities, that is, those dating from the *mukarrib* period and the period of the kings of Saba. Their regularity shows a certain uniformity in planning and execution, easily discernible in cities like Maʻīn (Qarnāw), Al- Bayḍā (Nashq), Barāqish (Yathil), Kharībat Saʻūd (Kutal), Mārib, Yalā/Al-Durayb (Hafarī), Hajar Kuhlan (Timnaʻ) and Shabwah (Shabwat), for example.

In other cities, however, the alternation of towers and indentations is so irregular that the perimeter walls do not appear to follow any clear route and the towns seem rather haphazardly planned. For this reason, we believe city walls like those at Kamnah (Kaminahū), Jidfir Ibn Munaykhir (Kuhal), Al-Asāḥil (ʻArarat), Ṣirwāḥ and Hajar Abū Zayd to be older. It appears that there were several reasons for their disjointed appearance (the presence of earlier structures, the continuation of building works, etc.) which must all have affected the cities' early attempts at building defences.

The Italian mission's investigations of the Yalā/Al-Durayb site proved that within the city there was an earlier, internal system of defence, made simply by juxtaposing the outermost houses and possibly putting short connecting walls between them (Fig. 40). This kind of defence, predating actual encircling walls, is still in use in Yemen today (at Shibām in Ḥaḍramawt, for example) and may have been the main reason why the above-mentioned cities have such irregular layouts. It must have been common during the protohistoric period in southern Arabia, that is, the centuries before the *mukarrib* Karib'īl Watar, son of Dhamār'ali, came to the throne (*c.* 700 BC) .

The later type of defensive walls was designed with bastions placed at regular intervals. This style may well have derived from the original arrangement, with the ring of houses joined together by protective walls.

This evolution in defensive planning is shown in the progress made in construction techniques, and particularly in the degree of refinement of the external wall faces. There is no need for us to describe the individual cities at this point, since we have already considered the history of each of the discoveries. We would, however, just add a few general observations on the techniques and stylistic development of the perimeter walls.

The blocks are usually of medium size and appear to be laid in horizontal rows at first, then covered by dry stone walling sometimes over ten metres high. The stones are rough-hewn and worked into rows of blocks of the same dimensions. However, although the facades seem quite well built, there are still a lot of gaps between the stones, which had to be filled in to give the impression of uniformity. Yalā is a typical example of this technique, as are Al-Asāḥil and Kharībat Sa'ūd[2]. Seen in section, these are clearly double thickness walls (an external and an internal wall), and the gap between them is filled in with rubble and earth.

Over time we see an evolution in construction techniques. Kharībat Sa'ūd was already more advanced than the nearby Al-Asāḥil, in terms of the standard of blocks used to build some of the bastions. This improvement is a foretaste of the major technical advances which would characterise the buildings (as well as the defences) in centuries to come. The blocks began to conform to a type; they became perfectly square and smooth (varying only in length) and walls built with them had no gaps at all. Often, the outward surface of the block would be decorated by creating a smooth frame around the edge of the block, and methodically chipping away at the central rectangle. This technique is characteristic of classical South Arabian architecture and is found throughout the major centres, from Najrān to Ma'īn, from Mārib to Hajar Kuhlan, from Shabwat to Khawr Rūrī, remaining in use, with little alteration, until almost the end of the pre- Islamic period[3].

We have mentioned that double thickness walls with filled-in nuclei were common in the earliest phase. Later (probably from the seventh to sixth centuries BC onwards) the loose earth and rubble filling was replaced by a stronger filling of rough bricks, contained on the outside by the facade of smooth blocks and on the inside by a wall of smaller stones, well-squared but not smoothed. This method has been unearthed recently by our excavations in the southern sector of Barāqish. Besides stone of various types – according to the local geology – and rough bricks, another popular building material was wood, probably also used in defensive works. This was well proven by Breton's excavations at Shabwat[4].

Well-defended, monumental gateways were placed in the walls, often articulated by a double (Al-Asāḥil, Al-Bayḍā, Kamnah, Mārib, Hajar Kuhlan, Shabwah, Al-Barīrah) or a triple entrance (Ma'īn, Ḥinū al-Zurayr, Khawr Rūrī[5]). The west gate of Ma'īn is particularly impressive, where a structure, leaning against the great towers which flanked the double entrance in the walls, contains an antechamber which was carved out and decorated with a portico set on pilasters, a staircase for the lookouts, and many inscriptions (Fig. 11).

The latest hypotheses all agree that monumental writing began in the eighth century BC. This, then, is a useful *terminus ante quem* for dating those defensive walls which do not contain inscriptions and a good way of proving what we said earlier, on the basis of plans and construction techniques, about the evolution of city walls. Indeed, some of the city walls that we thought were the oldest because of their irregular perimeters and unfinished facades (Hajar Abū Zayd, Yalā) do not contain inscriptions.

Al-Asāḥil is the exception. Several inscriptions have been found incorporated into the stone blocks of the walls which were written by Yatha''amar Bayyin, son of Sumhu'alī, one of the earliest known *mukarribs* (federate kings) of Saba. This was towards the end of the eighth century BC, just a few decades after Karib'īl Watar son of Dhamār'ali came to the throne. This sovereign is famous for the extensive fortifications that he built around the cities he conquered. One such city is Khirbat Sa'ūd, which, as inscriptions in the walls tell us, he built not far from Al-Asāḥil. Here the walls take on a regular quadrangular plan, and in the uniformly spaced bastions we see the first indication of more refined work, prefiguring the perfectionism that was to characterise the following centuries.

In summary, we can confirm that the first South Arabian defensive walls were built during the so-called South Arabian protohistory, when they marked the external boundary of the settlement with the natural defensive barrier of the outermost houses' walls. Towards the beginning of the period of the Sabaean *mukarribs* (around 700 BC), free-standing walls began to be built, either to identify the boundaries of new settlements or to establish the extent of existing ones. During this and the subsequent period of the kings of Saba (fourth to first centuries BC) when we see the emergence of the states of Maʻīn, Qatabān and Ḥaḍramawt alongside Saba, the evolution of city walls reached its apex, at least as far as the principal caravan centres in the interior of Yemen were concerned.

From the end of the second century BC, profound political and economic changes occurred which led to the gradual destruction of the hegemony of the hinterland tribes, the strengthening of the highland tribes (Himyarites) and the progressive weakening of the cities bordering the desert. During the period of the kings of Saba and Dhū-Raydān, (first century AD onwards) while the ancient capitals of the interior like Mārib, Timnaʻ and Shabwat were still more or less prosperous, new centres began to appear in the highlands.

These new centres had no need for the impressive bastioned city walls that had guaranteed the safety and status of the desert cities. The new settlements were apparently less anxious to build themselves proper defences. Sometimes nature did their work for them, providing a natural barrier, as at Na'it, Ghaymān, Ẓafār, Baynun or Hammat Kilab, or a plain surrounded by canyons as at Madīnat al-Ahjur. In this case, the city would sometimes stand exposed on level ground, like Qaryat al-Fāw, Shibām Sukhaym and Al-Miʻsāl. The occasional defensive wall has, in fact, been discovered at Al-Miʻsāl but this seems to be due more to temporary needs than to an organised and coherent general plan of defence.

An interesting development within the settlements is that one building always seems to be particularly important, as it is larger than the others and stands apart from them. Like a sort of castle, this building tends to stand on higher ground than the rest, if the site's topography allows. These strongholds are found in almost all the sites mentioned above. However, they are particularly striking in cities built on flat areas, where they look like little fortresses surrounded by strong walls and bastions (e.g. the so-called *sūq* at Qaryat al-Fāw).

The imposing silhouette of the citadel of Mārib leads one to think that there may have been a similar fortress on the site, and it is possible that this was the hub of the Sabaean capital in the period of the kings of Saba. There are also many references to these "castles" in South Arabian texts of this period: castle Raydān at ẓafār, castle Salhin at Mārib, castle Ghumdān at Ṣan'ā, castle Shakar at Shabwat, etc.

We do not know much about the internal organisation of the cities. Apart from the ruins of temples, public buildings and private villas (Timna'), we cannot say for sure if there was a dense network of homes within the city walls. Indeed, to judge by the ruins, many of these ancient centres seem amazingly empty. It seems fairly likely that the walls were built to defend the population in times of need and that most people usually lived outside the city walls[6].

The lack of excavations has meant that we have no precise information on the layout of the cities as yet. We must, therefore, avoid making judgements on the exact nature of South Arabian cities. However, it does seem clear that most of the time people lived outside the walls. Traces of vast ancient fields have been found in the immediate vicinity of every centre. Judging by the ruins of the houses, farms, irrigation systems and dams, the city lived mainly on the produce of its flourishing agriculture, supplemented by what they made through commerce.

The dams were particularly important. The careful work executed on them clearly shows how much attention the cities lavished on their dams. Well-hewn, decorated blocks of stone and monumental epigraphy were used to embellish these important structures, the most glorious example of which is the Mārib dam[7].

A Typical Settlement: Yalā

To understand the close relationship between a city and its agricultural land, we might perhaps be well advised to take another look at Yalā and the ruins found in its territory.

These ruins stand about 35 kilometres south-west of Mārib, and are concentrated in the area contained between two small tributaries to the right of Wādī Dhanah, Wādī Yalā and Wādī Qawqah. The complex is divided into three distinct groups of ruins at Shi'b al-'Aql, the Al-Jafnah plain and the city of Yalā/Al-Durayb (Fig. 44).

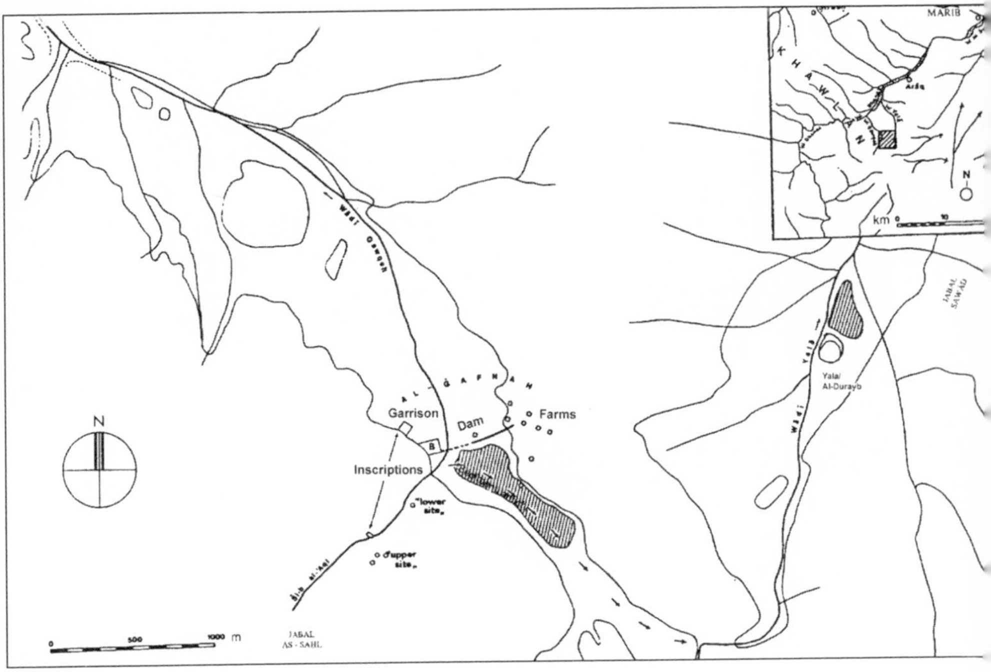

Figure 44
Map of the distribution of Sabaean antiquities around Wādī Yalā

The first group of buildings, which was also built highest up, stands right at the top of Wādī Qawqah, in other words at its steepest point, where the water has carved out a narrow gorge from the gneissic pre-Cambrian granite of the north face of Jabal al-Saḥl, the highest mountain in the area (about 2500 metres). There are ruins within this gorge, both low down (lower site) and high up (upper site). In the lower site, there is a charming villa (Plate 49) with a monumental staircase and three window openings still visible in the facade. Thanks to the particularly fine construction technique, the villa remains intact up to roof level.

Between this villa and the antiquities about 300 metres further up, the *wādī* bed is set between the rocks. It slopes gently and the bed is strewn with rocks and boulders. The pink granite has been smoothed and carved by water running down the *wādī* over the course of the millennia, giving the canyon an unusual, evocative aspect (Plate 52). The great boulders of the *wādī* bed and the walls of the

Plate 49
The Sabaean villa at the foot of the Shi'b al-'aql, near Yalā

gorge sometimes take on bizarre plastic shapes. During the rainy season, the water courses down towards the valley, gathering in great blue pools. These pools combine with the pink of the granite to give the visitor the impression of having landed in an enchanted place. The pools remain for days, even months, in the suffocating climate of this region on the very edge of the desert, whose altitude never exceeds 1200 metres, providing the only water source for the inhabitants (the Al-Ṭāhir tribe) and their flocks. There is an ancient path that runs alongside the left bank of the gorge. It starts at the lower site and one finds that, with a few steps cut out into the rock and the terracing, it can still be followed as far as the upper site.

The Social-Religious Zone

Here, in the middle of a wide clearing within the *wādī*, is a deep basin carved into the rock. A few steps cut into one

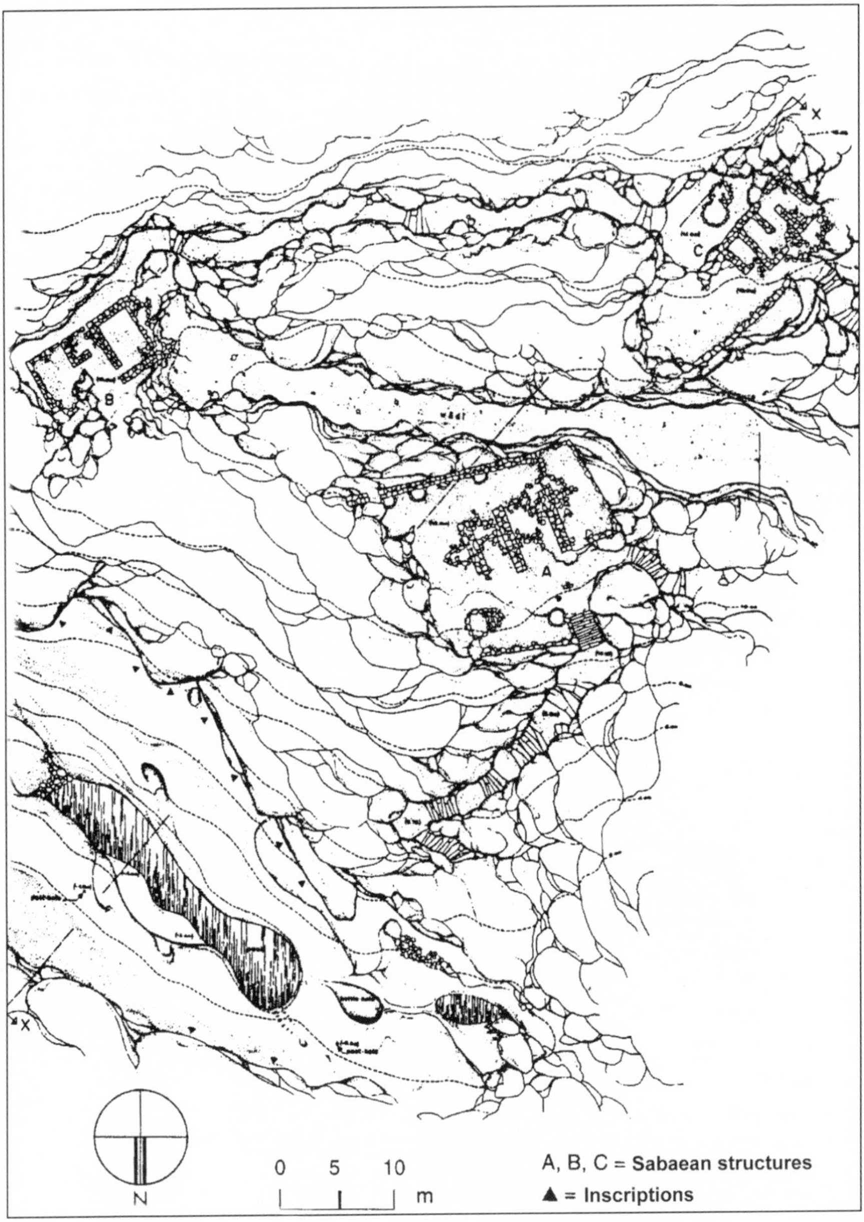

Figure 45
General plan of the Sabaean structures in the upper part of the Shi'b al-'Aql

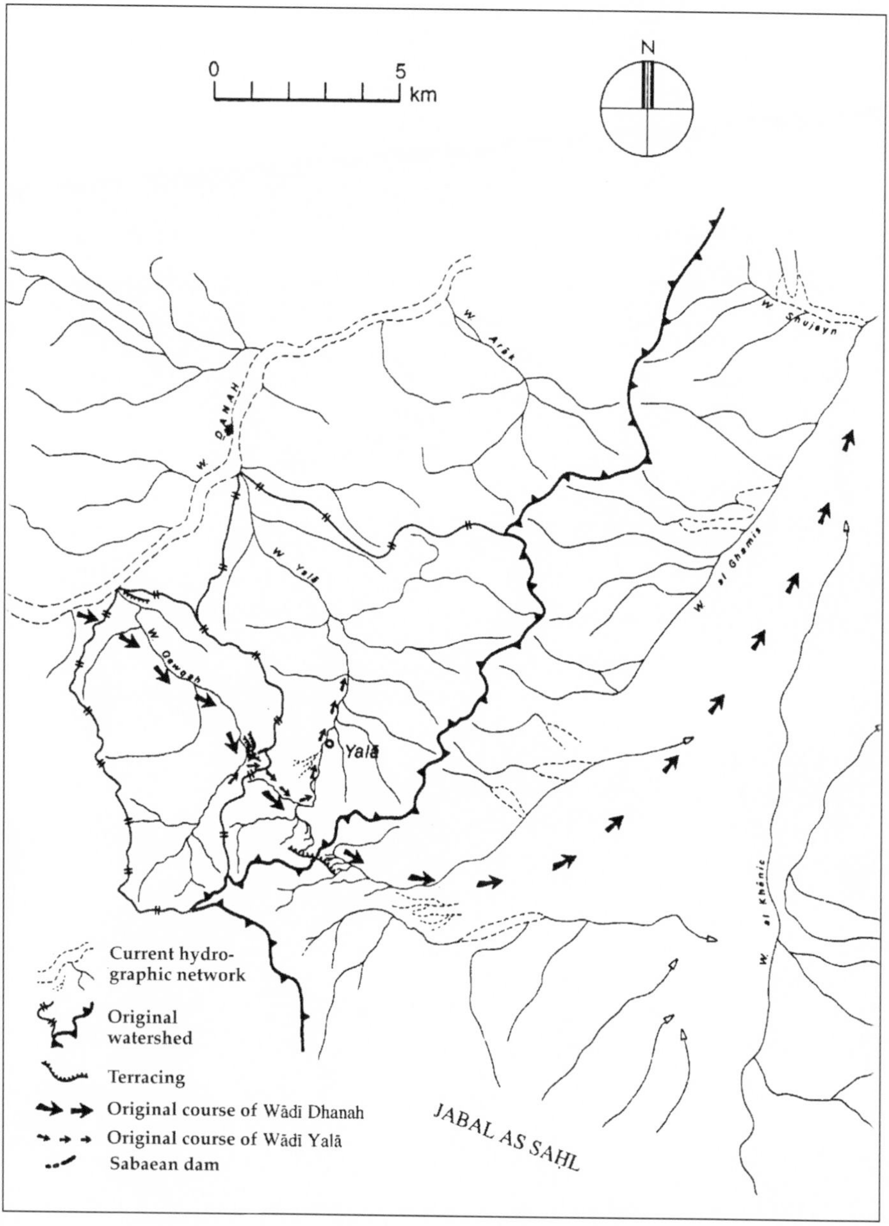

Figure 46
Interpretation of geo-morphological photos of the area around Wādī Yalā

Plate 50
The ruins of the dam across Wādī Qawqah, on the Al-Jafnah plain near Yalā

side, two square holes (possibly designed for wooden posts), and a smooth platform carved out at the water's edge prove that the basin was used in ancient times – possibly for ablutions. Its importance is emphasised by 28 inscriptions carved onto the vertical stone rim, which starts on the south side and runs all around the outside of the pool (Plate 53).

These are the famous inscriptions of Shi'b al-'Aql, precious documents which describe the evolution of the sacred hunt in this area, which was celebrated by the earliest known *mukarribs* of Saba, Yatha''amar Bayyin son of Sumhu'alī, and Karib'īl Watar son of Dhamār'ali (Karib'īl the Great).

A flight of stairs leads from the level of the inscriptions up to an artificial platform built on the rock and supported by a circular terracing wall. In the middle are the remains of a curious building; three thick foundation walls, standing parallel and of different lengths. From here there are paths and stone steps leading to two solitary houses situated nearby. A pre-Islamic tomb found to the north, some fragments of a calcareous basin found near the central building, and the wonderful view from this point suggests

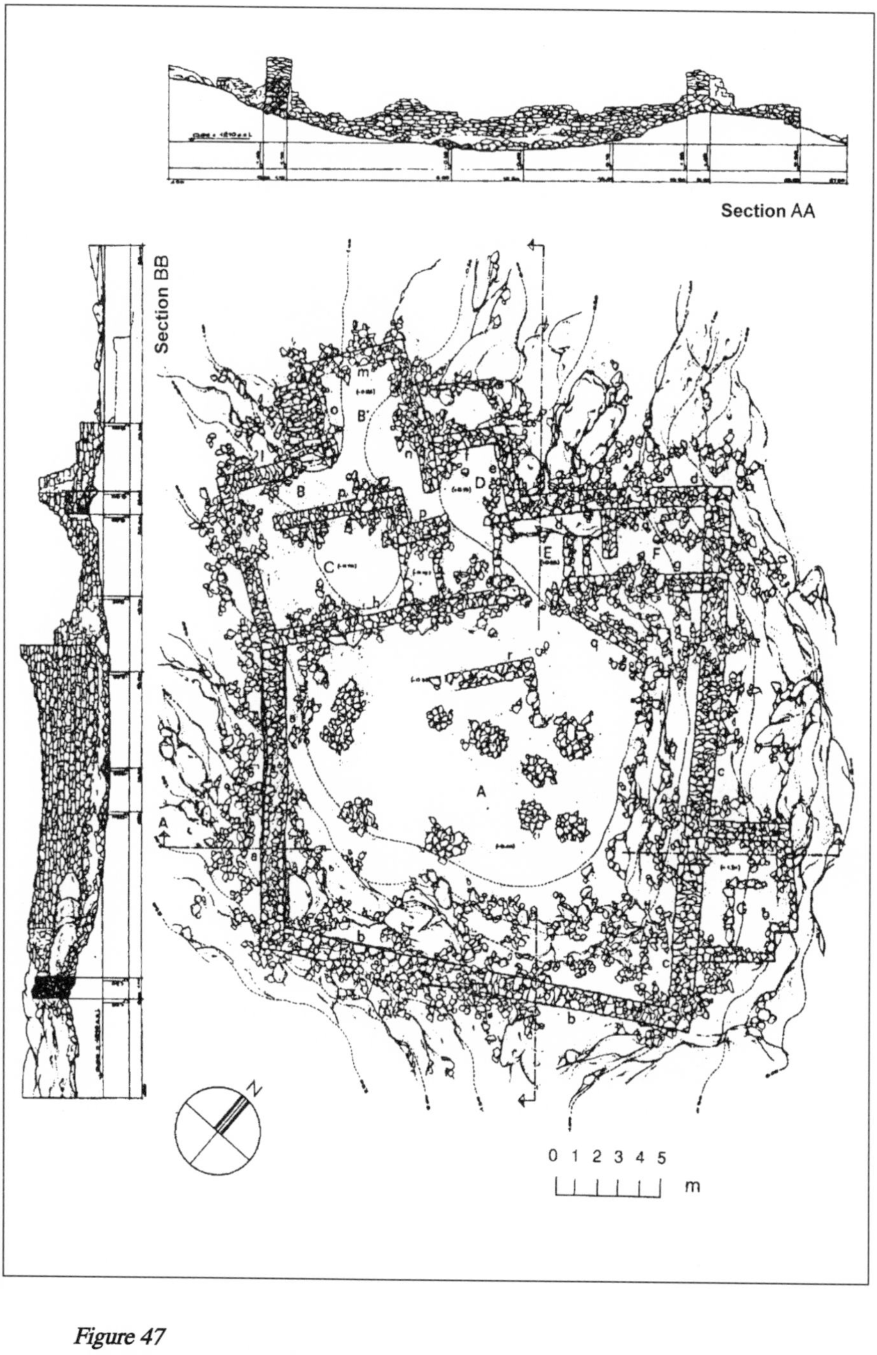

Figure 47
Plan of building G in Al-Jafnah

that a sanctuary could have stood here. This is further confirmed by the similarities between these structures and their location, and those of the upper temple of Jabal al-Lawdh (temple of the Shi'b Mushji').

The geological survey has shown that before the start of the Pleistocene era, the final stretch of Wādī Dhanah was different from how it is now. Before tectonic movements forced it to assume its current hydrographic shape, emptying into the Mārib plain, Wādī Dhanah actually ran through the area which subsequently housed the antiquities of Wādī Yalā, flowing inside the great fault that is now the bed of Wādī Qawqah (Fig. 46). The ancient Sabaeans noticed the wide delta area formed by the sediments of this paleo-Dhanah and were able to put their exceptional hydraulic skills to good use, taking advantage of the particular geomorphological characteristics of the area.

The Economic Production Centre

The site of Al-Jafnah lies on just such sediments. The houses built here were designed for the agricultural exploitation of this exact type of terrain. A stone dam was built across Wādī Qawqah to collect the abundant water flowing down from the Shi'b al-'Aql, and prevent the water from being lost to the north-west, in other words from following its natural course. The water was then directed towards the sedimentary area stretching to the south-east and used for irrigation. We can still clearly see the remains of the dam (Plate 50). The architects of the time managed to avoid the need for a massive construction by choosing to position the water management system at a point where the water flowed more gently, at the watershed between the basin of Wādī Qawqah and that of Wādī Yalā. A containing wall completed the water works, extending the function of the dam eastwards along the thin line of the watershed.

The southernmost point of the dam touched the corner of a large rectangular building, whose walls were particularly carefully constructed (building B). Among the rubble inside this house, we can make out dividing walls that must have separated huge open rooms. This immense and intricately designed building, whose function we can only guess at, is entered through a door which opens at a right angle. A flight of stairs that starts immediately outside the

Figure 48
Reconstruction of the section of the walls around Yalā/Hafarī

door probably led down to a small lake made by the dam. This would confirm that this building was linked to the area's specific designation, water management.

A little further south lies another important structure (building G), situated on a granite outcrop that dominates the expanse of sediments from the west (Fig. 47). Built in rather a refined style, it is made up of a large square room, with smaller secondary rooms opening off it to the north. This building, like building B, can only have been intended for public use.

Around the sedimentary area, and especially to the east, stand the remains of about 20 ancient houses which, although they were built in a rougher style than the two buildings already mentioned, are often fairly large with complex layouts. This is a sort of village made up of widely spaced houses. The plan of these houses tends to be of a type adapted to the agricultural uses made of the ancient fields. We know that these were farmhouses and the like from the consistent presence of stores and threshing floors.

About 300 metres north-west of Al-Jafnah, on the steep left-hand bank of Wādī Qawqah and protected by a rocky spur, there is a large rectangular space divided by long internal partitions, which reminds us of building B. Here, though, the external perimeter wall is thicker, suggesting a sort of stronghold. The nearby rocks bear a few short Sabaean inscriptions (mostly people's names), and one could imagine that a garrison of soldiers may have been stationed here, to protect the settlements from any attacks from the valley of Wādī Qawqah.

The water of Wādī Qawqah, once diverted from its natural course by the dam, irrigated the fields of Al-Jafnah, and turned to the south-east, converging naturally about two kilometres further on in the bed of Wādī Yalā. This *wādī*'s water supply, which was poorer than Wādī Qawqah, was thus increased, allowing it to supply water to the city of Yalā/Al-Durayb, one kilometre down the valley on the right-hand bank of the *wādī* (Fig. 44).

The Residential Centre

We have already discussed the city on several occasions. Now, however, we must simply bear in mind that the area contained by the walls has a total length of 230 metres (north-south), a maximum width of 170 metres and a surface area of almost two and a half hectares. About two-thirds (380 metres) of the original circumference of the walls (580 metres) is still standing, mostly up to the original height. Within the walls to the south-east is the so-called "upper city", a roundish area with higher-standing ruins that occupies almost two-thirds of the total area of the city.

The stone walls have regularly-spaced buttresses and indentations; the buttresses are about five metres wide and the indentations about 4.5 metres (Plate 48). Where the walls are best preserved, one can see an ancient walkway about 2.5 metres up (Fig. 48), whose width varies from 1.6 to 1.2 metres, depending on the presence or lack of buttresses. This was protected on the outside by a wall about 50 centimetres thick that must have stood a couple of metres high as it was designed to cover the height of a man. Seen from the outside, this wall does not seem to fit particularly well with the main body of the walls, which must have stood about 4.5 metres high in total. The main entrance was set into the walls to the north-east, and was flanked by two large rectangular towers, which remind one of the city gate at Barāqish.

The stone used for the walls is different in colour and type from the stone of the ruined "upper city". However, the architectural technique is essentially the same. It is not actually very different from the style of Shi'b al-'Aql and Al-Jafnah. We get the impression, then, that all these ruins were roughly contemporary, which appears to be confirmed by the pottery found on the surface. A study of this collection of various types of Sabaean pottery (Figs. 41-43) has shown clear parallels with pottery excavated by the Americans, especially in levels N-K of Hajar Bin Ḥumayd (eighth to seventh centuries BC)[10].

We have already seen how important the cities are for any attempt to understand the chronology of southern Arabia. Here, though, the city is particularly interesting because, seen in the context of the other antiquities found at Al-Jafnah and at Shi'b al-'Aql, it tells us a lot about the development of the typical Sabaean settlement at this very early date.

In order to establish the functions of the various buildings described above, we first need to establish how they were divided into three distinct physiographic groups. The mountains, the foothills and the plains are the respective locations of the antiquities of Al-'Aql, Al-Jafnah and Yalā. Although these areas differ in height, geology and vegetation, they nonetheless share the same water source, which clearly shows that they represent different activities performed by the same community.

At the start of the water's course, the magnificent gorge of Shi'b al-'Aql, we find evidence of religious-leisure activities; where the water slows down (Al-Jafnah) we find systems of water management and agricultural methods that supported economic/production activities; and where the water finally runs into the *wādī*, we have the great inhabited centre (Yalā/Al-Durayb), the decision-making nucleus.

We are inclined to make a rather bold comparison between this place and the situation in northern Italy, where plains, foothills and mountains are respectively used for cities, electricity production, and tourist activities.

An Integrated Community

This, then, confirms what we deduced from archaeological research: the antiquities from the settlement complex of Yalā reflect the life of a single, unified society. The community based in these valleys on the edge of the desert achieved social and economic integration through internal diversification within a single ecological framework, which they chose for its unusual and favourable water-rich situation.

We are standing at the foot of a high, isolated mountain, Jabal al-Saḥl, whose slopes naturally collect moisture. The mountain attracts water from the clouds that would otherwise pass by, and this water has had a profound, visible impact on the steep northern granite face. The desert is just a step away and the pools of clear water which stay for months in the caverns under the crags of the gorge, must have attracted Sabaean communities in the area.

We know what store the Sabaeans set by isolated mountains and it seems only natural that the antiquities of the upper site of the Shi'b al-'Aql should document ancient practices and cults. This is confirmed by the contents of the inscriptions, which limit themselves to declaring the importance of the activities and the types of ritual that accompanied them. It was here, in the gorge of Jabal as-Saḥl, that the ancient *mukarrib*s came to celebrate their sacred hunt. The sovereigns must have resided in the villa at the lower site during the period of the hunt, and the path cut into the right-hand flank of the gorge must have been their means of reaching the upper site, which was devoted to the cult and, perhaps, the practice of the rite.

The rare references to the hunt in the inscriptions specifically mention the ritual banquet, the federal pact between tribes of the Jabal al-Lawdh and the ritual of chanting names at Al-'Uqlah, and we must ask ourselves whether the various isolated mountains on the edge of the desert were each seen as the seat of a different cult.

At the foot of the mountain, where the water suddenly slows down, the Sabaeans found an ideal combination of natural elements and put into practice their capacity for technology, altering their environment to their best advantage. The dam and its accompanying containing wall bear witness to their ability to work nature. It was built where there was an exceptional flow of water, where fertile, muddy sediments covered vast stretches of land and, most of all, where, on account of a particular topographical circumstance, the water hesitated for an instant before flooding down Wādī Qawqah.

All this resulted in the construction of a modestly-sized dam. The size of the project is not remarkable in itself; the most striking aspect is the inhabitants' feeling for the land and their capacity to evaluate and combine those environmental aspects which justified their choice of a place to settle. Based on an objective, precise analysis of natural features, this project became workable and enabled them to divert the course of the *wādī,* bearing more water into the neighbouring one, and irrigating a pre-existing plain of fertile, cultivable sediments.

The old dam is now broken, and Wādī Qawqah has reverted to its natural course. In 1985, the sheikh of the Al-Ṭāhir tribe declared his intention to "do as the ancients did" to try and solve the problems of his poor agriculture. And in 1987 we found that a small, new dam had been built in exactly the same place as the old one. Although it meant losing all traces of the old structure, the dam has proved itself useful and the sheikh declared himself proud of "his" idea. It was certainly a good idea, but nothing compared to the vision of the first builders at the time of the *mukarrib*s of Saba.

Footnotes:

1. Ryckmans, J., "Villes fortifiées du Yemen antique", *Bulletin de la Classe de Lettres et de Sciences morales et politiques de l'Académie Royale de Belgiques, 5e Série,* 67 (1981-85), p. 255.

2. Robin, C. and Ryckmans, J., "Les inscriptions de Al-Asāḥil, Al-Durayb et Hirbat Sa'ūd", *Raydān* 3 (1980), p. 113-181.
3. van Beek, G., "Marginally Drafted, Pecked Masonry", in Bowen, R., and Albright, F.P., *Archaeological Discoveries in South Arabia* (Baltimore: Johns Hopkins Press, 1958), p. 287-298.
4. Breton, J.F., *Fouilles de Shabwa II. Rapports préliminaires* (Paris: 1992).
5. See Doe, B., *Southern Arabia* (London: McGraw-Hill, 1971); and *Monuments of South Arabia* (Naples: Falcon, 1983).
6. Beeston, A., "Functional Significance of the Old South Arabian 'Town'", *PSAS* 1 (1971), p. 26-28.
7. Schmidt, J., "Baugeschichtliche Untersuchungen an den Bauanlagen des grossen Dammes von Mārib", *ABADY* I, p. 123-125.
8. Beeston, A., "The Sayhadic Hunt at Si'b al-'Aql" in *Etudes sudarabes. Recueil offert à Jacques Ryckmans* (Louvain-la-Neuve: 1991), p. 49-57. See also Garbini, G., "The Inscriptions of Si'b al'Aql, Al-Jafnah and Yalā/Ad-Durayb" in de Maigret, A., *The Sabaean Archaeological Complex in the Wādī Yalā* (Rome: IsMEO, 1988), p. 21-40.
9. Marcolongo, B. and Palmeiri, A., "Environmental modification and settlement conditions in the Yalā area", in de Maigret, A., *The Sabaean Archaeological Complex in the Wādī Yalā*, p. 45-51.
10. van Beek, G., *Hajar Bin Humeid. Investigations at a Pre-Islamic Site in South Arabia* (Baltimore: Johns Hopkins Press, 1969).

XVI

THE TEMPLES

Distribution

Most of the pre-Islamic temples that we know of are situated in the hinterland of Yemen. This seems to be because, in the period of Saba and Dhū-Raydān, temples were not considered very important. As we saw in our study of the cities, urban planning in mountain communities of this period focused more on palaces than temples. With the advent of monotheism in the subsequent period (from the fourth century AD onwards), the pagan temples disappeared completely, and were replaced by churches and synagogues, for which we unfortunately have no archaeological evidence.

The temples situated along the caravan route are, therefore, both the most numerous and the oldest. Not all of these temples are situated within a city. Besides the *intra muros* temples of Al-Bayḍā and Al-Sawdā, Ma'īn, Barāqish, Kharībat Sa'ūd, Ṣirwāḥ, Mārib, Timna', Shabwat, Ḥurayḍah and Khawr Rūrī, there are numerous extra muros examples at Al-Sawdā, Kharībat Hamdān, Kamnah, Ma'īn, Barāqish, and, of course, at Mārib.

The Stone Sanctuaries

Given the relative antiquity of these *extra muros* temples, one would perhaps be tempted to think that they were older than the cities, and were situated in particular, established places of devotion.

Besides, there are many examples of isolated sanctuaries of great antiquity in Yemen. Most of these were built on mountains or plateaux, like those on the summit of Jabal al-Lawdh, on the hill of Darb as-Sabi near Barāqish, and at the top of Shi'b al-'Aql near Yalā. We have already seen how certain rocks and mountains were considered sacred in South Arabia as they represented a divinity; a temple situated on one of these was seen as being one step nearer to the divinity. These temples have irregular layouts and although they remained in use until a late date, they are very probably some of the oldest temples ever built in South Arabia[1].

We should probably look for their predecessors in prehistoric monuments like the lines of stones of Wādī al-Hamilī, near Al-Mukhā[2] (Fig. 49) , the groups of betyl found recently by the French in the desert north of Jabal al-Lawdh, and in structures like those found by our Italian mission near the village of Banī ‘Aṭif in the Al-‘Arūsh region (Fig. 50, Plate 51).

We can perhaps add to this category of temples, whose plans rely on the nature of their surroundings, the Awwam temple at Mārib, at least in terms of its great oval encircling wall; and a similar temple discovered at Riyām by the Soviets, on the high plain of ‘Amrān[3]. We should maybe also include the oval temple of Ṣirwāḥ in this category (Fig. 14).

From the various typological studies carried out on the square temples of the following period – from A. Grohmann’s[4], through J. Schmidt’s[5], to M. Jung’s[6] – we can trace separate evolutions for two principal categories of buildings, the first containing courtyards, and the second hypostyle, or without courtyards. Both types probably derived from the roofless temple with simple, non-fixed, internal partitions, a few examples of which we can see in the Mārib area: the temple of Dish al-Aswad (Fig. 51) and the temple on the Rahabah plain.

Courtyard Temples

Temple courtyards were made by dividing the rectangular interior of the building into two, producing a tripartite cell in the farthest third and a wide open courtyard nearest the entrance, which was placed on an axis (Fig. 52). One of the oldest examples of this type was discovered by the German archaeological mission on Jabal Balaq al-Awsaṭ near Mārib, which we can date, on the basis of the inscriptions, to the seventh to sixth centuries BC.

Later, a portico supported by pilasters was added to the courtyard and the entrance was adorned with a propylaeum, as we find in the temple of Waddum Dhū-Masma‘īm (Fig. 53), discovered by the same mission on the western slope of Jabal Balaq al-Qiblī, near Mārib[8], as well as in the lovely temple of ‘Athtar excavated by J.F. Breton east of Al-Sawdā in the Jawf [9] (Fig. 54), and in the temple of Al-

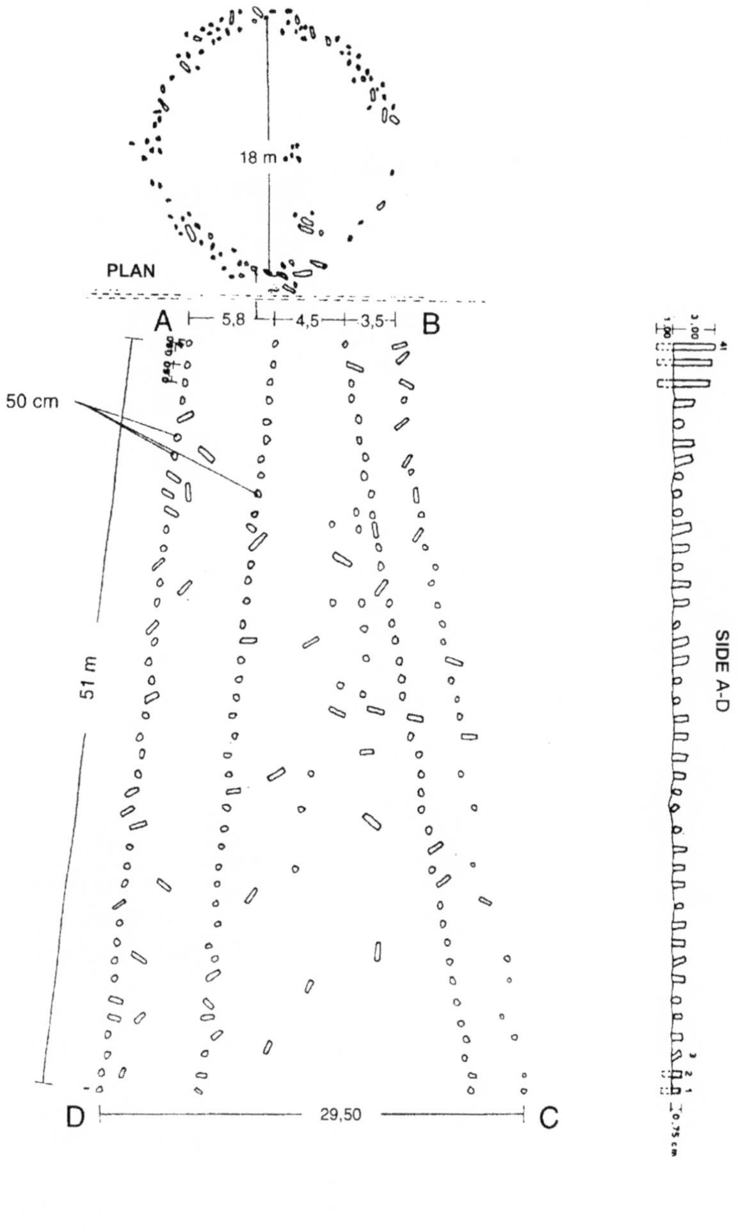

Figure 49
Plan of the megalithic complex of Wādī Al-Hamilī

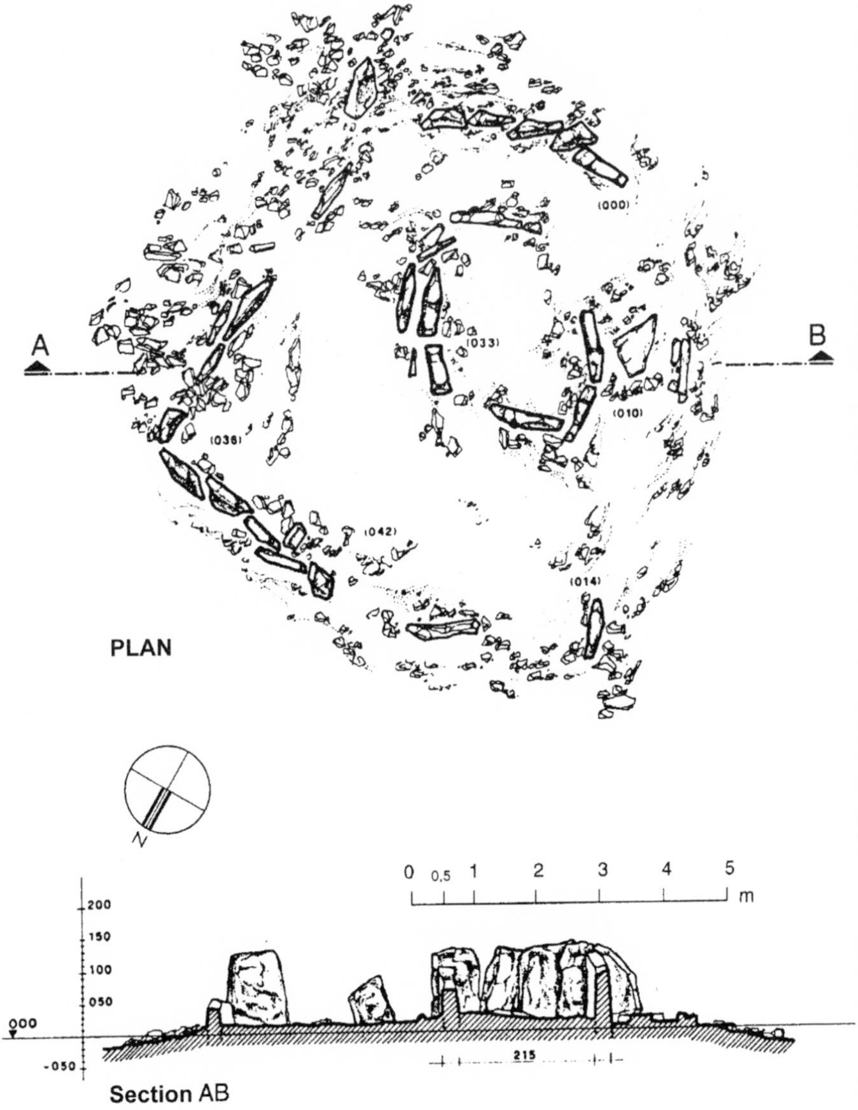

Figure 50
Plan and section of the megalithic structure in site 3 of Banī 'Atif *(BATiii)*

Plate 51
Bronze Age megalithic structure (BATiii), near Banī 'Atif (Khawlān al-Tiyal)

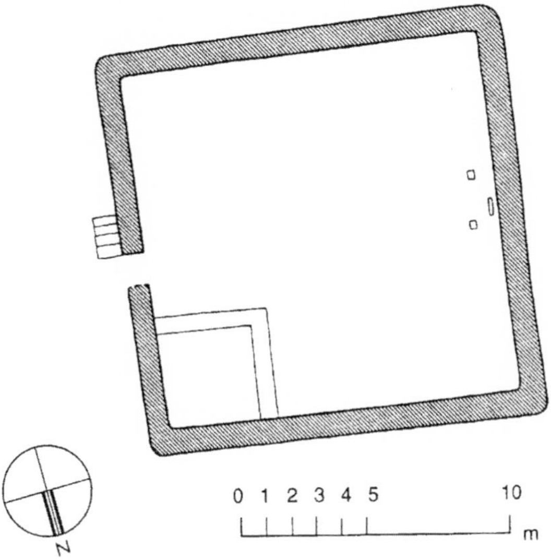

Figure 51
Plan of the temple of Dish al-Awsad

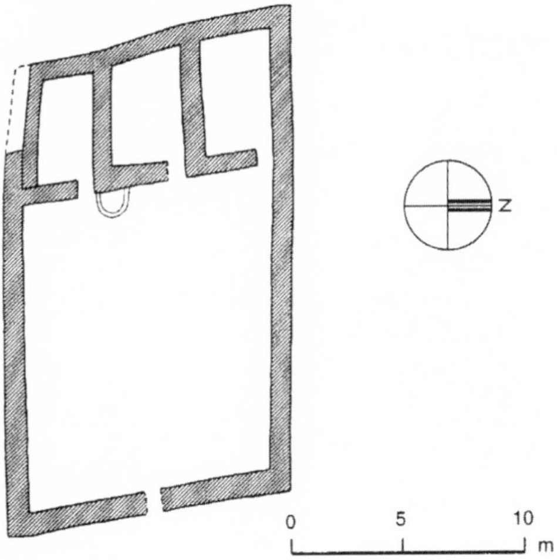

Figure 52
Plan of a temple on Jabal Balaq al-Awsat, near Mārib

Masājid (Fig. 55) about 30 kilometres south of Mārib[10].

Courtyard temples were used until a fairly late date, as the temple of Ḥuqqah (Fig. 56) shows, with its strong Hellenistic influence and clear signs of a change in the relationship between the width of the courtyard and that of the cell and the addition of rooms opening off the sides of the courtyard.

This expansion basically separated the courtyard from the cell and is therefore an important development for the history of religious architecture in Yemen. It seems to be a common feature, both in the highlands (at Ḥuqqah) and in the desert regions, as shown by the so-called temple of ʻAthtar at Timnaʻ (Fig. 22), the "royal palace" of Shabwat, which we actually believe to be a temple on account of its complex plan (Fig. 57), and – as far as we can tell at this point – the Bar'an temple at Mārib, currently being excavated by the German archaeological mission.

Hypostyle Temples

Hypostyle temples are composed of a single room and are almost cuboid in shape. They are small buildings, which may be why they are often very well preserved (in other words, up to roof level). The roof is supported by two,

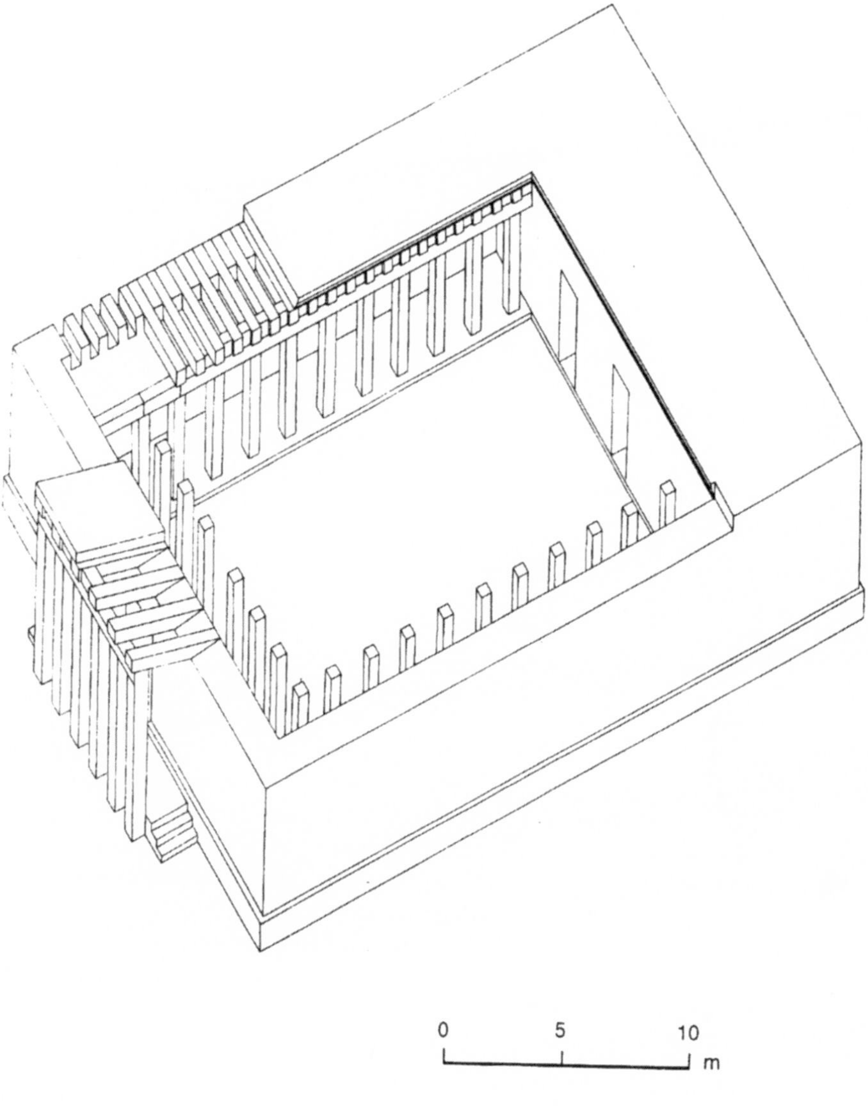

Figure 53
Axonometric reconstruction of the temple of Waddum Dhū-Masma'īm, near Mārib

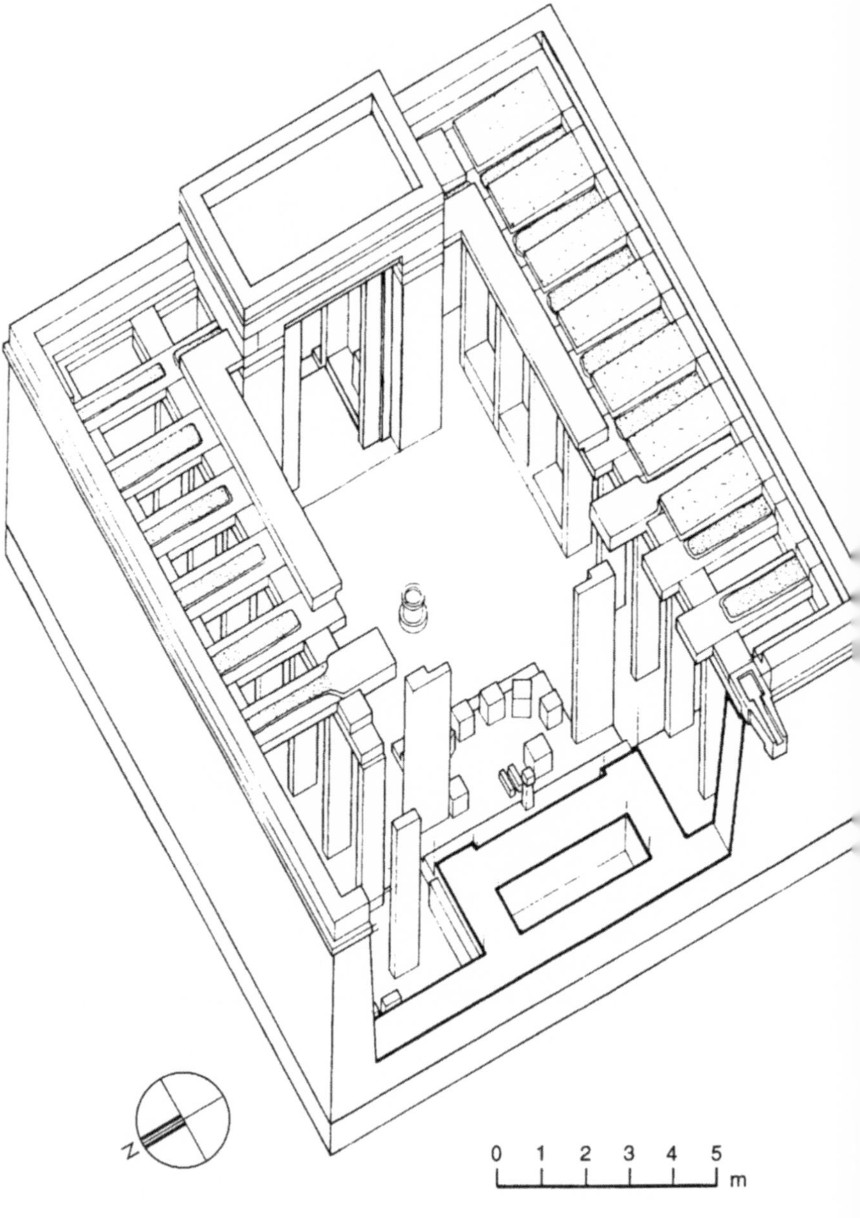

Figure 54
Axonometric reconstruction of the temple of ʻAthar, near Al-Sawdā/Nashan

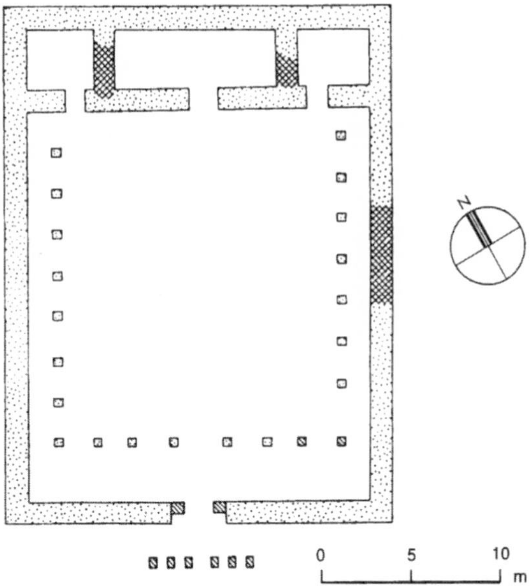

Figure 55
Plan of the temple of Al-Masajid

three, four or five rows of pilasters, which delineate the aisles within the room. A cell or cells would have stood slightly higher than the floor level of the hall.

One of the oldest examples of this type is the temple that stands on the left bank of Wādī al-Shaqab, a few kilometres south of Barāqish (Fig. 58). Both the five rows of pilasters and the monolithic roof beams are roughly shaped, and show no sign of refinement or decoration.

The hypostyle temples discovered by the French mission in Wādī Ḥaḍramawt (temples of Hajrah, Makaynūn, Ḥuṣn al-Qays and Ba Qutfah) (Figs. 59 and 60), and in Wādī Du'ān (temples of Raybūn) (Fig. 61), must also be relatively ancient, considering that the plans are not substantially different from the "moon temple" of Ḥurayḍah, (Fig. 5), whose oldest phase dates from the sixth century BC.

The Hadrami temples all stand on a high platform which is reached by a long monumental stairway. They are not large, and the inside rarely contains more than two rows of pilasters. We often find two twin temples positioned together on the same platform.

In the Jawf, there are hypostyle temples – besides the

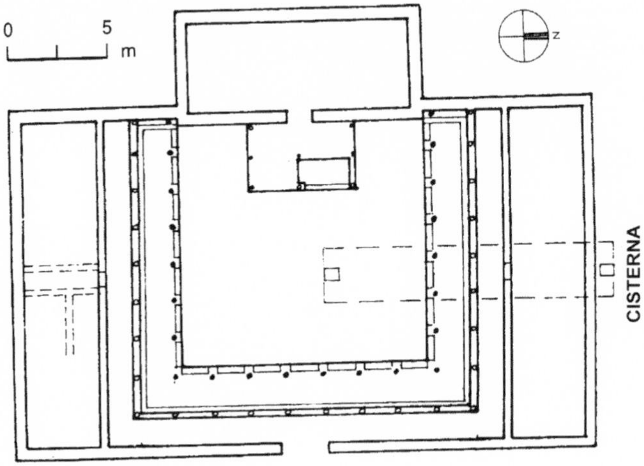

Figure 56
Plan of the temple of Ḥuqqah

Wādī ash-Shaqab examples already mentioned – at Barāqish (temple of Nakraḥ) and at Ma'īn (the so-called *intra muros* temple) (Fig. 62). As the Barāqish excavations found, hypostyle temples were in use in this area at least until the end of the kingdom of Ma'īn, in other words, around the beginning of the first century BC. This appears to be confirmed by the profusion of this type of temple on the plateaux at this time. A hypostyle temple has also been found at the ancient site of Kāniṭ, slightly east of Raydah, which shows clear Hellenistic influences in the type of columns used. (Fig. 63).

Schmidt finds that the two classes of temples, the courtyard type and the hypostyle type, represent two completely different concepts of space[11]. One type generally has a long directional axis that leads the devout along a predetermined route (propylaeum, main entrance, courtyard, cell door and *cella*), as he slowly but steadily approaches the divinity. The other style, by contrast, generally has an almost square plan and therefore has no preferential axis. Here the worshippers enter (through a gateway which is often not on an axis) and find themselves alone, surrounded by a forest of pilasters, in a room with no directional references. They are free to experience the divine in an individual way. The first type is conditioned by an established form of religious sentiment, which is far more abstract in the second type.

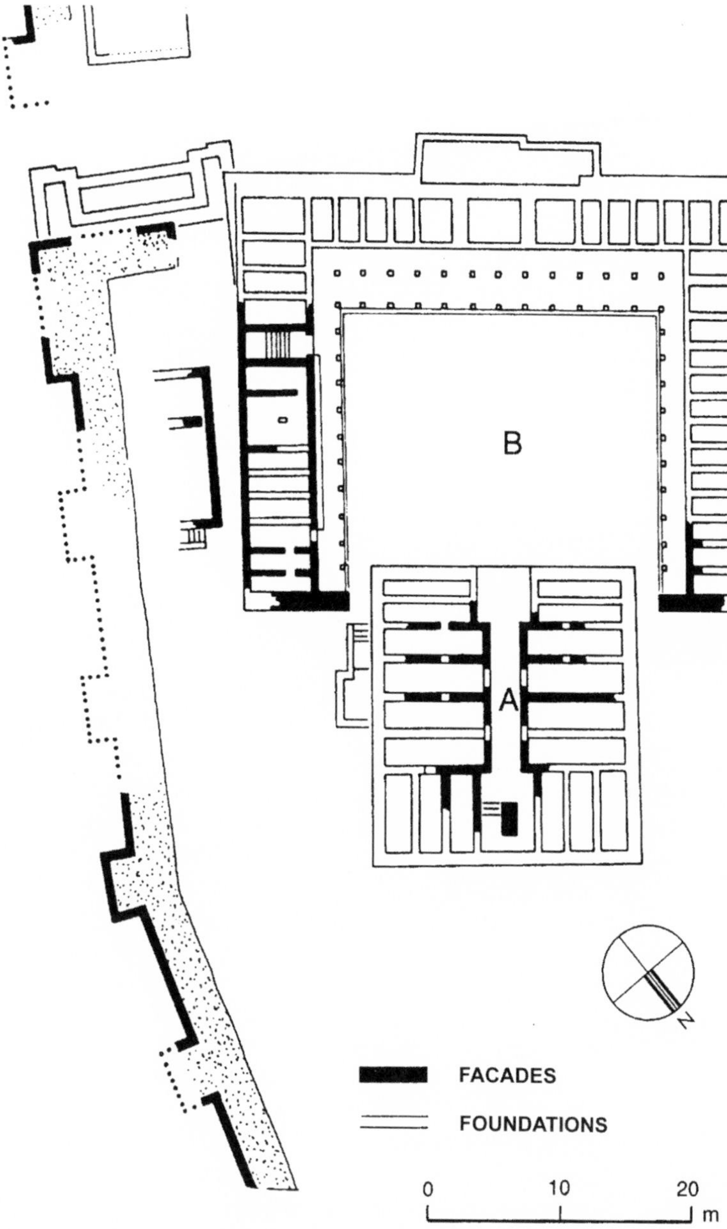

Figure 57
Plan of the so-called "royal palace" of Shabwat

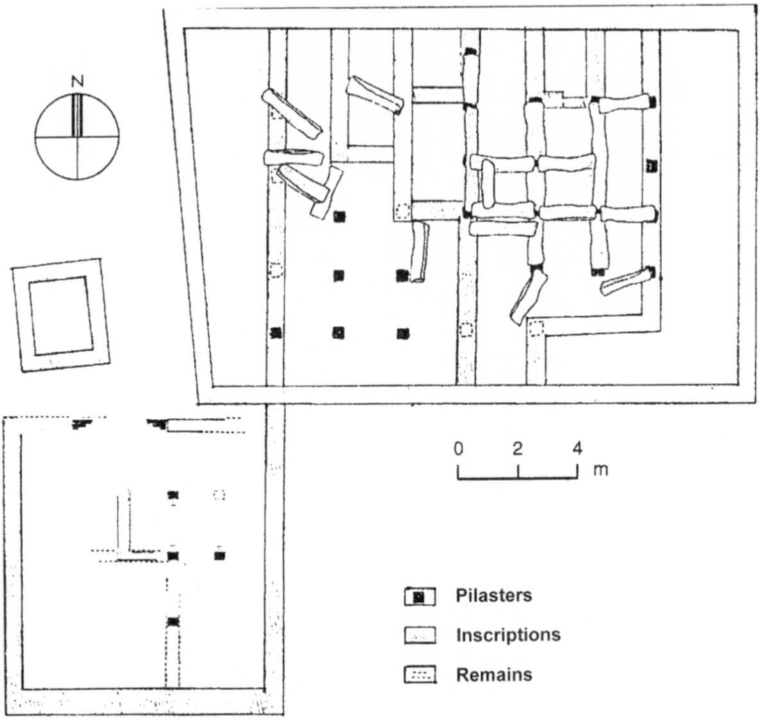

Figure 58
Plan of the temple in Wādī al-Shaqab, near Barāqish

We find Schmidt's theory valid, partly because he manages to highlight the influence of South Arabia on the religious architecture of the ancient Near East as a whole. While the courtyard temple clearly adopts some architectural elements and perhaps religious concepts that originated in the Syrio-Palestine area, the hypostyle temple is clearly the result of a genuine creativity based entirely on local inspiration and thoughts. This form of temple gives us the best sense of the geometry, formal abstraction and stereometry that are also evident in statuary and are the characteristic elements of art of the formative period and later, the mature period. This is a concept of a form, as real in its precision and rigorous geometric rules, as it is abstract and intangible in its overall simplicity and purity. This characteristic is never lost, even under the increasing pressure of foreign influences – Hellenistic, Roman, Ethiopian and Indian.

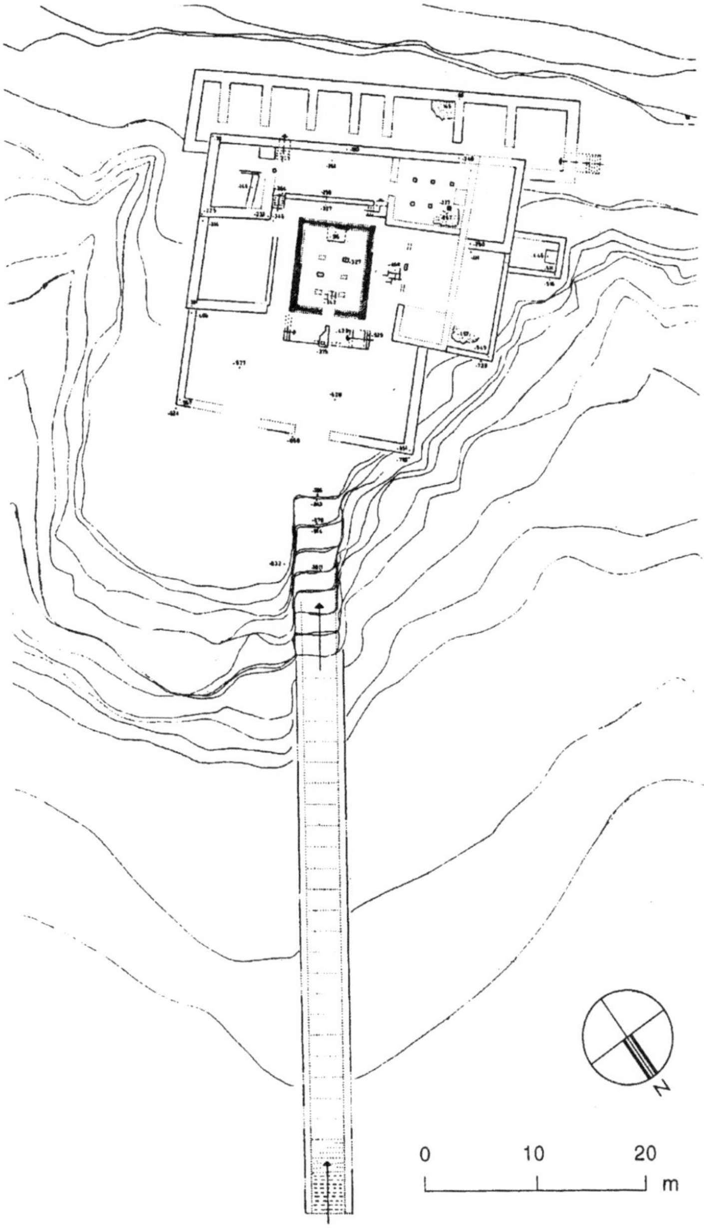

Figure 59
Plan of the temple of Al-Hajrah in the Ḥaḍramawt

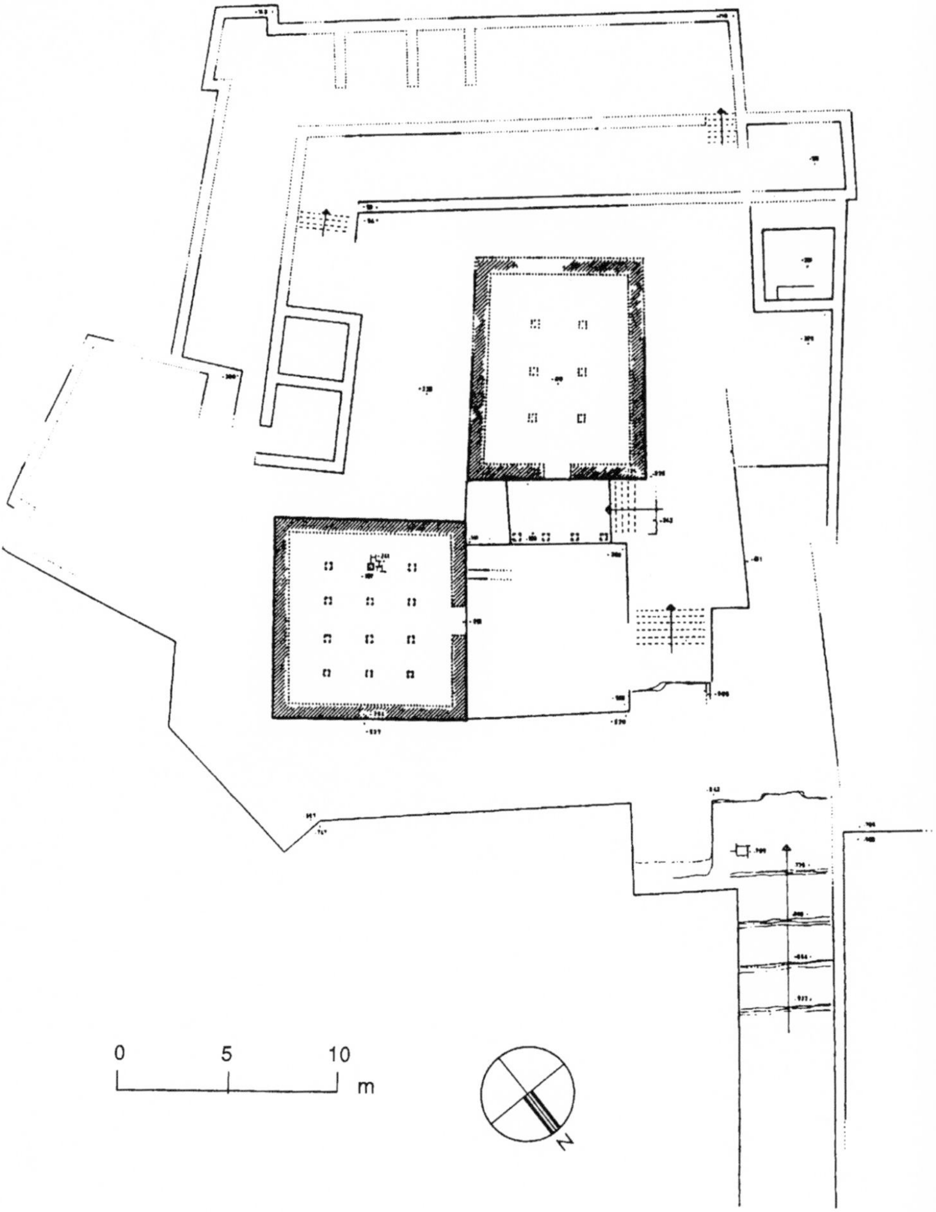

Figure 60
Plan of the temple of Husn al-Qays in the Ḥaḍramawt

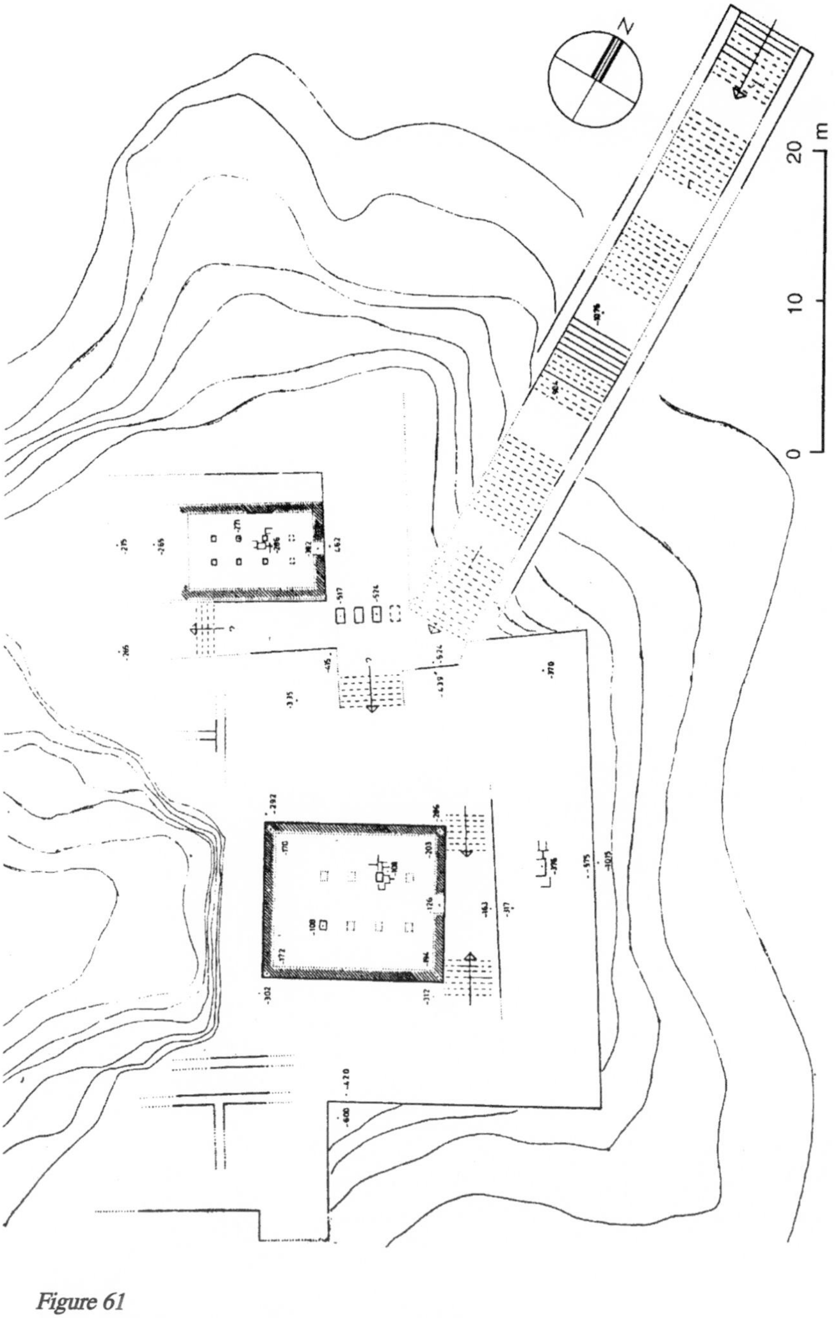

Figure 61
Plan of the temple of Raybun-west, in Wādī Hu'an

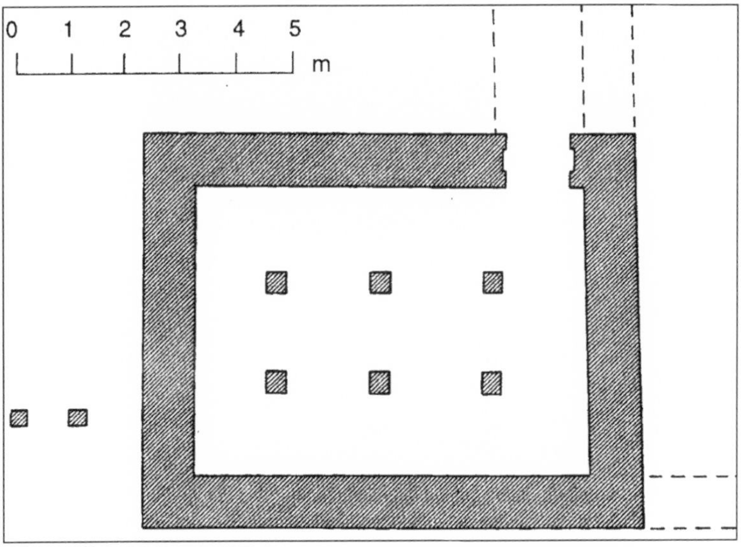

Figure 62
Plan of the *intramurros* temple of Ma'īn/Qarnāw (Schmidt 1982)

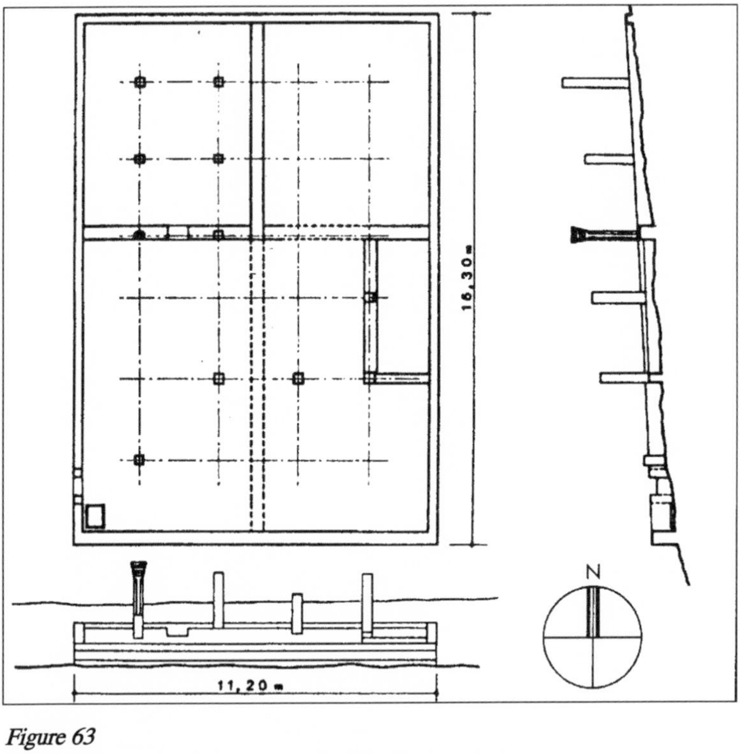

Figure 63
Plan of the temple at Kānit, near Raydah (Robin 1976)

Schmidt linked these two concepts of space found in temple architecture to two specific cultural areas: the courtyard temple with the Sabaean area and the hypostyle with the Minaean and Qatabanian area[12]. This is, of course, difficult to prove. On the one hand it is difficult to find examples of the hypostyle temple in Qatabān (while as we have seen, the style was common in Ḥaḍramawt), and on the other we find courtyard temples spread throughout Minaean territory (like the *extra muros* temples of Al-Sawdā, Kharībat Hamdān, Ma'īn and Kamnah).

We could perhaps phrase the question differently, considering its importance, and relate it to the origin of the hypostyle temple. I think that in this case – considering the results of the recent Russian excavations in Wādī Du'ān – we should consider the Ḥaḍramawt region as the birthplace of this original and important architectural form.

Footnotes:

1. Jung, M., "The Religious Monuments of Ancient South Arabia. A Preliminary Typological Classification", *AION* 48 (1989), p. 182.
2. Benardelli, G. and Parrinello, A.E., "Note su alcune località archeologiche del Yemen, I" *AION* 30 (1970), p. 117-120.
3. Grjaznevich, P.A., "K topografii contral'nogo Arhaba (Sirvah-Rijam-Itva)", *Drevnjaja Aravija* (1914), p. 56-71.
4. Grohmann, A., *Arabien* (Munchen: Beck, 1963), p. 157.
5. Schmidt, J., "Zur altsüdarabischen Tempelarchitektur", *ABADY* I (1982), p. 161-169.
6. Jung, M., "The Religious Monuments of Ancient South Arabia. A Preliminary Typological Classification", *AION* 48 (1989), p. 179-181.
7. Müller, W.W., "Sabäische Felsinschriften von Gabal Balaq al-Ausat", *ABADY* I (1982), p. 67.
8. Schmidt, J. "Der tempel des Waddum Du-Masma'im", *ABADY* I (1982), p. 91-99.
9. Breton, J.F., "Le sanctuaire de 'Athtar dhū-Risaf d'As-Sawdā", *CRAIBL* (1992), p. 429-453.
10. Schmidt, J., "Tempel und Heiligtum von Al-Masagid", *ABADY* I (1982), p. 135-140.
11. Schmidt, J., "Zur altsüdarabischen Tempelarchitektur", p. 163.
12. Ibid, p. 167.

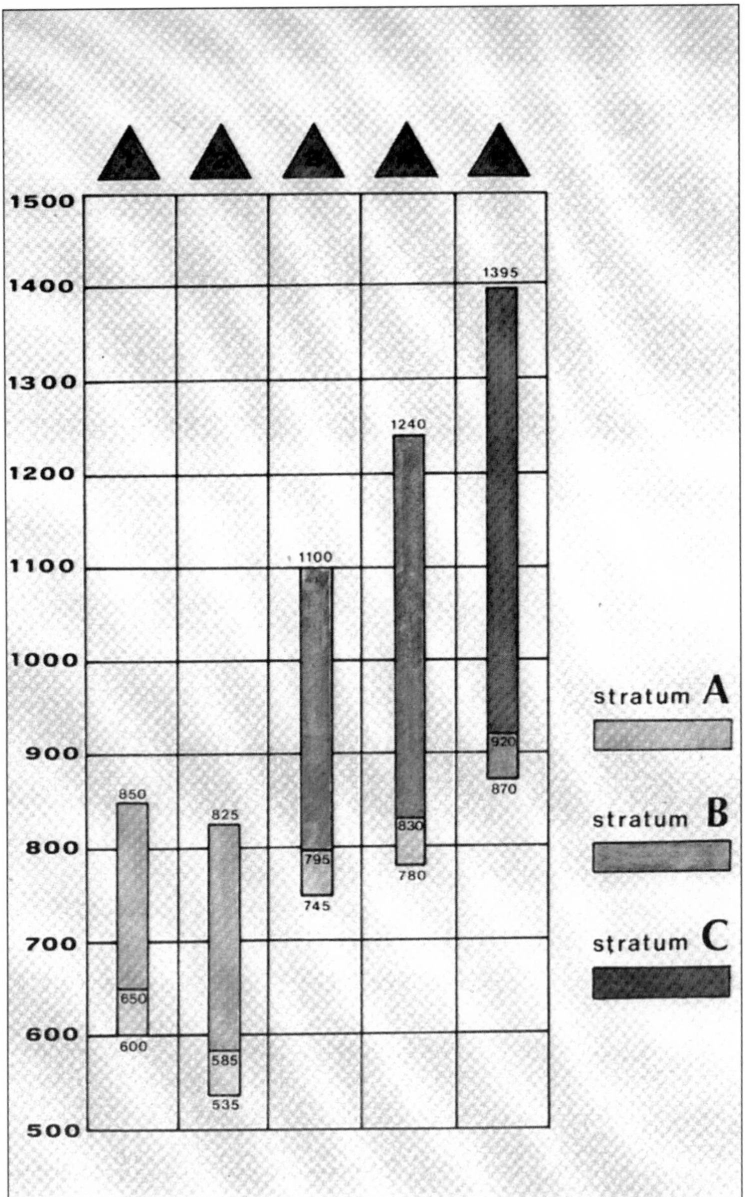

Table 9
Summarised outline showing the C14 dates found for carbon samples taken from the stratigraphic sequence of house A in Yalā/Al-Durayb

Plate 52
View of the Shi'b al-'Aql, near Yalā

Plate 53
Inscriptions on the rock at Shi'b al-'Aql, near Yalā

Plate 54
View of Barāqish/Yathil from the west

Plate 55
View of the temple of Nakrah (Barāqish) after the 1989-1990 excavations

Plate 56
Excavated area south-west of the temple of Nakrah (Barāqish)

Plate 57
Turret tomb in the Al-Makhdarah area (Ṣirwāḥ)

Plate 58
View of the northern sector of the Al-Makhdarah necropolis (Ṣirwāḥ)

Plate 59
Alabaster statues of two sovereigns of Awsān (1st century BC)

Plate 60
View of the walls of Barāqish

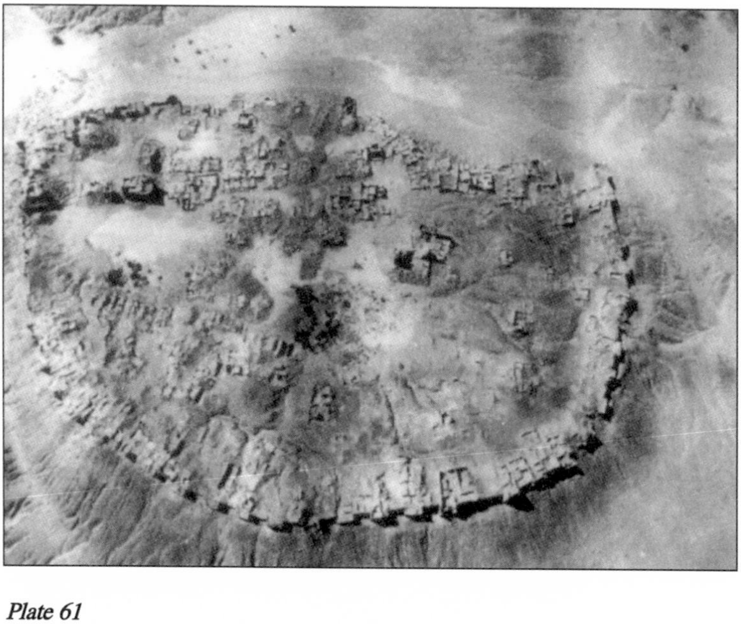

Plate 61
Aerial photograph of Barāqish/Yathil (by Christian Robin)

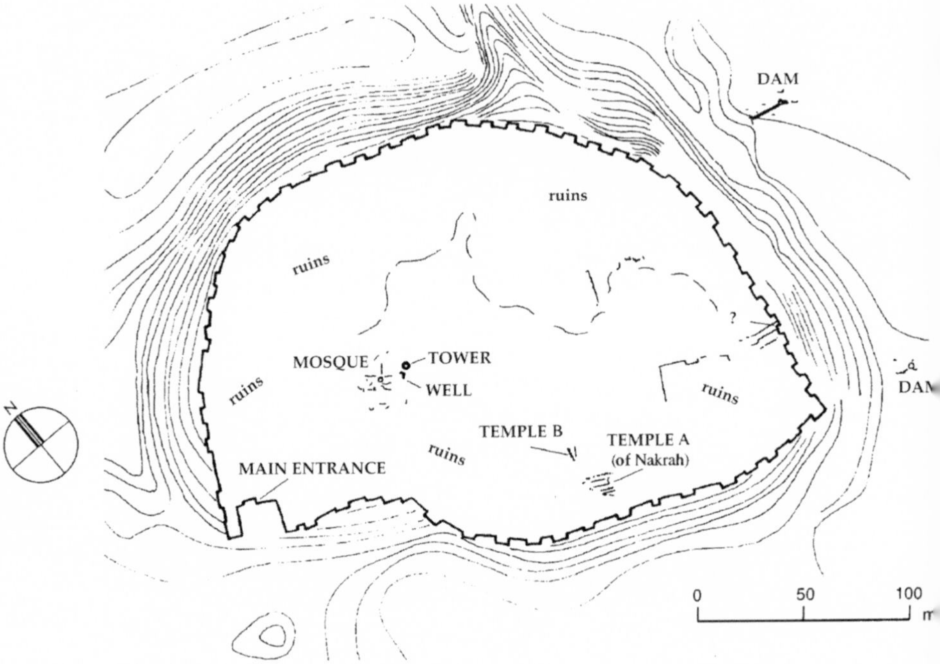

Figure 64
General plan of Barāqish/Yathil

XVII

THE NAKRAḤ TEMPLE EXCAVATIONS

Barāqish

The research carried out by the Italian archaeological mission in Yemen during 1989-90 and then in 1992 centred on the excavation of just such a hypostyle temple. This was the famous southern temple of Barāqish, which Ḥayyim Ḥabshush visited in 1869 and which Aḥmad Fakhry photographed in 1947.

We were given the opportunity to undertake the excavation by the General Organisation for the Antiquities and Libraries of Ṣan'ā's decision to entrust to Italy a new programme for the conservation and study of Barāqish. The Italian Foreign Office drew up an agreement for archaeological cooperation with the Yemeni Government, and the project was then entrusted to IsMEO and, therefore, our mission. Work was to begin with the excavation and restoration of the temple at the southern end of the city, which we conventionally call temple A.

Barāqish, previously named Yathil, was conquered by the Roman general Aelius Gallus in 24 BC. After the capital Qarnāw, it was the second city of the kingdom of Ma'īn (Plate 54). However, by the time of Augustus, Yathil had already started its steady decline. Having perhaps fallen into the hands of nomads, the city was coming to the end of a period of opulence and splendour (the Minaean period) which had probably begun in around the seventh to sixth centuries BC. But the history of Yathil reaches much further back in time than this.

A series of mechanical probes within the walls brought to light some polished reddish shards fairly similar to those found in the archaic Sabaean excavations at Yalā, all of which predate the seventh to sixth centuries. Together with the remarkable thickness of the pre-Minaean (or Sabaean) strata, this suggests that Yathil may have had a millennnium-long pre-Islamic history.

The encircling walls are in a good state of preservation (partly due to the city's re-occupation in Islamic times) and the ruins occupy a gloriously isolated position in the desert, making this city one of the archaeological marvels, not just

Plate 62
View of the temple of Nakrah at Barāqish after the 1992 excavations

of Yemen, but of the entire Near East (Plate 61). It is appropriate that the excavation of such an important site should include a comprehensive project to preserve and investigate the city, to encourage the discovery of the ruins and the restoration of the walls. This was an ambitious and difficult project and we were comforted by the knowledge that it was an historic opportunity to undertake the first ever continuous, thorough investigation of one of the greatest centres of South Arabia.

The fortified walls (Fig. 64) are about 766 metres long and surround a more or less semi-circular area of approximately 7.25 hectares. The city is 276 metres at its longest extent (the south-west diameter); and 188 metres at its widest point (taken along the north-east radius).

High up, the walls were fairly well repaired by the later

Islamic occupants, but the Minaean foundations, which are visible around most of the perimeter, bear witness to an exceptionally accomplished architectural technique, using large, well-hewn stones whose polished surfaces are decorated with a raised, rough area within smoothed frames. The average height of the walls must have been around 14 metres, which appears to be proven by one of the southern bastions which has miraculously remained intact right up to its crown of battlements.

The radiocarbon dates – which we gathered during a brief reconnaissance trip in 1986 – tell us that although Yathil was destroyed in the second century BC, it was still occupied around the time of Christ[1]. The city must, however, have been abandoned shortly after this and left for almost a thousand years, until it was re-occupied in the twelfth century AD, when the walls were rebuilt around an extensive, long-lasting settlement. The city was then definitively abandoned in the eighteenth century. The Islamic period of occupation has left an archaeological layer three to four metres thick, which has covered and protected the underlying layer, which dates from the Minaean era. While this may form an obstacle for the recovery of buildings of the classical period, it also had the advantage of protecting and preserving them intact.

Therefore, a walk around the great oval site of the city today reveals very little of the ancient settlement of Yathil. Of the mass of stones and mud which is all that remains of the medieval city, our only clues are in the recycled stones bearing decorations and inscriptions, the strong, neat foundations of the walls and the pilasters of some of the temples which, on account of their height, still protrude here and there through the later levels. The excavations centred on one such area, where a group of square pilasters (temple A) rose out of the ground[2] (Plate 62).

The Temple of Nakraḥ

Now, after two rounds of excavations, the temple which these pilasters belonged to has been completely excavated, and we can construct a structural framework for it, and perhaps even a complete chronology[3].

The temple (Fig. 65) consists of a hypostyle room (B areas), an access lobby (A areas) and an annex to the side (C, also called the sacristy). The total length of the building

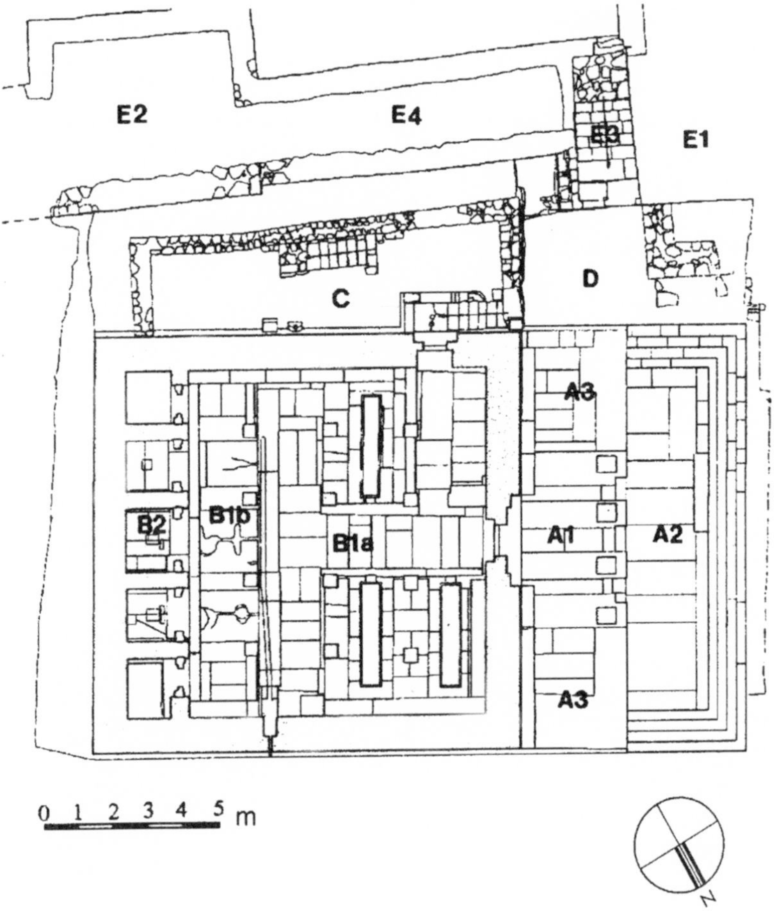

Figure 65
Plan of the temple of Nakrah at Barāqish (G Tilia and A Bizzarro)

is 18.7 metres; and the width (excluding the sacristy) is 11.6 metres.

The hypostyle room has kept its stone facade, in some places up to roof level. This is a complex trabeation of monolithic blocks of stone, all well-smoothed, decorated and covered with strong stone cladding (Plate 55). These final slabs, cemented in with plaster, are placed on calcareous joists about two metres long and 35 centimetres thick, which run across the axis of the temple and are placed in turn at regular intervals on top of larger girders, 45 centimetres thick and up to 4.5 metres long, this time aligned with the axis of the building's entrance. The gaps between the smaller beams are filled with rectangular metopes, decorated with a battlement motif. The trabeation rests on the perimeter walls of the room and the middle is supported by 12 pilasters standing at a height of about four metres and the same width as the principal beams. Both the pilasters and the beams are decorated in the typical way; a slightly rough-hewn centre within a smooth frame. The 12 pilasters, standing in four rows, divide the room into five parts. There is a sort of central nave about 1.7 metres wide and four side aisles (two on each side) each about 1.5 metres wide.

Entering the room through the main door, flanked by the two high monolithic jambs, which must have supported complex architraves, and with a room on the right leading to the outside, one walks down the central nave of the temple, which runs eastward and culminates in a small final cell (Fig. 66). To the left of this nave we find two sets of stone benches and great offertory plates, whose edges are decorated with reliefs depicting ibex. The slabs supporting the front of these plates bear inscriptions which describe how the two cenacles were dedicated by Basil dhū Ma's to bless the agricultural produce of autumn and spring. Underneath the rows of ibex along the edges of the plates, we find inscribed the words *ḫrf* (easternmost plate) and *dtʿ ʾ* (westernmost plate), which do indeed mean autumn and spring. There is another, similar, arrangement to the right of the nave. Here we find the word *dyṯ* inscribed under the ibex, although there is no inscription on the front supporting slab.

Beyond the offertory plates there is a large open space, marked off by a step running the width of the room which raises the height of the remaining, southern part of the temple. A channel has been carved out of the great square paving slabs. It runs under the step into a low opening and out through the hall's northern wall to emerge outside the building. Three drains are united in this channel, all originating in the raised level known as the antecell (Fig. 65). Here we find three oval hollows in the floor, designed to receive fluids that would flow in three small separate channels before amalgamating in the large channel situated

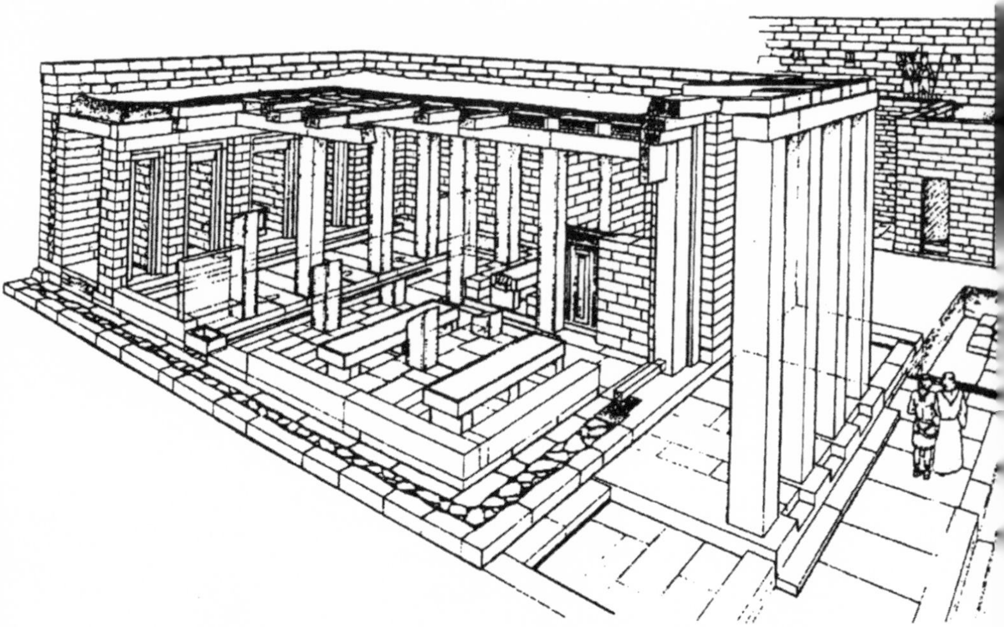

Figure 66
Axonometric reconstruction of the interior of the temple of Nakrah (by Edoardo Gatti)

under the extreme west of the step. This area is situated right in front of the five cells of the temple (B2) and this is where victims were sacrificed to the divinity. The small basins hollowed out from the paving slabs and the drainage system both helped to channel the blood outside the building, and the sacrificial area was probably washed down with water. The evidence that has been found on the floor seems to confirm that sacrifices were only carried out in front of the three central cells.

These five small cells stand at the ends of the temple's five aisles, and they therefore also reflect their different sizes. Thus, the central cell is the widest, and the remaining four are approximately equal. The only remaining dividing walls are those that mark off the central cell. This seems to have been contained within walls made of decorated blocks which still support an architrave and contain an inset white limestone cornice which was wide enough to frame the architrave. In the centre of each of the middle cells are the rectangular hollows in the floor which must have contained the divine statuettes and symbols.

The hypostyle hall was reached through a monumental entrance lobby; this created a sense of balance within the complex and has provided us with a hitherto unknown element of Minaean architecture[4]. This stone lobby is the same width as the covered hall, and is composed of a platform, with steps on three sides and a flat centre paved with large slabs aligned on an axis with the entrance (A2), plus a sort of terraced podium (A3) in the middle of which stands a lovely stylobate supported by four pilasters (A1). This

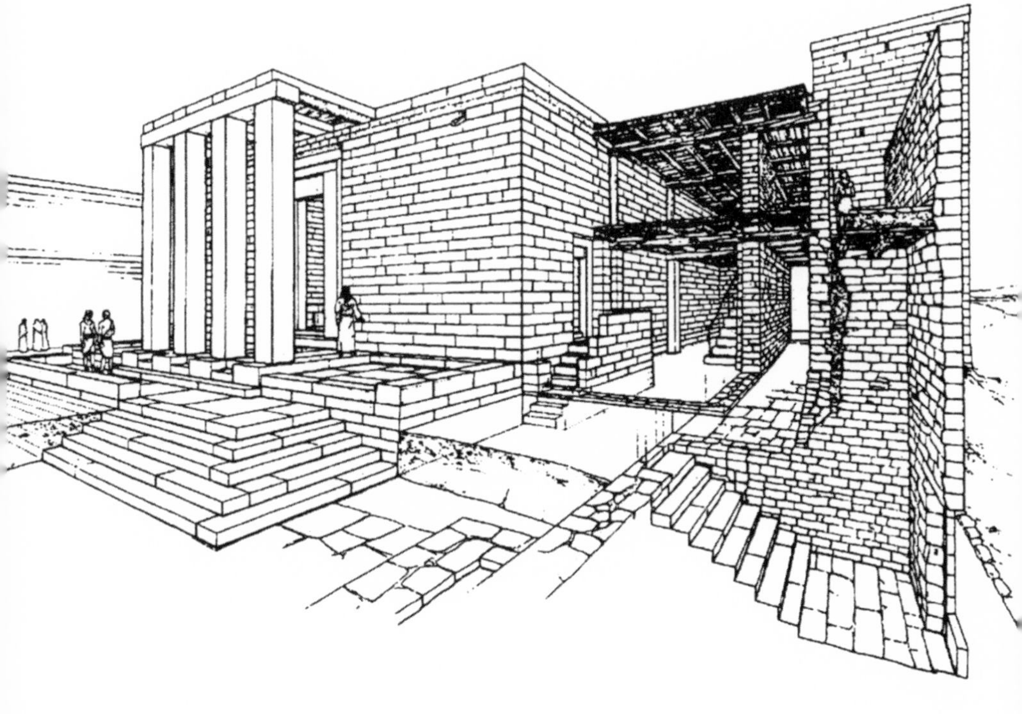

Figure 67
Axonometric reconstruction of the temple of Nakrah and the "sacresty" (Edoardo Gatti)

pedestal leads to the entrance of the hypostyle room. It is made of large, perfectly squared and decorated blocks of stone, which are also aligned according to the entrance axis, and the four pilasters stand at the front of it. It stands about 60 centimetres higher than the level of A2 and this height difference is emphasised by steps sculpted into the three spaces between the columns. The central one lies on an axis with the entrance. Only part of the base of the westernmost of the four great pilasters remains in place; the others have been removed or have fallen down, but their positions are marked by two centimetres deep rectangular hollows in the stylobate.

The pilaster that once stood atop the base which is still standing was found lying at A2 level, and we have been able to reconstruct the original height of the pilasters from its measurements: 5.58 metres. The pilasters were topped by a square tenon, suggesting that all four of them were connected at the top by a joist, which probably supported other joists linking the prostyle to the wall of the temple. (We deduced this by comparing it to other Minaean temples, like the external one at Ma'īn.) (Fig. 66).

The "sacristy" (C) is a two-storey building (Plate 56) that was connected at a later date to the southern wall of the temple (Fig. 67). It is important because it has provided us with a large number of religious objects. Of particular interest are the votive offerings of small plaster human heads, the stone incense burners and inscriptions, and the enormous quantity of pottery.

These excavations have not only unearthed the temple, but have also given us the opportunity to examine the interior facade of the massive city walls nearby.

The Adjacent Walls

Research has been centred around the two great towers T44 and T45 (E2 and E1) and the wall that connects them (E4). Excavations have shown that the walls were composed of: 1) a thick, compact nucleus of rough bricks (preserved in some places to a height of five metres above the level of the oldest Minaean flooring); 2) a facade of perfectly squared, polished and externally decorated blocks placed in even layers directly against the brick nucleus; and 3) an internal facade of smaller stones (also placed in even layers) which are squared off but not finished.

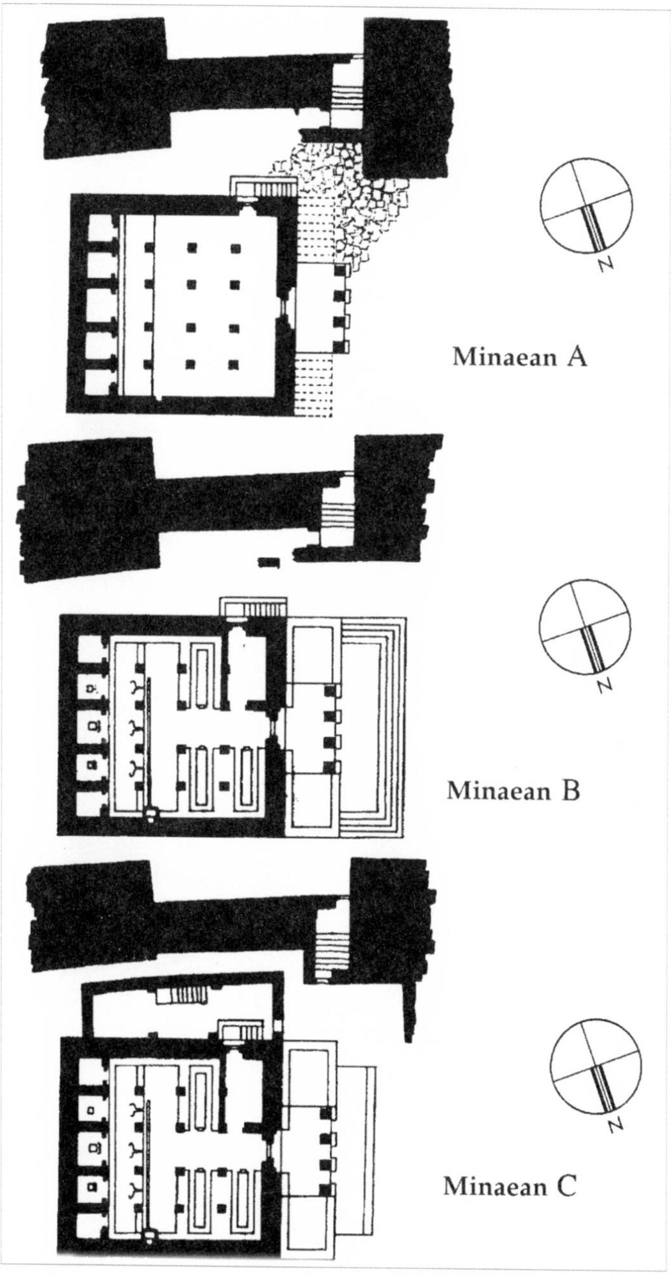

Figure 68
The three phases of the evolution of the temple of Nakrah in the Minaean period

The bricks of the Minaean walls must have formed a walkway level higher up, protected on the outside by a stone facade. Although it is unfinished on the inside (as we see in tower T48, the only one of the city's 57 Minaean bastions still intact), this facade would have been several metres higher still, culminating in a final crown of battlements.

It was here, in the section of walls overlooking the temple, that we were lucky enough to find, during our second round of excavations, a passageway leading to the outside (Fig. 65: E3 and Fig. 67). This is a particularly important area, as it includes a stairway leading down to the south, which connects the temple area with the outside of the city. It is contained within a break in the great connecting wall E4, behind the eastern wall of tower E1, which is about 1.8 metres wide. High up in the passageway's walls we can still see the square holes that would have held three or four large beams supporting an intermediate floor which in turn would have guaranteed the stability of the circular walkway around the top of the walls.

The entire room is taken up by a wide staircase made of great blocks of stone. At the bottom is a landing which must have had a door leading off it, through the narrow opening (63 centimetres) in the stone facade of the walls behind bastion E1. This opening is too small to be considered a city gate. It seems more likely that it was designed with a precise, limited purpose in mind, which I should imagine was almost certainly connected with the temple (or temples, if we count the nearby temple B). If this is the case, the discovery of a doorway and the first Minaean passage to be found in the city takes on particular importance. It may, for example, prove that there was a traditional need to link the interior and exterior of a city, possibly for the celebration of religious rites practised at the temple of Nakraḥ (and possibly at temple B). It would therefore be interesting to know when the side door was put into use, and how its date relates to that of the temple.

Stratigraphy and Chronology

To this end, it may help to look at the data found by the stratigraphic survey of the various elements of the temple and the walls, which is summarised in Fig 68.

To begin with, the great hypostyle hall and its prostyle entrance with the four great pilasters belong in the oldest phase (Min. C level). The city walls were already standing, along with the entrance leading into the temple from outside. As far as we can tell, this phase dates from the start of the height of the Minaean kingdom, that is the seventh to sixth centuries BC.

The stylobate with its four pilasters, situated in front of the hypostyle hall, was incorporated into the great stepped avant-corps at a later date (Min. B level). The space necessary for the new building was created by reducing the dimensions of the tower overlooking the walls (T45). It was probably during this time that Basil dhū Ma'ʿs restructured the inside of the hypostyle hall, building the three cenacles around huge decorated monolithic plates in the side aisles. This must be around the fifth to fourth centuries BC.

The sacristy was built in the final phase (Min. A level). To build it, they probably also had to reduce the dimensions of the northern tower (T44), in order to leave a passageway between the new building and the walls. Centuries had passed since the original temple had been built, and the external ground level had risen by about a metre, hiding the steps in front of the avant-corps. We can date this final phase to the third to second centuries BC, partly on account of the Hellenistic style of some small plaster heads.

We should remember, though, that besides this Minaean stratigraphy, the excavations have also enabled us to establish an Islamic stratigraphy for Barāqish. This is vitally important, as it is the first one of this period in the interior of Yemen. Working upwards, then, after the long post-Minaean period of neglect, we have a level that probably dates from the famous settlement at Barāqish of the Imām Al-Manṣūr bi-(A)llāh ʿAbd-Allāh ibn Ḥamza (Isl. D level, twelfth to thirteenth centuries AD), followed by evidence that the settlement was destroyed. Next comes a Rasulid-Tahirid era level (Isl. C level, fifteenth to sixteenth centuries AD), which dates from the first Turkish occupation of Yemen (Isl. B level, sixteenth to seventeenth centuries AD), and finally, a top layer that must be no later than the late eighteenth century (Isl. A level).

The excavations yielded 66 Minaean inscriptions, which are crucially important, not only because they allow us to identify temple A with one dedicated to the Minaean divinity Nakraḥ, patron deity, confessor and healer; but also because in providing the names of some of the Minaean kings, they contributed enormously – together with the archaeological data – to the reconstruction of the dynastic succession and history of the kingdom of Ma'īn.

The inscriptions are currently being examined under the direction of Christian Robin and Gherardo Gnoli. They contain numerous references to the temple, to its architectural elements and furnishings. Here too, a comparison with archaeological data would doubtless give us a better understanding of their true meaning and therefore the real essence of South Arabian religious architecture.

The Nakraḥ temple is the best preserved and is certainly the most spectacular example of a hypostyle temple found to date, clearly showing the individuality of conception that we discussed earlier. This type of architecture, employing faultlessly assembled, perfectly square blocks, combined with the exceptional state of preservation, reveals to us the character and expertise of the Minaean builders. Here we have tangible, concrete proof of their artistic originality and creative potential. We believe, therefore, that they are among the greatest monumental builders of the ancient Near East.

Footnotes:

1. de Maigret, A., "Himyarite Culture; Sabaean-Minaean Culture", *EW* 36 (1986), p. 384-388.
2. de Maigret, A., "The Excavations of the Temple of Nakraḥ at Barāqish (Yemen)", *PSAS* 21 (1991), p. 159-171.
3. For detailed analysis, see de Maigret, A., *Gli scavi della Missione archeologica nella città minea di Barāqish* (Rome: 1991); and de Maigret, A. and Robin, C., "Le temple de Nakraḥ à Yathill (aujourd'hui Barāqish), Yémen. Résultats des deux premières campagnes de fouilles de la Mission italienne", *CRAIBL* (1993), p. 427-496.
4. de Maigret, A., *La seconda campagna di scavi della Missione Archeologica Italiana a Barāqish* (Yemen 1992) (Rome: 1993).

XVIII

THE TOMBS

Heterogenous Funerary Customs

Many of the alabaster statuettes that have interested the art merchants of Aden and Ṣan'ā since the last century are said to originate from the tombs spread along the pre-desert strip of the Yemeni hinterland. So far, however, very few necropolises in the area have been studied (or even identified) and apart from the Timna' cemetery (Ḥayd Bin 'Aqīl), we are still not sure where the inhabitants of the great South Arabian cities buried their dead.

The little information that we have indicates that the types of burial were heterogenous. Indeed, in some instances, the form of the tombs and the funeral customs

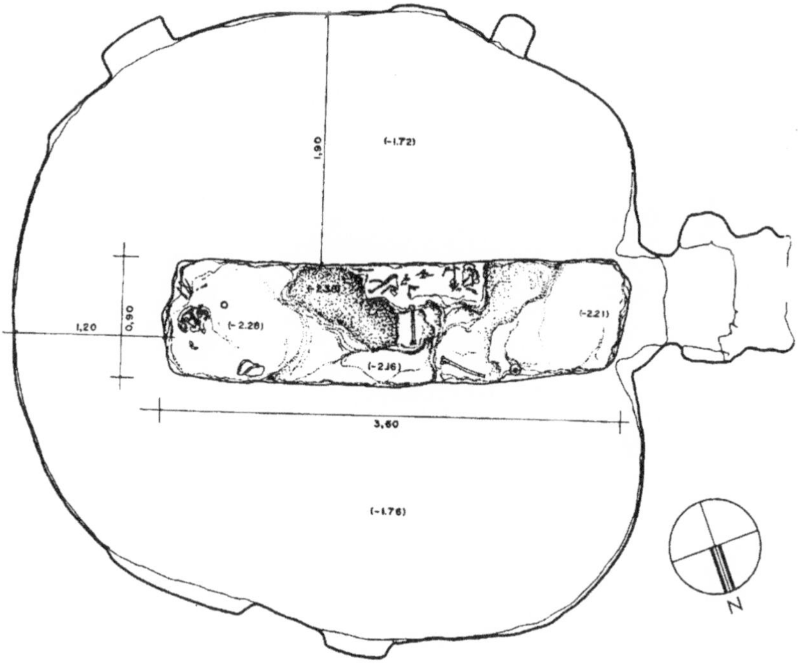

Figure 69
Plan of the hypogene tomb (T1) at Kharibat al-Ahjar, near Dhamār

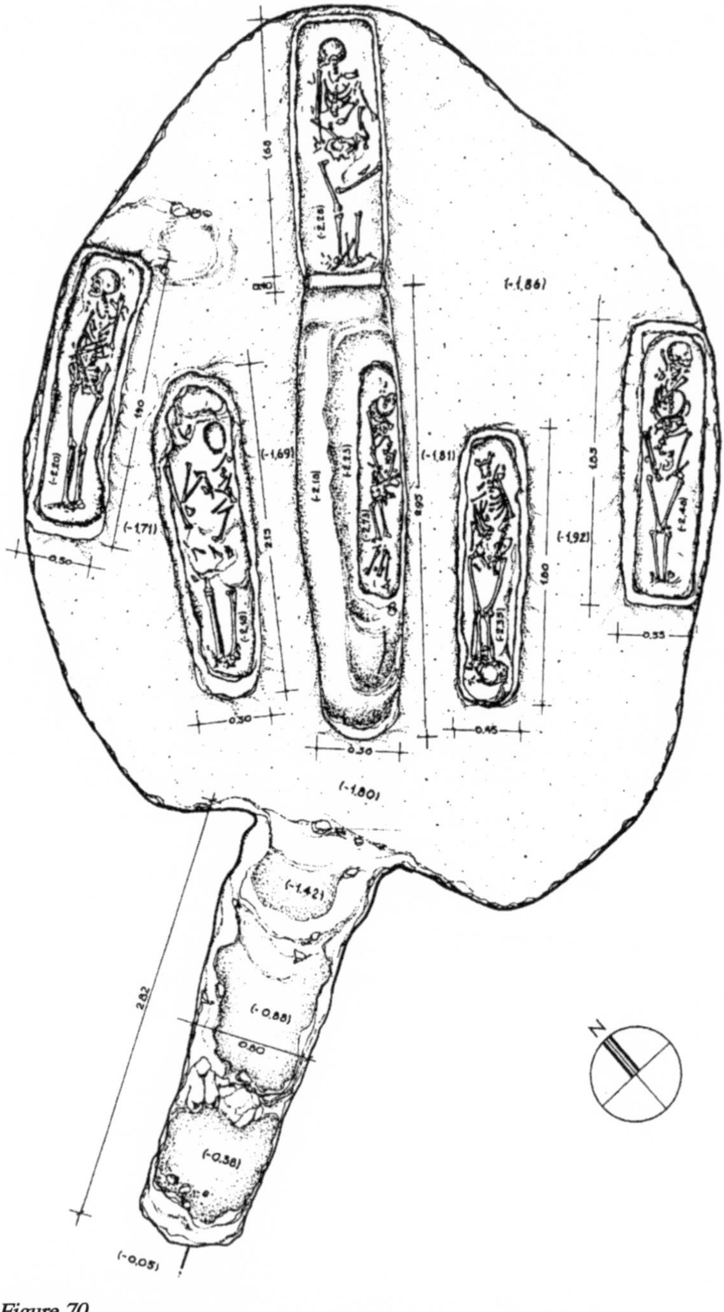

Figure 70
Plan of the hypogene tomb (T2) at Kharibat al-Ahjar, near Dhamār

appear to be so different that they suggest that the people had entirely different origins and spiritual concepts. Following is a brief typological summary of the five monuments known to date.

Masonry tombs with superimposed niches are only common in the necropolis of Ḥayd Bin ‘Aqīl (Fig. 23, Plate 23). *Ditch graves* (i.e. dug into the earth) like the ones we found in 1984 at the large necropolis of the Himyarite city of Madīnat al-Ahjur (Al-Ḥadā) record their position in the earth with a simple oval ring of large stones. *Rock tombs* are composed of a room with lateral niches, like those found on the side of Jabal Marmar above the site of Shibām Sukhaym, near Al-Ghirās (Ṣan‘ā), and those explored by the Soviet mission near Raybūn in Wādī Du‘ān (Ḥaḍramawt). The Shibām tombs also yielded the interesting mummified remains now kept at the little museum in the University of Ṣan‘ā. These date from the first centuries AD. There was a tradition of this type of burial in north-west Arabia too, specifically in the Al-‘Ulā tombs, and at Madāin Ṣāliḥ.[1]

There are also *tombs comprised of hypogean rooms*, like those excavated by the English at Ḥurayḍah and by the Italians at Waraqah (Dhamār) (Figs. 69 and 70). The two large tombs at Kharībat al-Ahjār, near Waraqah, which contain a series of niches dug out of the ground, are later than the Ḥurayḍah tombs and have been dated to the mid-first century AD on the basis of the ‘Amdan Bayyin coins[2] and the imported objects[3].

Turret tombs are distinguishable from the others by their shape – they look like small Sardinian *nuraghi*, as in Plate 57 – and their distributive layout. These were first seen by Philby during his return journey from Shabwat. They can be seen atop Jabal Balaq west of Mārib, for example and on the slopes of Jabal Yām, south-west of Barāqish.

Considering that these are the least known tombs, and that part of the Italian mission’s brief was devoted to them (in 1986 and 1987), it is only right that I should discuss them in greater depth.

Arabian Nuraghi

Turret tombs are common not only in Yemen but throughout the Arabian Peninsula (Oman, Saudi Arabia

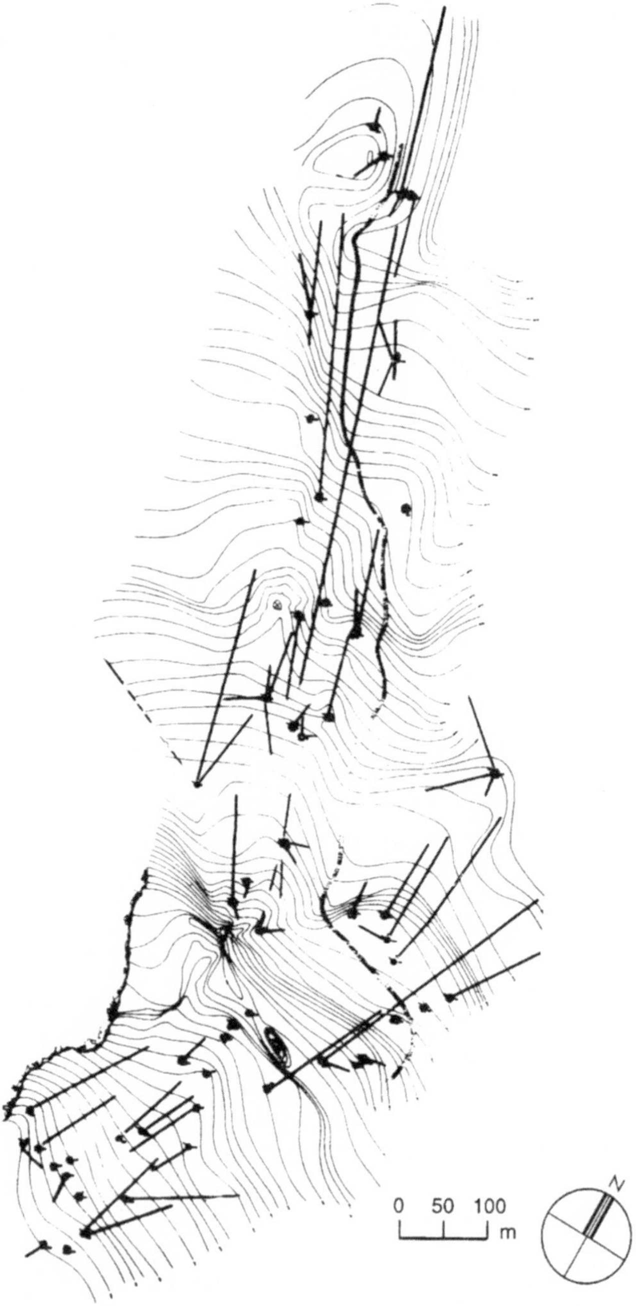

Figure 71
Plan of one of the Al-Makhdarah necropolises, near Ṣirwāḥ

and Jordan) and are distributed, in varying degrees of preservation, throughout those areas of north Yemen that we explored, from the desert to the highlands.

These tombs were always built relatively high up, and were visible from all sides. They were sometimes isolated (for example, those scattered across the Khawlān region), and sometimes formed part of huge necropolises, like in the mountains on the borders of the Jawf valley and the northern extreme of the Ramlat Sab'atayn desert.

Although ruins of this type have often been spotted and reported by travellers, their function has always been unclear and their chronology has been heavily debated[4]. Bizarre arrangements of stones (low walls, lines of slabs, piles of blocks, etc.) differing in number, length and orientation (some are several hundred metres long), which often accompany these small conical towers, only served to further complicate the theories, compounding the sense of mystery that has always distinguished this category of antiquities. The discovery of a series of necropolises along the pass leading from Mount Marthad and Mount Ḥaylān to the plains of Ṣirwāḥ (Plate 58) and the Jawf gave us the opportunity to face the problem through systematic research and excavations.

The Al-Makhdarah Necropolises

The tombs in this area (Al-Makhdarah) form a perfectly integrated architectural whole. The facade was formed by a double layer of dry stone walling, which was still covered at the top by large slabs (Fig. 72). Further stone slabs within the tombs marked out the burial room. Access was through a narrow, rectangular open doorway in the western side of the turret standing about a metre above the level of the site (Plate 63). Almost all the tombs were adorned by one or more arrangements of stones in the form of "rays" or "tails", like low walls. These led away from the circular tomb structures in various directions, sometimes for great distances.

Unfortunately, the tombs seemed to have been ransacked in ancient times. Excavations of six of the best-preserved tombs did, however, allow us to establish some of the principal elements of ancient funerary custom.

Multiple tombs may have belonged to a family group,

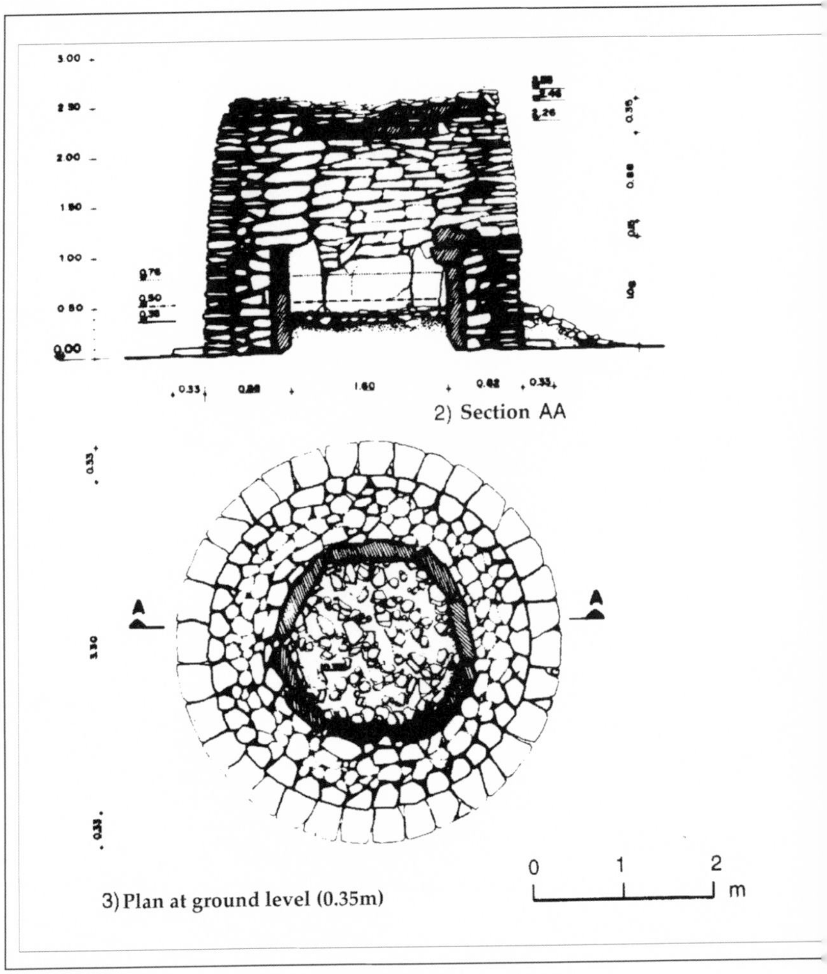

Figure 73
Plan and section of tomb 9 at Al-Makhdarah (by V Labianca)

with older remains being moved against the walls to make room for new arrivals (Plate 64). The most recently buried bodies still bore traces of cloth and vegeplate substances (inflorescence of *Arvaea japonica*), which is probably the result of a crude form of embalming. On the whole, there were only a few remaining funerary objects: glass beads, bronze and iron fragments.

Only one tomb (tomb no. 13, Fig. 73) yielded ornaments belonging to a young woman. These consisted of a necklace of semi-precious stones, shells and gold, a

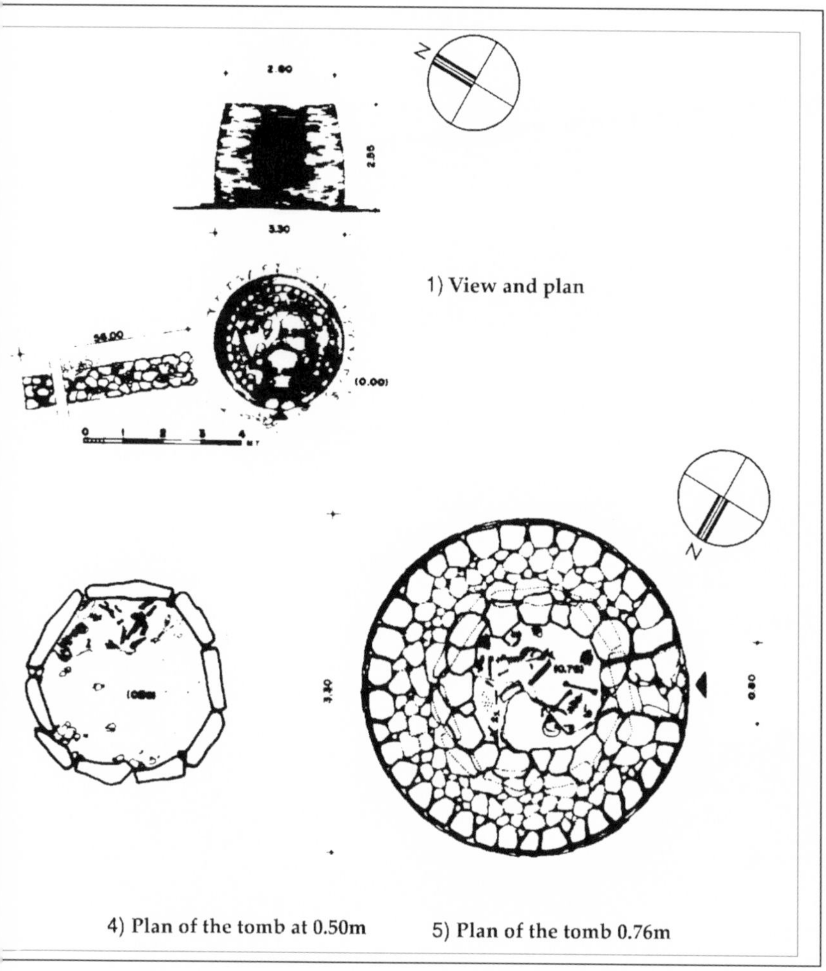

cornelian bracelet, a bone ring, and objects for preparing and applying eye make-up (Plate 38). Interestingly, there was no pottery, apart from two fragments.

We took samples from the tombs containing the most bones (tombs 5, 13, and 15) which were then subjected to C-14 analyses, providing the following dates: 60 BC, 630 BC and 830 BC, we are, therefore, dealing with the middle of the first millennium BC, and these tombs are contemporary with the South Arabian states.

This was surprising, though, since we would not have

Plate 63
Complete turret tomb at Al-Makhdarah, near Ṣirwāḥ

Plate 64
Burial layout of tomb 13 at Al-Makhdarah

expected these monuments to be so late in date, compared to other, structurally identical funerary monuments excavated in Oman. Indeed, we would have said that communal tombs in this late period belonged to one of the other four types.

But are these really late tombs, or exclusively late tombs? Of course, chronological assumptions made on the basis of analyses of only three tombs cannot *per se* lead to generalisations on the chronology of all the necropolises of this type found in Yemen. Besides, the tombs we found at Al-Makhdarah are obviously late. We need to be aware that the state of preservation of this type of monument undergoes various stages of decomposition. The first thing to crumble is the external facade of the building (Plate 46), then the interior facade, and in the end all that remains are the great slabs of the burial chambers fixed on end in an upright position (Plate 46). So, the fact that these tombs (the ones subjected to radiocarbon dating) are almost intact, showing only early stages of the ageing process, tells us that they are relatively late structures.

However, close by these complete turrets, there are often decidedly ramshackle ruins, remains of clearly older tombs of which only the upright slabs remain. We found tombs in this relatively advanced state of decay in almost every necropolis we visited, either alongside whole, obviously later tombs or standing on their own in the necropolises that were not reused in later times.

Unfortunately, so far, research into these older monuments has not produced much in the way of results. The decayed state of the structures makes it impossible to preserve the bones and belongings within the burial chambers. Some fragments of human bone that we unearthed in 1983 at a tomb in Khawlān (Al-Suhmān) did not, unfortunately, provide us with any reliable chronological conclusions.

However, the tombs that we excavated did provide us with some data which may help us to determine the antiquity of this funerary tradition. The collection of feminine ornaments in tomb no.13 of Al-Makhdarah (carbon dated to around 630 BC) includes one object, for example, which undoubtably has ancient counterparts. This is a pendant, found alongside the necklace it belonged to, which is made of a large gastropod's operculum. We found

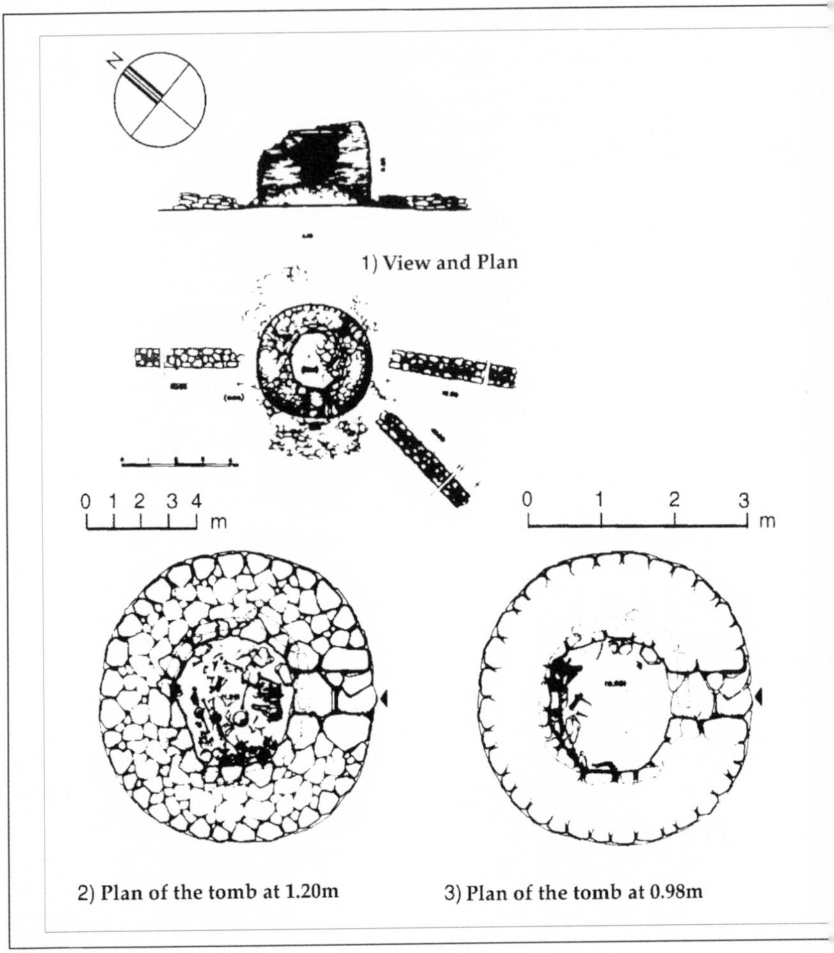

Figure 73
Plan of tomb 13 at Al-Makhdarah

an identical one during our excavation of a Bronze Age site of Al-A'rūsh, and it is a common ornament found in east Arabian sites of the third millennium BC.

The technique of building tombs with upright slabs supporting the roof is also common – as we have seen – in Bronze Age villages in Yemen. In this sense, the similarities between the tombs assume even greater significance when compared with the foundations of the apparently protohistoric monument that we discovered near Banī 'Aṭif in the Khawlān region (Fig. 50, Plate 51).

6) Section AA

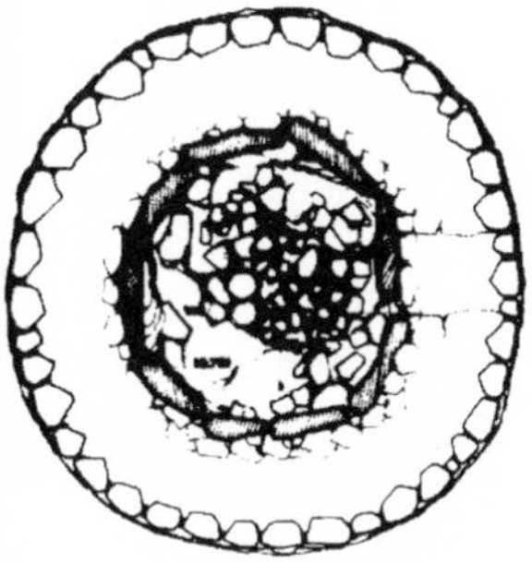

4) Plan at floor level (0.78m)

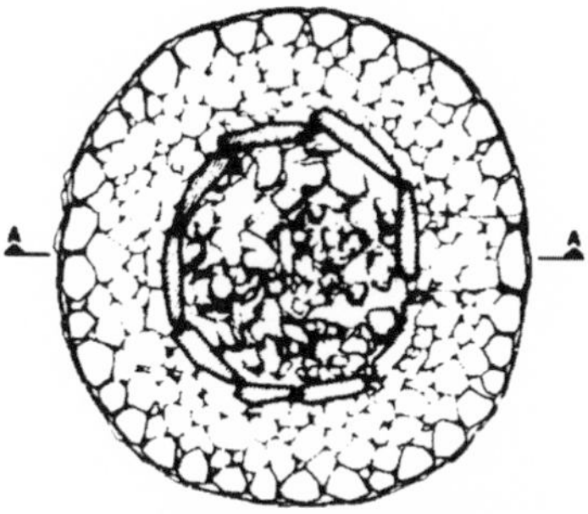

5) Ground level (0.42m)

I would conclude, then, by saying that the evidence available to date has led us to believe that there was a long tradition of this type of funerary custom, involving the turret tombs. However, the only way to provide definitive proof of this is to continue the excavations.

Intermediate Geographical Distribution

We undertook a series of expeditions into the interior of Yemen between 1985 and 1987, the results of which have given us quite a clear framework for the distribution of this type of monument in relation to ancient settlements in Yemen, both in the Bronze Age and South Arabian period.

Plate 65
Turret tomb at Al-Makhdarab, of which only the inside curtain wall facade remains

Plate 66
Turret tomb at ‘Alam al-Abyaḍ (Ramlat Sab‘atayn), of which only the vertical slabs of the funeral chamber remain

Necropolises with turrets tend to be placed outside the great fortified cities of the South Arabian period (Fig. 74). Tombs are occasionally found over a hundred kilometres from the nearest Sabaean or Minaean settlement. These are always situated on hillsides or isolated plains and are built using local materials (limestone, granite and basalt). Some areas contain an exceptionally high concentration of tombs; along the northern edge of the Ramlat Sab'atayn, for example, more than 4000 tombs have been sighted, partly with the help of aerial photographs.

The necropolises seem to be distributed according to a pattern which, surely, cannot have been accidental. They are lined up in long chains covering the intervening spaces between classical era settlements. So we find lines of tombs running across the desert between Ḥaḍramawt and Ma'īn, between Shabwat and the oasis of Al-'Abr, towards the Rub' al-Khālī and the highlands of Al-Najd, between Najrān and the faraway eastern province of Saudi Arabia.

We find the same kind of intersettlement distribution on a smaller scale as well. The traveller sees rows of turrets along the crests of the mountains from Mārib and Ṣirwāḥ, from Mārib to Yalā, from Ṣirwāḥ to the Jawf and from the Jawf to the highlands. This is how the idea originated that these funerary monuments marked the roads that linked the centres of the classical era.

We carried out a few reconnaissance missions which confirmed this theory. Following the lines of the turret tombs, we found traces of the ancient roads, which are otherwise unrecognisable. One example is the lovely route which crosses Jabal Ḥaylān, linking the Ṣirwāḥ area with the Jawf valley, and which is lined with this type of tomb.

Might we not, then, have an explanation for the long "tails" attached to the turrets? Since they are aligned with the ancient routes, and were therefore clearly visible to those following the routes, could they not have been intended – at least partly – to individualise and distinguish the separate tombs, which were otherwise identical?

Nomads' Tombs

Once complete, the study of the distribution of these burial sites will be of the utmost importance for a topographical and historical reconstruction of pre-Islamic Arabia. This

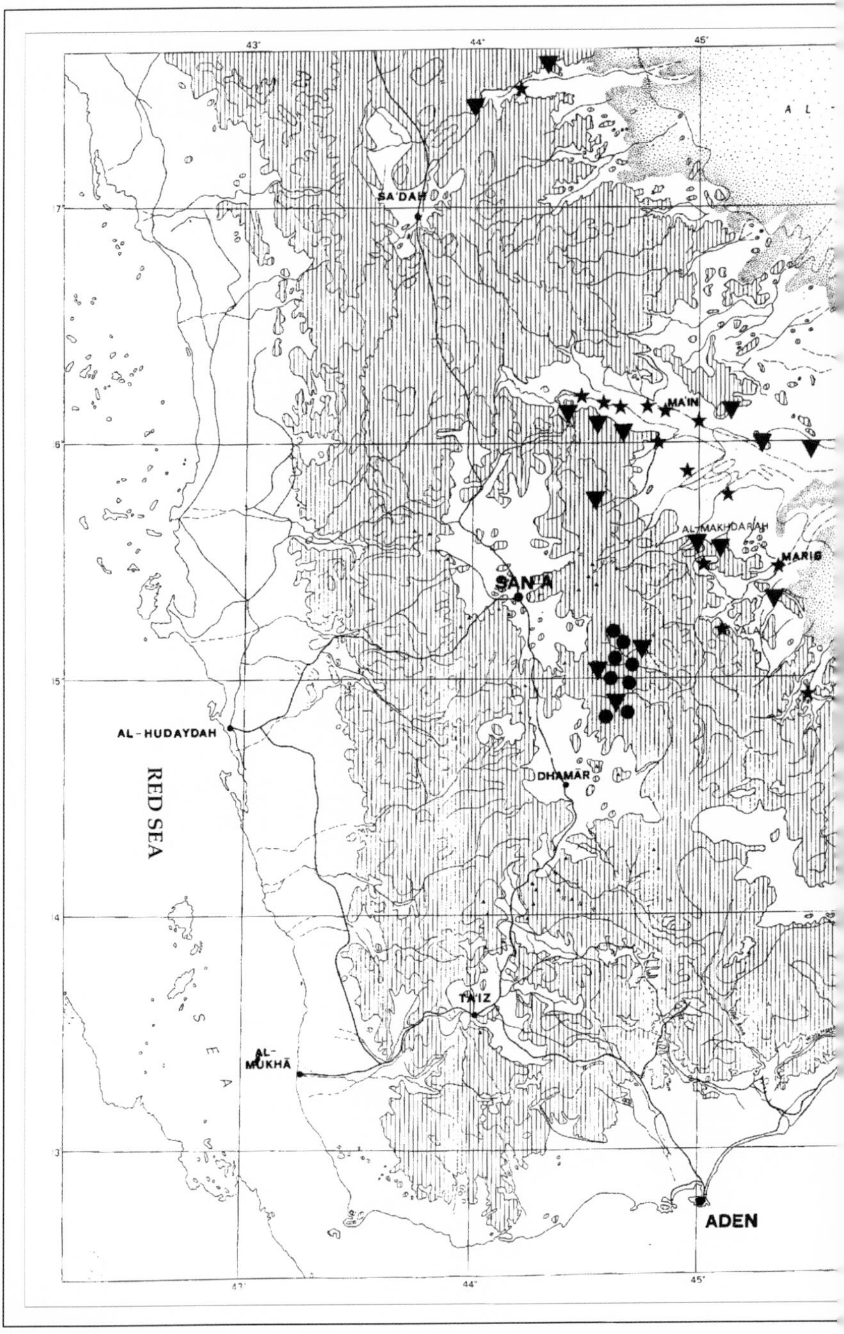

Figure 74
Map of the distribution of turret tombs in the interior of Yemen

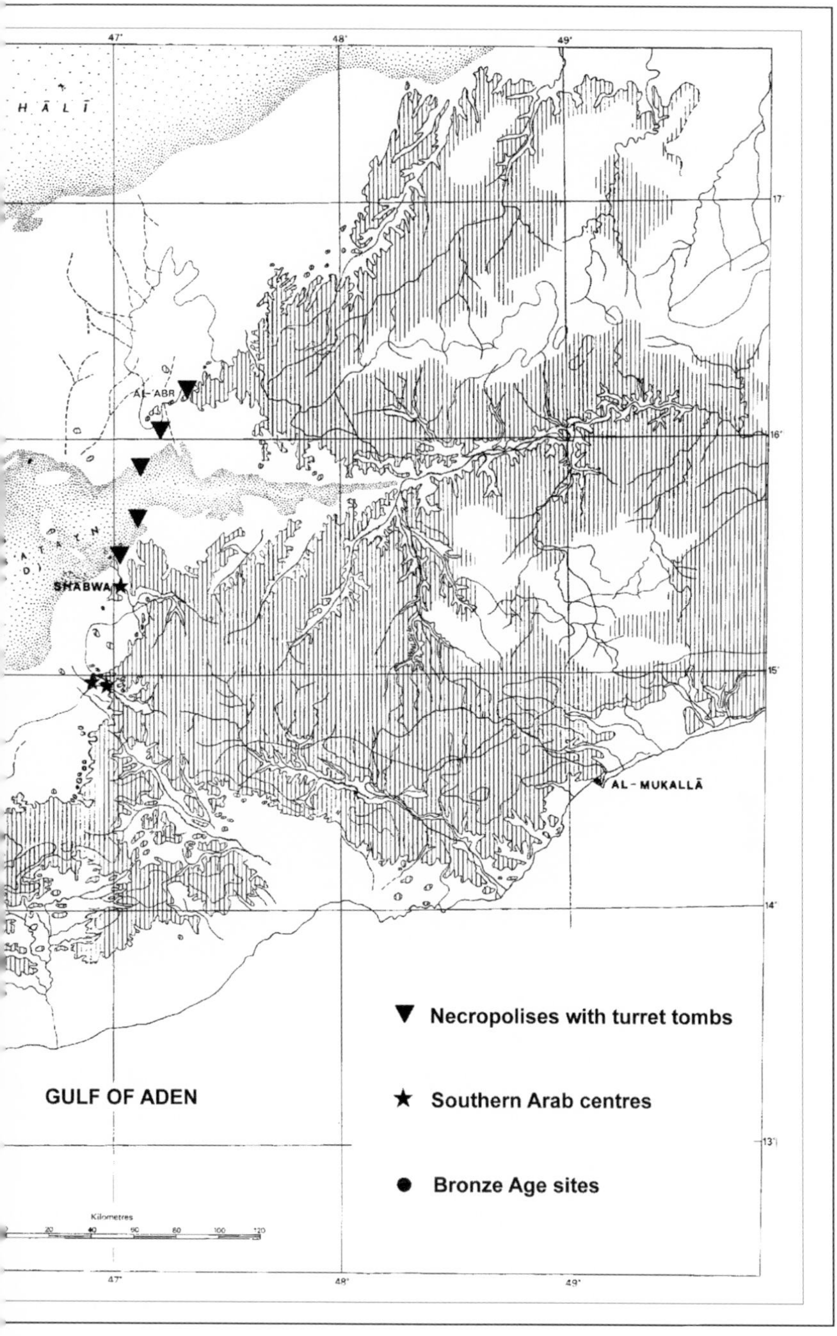

47°
48°
49°
17°
16°
15°
14°
13°
AL-'ABR
SHABWA
AL-MUKALLĀ
GULF OF ADEN
Necropolises with turret tombs
Southern Arab centres
Bronze Age sites
Kilometres

new documentation will also touch on some aspects of the birth of the South Arabian states, which we should like to briefly mention here.

Their particular distributive pattern seems to suggest that there was a link between these structures and ancient trade routes. On the other hand, we can see that the turret tombs belong to a different culture than that which produced the other types of tombs in pre-Islamic Yemen, a culture that is not classically South Arabian and that has most in common with the settlers in the Yemeni mountains in the third to second millennia BC. This is a culture that was diffused throughout the Arabian Peninsula from at least 3000 BC, as we know from the turret tombs of Oman and Saudi Arabia and which, given its unusual funerary habits, can be considered particular to the subcontinent. The few, important excavations at Al-Makhdarah prove, therefore, that this culture survived until about the time of Christ and that it lived alongside that of South Arabia, while preserving its own character.

The excavations also told us that: 1) the bodies buried showed clear signs of mummification, and 2) they were not buried with any pottery vessels. The first point tallies with the idea that the dead were carried to necropolises far away from centres of habitation, but seen together with the second point it seems to indicate that the tomb builders were travellers. Could this perhaps mean that in the Sabaean period there was a part of society with a particular ethnic identity which continued the ancient tradition of transporting merchandise from one place to another? Could these people be the only documented survivors of an aboriginal, ancient population of Arabia (perhaps the *rb* – Arabs, or "nomads" – whom we know from the South Arabian texts)? And could the Sabaeans not be seen as later newcomers with a flair for organising and hence exploiting the commercial links already established throughout the peninsula by this older section of society?

It is an exciting idea, not just because it has implications, as we have seen, that reach beyond the borders of Yemen, but also because it is the first time that archaeology has provided concrete evidence of the dimorphism of South Arabia. We believe that, considering the scarcity of information available on this ancient people, this is an extremely important discovery.

Footnotes:

1. Saudi Arabian Department of Antiquities and Museums, *An Introduction to Saudi Arabian Antiquities* (Milan: 1975), p. 56, 59-62.
2. Davidde, B., "Le monete di 'Amdan Bayyin Yuhaqbiḍ dalle tombe di Harabat al-Ahjār presso Qaraqah (Damar)", *Yemen 1* (1992), p. 41-54.
3. Antonini, S., "Oggetti d'importazione dalle tombe di Kharabat al-Ahjār (Dhamār)", *Yemen 1* (1992), p. 3-12.
4. Doe, B., *Monuments of South Arabia* (Naples: Falcon, 1983), p. 56.

XIX

THE FIGURATIVE ARTS

The Originality of South Arabian Art

In discussing the tombs, we mentioned the existence of a social dimorphism in southern Arabia in the historic period, and the related theory that this may have derived from the presence of two distinct ethnic groups, one of local origin (Bronze Age culture, which survived in the culture of the turret tombs) and the other of foreign origin (South Arabian culture). This idea becomes particularly attractive when we turn to the discussion of the figurative arts of the historic period. These observations could in fact help us to explain, for the first time, the most important and obvious characteristic which distinguishes South Arabian art, which is its particular, emphatic individuality compared with the other kinds of art produced within ancient Asia.

It is bizarre to think how little investigation there has been into this distinctive individuality. Everyone agrees that it exists, but few have stopped to consider what exactly it consists of, and where it may have derived from. Paradoxically, the favourite aim of studies so far has been to emphasise the similarities between the arts of South Arabia and other cultures. Thus, on the question of origins, some scholars have played up the influence of Mesopotamia and Egypt in the third millennium BC[1], while others have emphasised parallels with the arts of the Syro-Anatolian States in the second millennium BC[2], and still others have found derivations from Greek art of the seventh century BC[3].

Clearly, a preference for one influence over another results from the fact that scholars of South Arabia differ greatly over chronology. At the same time, this would explain why there has been more emphasis on the superficial aspects of South Arabian art, rather than the more fundamental points. It is therefore obvious why this way of looking at the question has not yet provided a penetrating study of the essence of this art, and its characteristic originality which jumps out at you the first time you look at a Sabaean statue, for instance. I use statuary as my example here because I shall attempt to

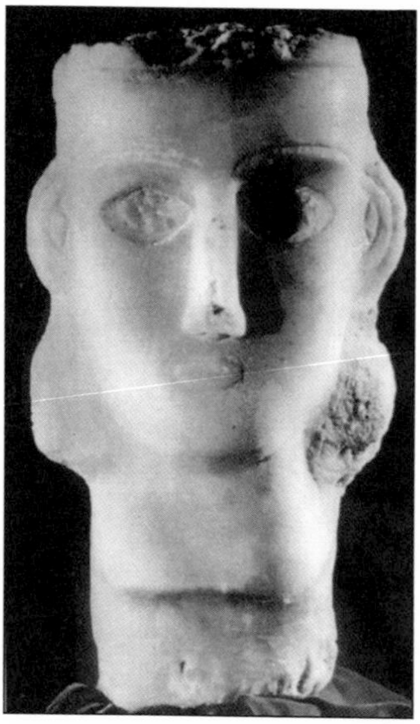

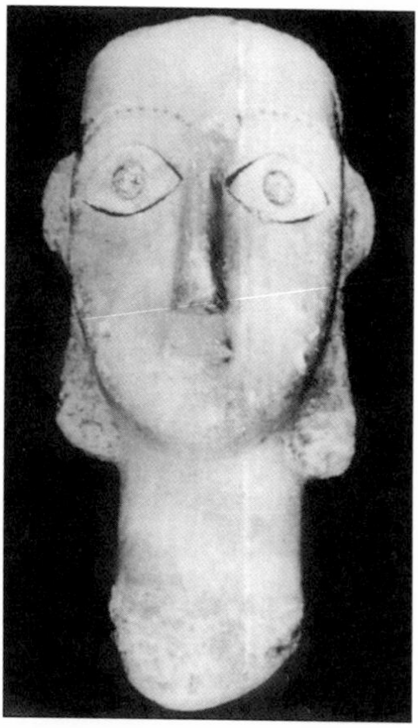

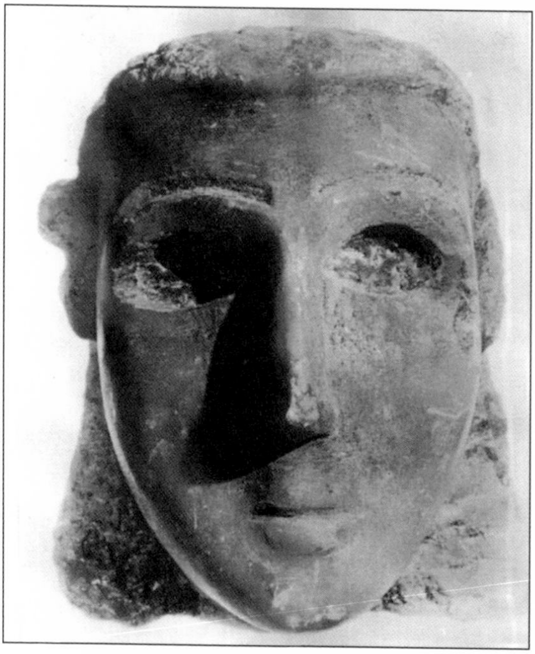

Plate 67, 68, 69
Funerary alabaster heads found in the Ḥayd Bin ʻAqīl necropolis, near Timnaʻ

explain my thoughts on the subject by looking first at the category of anthropomorphic statuary.

Statuary

When we look at a group of alabaster statuettes like that collected by Brian Doe, (Plate 39), or indeed the statues, busts and heads found at the Ḥayd Bin ʻAqīl necropolis (Plates 40 and 67-69), we are immediately aware of the meaning of "South Arabian art". These works, belonging to what we might call the middle or mature period, are fine examples of the full, integrated and autonomous flourishing of local artistic expression.

The first thing we notice about these pieces is their strikingly individual way of representing the old, originally Mesopotamian, motif of a worshipper praying. The squat, square figures, although they all have distinguishing features (could we be dealing with portraits?), seem unable to break free from the figurative limitations of a precise and rigidly imposed stylistic canon. This canon, which we find in all South Arabian arts, from statuary to architecture, is very distinctive in that (according to Grohmann) it favours symmetry and stability, imposing full, square forms and a robust style. This is a local taste, whose origins may become clearer if we review the evolution of statuary as a whole.

We have described the statuary mentioned above as belonging to the middle or mature period, to distinguish them from later ones, which show obvious signs of

Plate 70
Statues called the "forefathers", kept in the Museo d'Arte Orientale in Rome

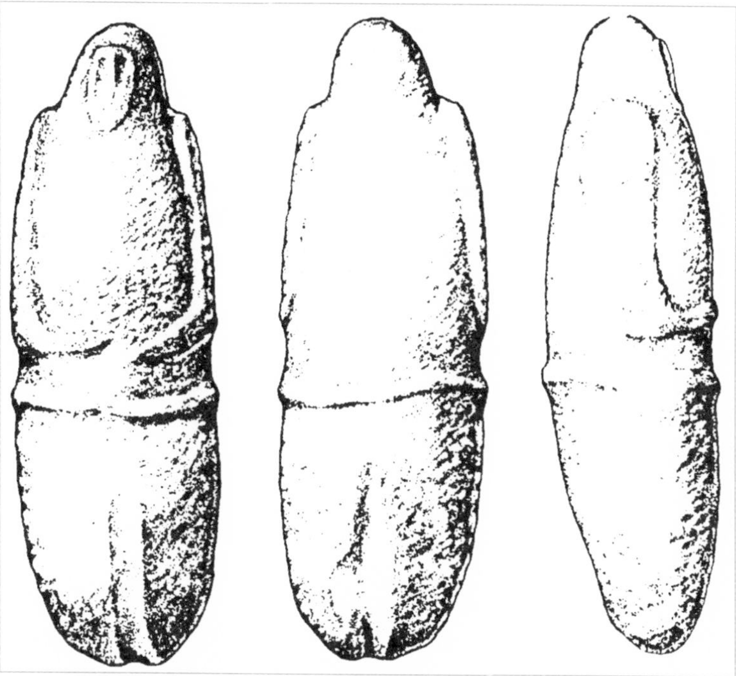

Figure 75
Granite idols from Banī Sulayḥ (Khawlān al-Tiyal)

Hellenistic contamination (in the late or decadent period), and from earlier ones, which we could place in an early or formative period.

I believe that we can justify this rather arbitrary division of South Arabian art into phases by the observations that this allows us to make. Pieces belonging to the earliest phase are typical and there are a lot of them. This phase includes the so-called "forefathers" statuettes. There is a fine collection of this type of statuary at the Museo d'Arte Orientale in Rome (Plate 70). They seem to demonstrate an even stricter iconographic canon.

Both male and female worshippers are shown, as Conti Rossini succintly puts it, "in a position of complete immobility, emphasised further by the position of the arms and legs"[4]. The only expressive features are the eyes. Looking at pictures of the profiles of these sculptures, we can tell that they were carved from stones no higher than 20-25 centimetres, squared off at the bottom, and rounded on top.

This must partly have dictated the size of the head, which is invariably disproportionately large compared to the body.

These "forefathers" statuettes give the impression of having been paralysed on their liberation from the stone, almost as if the ideological canon which inspired their creation imposed on them the immobility dictated by the stone, or as if the immobility of the stone itself was more important than the essential mobility of man. These are stereotypical motifs, and they turn up exasperatingly often. All this points to recognisable and established stylistic and iconographic norms. This in turn points to the existence of a long figurative tradition.

The Style of the Ancient Idols

Picture the stage before this form of expression, and imagine the human figure still further bound by its material, stone. These works must have been the merest outline, something, for instance, like the idol that we found in 1984 at Banī Sulayḥ in Khawlān: an elongated pebble, about twenty centimetres high, which shows the faintest traces of a rough outline of the human form (Fig. 75).

In this work, which we can date to the Yemeni Bronze age (late third to early second millennium BC), the stone completely imposes its rhythms on the figure, and this clearly reflects the artist's intentions. Trying to guess the artist's intentions would be a stab in the dark (life originating from the magical nature of stone, or the divine, life-giving qualities of stone?), but we can see that the artist felt that there was a link between the nature of the material and the form that he wished to represent. (We must remember that this was a worshipping figure, someone communicating with the divine.) This was an extremely strong link, strong enough to condition not only this first little idol from Khawlān, but also, later, the South Arabian statuettes of the early period and, later still, those of the middle period.

So, do we believe that the style of South Arabian statuary is based on that of the Bronze Age? Are we even sure that we have been following the right clues?

Four more small granite idols have been discovered, which are very similar to the one from Banī Sulayḥ and seem to prove that we are on the right track. Three of these

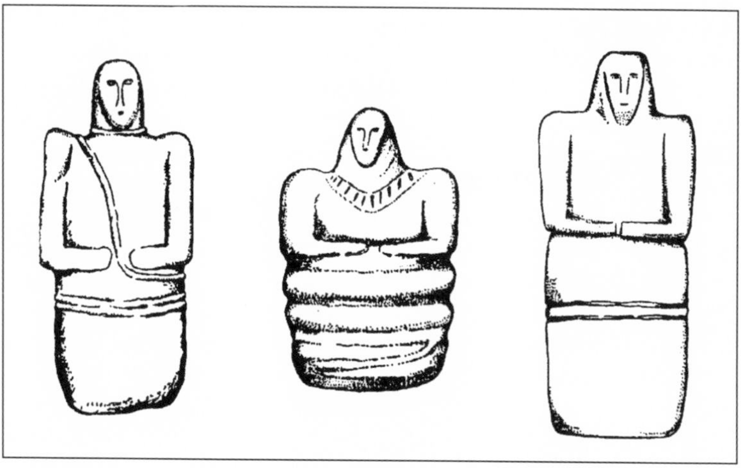

Figure 76
The three idols found by Russian archaeologists in Wādī ʻIdim in the Ḥaḍramawt

Figure 77
Stone idol preserved in the National Museum in Ṣanʻā (OGAB 1987)

were found by the Russian mission in Wādī ʿIdim in the Ḥaḍramawt (Fig. 76), and the other, whose provenance is unclear, was published on a recent front cover of a brief Arabic guide to the National Museum in Ṣanʿā (Fig. 77).

All these pieces show similar iconographic and stylistic traits, and together they form a sculptural group totally unknown until a few years ago that has been classified as the oldest known type in Yemen. In my opinion, the "forefathers" statuettes clearly belong in this group. The square set of the shoulders, the wide neck, the triangular face with wide eyes, long nose and small mouth, the position of the arms (interestingly, in Bronze Age sculptures the hands never meet in front, implying that the forearms extend forwards), and especially the division of the body into two distinct parts by means of a sort of belt, with the upper part (head and bust) being almost twice the length of the lower part (the legs), are all characteristics which clearly link the two groups.

In anthropomorphic South Arabian statuary, the lower part of the statue always takes up about a third of the whole, even once the legs have taken on their definitive shape. It has always been thought that the "forefathers" statuettes were seated figures, but this cannot be true, except for a few obvious cases. The origins of this stylistic type are not easy to establish, although they probably related to the specific function of the statuettes. The proportions of these statues remain the same over time, even when this meant that figures seem seated when they were actually standing, and at the expense of making the more evolved statues of the mature period seem out of proportion.

Take, for example, the three lovely Awsanite sovereigns in the museum in Aden (Plate 59 shows two of them). There is an astounding contrast between the persistent lack of proportion in the somatic measurements and the full and carefully-worked figures, which inscriptions date to a relatively late period (first century BC to first century AD, according to Pirenne). The contrast is particularly striking in the latest of the three statues, that of the king Yaṣduq'il Fariʿum Sharaḥʿat (Plate 59: right-hand statue). It shows clear signs of the Greco-Roman influence which would gradually come to dominate the final phase of South Arabian art, and which we therefore call the "decadent" phase.

The inscriptions that record the name of the person depicted and appear on the pedestals of nearly all the later statuettes (but which had also started to appear sporadically on those of the "forefathers") tell us about the function of the statues. Their purpose was simply to act as a substitute for the physical presence of the person represented. They may have been intended for religious or funerary use.

It is difficult to believe that this had been common practice since the Bronze Age. Idols of that period actually have certain characteristics which, although their interpretation is not entirely certain (like the folds of fat seen in the lower part of the little female statue from Wādī 'Idim, which makes us think of the earth mother, or the glans-like shape in the lower part of the Banī Sulayḥ sculpture, which had already led to its identification as a phallic idol), would seem to be most closely related to a fertility cult. However, an answer to the statues' function may lie in something completely different. It may seem absurd, considering its very different date, but if we had to name the civilisation that seems the most similar in ideological, and therefore iconographic, terms and especially in the way that its anthropomorphic sculpture is meant to stand in the presence of the gods, we would have to opt for Mesopotamia in the Sumerian period (third millennium BC).

The wealth of statues depicting worshippers from, for example, the temple of Abū at Tell Asmar, the oval temple of Khafajah and Mari are so like ours in concept that one cannot help but imagine that there is some kind of link. Looking at their similarities, one would almost say that the general iconographic scheme and the ideas behind South Arabian statuary belong to an artistic tradition which must have derived – fairly directly – from the arts of the Sumerian protodynastic period.

However, it is worth mentioning that while there are undeniable similarities, there are also obvious differences between the two styles. On closer inspection, one is immediately aware that there is something different. And it is something of the greatest importance.

The relationship between the length of the torso and the legs in the Mesopotamian figures is exactly the opposite of that found in South Arabian statuettes. In the former, the legs are almost twice as long as the bust, while in the latter they are about half as long. This means that while the South Arabian figures essentially follow a tradition that originated in the Fertile Crescent, they have adopted a different stylistic type, which, as we have seen, is of local origin. This ties in very well with the new framework that archaeological research has established for the origins of the South Arabian states.

If it is true, as we have said, that the states were born around 1200 BC, due to nomadic tribes gradually settling at the feet of the Yemeni mountains, having travelled the interior deserts of the peninsula for centuries, we should not be surprised if we find that the culture of South Arabia contains ideas, concepts, evidence and memories of far more ancient cultures, which these people had evidently once been in contact with (maybe before they became nomadic?). The weight of tradition, essentially Mesopotamian in origin, must have been zealously preserved in the collective memory of the nomadic world; a figurative repertory which was handed down in the form of minor works of art, like figurines (wooden, clay, etc.), and in rock carvings.

Once the process of settlement was complete, larger art forms, like stone statuary and architecture, could finally be realised. The only way this could happen was by following the methods and stylistic canons which these new settlers had learnt from Bronze Age civilisation, which was now several millennia out of date in the mountains of Yemen.

Engraved Drawings: the Banāt ʻĀd

The figurative details engraved on temples in the Jawf prove that South Arabian figurative art was influenced by ancient Mesopotamia. These figures are commonly known as *Banāt ʻĀd*, or "daughters of ʻAd" (the ancient Qur'anic people), from the name which the bedouin generally give to their similar female figurines (Fig. 78). During the last century Joseph Halévy saw these figures engraved on the portal of the temple of Kharībat Hamdān/Haram[5] and they were published for the first time in Aḥmad Fakhry's photographs. The graffiti is presented in a very unusual way. Most of the visible surfaces of the

Figure 78
Figurative decoration carved on the temple of ʻAthtar near Al-Sawdā/Nashan

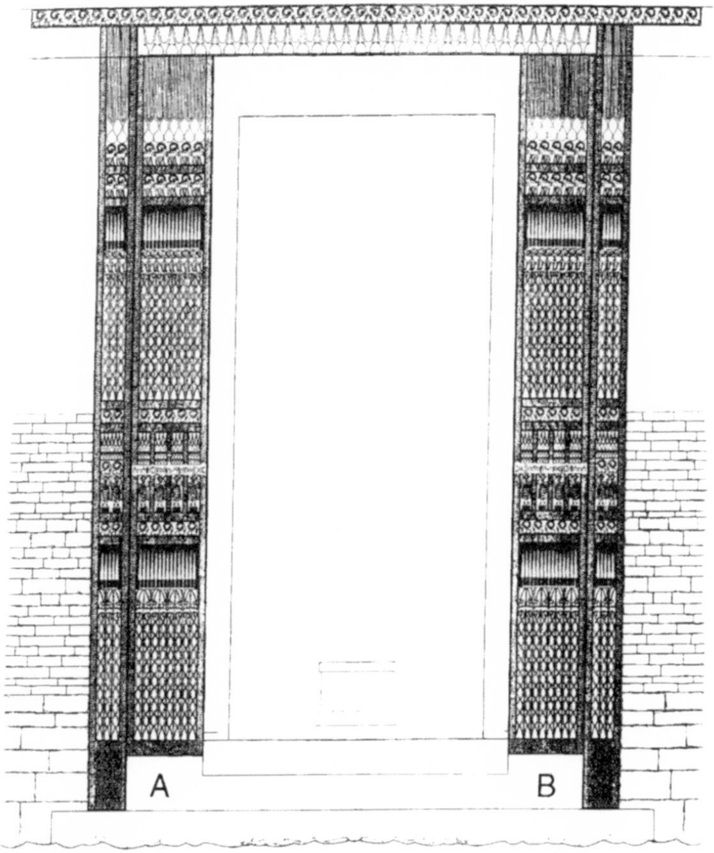

Figure 79
Decorative carvings on the portal of the temple of ʻAthtar near al-Sawdā/Nashan

pilasters and doorways of the temples are completely covered by the designs, which are arranged in long panels containing several layers of geometrically repeated motifs (Fig. 79). Standing in front of the two entrances of the external temples of Kharībat Hamdān and Al-Sawdā, where we can see the decoration in its entirety (it even covers the architraves), the dense and intricate composition gives one the impression that it is a kind of fine and elegantly woven brocade, which seems to swathe the naked architectural structures of the temples[6].

Among the repeated animal motifs (ibex, ostrich,

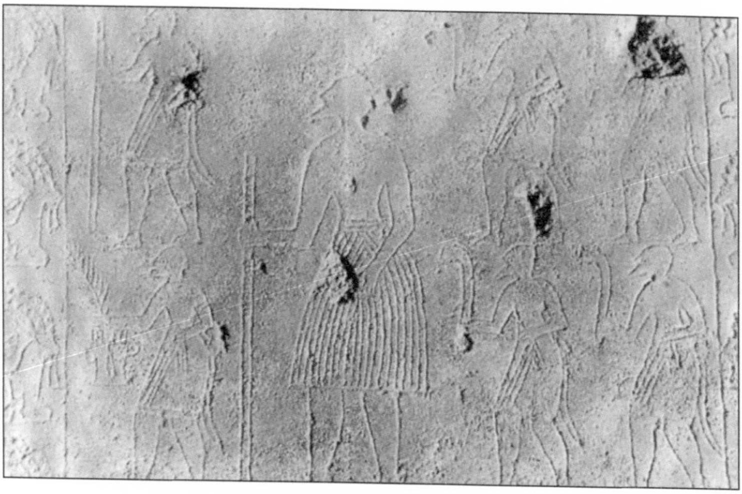

Plate 71
Stone slab with figurative engravings from Ma'īn

serpents, antelopes, etc.), we also find isolated panels depicting humans. The most common of these is a row of stereotypical female figures, seen from the front, and divided by spaces. These are the *Banāt 'Ād.* Not all panels are so static and constrained, though. Look at the scenes on the Ma'īn panels, which portray solemn-looking men walking in processions (Plate 71). These last are the only narrative scenes. The rest are purely concerned with symbols, repeated and juxtaposed until their original significance has turned into a *recherché* ornamental motif. Nonetheless, they give us a feel for the interior harmony that pervaded this ancient, complex spiritual world.

There has been a lot of discussion about the significance of the various iconographic motifs and the overall meaning of these works. Some believe that these engravings contain symbols of the sacred hunt[7], others that some of the specific rituals of the temple were illustrated here[8]. For the time being, our knowledge of South Arabian religion is too threadbare to allow us to grasp the true semantic value of these rock drawings, and we think it more useful to concentrate on some of their aspects that are perhaps more interesting, even if they are not so closely related to our topic.

The first thing we notice is that here too there are signs of Mesopotamian influences. The individual iconographic

Plate 72
Inscription carved on the portal of the temple of ʻAthtar near al-Sawdā/Nashan

motifs are again similar to the Sumerian work of the protodynastic period. The processions of ibex, interlaced serpents, male figures and harp players are all common motifs in the reliefs, inlaid work, and glyphs of that time and place. To get a better idea of this close link, we only need to compare, for example, the figures in the scenes from Qarnāw/Maʻīn with those of the famous standard of Ur. Sumerian art displays the same tendency to fill every available space. Compare the seals of the so-called "brocade" style, or those – still protodynastic, but slightly later – in which the rampant animals overlap each other so as not to leave any empty spaces[9].

How old are the Jawf inscriptions? They certainly belong to a very early period. This has recently been confirmed, following the French excavations of the exterior temple of Al-Sawdā. Breton found an inscription, between the rows of decoration on the entrance doorway, in which a certain Ab'amar Sadīq says that he built the temple of ʻAthtar. (Plate 72). The lettering of this inscription turns out to be fairly archaic; even more so than that used by the earliest known *mukarribs* of Saba (Yathaʻ'amar Bayyin bin Sumhuʻalī and Karib'īl Watar bin Dhamār'ali), whom we think probably reigned around 700 BC. More interesting

Plate 73
Stone slab with decorative relief from Mārib

still is the fact that – as Breton again observed – Ab'amar Sadīq built this temple reusing many decorated blocks of stone that belonged to an earlier era. This means that the tradition of decorating pilasters and temple door jambs with these figurative details must be very old indeed, perhaps even pre-dating the appearance of monumental writing. Here we have, then, one of the oldest forms of artistic expression in South Arabia. Within this art form we can still make out the individual iconographic, stylistic and technical elements that would later combine to form the original and distinctive characteristics of the art of the mature period.

Plate 74
Inscribed stone slab with decorative relief from Mārib

Art and Symbols

There is a prevailing trend, in the earliest phase, to use symbols as the base element of the composition. This is shown, for example, in the clay panel found at Yalā which dates from the eighth to the seventh centuries BC. The plate expresses its own function through a pure and simple string of symbols[10].

These symbols provide us with a fundamental aspect of South Arabian mentality. As we discussed in the chapter on religion, the South Arabians believed that they felt the

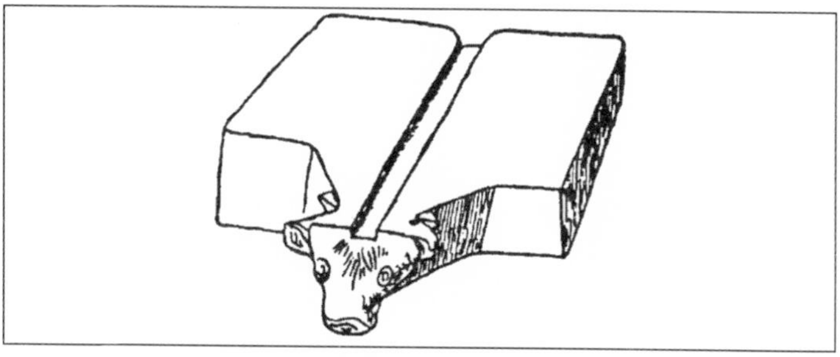

Figure 80
Drip-stone with bull's-head from the temple of Ḥuqqah

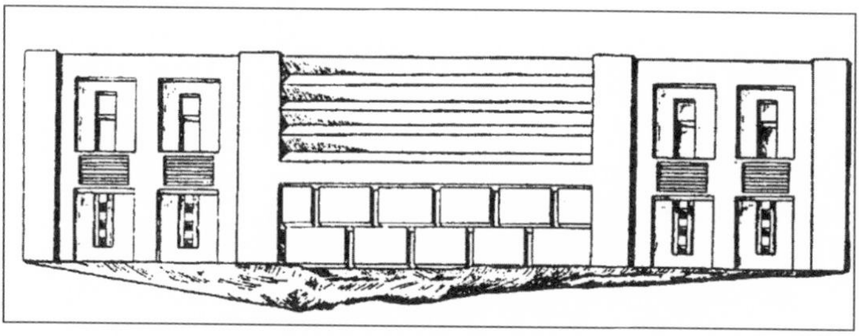

Figure 81
Architectural detail with "blinds", false windows and dentils

divine through the spirit, rather than the senses, and so they developed an individual and subjective concept of the supernatural. They had to turn to symbols if they needed to express the transcendental in objective terms. The temple was a place of communal worship, and the figural art destined for its entrance had to express the common denominator among the wealth of individual religious sentiment. Therefore, symbols became the conventional vehicle for an objective portrayal of the innumerable, inexpressible manifestations of individual spirituality. As a convention, its validity must have been unchallenged. So the iconography of these symbols was taken from their ancestral heritage, which, since time immemorial had jealously guarded the models they would need for the language of the image. These models had been preserved throughout the centuries when the Sabaean forefathers led a nomadic existence, thanks to their continual representation on rock and sand. They

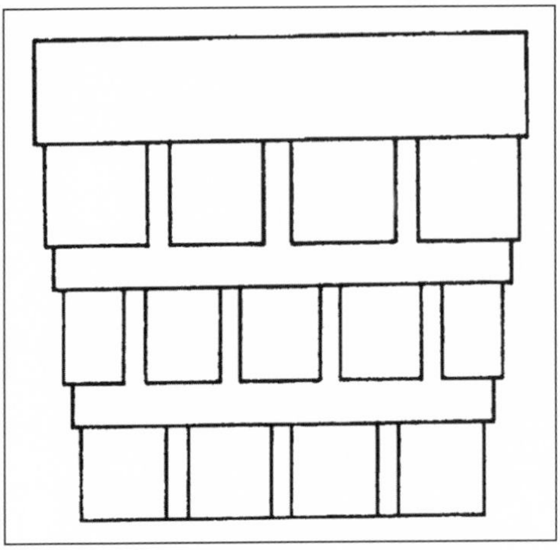

Figure 82
Capital with dentil motif from Mārib

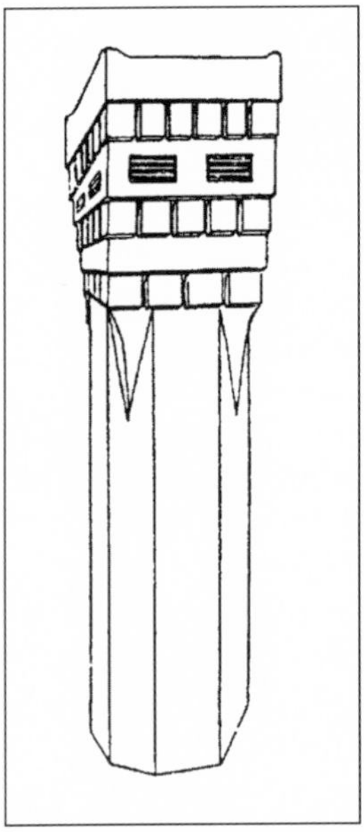

Figure 83
Octagonal column topped by a capital with dentil from Ḥuqqah

were conserved as memories that dated back to the age of Sumerian Mesopotamia.

It seems, then, that there are elements that were common to both statuary and rock graffiti, concerning the origin of their motifs and the development of their figurative canons. However, these two forms of expression are neatly divided on the subject of function. Although both statuary and drawing derived from a need to express a particular religious feeling, the former is more of a subjective art form, made for individuals, and as such is the purest, most genuine expression of individual religious thought; the latter, on the other hand, seems to be more of an objective art form, made for the community, and revealing a religious sentiment conditioned by the need for a conventional rendering that would be universally understood. While statuary expresses spirituality, figure carvings tend to represent more earthly thoughts.

Relief Sculpture

The progression from carved drawings to sculptural relief is documented by a stone slab reproduced by Pirenne[11] and by some pieces from Mārib, photos of which were given to me by the French archaeological mission (Plate 73). The *Banāt 'Ād* motif appears again, emphasised by the sunken background, which almost looks like it has been hollowed out.

The next phase is quite clear. The art form develops into classic relief work, which has come down to us in the form of numerous broken or fragmentary slabs, on which ibex, antelopes etc., are arranged in row upon row around a central panel containing a carved inscription (Plate 74).

In some examples of this category the relief takes on a truly modelled form, almost in the round. One example, a stela in the Barely Museum in Marseilles, shows a definite departure from the original technical and stylistic ideas. But it must be said that, despite the evolution of the techniques and compositions, these reliefs still had the same original functions as the *Banāt 'Ād* drawings. Indeed, in both cases, the border of figured motifs is designed as an introduction to the main attraction, using powerful symbols to emphasise the importance of the focus. In the case of the Jawf graffiti, this is the interior of the temple and for the stone slab reliefs, it is the dedicatory inscription.

Plate 75
Funerary stela with engraved eyes (*Augenstele*)

In later reliefs, the iconographic motifs are extremely simplified, and the border is reduced to the status of a purely decorative element. But we must not forget the original inspiration: only then will we understand the true meaning of a figurative art often simply, and wrongly, described as an "eminently decorative art".[12]

It seems, then, that reliefs were used to emphasise the sacred character of the temple. They are thus closely linked to the architecture. Look, for example, at the drip

Plate 76
Funerary stela with bull's-head, from the British Museum

stones and sacrificial slabs with bulls' heads projections (Fig. 80).

This would explain the wealth of obviously architectural motifs in South Arabian iconography: battlements, false windows, "blinds", etc. (Fig. 81). These occur throughout mature period sculpture, not just in pieces directly connected with architecture, like capitals (Figs. 82 and 83), but also in less related objects, like stone furniture, for example or incense-burners[13].

Plate 77
Sela showing the goddess Dhat Himyam from the National Museum of Ṣan'ā

Stelae

The category of funerary stelae is very important and must be included in our study of reliefs. They followed the same technical-stylistic progression as we have seen in other forms of sculptural relief. The figural work surmounting the inscription containing the name of the deceased is limited, in one type of stela, to a pair of eyes (hence the name *Augenstelen*) which are simply carved into the stone (Plate 75). The technique is not very different from that of the *Banāt 'Ād* carvings, and it is no

Plate 78
Some of the stelae containing framed heads, photographed in the fortress at Mārib by the American mission of 1951-1952

coincidence, as G. Garbini points out, that the "*Augenstelen*" originated in the Jawf[14]. It is true that these are relatively late works, but many aspects, including their content (symbolically abstract eyes), reflect an older tradition, typical of the Jawf.

Contemporary with these, or possibly a little later, we have stelae in which the inscription is surmounted by a flat relief of a human face. The triangular face, the eyes, small mouth, and long, thin nose are all very reminiscent of the "forefathers" statues. It is as if these stelae are continuing the process of evolution of reliefs, as well as that of statuary. On a level with statuary, one should also consider the high reliefs of stelae of the mature period. Both the lovely bulls' head projections (Plate 76), and the representations of the goddess Dhāt Ḥimyam (Plate 77) actually tend to stand out from the stone slab, remaining tied to it only as a reminder of the otherworldly status attributed to the stone itself by the cult of the dead.

Plate 79
Decorated panel with vine motif, from Bayt al-Ashwal

Pirenne observed that "statues originated from stelae, which represented the spirit of the deceased"[15]. This is how we should interpret the stone heads which were placed into rectangular niches and which Wendell Phillips saw a great number of and photographed in a Mārib warehouse during his expedition of 1951-1952 (Plate 78). In South Arabia, stone has a particular importance. This is shown, for example, by the fact that, even in a relatively late period, some stelae are left completely smooth, almost as if exalting in the intrinsic importance of the material[16].

Art and Stone

South Arabian art was born from stone; the slow development of the art and its period of full maturity are documented by the struggle of the image to free itself from the stone. We have seen that statues developed from pebbles. Material and form are so bound together in Bronze Age idols that we seem to see the slightest developments almost as life being born from nature, or the magical birth of the human from the divine.

Next, we have a period of growth. In the "forefathers" statuettes the relationship between material and form has already swung substantially in favour of form. It will change still more dramatically in the classical statuettes of the "worshippers". But the imprint of the mother-stone is never lost as, by binding images in a static solidity, it lends an aura of exquisite originality to the statuary.

Like statuary, relief work is also intimately bound up with the stone. We have seen how it originates from rock carvings, where the stone bears eternal witness to the magical relationship between man and nature. There is a logical progression from rocks to temple structures. It is also possible that the pilasters so characteristic of South Arabian architecture derive from the groups of standing stones that we still find in great numbers in Yemen.

Plates 80, 81
Capitals with acanthus leaf decoration in the Museum of Ṣan'ā

There is doubtless a close mystical link between the mountains, rocks and stones and that which man could represent on or with them. The link between the arts and stone in South Arabia was so strong that the appearance and spread of bronze statues more or less signalled the end of the most genuine phase of original artistic expression.

A Possible Chronology

We must begin with better definitions of those phases of art that we have called ancient and mature, although obviously we must still remain within extremely general boundaries.

Keeping one eye on the chronology outlined in Table 1, we could date all works of art that seem to precede the true flourishing of South Arabian art (idols, rock graffiti and standing stones, which are the origins of statuary, reliefs and stelae), to before 1200 BC, the date that we conventionally take as the start of South Arabian culture in Yemen.

South Arabian art, then, began in earnest during the long period that we have categorised a South Arabian protohistory (around 1200-700 BC), when the "forefathers" statuettes and the carvings of the *Banāt 'Ād* appeared. This phase, whose art we have designated as ancient period, continued into the period of the *mukarribs* of Saba (about 700-400 BC), which is when figured drawings must have given way to sculptural relief and potentially when the stelae, derived from the carved drawings of the Jawf (the *Augenstelen*), evolved into stelae with faces in flat relief. We have also called this phase formative because in this period all categories of art (including architecture) gradually develop their full expressive potential.

The arts achieve their full and complete development in the following period of the kings of Saba (fifth to fourth centuries BC) when the kingdoms of Ma'īn, Qatabān and Ḥaḍramawt emerge as strong independent states. In terms of the history of art, we can call this phase the *mature period.*

Later (at around the beginning of the decadent era), we enter into a *late phase,* which, obviously with various internal developments which are yet to be investigated, lasts until the appearance of Islam. We can date its start to the emergence of the Himyarite element, in other words the growth period of maritime traffic with the Mediterranean world. This phase in art may also be termed decadent, in that the true potential of local art is by now exhausted, and an increasingly abundant store of foreign iconographic and stylistic motifs (first Hellenistic, then Roman and Persian) begin to add themselves to – though they never displace the intrinsic nature of – South Arabian art.

Bronzes and External Influences

We cannot deny, though, that the influence of the Mediterranean had already been felt in earlier periods. It is interesting to note that this mainly occurred in categories of objects that were not really typical of South Arabian art, like bronze statuary.

In a sense, then, we are really dealing with imports, rather than influences. Consider, for example, the famous bronze warrior that R.A.B. Hamilton found in Wādī Jirdān, which is, for all intents and purposes, a Peloponnesian work of the sixth century BC, or the more famous bronze statue of Ma'ādī Karib found by the Americans in the Awwam temple in Mārib (Plate 35) which, given local taste, could have been produced by foreign artists in South Arabia between the end of the fifth and the beginning of the fourth centuries BC[17].

We know that Greek objects were imported or copied locally during the mature period, from the coins which began to appear in South Arabia from the third century BC onwards. But, as I have said, the distinctive characteristics of South Arabian art actually remain unchanged right up to the first century BC, thanks to the conservatism imposed by its strong, distinctive, formative precedents.

Bronze statuary only became widespread during the late period. Besides the Timna' lions, which we have already looked at, some good examples are: the famous horse in the Dumbarton Oaks Collection, which dates to the first to second centuries AD, the lovely head of the same date from Ghaymān, now in the British Museum, another, even lovelier, head, also from Ghaymān (now housed by the Museum of Ṣan'ā), which shows Parthian influences and probably dates from the second century AD; and finally the two great statues of the sovereigns Dhamār'ali Yuhabirr and Tha'rān Yuha'min (displayed in the entrance of the Museum of Ṣan'ā), found at Nakhlat al-Ḥamra in Jabal Kanīn and dating from the fourth century AD.

In the late period we find evidence of Roman, Alexandrian and Parthian influences. Bronze becomes the favourite material for statues and some entirely new motifs appear, in reliefs, for example. We can probably attribute the widespread use of the vine motif (Plate 79) to the infiltration of beliefs linked to the cult of Dionysis and of Atargatis, from Roman Syria. The same can probably be said of the various animal motifs, with bodies that form the roots of plant motifs. A deep love for these decorative elements can also be seen in the column capitals, which are

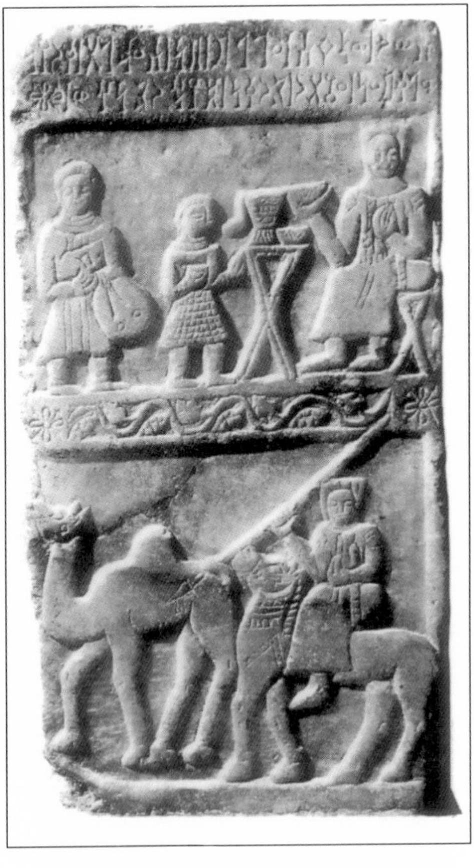

Plate 82
Funerary stela from the Louvre

decorated with acanthus leaves, in the Corinthian style (Plates 80 and 81).

Artists now started to abandon the moulded style, in favour of a design whereby the picture stands out against a dramatically recessed background. Even the letters of the inscriptions, which had always had a particular decorative value in South Arabia, now start to stand out from a sunken background. Next came funeral stelae in low relief, showing the deceased engaged in his normal pursuits: camel driver, warrior or peasant. These stelae are often divided into rows depicting scenes of daily domestic life (Plates 82 and 83).

Plate 83
Funerary stela from the British Museum

In this brief survey of the history of South Arabian art we have only mentioned the most important and famous monuments, but we must not forget that the artistic repertoire of pre-Islamic Arabia was extremely rich and included paintings, pottery, toreutics, seals, as well as sculpture in wood, ivory and other perishable materials.

The glorious palaces of the Sabaeans were highly decorated and filled with works of art, vividly described by contemporary Latin authors (in the words of Diodorus Siculus, "The Sabaeans have beds and tripods with silver feet ... they have high perisytle columns, some gilded, others adorned with capitals with silver figures"[19].) Their fame was destined to last well into the Islamic era.

The Yemeni historian Al-Hamdānī (tenth century) discribes Ghumdān, the famous palace of the Sabaean sovereigns of Ṣan'ā. Wondering at its striking ruins ("a huge mound that stands as high as a mountain"), he evokes the original dimensions ("twenty levels of ten cubits height"), the perfection of the architectural techniques and the beauty of the columns whose bases were decorated with bronze lions[20]. King Ilsharaḥ, who built the palace, had his bedroom built on top of the highest terrace, so that he could make out all the different birds that flew over him, through the great alabaster roof. Four hollow bronze lions stood in the corners of the room, and seemed to howl at the wind. The windows were framed in marble, and their fastenings were decorated with perforated ebony and protected on the inside by silk curtains. The alabaster roofing slabs were surmounted by a cupola containing an enormous lantern which stayed alight all night, and could be seen from the summits of all the surrounding mountains[21].

All this splendour is only feebly reflected by the few archaeological remains that we have looked at in this chapter. It was all lost, and so far very little has been found. But the memory of the past lingers on, far beyond the words of Al-Hamdānī. It is alive in Yemen today, in the architecture of the houses and the mosques, in the cities and the walls and the minds of the people. For in Yemen, the revelation of past glories is simply a kind of conscious reawakening. Surely, the knowledge of having produced a great civilisation and of being its current representative must be one of the most powerful sources of pride for a modern nation.

Footnotes:

1. See Rathjens, C., *Sabaeica, Bericht über die archäologischen Ergebnisse seiner zweiten, dritten und vierten Reise nach Südarabien II. Teil: Die unlokalisierten Funde* (Hamburg: Kommisionsverlag L. Appel, 1955); and Grohmann, A., "Arabia" and "Arabici preislamici, centri e tradizioni" in *Enciclopedia Universale dell'Arte I* (Rome: 1958).
2. Segall, B., "Sculpture from Arabia Felix. The Hellenistic Period", *AJA* 59 (1955), p. 207-214.
3. Pirenne, J., *La Grèce et Saba. Une nouvelle base pour la chronologie sud-arabe* (Paris: Imprimerie nationale, 1955).
4. Conti Rossini, C., "Dalle rovine di Awsān", *Dedalo* 7 (1927), p. 746.
5. Halévy, J., "Rapport sur une mission archéologique dans le Yémen", *JA* 19 (1872), p. 30.
6. See Breton, J.F., *Le temple de 'Athtar d'As-Sawdā* (Ṣan'ā: 1990), and "Le sanctuaire de 'Athtar dhū-Risaf d'As-Sawdā", *CRAIBL* (1992), p. 429-453.
7. See Serjeant, R.B., *South Arabian Hunt* (London: Luzac, 1976); and Ryckmans, J., "La chasse rituelle dans l'Arabie du Sud ancienne" in *Al-Bahit, Festchrift Joseph Henninger* (Bonn: 1976), p. 259-308.
8. Pirenne, J., *Inscriptions et antiquités sud-arabaes* (Louvian: 1977), p. 260.
9. Frankfort, H., *The Art and Architecture of the Ancient Orient* (Harmondsworth: Penguin, 1970), p. 77.
10. See Antonini, S., "Una tavoletta-portafortuna in terracotta dagli scavi di Yalā/ad-Durayb", in Robin, C. (ed.), *Arabia Antiqua. Early Origins of the South Arabian States* (Rome: IsMEO, 1996), p. 143-163.
11. Pirenne, J., *Inscriptions et antiquités sud-arabaes*, p. 269.
12. Pirenne, J., "Arabie préislamique" in *Historie générale de l'Art*, vol. I (Paris: 1961), p. 910.
13. Bossert, H., *Altsyrien. Kunst und Handwerk in Cypern, Syrien, Palästina, Transjordanien und Arabien von der Anfängen bis zum völligen Aufgehen in der griechisch-römischen Kultur* (Tubingen: E. Wasmuth, 1951), p. 1263-1265, 1275-1281.

14. Garbini, G., "Una nuova iscrizione minea su 'Augenstele'", *AION* 26 (1976), p. 308-315.
15. Pirenne, J., *Inscriptions et antiquités sud-arabes,* p. 309.
16. Ibid, p. 363-366.
17. Garbini, G., "La datazione della statua sudarabica di Ma'adkarib",*OA* 5 (1966), p. 64.
18. Hill, G.F., *The Ancient Coinage of Southern Arabia* (London: Oxford University Press, 1919).
19. Conti Rossini, C., *Chrestomathia arabica meridionalis epigraphica* (Rome: Istituto per l'Oriente, 1931), p. 8.
20. Hamdānī, Al-Hasan ibn Aḥmad, *The Antiquities of South Arabia (being a translation from the Arabic, with linguistic, geographic, and historical notes, of the Eighth Book of al-Hamdānī's Al-Iklīl),* trans. N.A. Faris (Princeton: Princeton Oriental Texts, 3, 1938), p. 17.
21. Pirenne, J., "Arabie préislamique", in *Histoire générale de l'Art,* vol. I (Paris: 1961), p. 924.

BIBLIOGRAPHIC ABBREVIATIONS

AAE *Arabian Archaeology and Epigraphy*
ABADY *Archäologische Berichte aus dem Yemen,* vol. I-VII (Deutsches Archäologisches Institut, Ṣan'ā)
AION *Annali dell'Istituto Orientale di Napoli*
AJA *American Journal of Archaeology*
AL *Allgemeine Literaturzeitung*
AO *Ars Orientalis*
AUAE *Archaeology in the United Arab Emirates*
BA *The Biblical Archaeologist*
BASOR *Bulletin of the American Schools of Oriental Research*
BSGP *Bulletin de la Société de Géographie de Paris*
BSOAS *Bulletin of the School of Oriental and African Studies*
BSRGE *Bulletin de la Société Royale de Géographie d'Égypte*
CIASA *Corpus des inscriptions et antiquités sud-arabes, 6 vol.,* Académie des Inscriptions et Belles-Lettres (Paris)
CIS *Corpus Inscriptionum Semiticarum. Pars Quarta, Inscriptiones himyariticas et sabaeas continens, I-III* (Paris)
CRAIBL *Comptes Rendus des séances de l'Académie des Inscriptions et Belles-Lettres*
DA *Dossiers de l Archéologie*

EVO *Egitto e Vicino Oriente*
EW *East and West*
GJ *The Geographical Journal*
IAAYAR *IsMEO Archaeological Activities in the Yemen Arab Republic, EW* (Rome)
IRM *IsMEO Reports and Memoirs*
JA *Journal Asiatique*
JAOS *Journal of the American Oriental Society*
JASB *Journal of the Asiatic Society of Bengal*
JESHO *Journal of Economic and Social History of the Orient*
JRAS *Journal of the Royal Asiatic Society*
JRGS *Journal of the Royal Geographic Society*
MAANL *Monumenti Antichi dell'Accademia Nazionale dei Lincei*
MUSJ *Mélanges de l'Université Saint-Joseph*
OA *Oriens Antiquus*
PPS *Proceedings of the Prehistoric Society*
PSAS *Proceedings of the Seminar for Arabian Studies*
RES *Répertoire d'épigraphie Sémitique,* I-VIII, Académie des Inscriptions et Belles-Lettres
RHR *Revue de l histoire des religions*
SEG *Sammlung Eduard Glaser,* vol. II-XIV, Österreichische Akademie der Wissenschafter, Philosophisch-Historische Klasse Sitzungsberichte (Wien)
Yemen *Yemen. Studi archeologici, storici e filologici sull'Arabia meridionale ZKM Zeitschrift für die Kunde des Morgenlandes*

INDEX OF PERSONS AND DIVINITIES

INDEX OF PLACES AND PEOPLE